Beautiful SOUTH SUDAN

The Heart of Africa

Achier Deng Akol Ayay

Beautiful South Sudan:
The Heart of Africa

First Published 2010

British Library Cataloguing-in-Publication Data

A catalogue record for this book is available from the British Library

ISBN: 1419678868
ISBN-13: 9781419678868
Library of Congress Control Number: 2001012345
Author: Achier Deng Akol Ayay

Home Address:
Pan Deng Akol Ayay
Kuajok, South Sudan

E-mail: bss2011@achier.org
Web site: www.achier.org
Publisher: CreateSpace, USA
Marketing: Amazon Company
Printed and bound in USA

Others that struggled hard like us achieved their full freedom, why not us in South Sudan?

A Cry for South Sudan Freedom

Beautiful South Sudan:

The Heart of Africa

To millions of our people
That relentlessly and selflessly
Paid ultimate sacrifice
For our total freedom

And to the few that survived
In South Sudan and beyond
To vote positively in Referenda
And Popular Consultations

Amorous means showing or feeling romantic love or sexual attraction.

Antagonisation is the act of causing a person or animal to be hostile.

Arabisation is making something conform to Arab customs or culture.

Assassination is the killing of a political or other public figure by a sudden violent attack.

Barbarism is a cruel or brutal act.

Bombing is the act of or process of dropping bombs from aircraft.

Contentious means causing or likely to cause disagreement and disputes between people with differing views.

Culture is defined as shared believes and values of a group: the beliefs, customs, practises, and social behaviour of a particular nation or people.

Deprivation is unfair treatment of one person or group, usually because of prejudice about race, ethnic group, age group, religion, or gender.

Discrimination is unfair treatment of one person or group, usually because of prejudice about race, ethnic group, age group, religion, or gender.

Falsification is deliberate misrepresentation of the truth or facts.

Folklore comprises traditional stories and explanations passed down in a community or country.

Hide is the skin of some larger animals, for example, deer, cow, or buffalo. Informally also a person's skin.

Genocide is murder of an entire ethnic group. The systematic killing of all the people from a national, ethnic, or religious group, or an attempt to do this.

Gorgeous means outstandingly beautiful or richly coloured.

Humiliation is the act of damaging somebody's dignity or pride.

Islamisation is conversion of people or countries to Islam or to cause people, institutions, or countries to follow Islamic Law.

Massacre is the vicious killing of large numbers of people or animals.

Marginalisation in a nutshell, is prevention from having attention or power. In other words, it is the taking or keeping somebody or something away from the centre of attention, influence, or power.

Nature is the appearance or aspect of a person, place, or thing that is considered to reflect reality

Obligation is something that must be done because of legal or moral duty.

Opposition is strong disagreement with a plan or activity and a trial to change or stop it.

Oppression is subjecting a person or a people to a harsh or cruel form of domination.

Poetry refers to all the poems written by a particular poet, in a particular language or form, or on a particular subject. A collection of love poems

Precious means highly valued, much loved, or considered to be of great importance.

Rejection is the rejecting of something or somebody, or the act of being rejected.

Referendum is an occasion when all the people in a country can vote in order to show their opinion about a political question.

Sacrifice is the giving up of something valuable or important for somebody or something else considered to be of more value or importance. For example, sacrifice of lives and vital body parts for one's homeland.

Self-determination is a free will of people to democratically determine their own future destiny.

Sharia is defined in Encarta as an Islamic, religious law, based on the Koran.

Slavery is the condition of being forced to work for somebody else for nothing or being completely dominated by another.

Starvation is the state of suffering or dying through lack of food.

Torture is the infliction of severe physical pain on somebody, for example, as punishment or to persuade somebody to confess or recant something.

Contents

Preface

In the Heart of Africa is a land so loved by its people that millions of them sacrificed their lives for it during over fifty years of contemporary war, and many more are ready to do the same until it is totally liberated. I am one of those lovers lucky to be still alive in a war where no soul was spared, young or old.

This land that is so gorgeous, so precious, so contentious, and so amorous is South Sudan. To me it is Heaven on Earth that I call Beautiful South Sudan: The Heart of Africa.

Born into this beautiful land, I thought I was going to enjoy it forever. Unfortunately for me and all fellow children of this land, that was not to be. First I could have starved to death when I was a small child during the war after the enemy burnt all our crops. Next I was also almost killed during the massive massacres of innocent civilians by government forces in our homeland in 1968. Worst of all, I ended up as a refugee in a foreign land where I went without gray hairs over twenty years ago and now I am at the edge of my grave. Missing my land for over twenty years to me is worse than death although others may think it was an opportunity for survival.

Read this book to see my emotions unfold from early childhood to my current aging adulthood in extreme love and dedication for my homeland beyond any imagination. Let me take you through its glamour, tell you some of its

folklore, and give you a glimpse of its history as well as its misery.
I believe this book will appeal to any human being on this planet who just wants to relax or enjoy romantic stories and exciting pieces of poetry, apart from indigenes of South Sudan themselves. It is not all to do with war, politics, and death.

It will also be useful to those who would like to glance at the history of South Sudan in a nutshell, understand why millions of its children sacrificed their lives for it and how its few survivors are likely to vote during the referendum in 2011. One can browse the pages of this book to locate twenty-one leading reasons that can justify secession of Southern Sudan and five principal criteria which, if met in full, may salvage Sudan from breaking up.

My prayer is to join the millions of our martyrs to whom I dedicate this book; but only after casting my vote in the referendum in 2011 if possible. This will give me a chance to go and tell them exactly when I arrive how the voting went. However, should I kiss the dust before then, I will have left behind this book as a romantic gift for our promised land.

Achier Deng Akol Ayay

Acknowledgement

I am grateful to Dr. Victoria Anib Stephen Majur Achut and Beck Awan Deng for transcribing some songs. My thanks also go to Amou Ring, Mary Mou Aken, Elizabeth Nyancol Makongo, Abuk Anei Yoor, and Akuol Parek for contributing stories. To Ajok Wek, Mogga Josephson, John Apurout Akec, John Amairi, Sunday Taabu Wani, Victoria Anib, Apuk Ayuel Mayen, Dr. Francis Mading Deng, and Deng Awur Wenyin for contributing poems, I register special thanks. The same goes to Wade Sir Anai for allowing me to reproduce a couple of poems of his late father, the poet Sir Anai Kelueljang, as a tribute to him.

In particular, I would like to thank my own children Nyibol (Mrs. Amet Amet Kuol), Deng Manger, Deng Adhongweth, and Ayay Marol along with other dependents who suffered from lack of vital paternal support when I abandoned work in UK for a year from July 2005 having been shocked by the sudden departure of our leader Dr. John Garang De Mabior. Nevertheless, they all remained collectively a vital source of motivation to me when I was writing this book during that time, apart from my little son Deng Dhukbaai who later arrived during the interim period of the Comprehensive Peace Agreement (CPA).

Some chapters of this book could not have been completed without the contribution of others like Islamic experts and notable singers of South Sudan whose names are indicated against their original songs and articles in the book. I am highly indebted to all of them. The same goes to the rightful owners of the photographs and diagrams used.

Notably, a young and talented lady that I thought I was training as my office manager, Miss Martha Ahok Ajiek Amet, turned out to be such a genius that she was the one training me instead! Her sharp eyes and brilliant brain helped me shape this book from a scratch. I have no better words to thank her than to completely agree with Dr. John Garang De Mabior and Salva Kiir Mayardit in their previous practical observation and sincere comment that she is truly a potential future leader of Southern Sudan.

This book might also have remained unpublished had I not received further encouragement and an energy boost from my bride Victoria Awit (Anok) Bona But Deng, a student of Law at Kampala International University and a young poet called Acai Chol of Abyei, a medical student of same university, that amazed me with her instantaneous poetry skills at a recent conference conducted in Juba. I can't find the right words that I can use to thank them sufficiently.

Above all, I would like to express heartfelt gratitude to all my courageous people, exemplified particularly by our leader Dr. Salva Kiir Mayardit, for protecting our beautiful land. Without their endless sacrifice, this land would have been completely snatched from us a long time ago and I would have had nothing to write about now.

Achier Deng Akol Ayay

INTRODUCTION

A Land So Curious

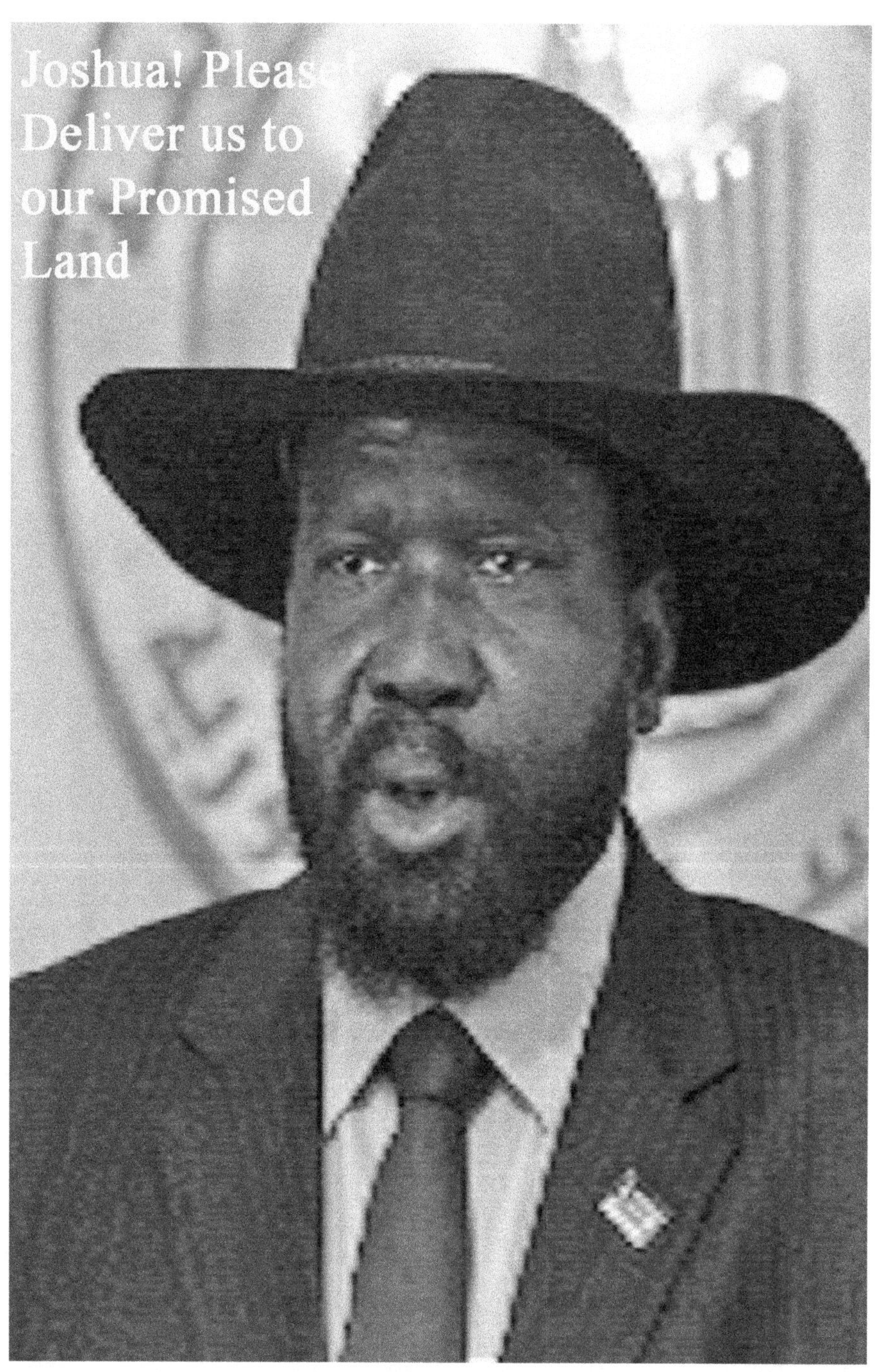
Joshua! Please!
Deliver us to
our Promised
Land

A lot of us that highly love our precious homeland of South Sudan usually weep openly when we listen to speeches or read reports about this land, especially those highlighting its enormous devastation and suffering. This prompts me at the beginning of this book to ask a general question: Why do we weep for our homeland? As reflected in an extract of one of my poems below:

Why do we weep?
For our motherland
When we think deep
About our destined trend
If you are tears of escapees
Now stop spilling over
If you are tears of esplees
Continue to flow forever

Indeed, the tears we shed for our homeland are not those of cowards or escapees. They are not crocodile tears either. They are tears of people I call esplees, borrowing from the French term that means "people that love their motherland."

The depth to which we love and cherish our homeland of South Sudan can also be derived from the following synopsis of another poem of mine called "South Sudan; Only You":

South Sudan
Only You

My Life
My Love
My Dream

Beloved land
Of billion martyrs
For freedom
For justice
For equality
For democracy
Only You
I want
Heartily
So much
Absolutely

Only You
I desire
To own
To love
To cherish
Forever

But the love I hold in my heart for my fatherland is only a tip of an iceberg. If you consider the millions if not billions of martyrs that paid the ultimate sacrifice for this homeland over many years of campaign for its liberation, it will give you a better clue of a more reliable thermometer of love.

Given the enormous sacrifice paid by our people, a common cry that vibrates in my mind or I murmur in my lips whenever I weep for my land is the following:

Others that struggled hard like us achieved their full freedom.
Why not us in South Sudan?

A Cry for South Sudan Freedom

Perhaps those who say our differences and bitterness against one another are core contributory factors inhibiting us from achieving our freedom are telling the truth. Therefore, at the beginning of this book of romance for our homeland, I would like to quote below a part of a song of the youth of South Sudan that appeals to any few of us that will survive to drop their differences for the sake of our homeland:

Even if our hearts differ, we should not concede and let our land down.
Any one of us that will survive can pick a pen, can pick a gun,
And raise it up and say: This is our land! This is our land!

Our Land of South Sudan!
Our Land of South Sudannnnnnnn!

Our Land of South Sudan it is indeed and it forms the theme of this book. I want you to read on and feel the deep romance we hold for this Promised Land as reflected and exposed in the vivid description, photographic depiction, romantic folklore, exciting songs, and moving poems inside this book.

So let me start this book by reciting one of my poems called **Vote Me Free in 2011.** This will give you a glimpse of more excitement to follow as you dive through the book. Most importantly, it will show you a hint of the secret behind my writing this book beyond mere historical documentation and utmost dedication. For, I believe even if I wept and wept to you until I filled one barrel after another with my miserable tears, it may not be enough to convince or support you to cast a proper decisive vote the way I want. Therefore, allow me to complement my tears by showering you, in good faith, with numerous outstanding romantic gifts of glamour, pictures, stories, songs and poems for you to browse and hopefully enjoy, starting with the one below:

Vote Me Free in 2011

Tell me you love me
Countless million times
I won't still believe you

Sing me love songs
Every day and night
I may still doubt you

Promise to jump down
From top of a mountain
It won't reach my ears

Just vote me free in 2011
Then I will believe you love me
For Words Words Words
Songs Songs Songs
Promises Promises Promises
All can be blown away
By the wind around

But your decisive vote
That vote for our freedom
No wind can blow it away
However strong that wind is

If you love me
Don't leave me a slave
In my own country

Vote me free in 2011

DEMOGRAPHY

A Land So Gorgeous

A glimpse of Beautiful South Sudan at Kuajok

It was around four o'clock in the morning when our father woke us up.

"You all know when I wake you up so early, it means there is something very important for us to either discuss or pray for," he said. "The rainy season has started and we do not want to run short of grain again next July. Therefore, this time we need to double our efforts and cultivate more.

"You may think that discussion about cultivation is not such an important matter for everybody to be woken up so early at dawn. It is, my children, for our life as farmers heavily depends on it. Do it right, we survive; do it wrong and we risk starving and dying," he elaborated.

I was still a bit drowsy and almost fell back to sleep being barely a five-year-old child. I was the last born of eleven siblings; the spoilt baby of the family. My father noticed that and immediately remarked, "Wake up, Achier. You can hold a hoe, you know, or at least spray some seeds on a farm if you think your hands are too small to grasp a hoe. The food that ends up in our hands to feed ourselves comes from the farm as a result of hard work."

"Let the little one sleep and talk instead to the bigger children," my mother tried to defend me. "Did your own dad have to wake you up to talk to you so early in age, so early in the morning, about cultivation, when you were that young?" she inquired, expecting to hear no as an answer.

"In fact, he did," my father responded. "And it stuck in my mind forever. Where do you think I learnt this from?" If you want children to remember something that important, something to do with their future survival, do not talk to them in the middle of the day when they are busy playing. Talk to them at a time like this."

"Ey, stop," my mother interrupted. "I was not inviting you to give me a lecture about the right time to speak to your children. I was just trying to ask you to exclude the little one for now. If you think he is old enough to be included in early dawn talks, just go ahead, please, without lecturing to me anymore."

The floor of the room we were sleeping in was smoothed and levelled with a shiny and reflective dark mud. You would think that was done by an engineer with a machine in order to leave no lumps and bumps to stumble on.

The beauty of our land of South Sudan does not start in the garden outside. It starts with the floor of the room inside. Smooth, shiny, and well levelled. And that is just the beginning of exceptional beauty even in the room itself.

On that floor lay various beddings ranging from softened hide and skin to woven grass and hay with different colours and consistencies. The pillows, which are intended for adults are especially curved strong wood that stand above the ground level like small cushions. Every one of them is smoothed, glittery, but hard enough to hold the head and neck up. Their colour reflects the type of wood used such as brown mahogany or ebony.

Tucked away to a relatively safer place at the end of the room are various utensils and pots of different sizes: spoons made of either wood or large snail shells, pots of clay, and plates of calabash among others. All give combinations of spectacular nice-looking but fragile essential items. Their beauty does not lie only in how they look. It extends to the art of how they were made in the first place and how they are subsequently handled. Fragile and precious as almost all of them are, they should be handled with utmost care.

Lie flat on the floor of the room and look up at the ceiling. You would think that all you would see are logs of wood and thatched grass. You are wrong. Tugged to those logs are delicate and more precious items. They include decorated gourds containing meals like dry fish preserved for a rainy day or special festivals. Other likely contents include decorative ornaments like beads and silvery metals. All are tugged away not to be trodden upon and destroyed or lynched easily. Behind the logs too, a few items may be hidden such as tobacco that is so precious to some elders who smoke. It is one of the precious gifts to offer elders among others when they visit a family.

One may allege that all the items and ornaments described so far are just items of poverty. That is not true. Beauty is simplicity in itself. The degree of preciousness of any is also relative to its use and stored value. Some of these ornaments are antiques that were inherited by one ancestor from the other over generations that may span beyond centuries. These antiques are more precious, more beautiful, and too admirable to describe in any words.

You may now think that the ceiling is the only place where things are hidden or tugged away. You would be wrong again. Ask yourself what might be beneath the floor of the room where you are and you would discover that you might be lying on top of a secret grain store. Such a store is a huge hole that is dug deeply into the ground to hide vital grain, especially away from destructive enemy agents like Mirihaleen or Junjaweet. The beauty of South Sudan lies too in our ability to devise strategies for survival in order to defy all attempts by our enemy to exterminate us on this planet. None of us would have made it until today were it not because of the genius defensive tactics and invincible strategies of our predecessors.

Step out now from the bedroom and do not let your eyes be caught yet by the amazing plains ahead of you. First glance at how our cottages and huts are arranged in a circle, usually around an elevated platform. The hut is the biggest of all the houses, inside which domestic livestock are reared such as cattle, sheep, and goats for those who keep them. It is also the one used as an entertainment or meeting hall for a large number of community members like people attending a wedding or harvest ceremony. The other buildings in the circle serve various purposes: master bedroom, guest bedroom, etc. Who doubts that we are descendents of the first human beings to discover civilisation along the Nile in Africa?

The beauty of South Sudan originates thousands of years ago when our great ancestors led the world in discovering architecture and how to write, just to mention two examples during our ancient kingdoms in the land of Kush and beyond.

Now take a stride with me to drive our herd of cattle, sheep, and goats to the grazing field or just stroll without them and start by looking at these domestic livestock or existing wildlife. The first thing to strike your eyes would be the extensive variety of multiple colours that our animals display. Think of any colour combination and you will find it on our heard of cattle or stock of sheep and goat in South Sudan. Take, for example, the top combination of black and white colours. You will find numerous ranges of the spectrum in that combination alone like Marial, Makuei, Mangar, Majok, Achol, and Yar, most of which lack equivalent English words to call them. Now add a third, fourth, fifth, or more colours to combine with or separately from black and white and you will end up with nearly an infinite number of colour combinations. All are there. All have unique names. This is beauty beyond description. Grasp it and you will never forget it in your lifetime.

Yet that beauty of South Sudan does not only lie in the spectrum of multiple colour combinations displayed constantly on our cattle, sheep, goats, chicken, other birds, wildlife, fishes, and flowers....whatever species you can think of in our marvellous piece of land. That is just what eyes see. It lies more in what is invisible to the eyes. It stretches, for example, up to our extremely rich languages to the extent that we have unique names for any colour combination imaginable as long as it is reflected in our domestic or wildlife.

At this moment, while trying to rest my fingers a bit from writing this book and my eyes from the computer screen in my small room in London where I have ended as a refugee, I glanced through the window and what did I see? I saw a small beautiful bird with white and black stripes on its neck sitting outside on a branch of a tree at my front garden, looking back at me through the same window. In my language this bird is called Areu.

For years I have always looked through this window and I have never spotted a bird sitting on a tree looking back at me. Why did it happen this time when I am writing about our beautiful land of South Sudan thousands of miles away twenty years since I last saw it? Could Areu have migrated too from South Sudan and ended up as a refugee like me in London in UK? Is another bird overseas thanking me for writing about their counterparts in South Sudan? No one will ever tell.

Twenty years abroad, in a foreign land, away from my homeland. Yet, I do not need to recall how glamorous our land is. It is fixed in my brain since I was born. See South Sudan even as a tourist for a second whatever your age. You would be struck by its enormous beauty and it will be fixed in your mind forever. And this is not simple advertisement. This is real truth and nothing else.

Let me go back to the stride I was taking with or without the domestic herd toward the grazing field amid their exciting moos and boos. To me the most exciting part of this stride is when one ultimately stands in the centre of the grazing field and looks around. I call this the most exciting moment in the heart of extremely Beautiful South Sudan. The wonderful wildlife grazing along the cattle, the astounding green scenery of grass and trees, the amazing spectacular colours of flowers and butterflies flying around, the eye-dazzling scenes of waterside along the springs, ponds, pools, streams, and rivers, the extremely beautiful birds in the blue sky and marvellous cloud, the fresh unpolluted air in our environment...Oh! My God! What have I forgotten to mention of all the gift of our natural beauty that you, the Almighty, and You alone bestowed on our precious land?

Yet all that beauty I have just described so far is merely a glimpse; all the glamour that is present in this small grazing field called Lil is only just a small fraction of what can be seen and enjoyed in a larger natural plain called Toic. Furthermore, even both Lil and Toic combined are still only a fraction of the overall indescribable beauty of the entire South Sudan. Add, for example, our beautiful mountains like Imatong, the marshes and swamps of the Nile, the tropical Equatorial Forest—you name it, we have it.

South Sudan, a land so gorgeous; the beauty and the Heart of Africa! Yet this beauty is sadly entrapped in a cage of slavery within a united Sudan. It is waiting to be released from the cage, by the votes of its people, in a 2011 Referendum lest it remain an imprisoned slaved forever.

In a nutshell the principal demographic features of this beautiful land can be summarised as follows:

Space

Southern Sudan is a region of Sudan that is so spacious that it is greater in size than countries like France. It borders Ethiopia on the east, Kenya, Uganda, and the Democratic Republic of the Congo to the south, and the Central African Republic to the west. To the north lies the predominantly Afro-Arab and Muslim region directly under the control of the central government.

Characteristics

The Southern Sudanese practise mainly indigenous traditional beliefs, although Christian missionaries have converted some.

The South also contains many ethnic groups and multiple languages as discussed under culture. For now, the official language of education and government function is English.

Legal and administrative structure

The relationship between autonomous Southern Sudan and the neighbouring areas of Blue Nile State, Nuba Mountains/Southern Kordufan, and Abyei has yet to be definitively determined, although for the time being these are effectively part of the North.

Southern Sudan consists of the ten states, formerly composing the provinces of Equatoria (namely Central Equatoria, Eastern Equatoria, and Western Equatoria), Bahr el Ghazal (Northern Bahr al Ghazal, Western Bahr al Ghazal, Lakes, and Warrab), and Upper Nile (Jonglei, Unity, and Upper Nile).

Pending elections, seats in both the Southern Sudan Assembly and the government of the Southern Sudan are to be divided in a fixed proportion between the SPLM (70 percent), the NCP (the former NIF) (15 percent), and "other Southern political forces" (15 percent).

Before his death on 30 July 2005, longtime freedom fighter and leader John Garang was the president of Southern Sudan. Garang was succeeded by Salva Kiir Mayardit who was sworn in as first vice president of Sudan on 11 August 2005.

Independence

Southern independence is foreseen as a strong possibility for the future if secession becomes the choice in the referendum in 2011.

Population

Pending a proper full census, the population of Southern Sudan is estimated to be around ten to fourteen million. The

2008 Census must have been abused in the Northern Sector because:

- Southern Sudan is not shown to be a third of the entire population of Sudan, contrary to what previous censuses consistently reflected.

- The population of Southern Sudanese in all the Northern States is said to be less than five hundred thousand when in Khartoum alone it was always officially reported during the war to be in the millions.

- The population of Darfur is extremely exaggerated to be almost equal to that of the Southern Sudan as a whole.

- In particular the population of Arab nomadic tribes in Darfur has been increased by over 90 percent.

- Men are falsely reported to be more than women.

- The Northern Census Committee declined to exchange raw census data collected with the committee of Southern Sudan as agreed before the census was started. This means they have something to hide.

"When you vote in 2011 Referendum, you will either choose to release Beautiful South Sudan, the Heart of Africa, from its cage of slavery to freedom or let it continue to languish in that cage forever."

PEOPLE

A Land So Courageous

Aweil youth singing an SPLA war song at a presidential reception: "If it is death, we accept it, that is why we left from the land of Bahr-el-Ghazal".

Serial No.	Ethnic Group	Originality	Locality	Language
1.	Acholi	Pure Acholi or Luo-Madi product	Magwe County, E Equatoria, N. Uganda	Leb Acholi
2.	Adio (Makaraka)	Azande	Yei River District	Kakwa and Mundu
3.	Aja	Gbaya living at Gbotu near Buma	Upper part of Sopo River and Raga	Mixed Kresh and Banda
4.	Anyuak (Anyuaa)	From Gilo, son of Mr. Ocwudho and Miss Akango	Pochalla and Akobo Counties	Dho-Anywaa
5.	Atuot (Reel)	Reel	Yirol County	Reel or Apak
6.	Avukaya	Undefined	Maridi and Congo	Avukaya
7.	Azande	Azande	W. Equatoria, Congo	Azande
8.	Bai	Ndogo and Bviri	Khor Ngoku, Bussere	Bai
9.	Baka	Undefined	Maridi, Yei, Congo	Baka
10.	Balanda-Boor	Bwor - the eldest son of Nyikango	Wau to Tambura	Boor dialect of Luo
11.	Balanda-Bviri	Migrated from the West to the East	Wau to Tambura and Raga	Bviri
12.	Banda	Central Africa	Raga-Central Africa	Banda
13.	Bari	Bari proper	Juba District	Bari
14.	Binga	From East to West	Raga-Southern Darfur	Binga
15.	Bongo	Undefined	Tonj to Wau	Bongo
16.	Boya (Larim)	Ethiopia	Kapoeta County	Larim
17.	Didinga	Lake Turkana	Budi County	Didinga
18.	Dinka- Jieng Muonyjang	From Deng son of Garang and Abuk	Upper Nile, Bahr-el-Ghazal, S. Kordofan	Thong Muonyjang
19.	Dongotona	Undefined	South of Torit Town	Lotuka dialect
20.	Feroghe	North to South	Raga to Hofra-Nahas	Kaligi
21.	Gollo	Undefined	West of Wau	Gollo
22.	Ifoto	From Lotuka	Imatong side of Torit	Lotuka dialect
23.	Imatong	From Lotuka	Imatong side of Torit	Lotuka dialect
24.	Indri	Undefined	Near Raga	Indri-Kaligi
25.	Jiye	Turkana area	Pibor County	Jiye
26.	Jurbel (beli)	Central Africa	River Gel-Mvollo-Yirol	Jur Beli
27.	Jurchol (Jo-Luo)	Dimo, a brother of Nyikango and Gilo	Wau-Tonj-Aweil and Alelthony of Kuajok	Dho Luo
28.	Mananger	From the West	Gogrial West County	Jur-Mananger
29.	Kakwa	From Yeki or Kui	Yei , Uganda, Congo	Kakwa-Bari
30.	Kara	Ethiopia-Darfur	Raga District	Kara
31.	Keliku	Madi -Lugbwara	Yei River County	Keliko
32.	Kuku	Bari Migration	Kajo-Keji area	Kuku-Bari

33	Lango	From East	Imatong-E. Equatoria	Lotuka dialect
34	Lotuka/Lotuho (Otuho)Otuko	East Africa Lopit Mount.	Torit District	Otuho (Lotuka)
35	Logir	Lake Turkana	Dogotono massif	Lotuka dialect
36	Lokoya	East Africa	Torit District	Lotuka dialect
37	Lulubo/Olu'bo	Undefined	Juba County	Olu'bo thi
38	Lopit	Lake Turkana	Lopit Hills of Torit	Lopit
39	Lugbwara	Gboro-Gboro/Meme	Yei River County-Uganda	Lugbwara
40	Maban (Maboano)	Soba near Kartuom	East of Renk up to Ethiopian Highlands	Burun,Maban or Chai
41	Madi	Rabanga	Torit District-Uganda	Madi
42	Mangayat Bugwa/Bukwa	Undefined	Sopo, Kagulu rivers, Khor Luju and Raga	
43	Moro	West Africa	Mundri and Maridi	Moru
44	Moro Kodo	Undefined	Amadi, Mundri, Yeri	Morokodo
45	Mundari	Bora-Bari	Terekeka,Tombe Tali	Bari dialect
46	Mundu	Cent. Africa	Maridi-Congo	Mundu
47	Murle	Ethiopia, Turkana	Pibor County	Murle
48	Ndogo	Mboro-Waye	Wau-Raga-D.Zubeir	Ndogo
49	Ngulngule	Darfur	Raga-Nyamlell	Ngulgule
50	Nuer (Naath)	Luel	Upper Nile, Ethiopia	Thok Naath
51	Nyangatom	Uganda	E. Equatoria-Ethiopia	Nyangatom
52	Nyangwara	Lake Turkana	Rokon Terekeka Juba	Bari dialect
53	Pari	Wi-Pach	Lafon County	Dhi-Pari
54	Pojullo	Undefined	YeiJuba Uganda Congo	Bari dialect
55	Sere	Mbomu River	Deim Zubier to Wau	Sere
56	Shatt(Thuri)	Othuru Dimo	Raga,Marial Bai, Aweil	Luo dialect
57	Shilluk (Chollo)	Nyikango	Upper Nile	Dhok Chollo
58	Suri (Kachipo)	Bor area	Boma to Ethiopia	Suri
59	Tenet	Lake Turkana	Lopit area	Tenet
60	Tid (Teuth)	Undefined	Natinga Mountain	Tid

61	Toposa	Uganda	Kapoeta County	Taposa
62	Uduk	East Sudan	Upper Nile-Ethiopia	Uduk
63	Woro	Undefined	Greater Equatoria	Woro
64	Yulu	Blue Nile	Kafia Kingi-Central Africa	Yulu

ETHNIC GROUPS OF SOUTHERN SUDAN

Ethnic Groups

There are a lot of ethnic groups in Southern Sudan as reflected above.

Localities

The ethnic groups live in defined entities all over Southern Sudan: some in mountainous areas, others on flat plains; some along the River Nile, others farther away from the Nile. The majority reside in rural areas.

Livelihood

Most people depend on subsistence agriculture. Others subsidize the agriculture with dairy such as cattle, sheep, goats, and fowl. Hunting and fishing also feature as an additional way of subsistence among most ethnic groups. Few that have minerals like gold in their areas conduct limited trade on them.

Originality

Most of the people maintain their African originality. However, some have had the names of their ethnic groups modified by their own neighbours.For example, some Dho Luo ethnic groups are referred to as Jur Chol and Jur Bel by Jieng ethnic groups.

Languages

Proudly, almost all ethnic groups preserved their African languages. Others have had their languages influenced by neighbouring groups. For instance, Ifoto and Imatong ethnic groups use Lotuka dialects.

Traditional Authority

Before the chieftainship system was imposed at the colonial era, African kingdoms and other forms of traditional authority existed.

Marriages

For most people in Southern Sudan, marriage starts with courtship. Then traditional approaches are made and dialogues initiated among families of potential couples. Thereafter, dowry is paid in various forms such as cattle, sheep, goats, spears, other ornaments, and money.

Birth

Ceremonies are held by most ethnic groups several days after the birth of a child. These are usually naming ceremonies during which prayers are conducted traditionally for good health and well-being of the newborn.

Naming

The name given to a child at birth can have a special meaning depending on the original ethnic group of the father. Some may reflect the day the child was born or an event that took place at that time. Others refer to the colour of their bulls or cows. However a lot assign a name of a predecessor or ancestor of that family.

It also depends whether one is a twin or follows twins. For example, the Rek would call a twin girl Anger and a twin boy Ngor or

Chan. A boy following twins is called Bol and a girl after twins is named Nyibol.

However names for triplets or more have to be worked out. Recently when a Southern Sudanese newly married lady gave birth to five children in the United States of America, I guess it was not an easy task to assign predetermined traditional twin-like names to them, as none might have existed beyond the two normally given to twins.

Black Africans take a special pride in remembering and stating their full names up to the last possible ancestor or predecessor in the family lineage. Take the author of this book for example; he can manage to trace his name only up to the thirteenth predecessor starting with his father. Thus his full name and pedigree are:

Achier Deng Akol Ayay Akol Kon Kuac Aguer Aluk Adup Achier Aguer Ajeng Ben

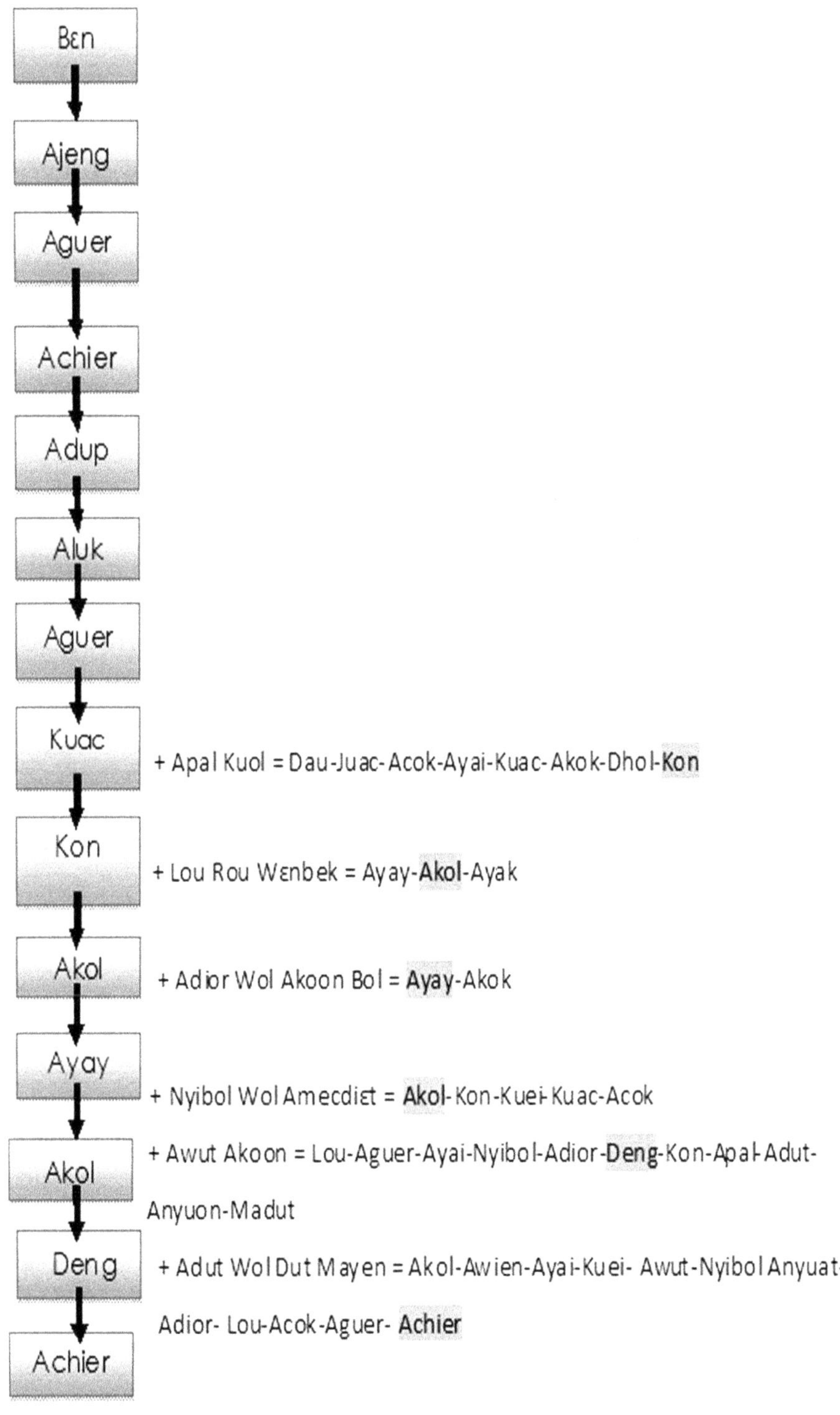
Bɛn
Ajeng
Aguer
Achier
Adup
Aluk
Aguer
Kuac
+ Apal Kuol = Dau-Juac-Acok-Ayai-Kuac-Akok-Dhol-Kon
Kon
+ Lou Rou Wɛnbek = Ayay-Akol-Ayak
Akol
+ Adior Wol Akoon Bol = Ayay-Akok
Ayay
+ Nyibol Wol Amecdiɛt = Akol-Kon-Kuei-Kuac-Acok
Akol
+ Awut Akoon = Lou-Aguer-Ayai-Nyibol-Adior-Deng-Kon-Apal-Adut-Anyuon-Madut
Deng
+ Adut Wol Dut Mayen = Akol-Awien-Ayai-Kuei- Awut-Nyibol Anyuat-Adior- Lou-Acok-Aguer- Achier
Achier

The squares and arrows signify the lineage of Pachier Pan Ayay where the author comes from. The plus indicates marriage to, and the equal symbol points to the children arising from that marriage staring from the first to the last born. The child referred to in the lineage is highlighted in gray colour. For example, Deng Akol Ayay married a lady called Adut Wol Dut Mayen, both of whom gave birth to eleven children, the last born of which is Achier who is the author of this book.

Perhaps if his traditional education was not interrupted by being taken to school, he could recall his ancestors up to more than simply thirteen.

Death

Most hold funeral ceremonies for the deceased, although the styles of burial and types of graves used differ. Burials of kings, spiritual leaders and chiefs tend to be greater than those of others.

Beliefs

Most of the Black Africans in Southern Sudan traditionally believe that there is a Creator given various names depending on ethnic origins. Prayers are conducted through intermediaries to the Creator. Spirits of the ancestors are adored and respected. Few believe strongly in witchcraft.

Courage

A common feature shared by almost all the People of Southern Sudan is courage. When challenged, most ethnic groups would fight vigorously to defend themselves against attackers. The advantage of this feature is that most of the ethnic groups in Southern Sudan have managed to survive a series of massacres and genocide perpetuated during the war. The disadvantage is that ethnic clashes are easily ignited and fuelled by rivals whose interest is to weaken the people of Southern Sudan and ultimately crash them and wipe them out. It is also intended to project them wrongly as people that cannot govern themselves. However when the people of Southern Sudan realise the malicious motives behind these clashes, they will stop and direct their courage entirely toward common defence for survival and existence. They will either continue to fade away in a united Sudan or begin to thrive in an independent South Sudan after 2011.

CULTURE

A Land So Courteous

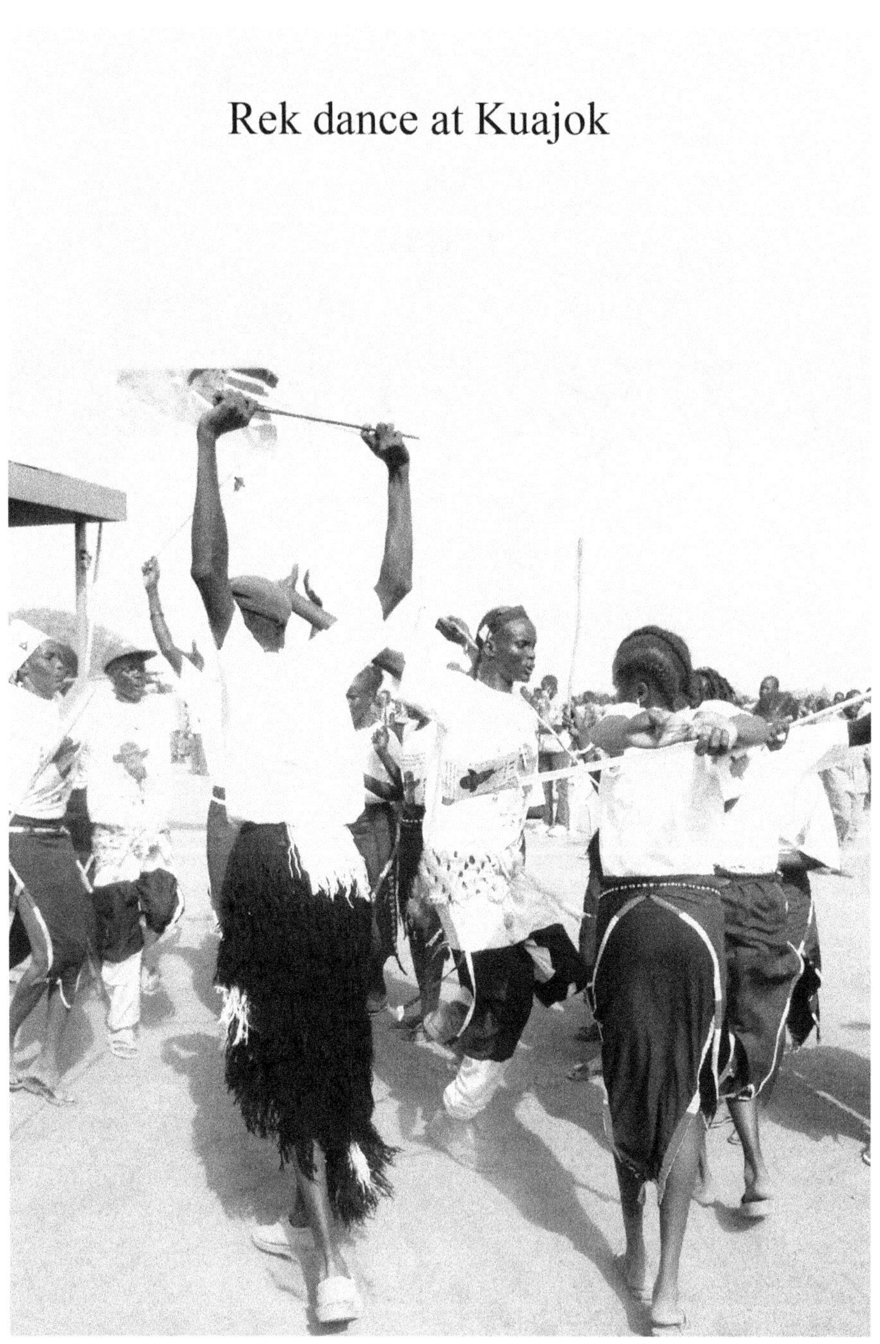

Rek dance at Kuajok

Earlier, I elaborated about spectacular colours on our livestock. Forget about how our animals look and glance at us ourselves too during a ceremony or celebration. You would be shocked to observe a range of exciting colorations, decorations, all admirations on us or of us apart from stunning variety of cultural performances themselves. When an African drum sounds, all beauty starts to flow in a stream unseen elsewhere on Earth, especially when it sounds in the Heart of Africa, in South Sudan to say to the world: See the beauty of Africa at its best: Ebony colour, shiny charcoal, tall and handsome people of Kush as described in the Bible, short and glamorous, black and proud.

My own feelings about our unique physical and cultural beauty are reflected in the following speech I recorded for Miss South Sudan Beauty Contest in the United States on 16 June 2006:

SPEECH FOR MISS SOUTH SUDAN BEAUTY CONTEST IN THE UNITED STATES BY DR. ACHIER DENG AKOL

Saturday June 17, 2006

Virginia–USA

Miss South Sudan Contestants
Brothers and Sisters

My name is Achier Deng Akol. Like you, I am a child and lover of South Sudan. I live in London, UK, from where I am now transmitting this speech. I was lucky to have attended this thrilling beauty contest in the United States but failed to deliver my speech then because the organisers were not aware that I had arrived at the ceremony that day. Nevertheless, I am grateful that they had considered me as one of the speakers and I hope my voice and message now reach all the participants in general and the very contestants in particular through their video and Web site.

This occasion may appear trivial. It is not. It is a great event that has put our unknown land in the spotlight worldwide. Those who will be watching anywhere, especially back home will feel a lot of joy and excitement to the extent that it will even heal any pains they have. Thanks to those who originally conceived the idea of this beauty contest and all of you who volunteered to participate.

I have travelled widely all over the world during my lifetime and can testify that I have not come across people who are more beautiful than us in South Sudan. This is not just something I am saying to appease you. It is true and we should all be proud of that.

There are two types of beauty: **External** and **Internal**. The external one is what is viewed physically while the internal one is manifested in the form of good behaviour. We as a People of South Sudan gladly possess both of them. This is contrary to lies that others say about us to project us negatively worldwide as horrible people. Forget about all those lies and continue proudly to feel and manifest both our external and internal beauty. Do not cover them up in long veils.

Internal beauty is more important than external. Please let the world know the good people we are through good behaviour above all.

We have missed out on so many nice things happening in the world because of long war. Let this be the start of our participation in good things and I hope one day we will ultimately take part in and win the Miss World Beauty Contest.

By taking part in this competition, you have shown the great extent to which you love and cherish our land of South Sudan. Please show your love to this land too by working hard wherever you are abroad and making sure you acquire a useful qualification. This will be invaluable for our land and people that desperately need vital services. Don't leave the United States, Canada, Australia, Asia, Europe and other African Countries empty-handed. Always remember your land needs you most and use that as a motivation to succeed. This advice applies to both boys and girls.

It is insignificant who takes the first prize today. To me, you are all winners in this exciting and positive competition. All you need to guard against collectively or individually is not to abuse your natural gift of exceptional beauty by using it in any bad way. Make sure you do not also throw away our beauty. It belongs to South Sudan and to a South Sudanese it should go, if you understand what I mean. For example, while I agree that love has no boundaries, I would prefer that the priority should go to a fellow South Sudanese if possible in terms of marriage. This way we can succeed to conserve our indigenous South Sudanese African species on this planet against the threat of genocide. Having said so, I have no prejudice at all against non-indigenous marriages.

And to young boys of South Sudan, please listen to this. Please aim to be good, caring, loving, gentle, and considerate to your future wives. For a wife is cuddled, not mishandled. She is amused, not abused. Don't reward them with torture, neglect and abuse in any form for offering you their love and beauty. Don't waste your lives and theirs away through addictions like alcohol, illegal drugs, domestic violence, or crime. Let the world be proud of us as good people wherever we live and let our girls not regret accepting to marry you. Let them not feel they have thrown their beauty away when they offer it to you in marriage and friendship. I am grateful to a sister called Susan Andrua for reminding me to emphasise these essential points to you gentlemen. We from marginalised Sudan have suffered too much in the course of our long struggle and we can do without additional self-inflicted pains of domestic violence and abuse. Let us instead enjoy ourselves through sweet friendship and happy marriage.

Oh! Spectacular flowers of South Sudan! You are charming and lovely and so is our land. I call our land **Beautiful South Sudan: The Heart of Africa**! It is a land so gorgeous, so precious, so amorous, and therefore so contentious. No wonder others want to rob it from us. We will not allow it to be taken away from us whatsoever.

Sometimes we start good programs and fail to sustain them. Let this not be the first and the last Miss South Sudan Beauty Contest. Let it be the beginning of more to follow.

You are all stunning and were I to think of marrying again, I would be confused about which one of you to choose. I believe your judges are finding it very hard to select the overall winner among you. Keep up that glamour. Remain forever world leaders in both external and internal beauty.

Since this is an occasion of beauty of South Sudan and I have come all the way from London, UK, with an empty pocket, let me conclude my speech with a little poem as a gift to all of you. Of course, had I a nice voice like brother Emmanuel Kembe and other wonderful singers of our land now taking part in this ceremony, I would have sung you this poem of mine called **BEAUTIFUL SOUTH SUDAN** instead of simply reciting it. Besides, were I a millionaire, I would have offered you millions of dollars to sponsor this event and not just a little poem:

BEAUTIFUL SOUTH SUDAN

Beautiful South Sudan
The Heart of Africa
Shall thrive and glamour
Once again as before
It shall shine with power
Like a star and even more

It will grow
From a weakling
To an independent bow
With a mighty string

Its dry plains
Will become green
To produce grains
As it had been

Rivers lakes and streams
Will fill and flow
Rusty golden beams
Will begin to glow

All destroyed cities
Like Juba Wau and Malakal
Will be reflourished
New ones like central Ramkiel
Will be established

Multiple wonderful flowers
Will spring up once again
With spectacular colours
To relieve longstanding pain

The painful years
Of long war
With miserable tears
Of absolute poor
Will all change

Dying forests
Destroyed plantains
Ruined harvests
Eroded mountains
Will all blossom
Once again

Beautiful South Sudan
The Heart of Africa
Shall thrive and glamour
Once again as before
It shall shine with power
Like a star and even more

Thank You and God Bless

Wait also for nighttime to come in order to add the shining stars and moon in the sky apart from wonderful cultural displays in the form of all-night-long dances and ceremonies.

The beauty of our land is never darkled or masked when night falls. It is sparkled with natural fireworks of twinkling stars and moonshine. It remains glamorous day or night.

Common cultural features shared by most of the people in South Sudan can be summarised as follows:

Source

The culture of South Sudan remains predominantly traditional African despite influence of the Western World and Middle East.

Religion

The leading religions professed in South Sudan are Christianity and indigenous African faiths followed by limited Islamic infiltration. When people like Jieng believe in Nhialic as the Creator anonymous to Almighty God or Allah, their religion cannot be dismissed or described as paganism.

Dress

Before cloth was discovered, South Sudanese were not necessarily naked. In the presence of dense tropical forest, thick grass, and colourful wildlife, they were among the first people to first use knitted grass, animal hide, and shaped leaves as dresses. Some of these original wears survived up to the present era. Take Jieng ethnic group (Dinka) for example, they still proudly use soft hide of sheep called "buong" that has edges beautifully decorated with colourful beats; "ajom," that is a beautiful hat composed of black ostrich feathers; and "dhok," that is a wonderful leopard hide worn particularly by bridegrooms. Other ethnic groups have or had similar kinds of traditional non-cloth dresses.

Various beautiful dresses exist in South Sudan such as Acuat or Lawa. The turban or jallabia tend to be associated with Arabism and Islam and therefore limited by others into pyjamas or for herding.

The African Cultural Society of University of Khartoum in conjunction with sisters at Ahfad University designed a provisional African national wear for the African majority in Sudan in the year 1978. There was one costume designed for either sex. These were neither "tob" nor "jalabia." They were derivatives of existing African costumes in Equatoria, Upper Nile, and River Lol (Bahr-el-Ghazal) regions. They can be revived, finalised, and applied.

Decorations

Nothing is spared from colourful decoration in South Sudan. Human skin, livestock, gourds, and ornaments are particular examples.

Hospitality

A common feature of South Sudan culture is an exceptional spirit of hospitality. Guests or visitors are not left to starve or remain thirsty. The last drop of water in a pot or grain in a basket is offered to them. They are also offered places to sleep free of charge.

Ceremonies

Various ceremonies and celebrations provide opportunity for wonderful cultural displays of dances and songs using various traditional musical instruments as detailed in the preceding chapter on people. Harvest festivals and wedding ceremonies are common examples.

Characters

In the absence of provocation and enmity, one can assert that most if not all South Sudanese are kind and welcoming among themselves and to others. This uniform character is featured in an extract of my poem that says:

Come and live with us

Come and live with us
For even a single day
You will know instantly
How good a people we are

Visit any part of South Sudan
When our cottages are re-erected
You will not be neglected
To sleep in the cold outside

Knock on any door
Of a South Sudan home
When you are thirsty
You will be offered
The last drop of water

Unfortunately, we are offspring of the Kush Kingdom that feared no other existing people in ancient history. Thus, if we are provoked or attacked, we fight up to the last drop of blood in full defence. This is a feature of heroism and protectiveness more than unnecessary hostility or brutality that has allowed most of our ethnic species to survive till now. Yet, the future of this beautiful culture hangs in a balance pending the outcome of 2011 referendum.

FOLKLORE

A Land So Mysterious

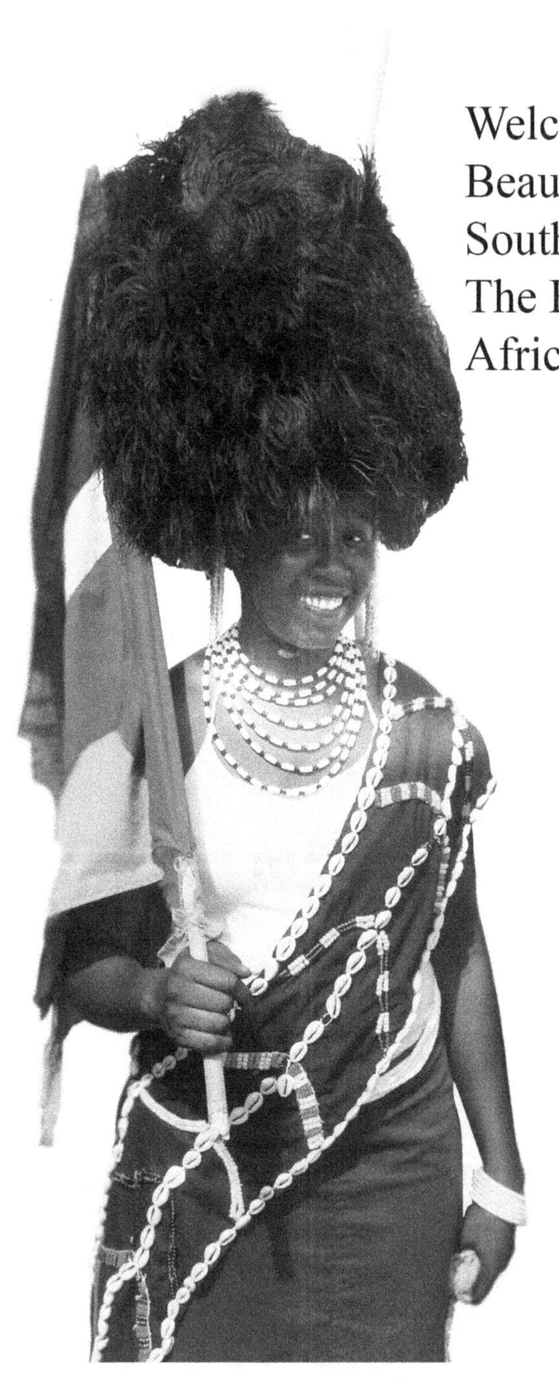

Welcome to Beautiful South Sudan; The Heart of Africa

F1 INTRODUCTION OF FOLKLORE

Indeed, when I was a child the best part of any day I longed for to come soon was not the early morning when I rushed for sweet corn or sugar cane on our farm, nor the afternoon when I joined other children to play in a group. It was the nighttime simply because of an opportunity to listen to exciting bedtime stories. All the nice things that daytime brought were overshadowed the moment the family circle in a room launched marvellous stories in turn. A family circle that goes on clockwise or anticlockwise to narrate one after another, stories that aimed to outstrip one another in excitement. And the rule of thumb was: Anybody in the circle that is still awake must respond with a story until all fall asleep lest something frightening might happen to the storyteller. Thus the last person to say a story would know only that everybody else had fallen asleep when the room is dead quiet apart from breath sounds and occasional air-letting, a polite term I learnt in my childhood to represent farting. You know, even in language we were taught how to speak politely. That is why I now prohibit all my children from echoing bad expressions like "shit" or "fuck you," and I am glad they listened to me.

So heartthrobbing and brain-stimulating were the nighttime stories that a good number of them stuck in my mind and I would like to gladly share some of them here with anyone interested. Of course, I must have forgotten fragments of those I heard when I was under five or so, as I was probably the first to fall asleep at that age and missed out on a lot. However, the later teenage stories with sweet honeymoon content that kept my eyes opened whenever I heard them never left my memory. In the following pages of this section, are some of them, for any family circle or individuals to enjoy, especially those contemplating, anticipating, participating in, or celebrating a wedding and honeymoon whether in a traditional wooden cottage or a luxurious five-star hotel.

F2 HOW TRUTH HELPS

Once upon a time a man called Awer was being chased by a group of people who wanted to kill him. He ran as fast as he could for his life; but, the people nearly caught up with him when he reached the cottage of an old man in the country-side. The old man was busy clearing weeds off his front garden by the side of a heap of straw.

"Help me, help me, please," Mr. Awer pleaded. "Those people chasing me are determined to kill me"

The old man thought fast of what to do to rescue Awer. Suddenly he responded to the plea.

"Enter quickly into that heap of hay before they see and never move an inch," ordered the old man.

When the people arrived, they immediately questioned the old man.

"Have you seen the young man that we were chasing?" One of them asked aggressively.

"Where did you hide him?" added another angrily.

The old man remained calm. He continued to clear the weeds off while gazing toward the forest nearby. Then he slowly put down the hoe and pointed toward the same heap of clay where he had instructed Awer to hide.

"There, inside that hay." The old man honestly replied. "I have hidden him in that heap of clay."

Awer was shocked inside the hay when he heard the old man reveal where he was exactly hiding. He wondered whether the old man he trusted as his angel might have been an accomplice.

He feared that the end of his world was about to come. However, he tried to control himself from shivering so that the hay did not shake or fall apart to expose him. As for the water, well, only few people on Earth would hold it at this stage and he was not one of them; he felt a dribble down his thighs and tried his best to limit the flow of urine so that some of it did not leak outside the hay as a matter of life and death.

"That is a pure lie," shouted one of the attackers. "How on Earth can a person be hidden inside hay?"

"This old man is misleading us," grumbled another aggressor. "Let us search the entire house and if he is not there let us quickly run to the bush to catch up with him."

A light of hope started to shine in Awer. A miracle was about to happen. His life could be spared.

There was no soul to be found anywhere in the house and to the bush the crowd dashed in disbelief, hoping to overtake their targeted victim there and finish him off.

When they had gone far out of sight, the old man said, "What are you still doing inside that hay? You can come out now."

Awer jumped out paradoxically in anger and shouted at the old man, his body still wet with sweat and what have you.

"Why on Earth, did you ask me to hide inside the hay and then reveal it to my enemies? Supposing they had believed you and ripped that hay apart, would they not have found and killed me?" he complained bitterly.

The old man had already resumed his work of clearing off the weeds. He was not bothered at all about Awer's complaint. Of course, if anything, he had expected gratitude and not blame. Nevertheless, he felt duty bound to clarify for future reference.

In a calm low voice and with full confidence so as to emphasise that he did the right thing, the old man responded.

"Young man, Almighty God helps you when you tell the truth. Had I told them a lie, that you were hiding in my house or ran to the bush, for example, they would not have believed me. They would then have looked in the hay where you were hiding.

"Remember, my son, God helps you when you tell the truth." The old man concluded.

In comparison, it is nothing else but the truth when we say that the land of South Sudan belongs to us and God will surely help us to liberate it fully.

F3 WAVERING RISKS PEOPLE'S LIVES BEFORE OLD AGE

Chol Muong (Choldit) had two wives. Both of them were preparing dinner for the family in their different houses. The houses were within walking distance of their husband.

"Whose meal will come out first?" Choldit wondered. "Is it that of my first or second wife? I am so hungry, I want to eat. Let me keep a close eye on them.

"I can see my first wife has just started. Let me go and check if my second wife will finish cooking first."

So Choldit walked to the house of his second wife only to find that she was only just about to begin cooking.

"Goodness me! She is miles away. Let me return to the house of my first wife to see how far she is gone." So he walked back to his first wife. Things were still boiling then.

There, he waited for a short while hoping it would soon be over. He could smell things still roasting endlessly.

"Maybe my second wife has completed her cooking now even though she started late. Some of these wives can be quick with cooking. Why don't I return to check up with her, just in case?"

Choldit thus impatiently walked back to the house of his second wife. He could smell from a distance the delicious odour of things being roasted.

"Didn't I say some of these wives are quick?" he comforted himself before reaching his second wife's house. He sat down in anticipation with a heart pumping eagerly. Unfortunately, the sweet smell was all that seemed forthcoming. Things were still being boiled.

"What am I doing here now? My second wife that I thought to be quicker does not seem to be. She is just going on endlessly. Anyway, perhaps she is about to complete the process. But, I am worried that I might miss the other delicious meal being prepared by my first wife. She might have finished preparing it now. Why don't I rush to her house to consume that first and return here later to enjoy this one too." Choldit went on contemplating and calculating his best chances of dual success.

Determined to catch up to the meal of his first wife, he left the one which was about to be completed by his second wife and ran to the house of his first wife.

Unfortunately, when he arrived there, he found that the cooking had not only finished there; but the entire meal had been consumed by the rest of his family. Nothing was left for him to eat on the assumption that he had decided to have his portion that day at his second wife's house.

"Oh my God!" he remarked "My only chance for a meal now is to fly back to my second wife."

Choldit had no more seconds to lose. He took off on his feet and wished he had wings. Back to the house of his second wife he really dashed like a wind.

To his bad luck too, his second wife had thought he did not want to eat in her house that night when he left at the time when the meal was almost ready. She thought too that he had opted to dine at the house of his first wife then. So everything was cleared by the time he arrived back to the house of his second wife. All the pots and gourds had even been washed with nothing at all left for him.

"What the hell!" he shouted. "What am I going to eat now when I am so hungry?"

"We thought you were going to have a meal at your other house," the second wife defended herself.

Thus Choldit ended up eating nothing for being impatient. Had he just felt contented and patient to wait in either house, he would have had a bite of something at least. He would not have ended up missing both meals.

And so it is said in Jieng (Dinka) language: "Akangkang akor dhiop." In other words, "Wavering in between options risks people's lives before old age. For since then, Choldit has been the principal advocate against wavering. Similarly, people who waver between political parties risk the lives and futures of those they represent.

F4 ONLY FOOLS KILL THEIR MOTHERS

This is the favourite story of my children that I had used many times to put them to sleep at night while struggling to bring them up abroad far away from their own motherland. Please read it to your small children too if you have any. They will like it.

Once upon a time, all the animals wondered what to do about their mothers who frequently smacked them when they committed mistakes as a disciplinary procedure.

The pain inflicted on them, though arguably justifiable as disciplinary in good faith, was too much for them to bear. So, all the animals decided to call a meeting to discuss what to do about their mothers.

They gathered all over, big and small. Rats, rabbits, sheep, goats, rams, cows, bulls, lions, giraffes, zebras, hyenas, foxes, elephants, rhinos, buffaloes, antelopes—almost every animal species you can think of was represented. The air was full of all animal noises and sounds: boos, moos, croaks, and many more.

Suddenly, Mr. Lion, the king of the jungle, stepped forward to chair the meeting.

"Silence everyone," the lion roared. And of course, no animal would dare to disobey the king. So all the moos, boos, and other sounds were suddenly gone.

"You all know why we have gathered here today," he started. "Our mothers have been smacking us painfully and we need to decide now how to prevent that or what to do about it. Let us hear what you have to say.

"Why don't we just run away from them every time they pick a whip or raise their hands," squeaked a rat.

"Run away from them?" A cat mewed. "Is that always successful?" it added sarcastically. "Let us come up with a better idea.

"How about locking them up on a ranch?" mooed a cow.

"They can still find their way out of the ranch," a dog barked.

Then the fox came up with what appeared to be a popular idea. "Why don't we just all kill our mothers? That way we can guarantee they can never hit us again."

"That is a splendid idea," all the animals instantly and unanimously agreed.

So every animal went back apparently to implement the decision letter by letter the same day.

The following day all the orphans of animals were hungry. They had no food to eat. No breakfast, lunch, nor dinner. They were all screaming with hunger as there were no mothers to fetch, prepare, and offer them something to eat. The breadbaskets of the families were dead and gone.

All were crying in sorrow and hunger except one animal: The fox. While all were hungry, the fox appeared satisfied and satiated. It was the only animal jumping around with full energy and paradoxical excitement. This was soon noticed by the rest of the animal children. So they called and asked him:

"Fox, why are you not crying like us? Why are you the only one laughing? Why are you not hungry too? Where did you find something to eat?"

"My mother cooked something and gave it to me to eat," the fox replied.

"What!" the animals shouted. "Did you not kill your own mother like all of us did as suggested by you and agreed?"

"I could not," defended the fox. "Where would I have found something to eat if I had killed my mother? I had a second thought and changed my mind."

"Only fools kill their mothers," the fox concluded.

F5 REMEMBER THESE BONES!

Once upon a time, a great famine occurred in Southern Sudan. Everybody was starving. The famine was precipitated by severe draught.

A gentleman called Mangok managed to catch two small fish from a river and decided to roast them under a tree by the river bank. An old woman called Ayuen, that was obviously starving, coincidentally decided to rest under the same tree before proceeding on her return journey home. She noticed Mr. Mangok roasting the fish.

It was dry season, in the month of July when the rivers were relatively dry and fish were even rarer. Fish is one type of food that you can hardly hide from others and eat secretly because of its smell that becomes even more remarkable during starvation. Dry wind was blowing toward the old man carrying along the nice smell of fresh fish which Mr. Mangok was roasting. Somehow, she had expected to be offered a small piece of the fish or at least to be invited.

During a famine there are two types of hearts. There are the tender ones who might even offer whatever little food they come across to victims who are frailer like children and the elderly that are more likely to die first from starvation.

Unfortunately there are the direct opposite ones who will think of themselves first and gallop any little food they can find without allowing anyone else to have a small bite even though the others may be the ones that are nearly dying.

When famine occurs it makes tender hearts more tender and cruel hearts harsher. It also exposes the true colours of individuals. It brings to the open the true colours of chameleons—people who used to show green light when there is plenty begin to show red light when things are scarce. Indeed, it is not green that is their true colour. It is red.

The old woman was frail, thin, and obviously starving. She had hoped that the heart which Mr. Mangok had was a tender one like that of most people during difficult times. She thought his colour was green.

The two small fish were visible on the sticks of firewood where they were being roasted. Mathematicians would agree that a kind-hearted man would at least offer a little piece if not an entire one of the two fish to the old woman. Unfortunately she waited and waited silently while Mangok consumed the two, one after the other. The old woman, who happened to be a Christian, recalled what the Bible says: "Knock and the door will be opened for you. Ask and you shall be given."

As an elderly person would not normally be expected to beg for food, she decided to tactfully "tease" Mr. Mangok just as he was about to take the final piece of the last fish.

"My son, where did you catch your fishes?" she asked.

"Mangok pretended not to have noticed her and first made sure he swallowed the last piece before he raised his head and turned toward her. "They were just two tiny ones that I luckily caught in that river" he replied defensively.

The old woman had an opportunity then to take a good look at his face and noticed a distinctive birth mark on the right cheek.

"I wanted to know where you luckily caught them, and not how big or small they were," the old woman explained.

Mr. Mangok got up and headed off, leaving behind barely the fish bones.

"You never know what may happen in the future, especially when I have attractive daughters," the old woman thought.

"Maybe this selfish and greedy man will become interested in one of my daughters later and even propose to marry her. Let me collect and keep these bones as a reminder to him if ever he has the guts to approach any of my daughters in the future." She picked up all the bones, wrapped them in a piece of cloth, and hid them safely in the roof of her house when she reached home.

After ten years, Mr. Mangok indeed developed interest and proposed to marry her younger daughter. Her prediction had come true. She decided not to interfere initially and waited toward the end when the marriage was on the verge of at its implementation phase. However, her daughter had observed that her mother did not seem to like Mr. Mangok. Every time she asked her opinion she did not come out with a clearly positive reply. She would also either engage herself with other duties or decide to go elsewhere when Mangok paid a visit to the house. So she decided to seek the assistance of her father to find out what her mother was up to.

"Daddy, I do not think my mother is interested in my marriage to Mangok. She seems to be behaving differently compared to when my elder sister was married. Could you please ask her?"

"We have all noticed," her father replied. "We shall ask her to tell us why. All I know is that she loves you dearly and it is puzzling for her not to show any interest in your marriage unless she has a strong reservation about Mr. Mangok." Her father decided to call a close family meeting soon after speaking with his daughter.

"All of us gathered here have noticed that you are not interested in the marriage of your daughter to Mr. Mangok. Can you please tell us why?" he initiated the consultation.

"Yes, I can," she replied. "Thanks for asking me. However, I would like Mr. Mangok to be also around so that he hears directly from me why I am reserved or, in fact, unwilling."

This was speedily arranged and in the presence of Mangok, she went upstairs to fetch the fish bones still wrapped in the cloth. Everyone, including Mr. Mangok, was observing her closely and wondering what was tied inside the piece of cloth. The old woman sat down in front of everybody and first glanced at the right cheek of Mangok where the birthmark lay so as to confirm that she was indeed talking to the right person.

"Do you recall having met me anywhere before about ten years ago?" The old woman asked Mr. Mangok.

"Ten years is a long time ago but I do not seem to recall having met you before I recently developed interest in your daughter," he replied. "Can you please refresh my memory in case I may have forgotten?"

Everybody was quiet. The air was still and the attention of the audience present was at its maximum level.

She silently opened the piece of cloth and exposed the dry fish bones for all to see.

"What is going on?" a few people murmured while the majority remained silent.

"You may have forgotten me," she continued, "but, do you remember these fish bones? Have you forgotten the great famine that occurred ten years ago when most of our people died and when you had the great luck to catch two fishes, or, to put it in your own words, just two tiny ones you luckily caught in that river? Can you recall that there was an old woman who was sitting under the same tree where you were roasting and enjoying the fishes without having the heart to even notice her, leave alone invite her? I was that very old lady. I collected and kept the fish bones after you left in order to remind you about them when an opportunity like this arose. I was worried that I might never get a chance at all to do so and I am happy that this chance has now been created by your interest to marry my beloved daughter."

The air remained still. The room was silent Mangok clearly re-called everything.

"How dare you come and ask for my daughter's hand for marriage when you are greedy as you are, heartless as you are?" she wondered.

Her daughter broke the silence. "People may be greedy but not to the extent of allowing others who are weaker than them to starve possibly to death while they consume alone whatever little food they managed to obtain from anywhere. No wonder why my mother had never shown any interest in you. You can now get up and go away to look for another girl with a similar heart to yours."

"I totally agree with you, my daughter," her mother said. "No mother who loves her daughter will be too inconsiderate to allow her to be married to a man as heartless as Mangok. In fact, I would rather my daughter remains unmarried until she dies, even if he was the only man left on the Earth," she concluded and everybody agreed with her.

The greedy Mangok got up, wiped his bumps of dust and left shamefully.

F6 WHAT ARE YOU AIMING AT, MY DEAR?

Once upon a time there was a newly married wife who used to cook nice meals for her dear husband. Her routine was always to put a soup of meat on the fire, and while it was roasting she would go to fetch some fresh spicy vegetables from the farm to add.

Unfortunately, whenever she returned she would notice some lumps of meat missing from the cooking pot.

"Who pinches the meat when I am away?" she wondered. "Who has the courage to dip the fingers into a boiling soup to extract the meat"?

Their house was a bit far from the neighbours and no one else apart from her husband resided in it with her. They did not yet have any children of their own to suspect.

"Could it be my husband?" she asked herself. "But why would he do so when I am actually cooking for him and when I always give him the lion's share of the entire food anyway? I don't think he is the one; but who else can it be? Is it possible for any rat to do so when the soup is hot?" she wondered.

One time she decided to come back earlier from the farm in an attempt to catch the culprit. By that time her husband had extracted a large lump of meat and he was just trying to cool it when he suddenly spotted his wife returning from the garden.

It was summertime. The grass was high. The farm was thick with crops and vegetables, especially pumpkin leaves and ladies fingers (okra). His wife was, in fact, negotiating her way back to the house through the thick farm. She was carrying a tray containing the vegetables. She could not see her husband from afar.

"Oh my goodness, what am I going to do with this lump of hot meat in my hands?" her husband quickly thought.

He had a few options. He could quickly throw it back into the cooking pot and dash away from there but he was very reluctant to do so as it would not serve his immediate purpose. He could hide it in his pockets but the long dress he was wearing did not contain any pockets. It was also too hot and too large to either hide in his mouth or to chew and swallow before she arrived.

His options had run out. There was only one left and that was to throw it far out to the farm and go later to fetch and eat it secretly from his wife. He did exactly that as quickly as possible. Unfortunately for him the lump of meat fell onto the tray that his wife was carrying on her way back to the house without him knowing.

She quickly glanced at what dropped into the tray. At first she had thought it was a small stone which her husband might have thrown to the farm to chase away birds from the crops. To her amazement she discovered that it was a hot lump of meat.

"There is no kite that can succeed to swoop a piece of meat from the bottom of a cooking pot especially when the water is boiling." She thought, "It must have been thrown off by my husband, especially when it seems to have come from that direction."

Silently she bypassed her husband after covering the meat in that tray with the vegetables. She pretended as if she had not known what happened to the meat, replaced it in the pot and carried on with the cooking.

After a short time her husband got up and walked out to the farm to look for the meat. Of course he could not locate it. He returned to the house, picked a large stone, and, after aiming exactly toward where he had thrown the piece of meat, he threw the large stone in that direction. He hoped it would drop at the same spot where he had previously thrown the meat in order to help him locate it. He also made sure he used the same amount of force so that the stone would not fall beyond or before the spot.

After throwing the stone he traced it and unfortunately failed still to locate the meat.

"May be I had not aimed correctly," he felt. "Let me try again."

After making several throws, his wife inquired, "What are you aiming at, my darling?"

"Oh! At the birds, my dear" he replied. "They are destroying our valuable crops you know." She almost burst into laughter. She knew of course that he was lying.

"Why are you using big stones this time?" she asked again.

"Well these destructive birds do not seem to be frightened again by small stones this time." He wisely responded, still assuming that his wife did not understand what he was exactly trying to do. He did not give up in time. He went on and on, aiming here and there until he got tired and gave up.

"Perhaps it had been picked away by a wondering cat or dog before I arrived," he concluded and sat down to wait impatiently for the small portion he had left in the pot.

His wife decided to isolate the large piece of meat which he had previously picked and prepare it more deliciously. Then she delivered it to him in a decorated calabash and then waited for him to take a bite from it before teasing him.

"Is that what you were looking for?" she asked. "Is that what you were aiming at in the farm?" she repeated mockingly. He was silent with shame, having now known where the meat had dropped if not who picked it up where it had dropped.

One does not need to steal one's own meat you know, if one is not brave enough to ask a wife for it in advance," she whispered.

For many years that followed, no more pieces of meat disappeared again from the cooking pot.

F7 A HIDE ON WHICH NO GUEST LIES

The weather was cold. Adut decided to warm water for her only son Dhol to have a bath in the evening. As she was carrying the warm water to her twenty-five-year-old son her husband shouted at her.

"Stop doing that now," he shouted "Don't you know it is about time he should have married his own wife," he added.

Dhol could not sleep. He thought overnight over his father's concern. In the morning he got up with a plan to look for a girl of his dreams. He walked to a nearby pond and caught two fishes and one frog. He tied all the three on a string and carried them on a stick and walked from one village to another.

"Can any one of you please care to cook for me what I am carrying?" he requested the first four girls he met. "I am hungry" he added.

The girls noticed a frog among the fishes and burst into laughter.

"You must be joking," they replied and walked away.

Dhol repeated the same request to the second girl he met next. She also noticed the frog.

"Don't tease me," she replied, "and don't waste my time," she added.

After three days of fasting, he was becoming weak with hunger and exhausted from walking. The fishes and the frog were also getting rotten and they attracted a lot of flies. Every night he slept under a tree while making sure that the fishes and the frog were not taken away even though they were rotten.

As he continued his journey, he received similar negative replies and even more laughter. At last he came across three sisters who were on their way to fetch drinking water from a nearby well.

"Can one of you please care to cook for me these food items of mine?" he further inquired. "I am very hungry," he stressed.

The two older girls burst into laughter like all the others before them.

"You must be mad," they remarked. However the younger girl called Adau appeared more concerned. Although she noticed the rotten fishes and frog surrounded by flies, she also observed that the gentleman carrying them looked weak with hunger.

"Give them to me and come along to our house," Adau said. "I will cook them for you," she agreed.

"Are you out of your mind?" her sisters remarked. "Don't you see he is a madman?" they added.

"He might be mad but he is hungry," Adau replied.

When they reached their house the two sisters rushed to report to their mum.

"Look at what your daughter Adau has done," they complained. "She has brought that madman to our house with rotten things which she has agreed to cook for him," they added.

"For God sake, Mummy, look at that man they call mad. He is weak and hungry and he needs something to eat," she emphasized.

"OK, Adau, you can do whatever you think necessary," her mother ruled, after a quick glance at Dhol.

Adau threw away the rotten fishes and frog and instead cooked for him fresh food consisting of delicious porridge mixed with milk and butter, traditionally known as "kuin-ci-diong."

"If you will accept me, I will marry you," Dhol thanked Adau. "I am not a madman, I am the only son of the local chief," he added.

While he was away, both his parents and members of his village community were worried.

"You made him disappear," Dhol's mother asserted.

"No, I was only trying to encourage him to get married," replied his father.

Suddenly Dhol returned.

"Thank God you are alive," his mother quickly remarked as she hugged him.

"Daddy, I have found the girl of my dreams," Dhol revealed.

"I am pleased" said his father. "Thank God too that you are alive, as your mother said. Now tell us about her."

He told them all about Miss Adau ad how he chose her.

After a series of family meetings to approve the marriage, arrangements were subsequently concluded. Dhol and Adau were happily married.

Soon after starting their new home, one of the cousins of Dhol killed a man from a neighboring village. The relatives and friends of the deceased decided to choose Dhol as the most valuable relative of the murderer whom they should kill in revenge.

While cultivating in his new farm near his house, Dhol was suddenly surrounded by ten powerful men carrying spears.

"We have come to kill you in revenge for our brother who has been murdered by your cousin," one of the invaders stated. "The reason we picked on you particularly is not only because you are the only son of the chief. It is also because you are a popular man in the community apart from the fact that you are a bridegroom. We therefore feel you are the most precious person we can revenge our dear brother with," they claimed.

"However, before we kill you, let us give you a chance to say a few words."

"Thank you for giving me that chance," Dhol spoke." Please let one of you go to my wife and tell her to seat him on a seat or hide on which no guest lies while she fetches a piece of tobacco I have hidden on the roof of our house." Then bring me that piece of tobacco to smoke before you kill me."

The farm was hidden by surrounding shrubs and tall grass and no one could spot from afar that Dhol was in danger.

The attackers agreed. One of them was sent as Dhol requested.

"Your husband, Dhol, wants you to seat me on a hide on which no guest lies while you go upstairs to fetch a piece of tobacco for me to take to him. He is busy on the farm and badly desires to smoke the tobacco."

Adau's heart jumped and she immediately sensed that her husband was at imminent danger even though the stranger appeared friendly.

"Oh! Look at my husband with his poor memory." Adau pretended. "He has forgotten that he has actually smoked that last piece last night. Please wait here and I will just run next door to get him another piece of tobacco," she added.

The messenger believed her and agreed to wait while she dashed to the neighbors.

"You will not catch my husband alive if you do not all go quickly to the farm," Adau pleaded with the neighbor. "I am sure there must be some people on the farm who are about to kill him."

Within minutes a crowd of people rushed to rescue Dhol. They formed a second huge circle around the invaders with Dhol in the middle of all. Everybody in the crowd was surprised how Adau knew that her husband was about to be killed.

"We shall not proceed to kill you, not because we are afraid of being subsequently killed but because we are amazed by the genius wife you have," the attackers spoke. "Please let your wife tell us how she detected the imminent danger on your life."

"First of all, my husband does not smoke at all, but above all, a hide on which no guest lies is a wife as long as her husband is alive. In short, what my husband meant by his message to me was that he was about to be killed and leave me as a widow who could be taken over by somebody else," explained Adau.

"You can now see how it pays to be patient until one finds an intelligent wife of one's dreams," Dhol boasted. "Had I not married a genius wife, I would have lost my life," he finally and proudly concluded.

F8 WHY DID YOU WASTE TIME STUDYING MEDICINE?

A medical doctor took his car to be hand washed by a manual labourer in Khartoum.

That labourer would normally wash up to ten cars a day for a charge of two thousand Sudanese pounds per car. Thus he would expect to earn twenty thousand pounds a day or six hundred thousand a month. That is well above the monthly salary of a qualified medical doctor serving in Sudan.

After he finished washing the car, the doctor asked him.

"How much do you charge?"

"Two thousand, sir," he replied.

After paying him, the doctor continued to inquire: "How many cars, by the way, do you wash a day?"

"On average, I wash ten, sir."

"So you get twenty thousand per day or six hundred thousand a month?"

"Yes, sir," he replied.

"That is far more than what I earn per month as a salary from the Sudan government," the doctor grumbled.

"Why did you waste your time to study medicine?" The car-washer concluded.

F9 THE FOX AND THE HERON

Once upon a time a fox and a heron became great friends.

One day, the fox decided to invite the heron for dinner. The heron accepted happily.

The fox prepared some tasty semolina and served it on a flat plate. When the guest arrived she said, "I cooked all this dinner alone, my dear friend. Please enjoy it."

The heron started to peck, but, he could not manage to eat from a flat plate. So the fox consumed it all. After the dinner, the fox said, "Sorry. That was all I prepared! I do not have anything else to offer you."

The heron replied, "Thank you, dear friend. I am full to my neck. Now please come to my house too for dinner tomorrow."

The heron cooked the food he knew the fox liked a lot. He put it in a jar with a very narrow neck.

When the fox arrived, he offered the nice meal in the jar to her saying, "Please help yourself. I cooked all this myself."

The fox walked around the jar feeling so hungry! The neck of the jar though was far too narrow for her to be able to reach and eat anything.

So the heron ate it all and said too, "Sorry, my dear friend, that was all I prepared."

The fox got very upset. She had hoped for a big dinner and came back home really hungry.

As they say: Every dog has its day!

F10 THE FOX AND THE LION

All animals wondered what to do to save themselves from the lion that killed and ate any of them all the time.

"Uncle Lion," the fox started, "If a bell is tight on your neck, all animals will be able to hear you when you are coming and gather around you. Then you can easily just select the fat ones you would like to eat. What do you think?"

"That is a splendid idea" the lion replied. "Please tie it on my neck straightaway."

The fox happily complied.

From then on, the lion would go and rest in the bush. Whenever it came out shaking its neck, the bell sounded loudly to alert all animals about its presence around. They all then ran away quickly and hide for their lives.

In the end the lion could not catch any prey and simply returned hungry to lie in the bush. This went on and on, until the lion was starving to death.

Then the fox paid the lion a visit and asked:

"Uncle, how is it going?"

"Things were better when the bell was not tied on my neck," the lion lamented.

Those who thought that SPLA/M would collapse with the death of Dr. John Garang De Mabior will be proved wrong. His death is tied around their necks.

F11 THE HYENA AND THE LION

A hyena and a lion shared a cattle camp. Then the lion ate its own cattle every day till only one bull was left.

At night, a cow belonging to the hyena gave birth to a heifer. Then the lion got up at night, picked the heifer and placed it in front of its bull.

In the morning, when the hyena woke up, it noticed its cow has given birth and wondered where its heifer was. Looking around, the hyena spotted the heifer lying in front of the lion's bull. So, the hyena asked the lion, "What is the heifer of my cow doing in front of your bull?"

"It's my bull that gave birth!" the lion responded.

"No, lion, it is my cow that delivered," the hyena asserted.

The lion became furious and started to look fierce. The hyena was frightened and decided to seek the help of the animal court of law. So, all animal species gathered to attend the court and try to resolve this dispute.

After listening carefully to both sides, all animals present resolved unanimously that the heifer indeed belonged to the cow of the hyena. The lion became wilder and threatened to kill and eat up all the animals. So the animals wondered how to save their own necks, leave alone resolve this case.

The air was tight and every animal was frozen with fear. Suddenly they noticed the fox approaching carrying a bundle of firewood on its head and a gourd tied on its back. So all the animals called the fox to come to their rescue saying, "Mr. Fox, since you have come, please sit down here to join us in this court. What is being judged is a case pertaining to all animals and you are one of them."

"Thank you for inviting me to join. Unfortunately, I am unable to sit down, as I am in a hurry," the fox replied.

"Mr. Fox, please wait a minute, what are you hurrying to go and do?" the animals inquired.

"Why do you ask again when you can clearly see me carrying firewood and a gourd? I am just going to throw down the fire-wood and fetch water so that I can prepare something for my father who has just given birth," the fox explained.

The lion jumped in to be the first to comment and said, "What is this nonsense the fox is saying? Where on Earth do men give birth?"

Then all the animals burst into laughter and the fox added say-ing, "Why then, Mr. Lion, did you snatch the heifer of the hyena?"

The lion was furious but turned its eyes away. Then the hyena got up, picked up its heifer, and made it away quickly with the fox following speedily behind.

The lion was left with nothing else to do, as all the other animals in the court were watching his next steps closely.

In analogy, our motherland was snatched away from us with lies and we will rise up and recover it if the verdict passed is secession in the 2011 referendum under the watchful eyes of the international community.

F12 THE WIFE WHO WILL ACCEPT MY LIES

A man had ten wives. During the dry season, when things were scarce, he collected some items, tied them in a bag and wondered to which of his wives he would offer them.

"Why don't I just create a lie and offer them to the wife who will readily accept my lies?" he thought.

Having made up a lie, he hid the items in a secret place and started by visiting his last wife and told her, "You know, that hyena you hear crying far away—it was exactly the one that had eaten the dog."

"That's a pure lie," she said. "How can you tell it is the one among so many hyenas around when you can't even see it?"

He got up and left quietly heading for his second-to-the-last wife and repeated the same lie to her.

"Go away with your lies," she said. "There are many hyenas out there, how can you tell blindly?"

One after another all nine of his ten wives echoed similar remarks, refusing to accept his lies. Then he paid the last visit to his first wife who had known him most.

"You know, that hyena you hear crying far away; it was exactly the one that killed and ate up the dog."

"Oh. Yes, you are perfectly right. No question about that," she responded readily. "I was actually waiting to share the same information with you."

"This is the one," he murmured quietly.

Then he went straightaway and fetched the hidden items and offered them to her.

Analogously, we certify that the nation that will readily support us to the end till we lift the flag of our independence in South Sudan, whether they view our claim for self-determination to be genuine or not, will be the one that will remain in our hearts forever.

F13 THE ZORRILA AND ITS TAIL

Once up on a time, a zorrila was running away to hide and save its life from a predator. It was a matter of life and death.

Then it managed to squeeze its body into a small hole in the ground that could not also accommodate and hide its tail. So it said to its own tail, "It's up to you and the predator, Mr. Tail. There is nothing I can do to protect you too."

The zorrila talked as if the tail was not part and parcel of itself, ignoring the fact that it is a fatal mistake to leave a visible trace outside for a killer.

When the hunter arrived, it did not become the problem of the tail alone as the zorrila thought. It ended up costing its entire life.

Let those who cooperate with our bitter rivals thinking their lives will be spared know that they are part and parcel of the entire South Sudan.

F14 A SLIGHT RAIN IN APRIL

There was a slight rain in the month of April toward the dry season. So, a black ant called Acuuk decided to bring its children outside the wet hole to dry them up in the sunshine. Then a francolin bird named Awec came and picked them up one by one and ate them all. The ant was angry and decided to spray salty water into the bird's eyes. The bird ran away from the ant and sat on top of a tree. The tree fell down on a blue duiker antelope called Amuk resting under it. The antelope ran inside a cottage and broke the teeth of a wife of the chief.

So the wife of the chief went to the chief's court of law to open a case against the antelope for breaking her teeth. So the chief called everybody around to look into this case and collectively pass a judgment. The court convened and asked the antelope, "Blue duiker, why did you break the teeth of the chief's wife?"

"If a big tree falls on you, won't you run away for your life?" it defended.

"What about you, tree, why did you fall down on the antelope?" the court inquired.

"Well, if a mighty francolin bird sits on you heavily, won't you fall down?" the tree replied

"Why did you sit on the tree, francolin bird, and cause it to fall?" The court continued its inquiry

"If salty water is splashed into your eyes by black ant, would you not flee for your life and sit safely away on top of the tree?" francolin bird responded.

"What about you, black ant, why did you splash salty water into francolin's eyes?" the court asked.

"Well if a heavy rain falls on you won't you take your children out of the wet hole and dry them up in the sunshine afterward? If then a wild bird attacks and eats up your little children, would you not react to defend them?" black ant replied

"And you rain, why did you fall?"

"If the huge elephant continues to defecate on the grass till it dries up, won't you water it?"

"Why on Earth, elephant, do you defecate on the grass?"

"Don't ask me again; if the big stomach I am carrying has things spoilt in it, won't I empty them on the grass?" the elephant explained as the case went on and on endlessly.

Similarly, our case in Sudan could go on and on endlessly with one excuse after another given now and then by chameleons in Khartoum. The only way to put an end to it once and for all is to cast a decisive vote in 2011.

F15 THE VALUE OF ELDERS

The youth thought the elders were useless. They only bombard them with one bit of advice after another. So they held a meeting and proposed to kill them all. However, some of the youth objected and the meeting was postponed for further consideration.

Successive meetings were called subsequently and the same proposal of killing all elders was advanced and rediscussed. Ultimately, all the youth concurred except one.

"Why don't you want elders to be killed," the single exception was asked.

"If something happens which needs the advice of an elder to resolve it, what shall we do after killing them all?" he argued.

"Nothing that we cannot resolve ourselves will happen," they tried to convince him.

He closed his mind and decided to hide his father in the bush while the rest waited for a ceremony and struck the heads of all their elders to death.

Then, a snake entered a girl's throat and curled around to peep outside through the mouth. She was scared and started to cry for help.

"What shall we do now to rescue this girl?" The youth wondered. "It is only an elder that could have advised us on what to do to resolve a problem like this, but, where can we find one of them when we have killed them all?"

"If I bring one elder to help, will you not kill him or her?" The single exception asked.

"No we will not kill him or her," they answered.

"Promise me first," he insisted.

They all promised. Then he went and fetched his father from the forest where he hid him.

"We are in trouble," the youth pleaded. "What shall we do to save this young girl with a snake in her throat?" they consulted the elder.

"Oh! That is a simple problem," the elder remarked. "All you need to do is bring a rat and tie it there and let the girl come near to it. Then see what happens."

They complied. As soon as the snake noticed the rat, it sprang out of the girl's throat and attacked its prey outside. Thus the girl was saved with the advice of the elder and all the youth celebrated.

No one with a sound mind should consider all elders to be useless and wish they were dead. No leader of South Sudan should pension all our elder officers when we do not know what may happen in the future.

F16 ACOK AND DUT MAKUAC

A lady called Acok was married to a man named Dut Makuac. They decided and promised themselves as a loving couple that if one died, the surviving spouse should volunteer to be buried alive with the dead one in the same grave instantly.

When his wife died, Mr. Dut Makuac initially requested for her grave to be dug wide enough for two bodies, considering the promise he had given her. This was done. However, fear soon rained on him and he started to jump to and fro over the corpse of his wife afraid to be buried with her.

"Why are you jumping up and down, Dut?" asked some close people that knew about the promise he had made to his wife.

"My eyes are the ones stopping me," he replied, meaning that the sight of his dead wife was preventing him from keeping the promise he had made to her.

Not all husbands are reliable, so they say.

Likewise, not all political partners are reliable. Indeed, one wishes the partnership between the Sudan People's Liberation Movement (SPLM) and the National Congress Party (NCP) was free of people like Dut Makuac; the implementation of the Comprehensive Peace Agreement would have run very smoothly!

F17 A MOTHER AND HER STARVING CHILDREN

Once up on a time, there was a mother with her several children. They were all starving and there was no food in the house. The children were crying and asking for food. So she thought and thought of what to do. Then an idea came into her mind.

She decided to light fire and put some water in a cooking pot. She added an axe to the water and then covered the pot and allowed it to boil.

The kids thought that their mum was actually cooking real food. So they eagerly began to wait and their spirits were lifted.

Now and then they asked their mother, "Mummy, when is the food going to be ready?"

"Just be patient, my children, it is nearly cooked."

This went on for hours until suddenly a hyena came running carrying the meat of a ram in its mouth and dropped it accidentally near the door of the house where the children were starving. The mother ran quickly and snatched the meat and cooked it. And they all ate the food happily and survived

If the mother had not kept up the spirits of her children, they could all have died. Likewise, we the marginalised People of South Sudan should continue to keep up our spirits and hope eagerly for our independence to come.

F18 THE RACE OF THE FROG TO THE TOWER

Once upon a time there was a race of frogs. The goal was to reach the top of a high tower. Many frogs gathered to see and support the others trying to reach the tower. The race to the destination began...In reality, the normal frogs probably didn't believe that it was possible that any of the frogs could reach the tower...all the phrases that one could hear were:

"What a pain! We once tried it!

"They'll never make it!"

The frogs began to resign, one by one except for one who kept on moving to climb...The crowd continued: "... Impossible! She will never make it..." No frog has ever achieved such a difficult task and most frogs admitted defeat, except for the one frog who continued to attempt...

At the end, all the frogs quit, except the one who, alone and with an enormous effort, reached the top of the tower. She arrived safely and accomplished the target and aspirations... The others wanted to know how she did it. One of them approached her and asked how she had done it, finished the race. They discovered that the winner frog was deaf.

The moral of the story to South Sudanese is: Never listen to people who tend to be negative because they remove the best aspirations from your heart! As South Sudanese our destiny lies within our hands to determine the way forward whether through procession or other means provided that the race is on and has just begun. Always remind yourself of the power of the words that we experienced. That's why you always need to think positive and challenge yourself!

Lesson:

Always be deaf to someone who tells you that you can't and won't achieve your goals or make your dreams come true. Don't give up the battle for implementing the 2011 referendum. Don't run away from the course of the struggle at this crucial time of referendum when we all need to rely on one another. As Mr. Lual Garang De Lual recites, "Winners don't quit and quitters don't win! And your attitude determines your altitude."

F19 WHY A CAT ALWAYS CHASES A RAT

A cat and a rat agreed to construct a boat to cross a river. They both managed to complete building the boat and they rowed it jointly up to the middle of the river. There, the rat started to say it was hungry and began to dig and eat up the boat until it made a big hole. Then the water began to flow into the boat through the hole, thereby putting the boat at risk of capsizing.

The cat was very annoyed and asked the rat to explain why it dug the hole into the boat and put their lives at risk in the middle of a deep river. The rat could not give a satisfactory explanation.

Although the cat was very annoyed, it decided to work hard to cover up the hole and slow down the influx of water into the boat while continuing to row it speedily until they reached the other side of the river safely. Then the rat jumped out quickly and ran away from the angry cat, having realised its grave mistake. And the cat started to chase it.

That is why, whenever a cat sees a rat, it continues to chase it until now.

This story is similar to that of the Addis Ababa Agreement. The People of South Sudan via the Anya-nya movement signed the Addis Ababa Agreement with Khartoum government to live in peace with their counterparts in North Sudan. Unfortunately the Khartoum government ripped that agreement apart in utter violation. The People of South Sudan were provoked by that and their trust in the Khartoum government was shattered. That is why whenever any agreement is signed between South Sudan and any Khartoum government, the People of South Sudan remain sceptical and fear that it will end up in the dustbin like the Addis Ababa Agreement.

F20 WHAT AKOL ACIIR WAS LOOKING FOR

Once up on a time, a man called Akol Aciir wondered if there might be a dog with horns on its head and a sheep with a striped hair. Everybody told him none of them existed anywhere. He did not believe anyone. So, he set off to search all the ten areas of Gogrial hoping to find a dog with horns and a striped goat. Then he would prove everybody wrong.

He went to all the ten areas he knew, namely Kuac, Aguok Baar, Aguok Ciek, Apuk, Awan Mou, Awan Chan, Tuic Amuol, Tuic Awic Ayuel, Tuic Cier Rehan, and Akuar. He could not find the types of animals he was looking for.

Eventually he returned to his home section.

"Did you find a dog with horns or a striped sheep?" he was asked

"I did not follow the right road," he answered.

"Akol Aciir, you are lying," they concluded

In comparison, let anyone set off to search the whole world around for an option that can make unity of entire Sudan attractive to all the People of South Sudan and let us hope it will not be what Akol Aciir was looking for.

F21 A MAN AND A SKULL

Once upon a time, a man came across a human skull at a roadside. He started to laugh at it saying, "What a skull! Who killed the person that had this skull?"

Then the skull spoke, saying, "Don't laugh at me. You will also meet your own fate."

He was stunned to hear a skull talking. So he rushed to people in the neighbourhood and broke to them news of a skull that talks.

People did not believe him. But, he insisted it was true and requested them to go with him and see for themselves.

People agreed to go with him on one condition: if the skull did not talk, they would kill him. He accepted this condition confident that the skull would definitely talk like it did to him.

Surprisingly, when the people arrived with him, the skull refused to talk. So, the people implemented what they said they would do. They killed him and left his corpse on the ground beside the skull.

After people left, the skull spoke again, saying, "Did I not tell you before that you would meet your own fate as a result of laughing at me?"

Similarly, let those that jeer at the bones of our martyrs that they might come across over our soil note that they could also meet their own fate. Whenever you come across them anywhere, please care to respectfully bury them.

F22 LOVERS' VOICES FROM A GRAVE

A long time ago, there were two great lovers called Aguer and Nyandeng who were about to get married.

Aguer decided to pay a visit to his fiancée Nyandeng prior to their final wedding arrangements. They had both been engaged for several months and were looking forward to their wedding.

It was afternoon on a sunny day. As he was approaching the home of his fiancée, he noticed a large crowd of people outside the house. Normally there would be only a few unless there is an occasion; but, what occasion would it be which he did know about in advance? Well he was going there anyway and he would soon find out when he arrived.

As he came closer, he started to hear people crying in loud voices. His heart jumped. He started to feel very sad. Apart from the fact that a relative of his fiancée might have died, which in itself is tragic, he felt their wedding would be postponed after waiting for it for a long time.

On coming even closer, he could not notice his fiancée among the crowd outside and he wondered if she might be either inside the house or away from the home at that moment.

He reached their home and was immediately received by Acok, the younger sister of his fiancée, who came to him crying.

"What happened, Acok?" he inquired.

"Something very sad occurred," replied Acok. "My sister Nyandeng has just died suddenly. She was never seriously ill, as you know. She woke up this morning and complained of severe headache and dizziness. Before she could be taken to a dispensary or a traditional healer, she passed away."

Aguer was shocked. Although he feared someone had died when he first noticed a crowd of people crying, it had not occurred to him that the deceased could have been his fiancée.

"What wrong have I done, Almighty God, that you should deprive me of my love and my soul?" he lamented as he joined the mourners.

Nyandeng was an admirable girl who was loved by many friends and relatives. Her body was inside the house when he arrived. Later, it was transferred into the hut where her grave was being dug. Aguer immediately joined the people who were assigned to dig the grave.

"I want my fiancée's grave to be as deep and wide as possible," he said. Then, he carried on, digging it even deeper at the time when almost all the other people had stopped digging.

"Please lower wide sheets of soft hide to cover the floor of the grave" he requested, while he remained inside the grave. "I will be the one to receive and lay her body on the soft hide."

His request was granted. Nyandeng's body was lowered into the grave where he laid it.

"I do not want the body of my fiancée to be covered directly by any mud or sand," he directed. "Please fetch me some logs and grass to thatch a roof of a tomb at the bottom of the grave." This was obeyed and he prepared a thick roof as he planned.

"You can now start to pour the mud or sand into the grave" he shouted, while he remained inside the grave.

"Are you not coming out?" people asked.

"Come out to whom when the only girl I cherished and was about to marry is not up there with you?" She is here lying dead by my side inside this grave. Please bury us together. "

No one was prepared to bury him alive with his fiancée. Almost all his closest relatives including his own parents were called in to try to persuade him to come out of the grave.

"My son, we all understand your extreme sadness and entirely share with you the sorrow of this tragedy," his father said. "We do not believe that what you are now doing is what your own fiancée would have liked you to do if you had had a chance to discuss it before she died. We also believe she would have joined us in our plea for you to come out of the grave and not to be buried alive with her if she knew what you are doing now. Please listen to us and come out of the grave."

He refused to listen. Despite one plea after another, Aguer could not be dissuaded, until everybody gave up.

"May be it is God's will and not a devilish idea," all the elders present concluded and directed the burial to be completed.

They also ordered that the whole house be vacated for some time since a person is buried alive and people could move back later.

Several days after the funeral, while the house was still vacant, a man called Muorter reached that village late at night. He was on his way to a distant location and he decided to call at the house where Aguer and Nyandeng had been buried in order to request to spend the night there and to continue on his journey in the morning. He had no idea that the house had been vacated. He did not know about the funeral either.

When he approached the house he could not see any lights and he thought all the people were asleep. However, on coming closer to the hut, he could hear two people talking clearly inside it.

"Now I know you really loved me," a voice said. "That is why you decided to be buried with me."

"I very much love you, Nyandeng. In actual fact, I adore you," another voice answered.

"I was only paying a visit to see you before our wedding day when I was shocked to discover that you had just died. I am grateful to the Almighty God for bringing you back to life but I do not know how we shall be excavated."

"Do not worry," she replied, "the same Almighty that revived me shall have us excavated."

Muorter was frightened to hear these voices. However he decided not to run away. He wanted to be sure that the voices were actually from a grave. He collected all his courage and entered the hut quietly and checked every comer of it. Apart from a fresh grave located at its end, it was completely vacant. He also checked all the other rooms in the compound. They were also vacant. There was therefore no doubt in his mind that the people who spoke did so from inside the grave.

He walked to the neighbouring house where he was offered a room to spend the night. He could not sleep. He spent the whole night thinking about the two people who were speaking in the grave and analysing their conversation.

In the morning he decided to consult the neighbours that hosted him.

"What happened in that house nearby? Why is it deserted?" he inquired.

"A person has been buried there alive with his fiancée who had suddenly died," he was told.

"How long ago was that and where are their relatives?" he asked again.

"Several days ago," they replied. "The immediate relatives of the girl have moved temporarily to the house of their uncle next door and the home of the man is not far from here."

"I want to meet all their relatives," he requested. "Please call all of them here. I have good news to give them."

"What good news to tell them when they are bereaved? Can you give us a hint before we call them?"

"Yes, I can. I am sure both the people who were buried there are alive. I heard both of them conversing last night when I passed through that home hoping to spend the night there before proceeding to this house."

At his request, all the prominent relatives of Aguer and Nyandeng were called. He broke the news to them.

"To what extent are you sure that they are alive and why should we believe you?" they asked.

"I am prepared to pay you all my cattle if you excavate them and do not find both of them alive," he promised.

"It will not be your cattle we shall take if we do not find them alive. We shah add you to the same grave and bury you with them. Only under this condition can we agree to exhume them."

Muorter agreed. He was not afraid of his own death because he was sure they would be found alive.

Excavation was implemented and the two lovers were found alive. Everybody was amazed. A large thanksgiving ceremony was conducted and the wedding that followed was more spectacular than any that had ever been conducted before anywhere in that area. Generations after generations in that community have continued to remember the wedding of Nyandeng to Aguer and their miraculous revival. Up to the present day sceptics who do not believe this story are regarded as doubting Thomases by the descendants of Aguer and Nyandeng in Southern Sudan.

Likewise, from the ashes of destructive war shall rise again our devastated land of South Sudan along with all its lovers that voluntarily sacrificed their lives for it and live happily ever after in a new world free of death, pain, and misery.

F23 CONCLUSION OF FOLKLORE

When the cocks crow to announce the arrival of dawn and wake us up, as our natural alarm clocks, I would always wonder in my mind, as the youngest child of the family, about how many exciting stories were narrated last night. Then I longed for the sun to set soon and another round of stories to begin.

Interestingly though, I must seize this chance to reveal a secret I have kept in my heart for a long time. My elder brothers, sisters, and cousins had deliberately left romantic stories to narrate when I was asleep. They thought it was inappropriate for them to talk about topics like sex when I was awake.

"Is he asleep?" they will would ask themselves. Then they would either glance at my eyes to see if they were closed or push me gently to discover if I would respond.

"Yes, he is," they would assume. Then, they embarked deeply into romantic and sexy folklore. What they did not know was that I simply pretended to be asleep at that time and quietly enjoyed whatever my little brain could understand in the romantic tales.

Children have their own ways of tasting what adults think they are enjoying alone. In retrospect, I admire the extent to which responsible adults in our society will go to protect small children from advanced stuff!

Nevertheless, all this wonderful and indigenous African folklore shall disappear. Indeed, the practise of sitting in a circle and relating stories may have started to dwindle away, especially in urban areas, due to both adverse modernization and antagonistic Arabization. If Africans in Sudan are not careful, in years to come, their witty fox in the dense African forest will be replaced by a dull donkey in a desert, when narrating stories.

ECONOMY

A Land So Precious

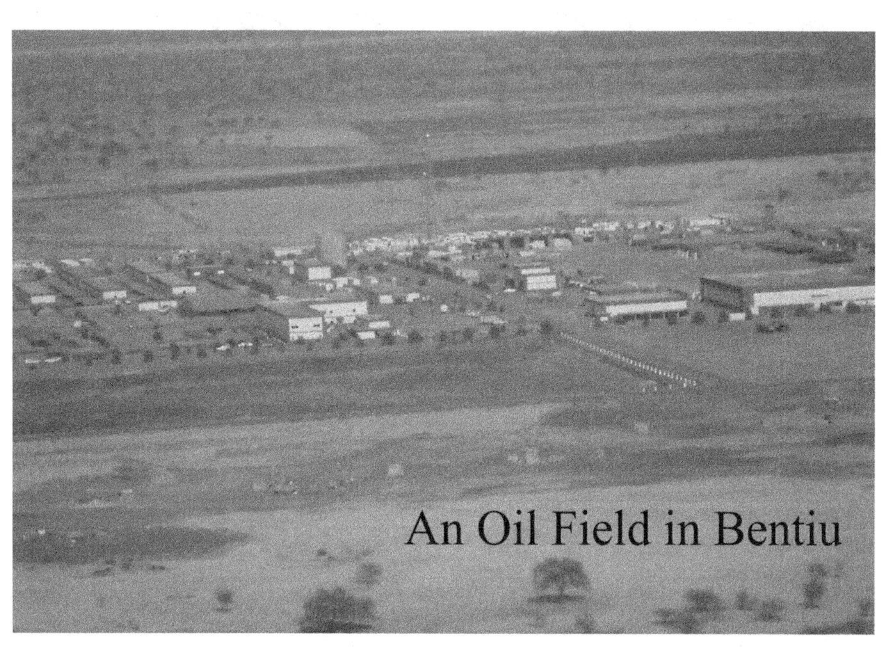

An Oil Field in Bentiu

If it makes one feel like flying to be part of a land so great and so beautiful, what will one do if that same land is also so rich? Great, rich, and beautiful—a land that combines all three and even more. Any child who belongs to such a land should feel more than gifted and ecstatic.

Indeed, the economy of South Sudan is predominantly a rural, subsistence economy enriched with discovery of oil over and above other minerals. The oil, though, is being exploited by foreign companies. The largest overseas consortium is controlled by China, with a 40 percent stake; Malaysia, with 30 percent; and India, with 25 percent. Canadian-based oil company Talisman withdrew operations in Sudan in 2003, due largely to external lobbying and pressure over political and human rights issues.

A lot of the oil of South Sudan was falsely claimed by North Sudan during the interim period of the Comprehensive Peace Agreement. An example of such oil fields is that of Panthou, misnamed as Heglid. Panthou and Aling, where this huge oil reserve is located, are indigenous areas of Ngok Rueng in the Greater Upper Nile Region of South Sudan. They fall well below the 1/1/1956 boundary deep in South Sudan.

Apart from oil, its wealth lies principally in its natural resources. The fertile soil, combined with tropical rain, provides the medium to produce any agricultural products. Sudan was once described as the basket of Africa. Where in Sudan does that basket lie? It lies mainly if not entirely in the South. There you need no artificial irrigation to cultivate cotton, the so-called white gold of Sudan. More of that white gold could have been more easily produced and of even better quality if the cotton scheme was located in the more fertile and rainy South Sudan.

Look at the green grass, the fruity trees, and various crops in the South; all bear testimony to the enormous fertility of the South. Tell me what tropical tree, crop, or grass cannot grow there. And all these are not just reflections of natural beauty; they are also markers or sources of potential wealth. We can compete in the world market with various crops, fruits, and flowers and if you say an orange produced elsewhere is sweet, you haven't tasted anything yet. Wait to taste an orange of South Sudan. Not Tamur el Hindi but Tamur El Junub!

Glance at our swamps before you even reach the lakes and rivers and see fish just wandering around. It will leave no doubt in your mind that we have the potential to cultivate fish and market it. It is nature's own way of telling the world, this is the land that can supply you with nutritive resources.

See the spectrum of domestic and wild life feeding in the grassy plains—cattle, sheep, goats, giraffes, leopards, lions, elephants, white rhinos, buffalos, antelopes, zebras, hyenas, foxes, chimpanzees, hippos—you name it, we have it. All are precious, most are rare species valuable to our lives and attractive to tourists. Interestingly, these precious wildlife that had migrated to neighbouring countries during the war, spontaneously decided to come back home, for example, to Boma Park to rejoin few fellow herds that had decided to stay at home despite the disastrous war and managed to survive.

Peep deep into our soil. You will see numerous precious minerals. The gold in Kapoeta, copper near Raga, and top-quality oil in Bentiu, Akobo, Abyei, and other locations are a few examples. We even have uranium somewhere that could be indispensable for our future military strength—who knows. Exploit these minerals and our land would undoubtedly be one of the wealthiest nations on this planet.

Look up to the sky, and you will see we have mountains too. Even though we have left behind our pyramids in Egypt, these mountains, like Imatong, and huge plantains are potential tourist attractions to boost our economy.

Our numerous rich cultures are second to none. Just watch us perform in a cultural anniversary and you will take away an exciting experience to cherish all your life. There is no price tag that can be put as a value for our multiple cultures.

Nature has blessed our Land of South Sudan with a lot of oil and non-oil resources. Overreliance on oil revenue only is a recipe for disaster, as happened during the 2008 global economic crisis, when the price of oil crashed too low. There is, therefore, a strong need for South Sudan to develop more non-oil revenue to offset any deficit arising from depreciating oil prices.

Dare I say more about our enormous wealth? Thank you, God, for the gift of South Sudan and all it contains. No wonder others do not want to set us free. Others strive to finish us, so that they can rob us of our land and all its precious and enormous wealth. That is why we will also fight to the finish. Even when only one person is left, he or she will continue the battle for our land and all its resources.

With enormous real and potential wealth, surely South Sudan can stand on its own feet and thrive if it becomes an independent country. Therefore, using poverty as a reason against secession of South Sudan in the 2011 referendum is nothing more than a cheap argument and a lame excuse to continue its exploitation and slavery.

HISTORY

A Land So Glorious

We were great people of Kush before and we shall be great again

H1 INTRODUCTION OF HISTORY

t makes one feel like flying with one's own wings to be part of a great history, to be an offspring of great ancestors, if not the greatest of all mankind.

As Mr. Wani Igga, the current speaker of the Southern Sudan Parliament says, "We were a great people in history before and we will become great people again."

Just spend the next few minutes sailing through this snapshot of our exceptionally marvellous history. It is summarised.

H2 PRE-BIBLICAL ERA

Our historical roots date back long before Christ, as illustrated by the following eras:

25000 BC KEM
10000 BC NABALIA
2000 BC KUSH

During the ancient period, the area that today is northern Sudan was known as Nubia. Egyptians and people of the Mediterranean world also referred to it as Ethiopia. The area of the Nile valley that lies within present day Sudan was home to three Kushite kingdoms during antiquity: the first with its capital at Kerma (2400–1500 BCE), another that centred on Napata (1000 – 300 BCE), and, finally, that of Meroë (300 BCE–300 CE).

Each of these kingdoms was culturally, economically, politically, and militarily strongly influenced by the powerful pharaonic Egyptian empire to the north—and the Kushite kingdoms, in turn, competed strongly with Egypt, to the extent that during the late period of ancient Egyptian history the kings of Napata conquered and unified Egypt itself, ruling as the pharaohs of the twenty-fifth dynasty. One of the more notable ones was

Taharqa, who was involved in war with the advancing Assyrians during the period the Nubian pyramids were built.

The Meroitic Empire disappeared by the fourth century AD. By the sixth century a group of three Christian states had arisen in Nubia. The northern most states eventually merged into Makuria, leaving two kingdoms. These were Nobatia, south of the First Cataract of the Nile and Alodia. Makuria was situated at Old Dongola, and the kingdom of Alodia was around Soba on the Blue Nile.

Pyramids were built by the Kushite Kingdoms.

During these eras, many of our kings and queens reigned, for example: Namer, Menes, Kufu, Darhaka, Remsis, Memphis, Abidos, and Meroe, just to mention few.

Proudly, we were the first human beings on Earth to discover civilisation, long before all others.

4500 BC: We discovered the cloth
3500BC: We invented writing
3200 BC: We discovered metals
2800 BC: We build pyramids
2500 BC: Chinese civilisation
1500 BC: Greek civilisation
753 BC: Roman civilisation

H3 BIBLICAL ERA

We are mentioned in the Bible as a people who are mighty in history inhabiting along the Nile in Isaiah chapters 18 and 20:

ISAIAH CHAPTER 18

A PROPHECY AGAINST CUSH
18 Woe to the land of whirring wings along the rivers of Cush,
which sends envoys by sea in papyrus boats over the water.

Go, swift messengers, to a people tall and smooth-skinned, to a people feared far and wide, an aggressive nation of strange speech, whose land is divided by rivers.

All you people of the world, you who live on earth, when a banner is raised on the mountains, you will see it, and when a trumpet sounds, you will hear it.

This is what the LORD says to me: "I will remain quiet and will look on from my dwelling place, like shimmering heat in the sunshine, like a cloud of dew in the heat of harvest."

For, before the harvest, when the blossom is gone and the flower becomes a ripening grape, he will cut off the shoots with pruning knives, and cut down and take away the spreading branches.

They will be left to the mountain birds of prey and to the wild animals; the birds will feed on them all summer, the wild animals all winter.

At that time gifts will be brought to the LORD Almighty from a people tall and smooth-skinned, from a people feared far and wide, an aggressive nation of strange speech, whose land is divided by rivers.

The gifts will be brought to Mount Zion, the place of the Name of the LORD Almighty.

ISAIAH CHAPTER 20

A PROPHECY AGAINST EGYPT AND CUSH
20 In the year that the supreme commander, sent by Sargon king of Assyria, came to Ashdod and attacked and captured it—at that time the Lord spoke through Isaiah son of Amoz. He said to him, "Take off the sackcloth from your body and the sandals from your feet." And he did so, going around stripped and barefoot.

Then the lord said, "Just as my servant Isaiah has gone stripped and barefoot for three years, as a sign and portent against Egypt and Cush, so the king of Assyria will lead away stripped and barefoot the Egyptian captives and Cushite exiles, young and old, with buttocks bared—to Egypt's shame. Those who trusted in Cush and boasted in Egypt will be afraid and put to shame. In that day the people who live on this coast will say, "See what has happened to those we relied on, those we fled to for help and deliverance from the king of Assyria! How then can we escape?"

The Greeks found us in 1350 and renamed our land Egypt, which means in Greek a land of the black. Indeed we had named the Mediterranean Ocean as Adek Diet, which means a river that no bird can cross or it will die on the way because it is too wide. We also named Cairo as Kar rou, which literally means where two rivers unite.

Indeed the longest river on Earth, the so-called Nile was originally inhabited by us, all the way from the Mediterranean Ocean.

H4 POST-BIBLICAL ERA

The Arrival of the Arab Enemy

Arabs came to Egypt in the **640s** and pressed southward; around **651** the governor of Egypt raided as far south as Dongola. The Egyptians met with stiff resistance and found little wealth worth capturing. They thus ceased their offensive and a treaty known as the **baqt** was signed between the Arabs and Makuria. This treaty held for some seven hundred years. The area between the Nile and the Red Sea was a source of gold and **emeralds,** and Arab miners gradually moved in. Around the **970s** an Egyptian envoy **Ibn Sulaym** went to Dongola and wrote an account afterward; it is now our most important source for this period. Despite the baqt, northern Sudan became steadily **Islamized** and **Arabized;** Makuria collapsed in the fourteenth century with Alodia disappearing somewhat later.

Far less is known about the history of Southern Sudan. It seems as though it was home to a variety of seminomadic tribes. In the **sixteenth century** one of these tribes, known as the **Funj**, moved north and united Nubia forming the **Kingdom of Sennar**. The Funj sultans quickly converted to Islam and that religion steadily became more entrenched. At the same time, the **Darfur Sultanate** arose in the west. Between them, the **Taqali** established a state in the **Nuba Hills.**

The economy of Sudan was **feudally** based, with a large number of **slaves** supporting the ruling **Jellaba** class. The Jellaba were Arab merchants who had come to Sudan with Islam. They traded across the region, but did not build up much industrial or productive capability in Sudan. Through the centuries millions of slaves were captured and sold in Sudan, many being exported to the Middle East and eventually the Americas. The slave trade made southern blacks hostile toward Islam, preventing its spread in those areas.

Series of Dispersals

We were dispersed by war from near the ocean backward to our present position in the Heart of Africa. This dispersal occurred in three stages:

641 First Dispersal. This occurred in a war involving General Ibu Elas.

651–1316 Second Dispersal. This followed an attack on Dongola by Kabib Abdullah after a cease-fire was concluded with General Kalidosus in 651. The Arabs were defeated by our kingdom in Dongola and forced to withdraw back to Cairo where they were confined for six hundred years. Despite our victory at that stage, some of our people had been dispersed backward then.

1316 Third Dispersal. The Arabs regathered their strength and attacked Dongola again when Kerembas was defeated as our last Black African kingdom in that border. I bet they spent the six hundred years studying how to defeat our ancestors in Dongola.

1821–1885: The Ottoman Empire of Turkey

In 1820–21 an Egyptian-Ottoman force conquered and unified the northern portion of the country. The new government was known as the Turkiyah or Turkish regime. They were looking to open new markets and sources of natural resources. Historically, the pestilential swamps of the Sudd discouraged expansion into the deeper South of the country. Although Egypt claimed all of the present Sudan during most of the nineteenth century, and established a province Equatoria in Southern Sudan to further this aim, it was unable to establish effective control over the area, which remained an area of fragmented tribes subject to frequent attacks by slave raiders. In the later years of the Turkiyah, the British missionaries travelled from what is now modern-day Kenya in to the Sudd to convert the local tribes to Christianity.

During the 1870s European initiatives against the slave trade caused an economic crisis in southern Sudan, precipitating the rise of Mahdist forces.

Mahdism and condominium

1884–1898: The Mahdia

In 1881, a religious leader named Muhammad ibn Abdalla proclaimed himself the Mahdi, or the "expected one," and began a religious crusade to unify the tribes in western and central Sudan. His followers took on the name "Ansars" (the followers) which they continue to use today and are associated with the single largest political grouping, the Umma Party, led at one time by the descendants of the Mahdi, Sadiq al Mahdi. Taking advantage of conditions resulting from Ottoman-Egyptian exploitation and maladministration, the Mahdi led a nationalist revolt culminating in the fall of Khartoum in 1885, where British General Charles George Gordon was killed. The Mahdi died shortly thereafter, but his state survived until overwhelmed by an Anglo-Egyptian force under Lord Kitchener in 1898. Sudan was proclaimed a condominium in 1899 under British-Egyptian administration. The governor-general of the Sudan, for example, was appointed by "Khedival Decree," rather than simply by the British Crown, but while maintaining the appearance of joint administration, the British Empire formulated policies, and supplied most of the top administrators.

1898-1955 British Condominium or Anglo-Egyptian Rule

In 1892 a Belgian expedition claimed portions of southern Sudan that became known as the Lado Enclave. The Lado Enclave was officially part of the Belgian Congo. An 1896 agreement between the United Kingdom and Belgium resulted in the enclave being turned over to the British after the death of King Léopold II in 1910.

At the same time the French claimed several areas: Bahr el Ghazal, and the Western Upper Nile up to Fashoda. By 1896 they had a firm administrative hold on these areas and they planned on annexing them to French West Africa. An international conflict known as the Fashoda incident developed between France and the United Kingdom over these areas. In 1899 France agreed to cede the area to the UK.

From 1898, the United Kingdom and Egypt administered all of present day Sudan, but Northern and Southern Sudan were administered as separate colonies.

Sadly, in **1905,** a controversial decision was made to annex Abyei Area of South Sudan to North Sudan. It was part and parcel of Greater Bahr-el-Ghazal Region and it was transferred to Kordofan. This decision has subsequently led to serious conflict. The deadly clashes between Messiriya Arab Nomads and the Ngok of Abyei over water and grazing areas meant whatever advantages expected of the annexation became secondary. Indeed, the dispute over Abyei escalated with discovery of oil in the area. Abyei was part of the reason for the Anya-nya and SPLA war.

The NCP and SPLM could not agree over Abyei at Naivasha peace negotiations. They only conferred to let the boundary of Abyei be drawn by international experts referred to as the ABC or Abyei Boundary Commission. The parties were expected to accept the decision of the ABC. Unfortunately the NCP did not, arguing that the ABC exceeded its mandate. It took a ruling of the International Arbitration Court in Hague for a permanent boundary of Abyei to be drawn, especially its Northern boundary. This decision, announced on 22 July 2009, is expected to be binding and permanent and marks a significant milestone in the history of Abyei.

The Messiriya Tribes appeared to be unhappy with the ruling of Hague although their access to grazing areas and water in South Sudan is guaranteed by the ruling in line with the Comprehensive Peace Agreement. Besides, a tactical claim of Mr. Didery, an NCP delegate to Hague, that Panthou Oil Field, misnamed Heglig, belonged to Kordofan provoked South Sudanese. The Hague simply mapped Panthou outside the boundary of Abyei without indicating that it fell inside Kordofan. Therefore, it was a mere pre-emptive claim that Didery did before the drawing of the South-North Boundary, which will undoubtedly indicate that Panthou Oilfield lies inside South Sudan.

1922–1930 Closed District Ordinance was imposed by the British in attempt to protect the Christian and African South Sudan from Arabisation and Islamisation. During that period, intermarriage between Arab Muslims and Africans was prohibited. Visas and passports were required for Arabs to enter South Sudan. Permits were required to conduct business in the other zone, and totally separate administrations were established.

During these periods, our kingdoms that were found in "**Soudan**," an Arabic name for land of Black people, were further attacked. These kingdoms included the Nuba, Funj, Fur, and Celock. Anyuak, "Nuer," "Jieng," Bari, Latuka, Luos, Azande, Morus such as King Deng Kak and King Kitayengkopio, and many more. Under these kingdoms existed more than eight hundred ethnic groups. These ethic groups are primarily grouped into Nilotics such as Nuers, Jieng and Cellock, Nilohamides such as Bari, latukas and Luos and Sudanic such as Morus and Azandes. These tribes continued to resist the Condominium Rule until it was ultimately abolished.

In the South, English, Dinka, Bari, Nuer, Latuko, Shilluk and Azande were official languages, while in the north Arabic and English were used as official languages. Islam was discouraged in the south, where Christian missionaries were permitted to work. Colonial governors of South Sudan attended colonial conferences in East Africa, not Khartoum, and the British hoped to add South Sudan to their East African colonies.

Most of the British focus was on developing the economy and infrastructure of the north. Southern political arrangements were left largely as they had been prior to the arrival of the British. Until the 1920s the British had very little authority in the south.

In order to establish their authority in the north, the British promoted the power of Ali al-Mirghani, head of the Khatmiyya sect and Abd al-Rahman al-Mahdi, head of the Ansar sect. The Ansar sect essentially became the Umma party, and Khatmiyya became the Democratic Unionist Party.

1924 Heroes like Tok Mac Miir, misnamed as Ali Abdel Latif, led a White Flag revolution in Khartoum against the mistreatment of Black Africans in Sudan.

1943 The British began preparing the north for self-rule, establishing a North Sudan Advisory Council to advise on the governance of the six North Sudan provinces: comprised of Khartoum,

Kordofan, Darfur, and Eastern, Northern, and Blue Nile provinces. This involved an "Arab" lawyer called Mohammed Salih Singetti

1946 Protocol was signed in London giving South Sudanese the right to **self-determination**. Suddenly, Abderahaman El Mahdi offered King George of Britain a sword (which was later returned) to abolish the self-determination protocol.

1947 Juba Conference was held. Egypt threatened the British to either let the South remain part of Sudan or lose the Suez Canal. On the other hand our delegates to Juba conference asserted counterarguments in an attempt to win our separation, such as "How can you make a viable partnership between a boy of twelve and a man of forty" that was put forward by both Chief Rehan and Lolik. Nevertheless, the Self-Determination Protocol was cancelled

1948 Legislative Assembly Formed in Khartoum

Thirteen delegates, hand-picked by the British authorities, represented the South on the Sudan Legislative Assembly.

Many southerners felt betrayed by the British because they were largely excluded from the new government. The language of the new government was Arabic, but the bureaucrats and politicians from southern Sudan had, for the most part, been trained in English. Also, the political structure in the south was not as organised in the north, so political groupings and parties from the south were not represented at the various conferences and talks that established the modern state of Sudan. As a result, many southerners do not consider Sudan to be a legitimate state.

14.12.1950 A serious debate took place at the legislative assembly about self-determination for South Sudan. Singetti deceptively stated, "Let us just send the British away and self-determination for the South is a given thing." This was to soon become a pure lie. The Graduates' Conference was held in Egypt to discuss some form of self-rule for South Sudan and not a single Southern Sudanese was allowed or invited to participate in that conference.

1953 The United Kingdom and Egypt concluded an agreement providing for Sudanese self-government and self-determination.

1954 The transitional period toward independence began with the inauguration of the first parliament in 1954. The first parliament was held and Sudanisation of Civil Service was implemented to take over up to fifty thousand civil posts including eight hundred senior positions. Of all these posts, only four were offered to southern Sudanese and zero posts to Nubas and Angasnas.

1955-1972 the Anya-nya Civil War

18.8.1955 At 8:00 a.m. on Friday, the Torit Uprising ignited the Anya-nya Civil War between South Sudan and North Sudan that lasted seventeen years.

01.01.1956 with the consent of the British and Egyptian governments, Sudan achieved independence on 1 January 1956, under a provisional constitution. The United States was among the first foreign powers to recognise the new state. However, the Arab-led Khartoum government reneged on promises to southerners to create a **federal system**, which had led to a mutiny by southern army officers as stated above that sparked the seventeen years of civil war (1955–1972).Therefore, South Sudanese do not recognise the so-called independence of the Sudan.

1960 Adverse Missionary Act legislated to deport all missionaries away from South Sudan.

1962 Forcible expulsion of all missionaries from South Sudan was done. This deprived the needy People of South Sudan of all the humanitarian help they received from the missionaries, thereby compounding their suffering.

1964–1972 Massive Massacres of Innocent Civilians

14.12.1964 on Sunday, over fourteen thousand South Sudanese and other Sudanese Black Africans were massacred by Sudan government forces in Khartoum including those who tried to seek protection by going to police stations. This massacre followed a riot sparked by a lie created by the Sudan government that Mr. Clement Umboro, a key South Sudanese leader, was killed.

1965 Massive massacres of innocent South Sudanese civilians including women, children, elderly, and disabled people, was done by Sudan government forces all over the whole of South Sudan. Examples are massive massacres inflicted in Wau, Juba, Malakal, Bor, Gakrial, Rumbek, and many other towns and villages when thousands of people were killed initially. Nobody was spared, even those who were innocently attending Church masses, hospitals, and wedding ceremonies. In Wau, for example, people who were attending two wedding parties of Cebriano Cier and Mr. Ottabo were massacred by the Sudan army including a district commissioner called Victor Bol Bol. The only crime these civilians committed was to hold a wedding ceremony inside a government-controlled town to celebrate marriage.

1965–1972 The massive massacres of South Sudanese innocent civilians by the Sudan government, that was meant to protect its own citizens continued unabated, tantamount to genocide. Examples of such massacres included that of Bor District when twenty-four chiefs and many civilians were murdered and Gakrial District where everybody found who was not an Arab was killed and bodies were piled like wooden logs in metres. Any South Sudanese who attempted to come and collect a body of a relative to bury was also killed and added onto the piled metre. No town or village in South Sudan was spared during this period when at least two million civilians were massacred. These martyrs included notable South Sudanese leaders who were assassinated by Sudan government forces like William Deng Nhial and Father Saturnino. William Deng Nhial had won elections as an MP to Khartoum at a time when Sadig El Mahdi failed in the elections and, had William Deng made it then to Khartoum, he would have been the head of the majority of the opposition parties. He would have been the one to be elected to become the president of Sudan then. This was not acceptable to ruling Arabs that will not allow any Black African Sudanese to occupy the top seat of Sudan government. To stop him from reaching Khartoum, he was waylaid and assassinated between Tonj and Rumbek Town in 1968.

The Murderous Khartoum Governments

1956–1958 Azhari Era

The National Unionist Party (NUP), under Prime Minister Ismail al-Azhari, dominated the first cabinet, which was soon replaced by a coalition of conservative political forces.

1958–1964 Abboud Era

In 1958, following a period of economic difficulties and political manoeuvring that paralyzed public administration, Chief of Staff Lt. Gen. Ibrahim Abboud overthrew the parliamentary regime in a bloodless coup.

Gen. Abboud did not carry out his promises to return Sudan to civilian government, however, and popular resentment against army rule led to a wave of riots and strikes in late October 1964 that forced the military to relinquish power.

1964–1969 Mahjoub and Others

The Abboud regime was followed by a provisional government until parliamentary elections in April 1965 led to a coalition government of the Umma and National Unionist Parties under Prime Minister Muhammad Ahmad Mahjoub. Between 1966 and 1969, Sudan had a series of governments that proved unable either to agree on a permanent constitution or to cope with problems of factionalism, economic stagnation, and ethnic dissidence. The successions of early post-independence governments were dominated by Arab Muslims who viewed Sudan as a Muslim Arab state. Indeed, the Umma/NUP-proposed 1968 constitution was arguably Sudan's first Islamic-oriented constitution.

1969–1985 Nimeiri Era

Dissatisfaction culminated in a second military coup on 25 May 1969. The coup leader, Colonel Gaafar Nimeiry, became prime minister, and the new regime abolished parliament and outlawed all political parties.

Disputes between Marxist and non-Marxist elements within the ruling military coalition resulted in a briefly successful coup in July 1971, led by the Sudanese Communist Party. Several days later, anti-communist military elements restored Nimeiry to power.

In 1972, the Addis Ababa Agreement led to a cessation of the north-south civil war and a degree of self-rule. This led to a ten-year hiatus in the civil war.

Until the early 1970s Sudan's agricultural output was mostly dedicated to internal consumption. In 1972 the Sudanese government became more pro-Western, and made plans to export food and cash crops. However, commodity prices declined throughout the 1970s causing economic problems for Sudan. At the same time, debt servicing costs, from the money spent mechanizing agriculture, rose. In 1978 the IMF negotiated a Structural Adjustment Program with the government. This further promoted the mechanized export agriculture sector. This caused great economic problems for the pastoralists of Sudan (see Nuba Peoples).

In 1976, the Ansars mounted a bloody but unsuccessful coup attempt. In July 1977, President Nimeiry met with Ansar leader Sadiq al-Mahdi, opening the way for reconciliation. Hundreds of political prisoners were released, and in August a general amnesty was announced for all opponents of Nimeiry's government.

1985–1986 Siwar Al Dhab Transitional Military Council

On 6 April 1985, a group of military officers, led by Lieutenant General Abder Rahman Siwar el Dhahab, overthrew Nimeiri, who took refuge in Egypt. Three days later, Dhahab authorized the creation of a fifteen-man Transitional Military Council (TMC) to rule Sudan.

1986–1989 Sadiq Al Mahdi and Coalition Governments

In June 1986, Sadiq al Mahdi formed a coalition government with the Umma, the DUP, the NIF, and four southern parties. Unfortunately, however, Sadiq proved to be a weak leader and incapable of governing Sudan. Party factionalism, corruption, personal rivalries, scandals, and political instability characterized the Sadiq regime. After less than a year in office, Sadiq al Mahdi dismissed the government because it had failed to draft a new penal code to replace the sharia, reach an agreement with the IMF, end the civil war in the south, or devise a scheme to attract remittances from Sudanese expatriates. To retain the support of the DUP and the southern political parties, Sadiq formed another ineffective coalition government.

1989–2010 Omar Hassan Amed El Bashir

In 1989 it appeared the war would end, but a coup brought a military junta, Omar Hassan El Bashir, into power, not interested initially in compromise. Since that time the war raged across Sudan.

The ongoing civil war had displaced more than four million southerners. Some fled into southern cities, such as Juba; others trekked as far north as Khartoum and even into Ethiopia, Kenya, Uganda, Egypt, and other neighbouring countries. These people were unable to grow food or earn money to feed themselves, and malnutrition and starvation became widespread. The lack of investment in the south resulted as well in what international humanitarian organisations call a "lost generation" who lack educational opportunities and access to basic health care services, and have few prospects for productive employment in the small and weak economies of the south or the north.

Peace talks between the southern rebels and the government made substantial progress in 2003 and early 2004, although skirmishes in parts of the south have reportedly continued. The two sides have agreed that, following a final peace treaty, southern Sudan will enjoy autonomy for six years, and after the expiration of that period, the People of southern Sudan will be able to vote in a referendum on independence. Furthermore, oil revenues will be divided equally between the government and rebels during the six-year interim period. The ability or willingness of the government to fulfil these promises has been questioned by some observers, however, and the status of three central and eastern provinces remains a point of contention in the negotiations.

Whether this government will survive elections, initially planned for 2009 and later postponed to February 2010, remains to be seen. I guess it shall depend on their level of commitment to respect peace agreements they signed including Darfur Peace Agreement (DPA), Eastern Sudan Peace Agreement (EPA), and Comprehensive Peace Agreement (CPA).

The Suppliers of Murderous Weapons

Sudan relied on a variety of countries for its arms supplies. After independence the army had been trained and supplied by the British, but after the 1967 Six-Day War, relations were cut off.

At this time, relations with the United States and West Germany were also cut off.

1968–1972 the Soviet Union and eastern bloc nations sold large numbers of weapons and provided technical assistance and training to Sudan. At this time the army grew from strength of eighteen thousand to roughly fifty thousand men. Large numbers of tanks, aircraft, and artillery were acquired at this time, and they dominated the army until the late 1980s.

Relations cooled between the two sides after the coup in 1972, and the Khartoum government sought to diversify its suppliers. The USSR continued to supply weapons until 1977, when their support of Marxist elements in Ethiopia angered the Sudanese sufficiently to cancel their deals. China was the main supplier in the late 1970s.

Egypt was the most important military partner in the 1970s, providing missiles, personnel carriers, and other military hardware. At the same time military cooperation between the two countries was important.

Western countries began supplying Sudan again in the mid-1970s. The United States began selling Sudan a great deal of equipment around 1976, hoping to counteract Soviet support of Marxist Ethiopians and Libyans. Military sales peaked in 1982 at US$101 million. After the start of the second civil war, American assistance dropped, and was eventually all but cancelled in 1987.

1972–1983 Addis Ababa Peace Agreement

1972 A Peace Agreement was signed in Addis Ababa called the Addis Ababa Agreement, between Sudan government and Anya-nya leaders. This ended the Anya-nya War. It offered South Sudan a very limited autonomous rule, referred to as a High Executive Council.

1972–1983 Mistreatment, torturing, lynching, oppression, enslavement, and marginalisation of South Sudanese and other Black African Sudanese continued despite the Addis-Ababa Peace Agreement. For example, many South Sudanese Students were killed when they protested against the digging of Jonglei Canal without any due consideration to the local people and environment and without seeking the approval of People of South Sudan. Similarly, local inhabitants were forcibly evacuated and killed in 1978 to phase the way for robbing their own oil. The South as an entity was also forcibly split into separate regions in a style analogous to the colonial system of divide and rule. This was aimed at weakening the South before serving it with a heavy blow of cancelling the Addis-Ababa Agreement and related limited Self-Rule or Southern Regional Government. Protestors against Sudan government on any issue that was harmful to South Sudan were arrested and tortured or killed. As a university professor said, and I quote: "Southerners are only respected and valued to some extent when they pick up a gun and start a war."

Thus the ten-year peace interval between 1972–1983 was a period of more misery that culminated with sudden abolition of the Addis-Ababa Agreement by President Jafar Numeiri, who said, "Addis-Ababa Agreement was not a Bible nor a Koran." The same president who had valued and signed that agreement dishonoured and cancelled it. Simultaneously, he enforced Sharia Islamic Laws to be applied all over the country including Christians and other non-Muslims.

1983–2005 SPLA/M CIVIL WAR

16.5.1983 A military garrison of South Sudanese soldiers from previous Anya-nya forces were ordered to be amalgamated into the Arab-dominated Sudan army and transferred to North Sudan. This sparked a mutiny in Bor when the Southern Sudanese soldiers defected to Ethiopia, thereby marking the start of a new war and a birth of a movement called the Sudan

People's Liberation Movement (SPLM) with a military wing called the Sudan People's Liberation Army (SPLA), led by Dr. John Garang De Mabior. Apart from enforced amalgamation of Anya-nya soldiers, many factors triggered the SPLA/M war including the following:

- Compulsory introduction of brutal Islamic Shania laws
- Cancellation of the Addis Ababa Agreement
- Continuation of all the primary causes which had led before to the Anya-nya War such as oppression, marginalisation, injustice, slavery, and lots of human rights violations against South Sudanese and all other Black African Sudanese. Apartheid did not exist only in South Africa.
- Killings around Jonglei Canal
- Robbing of South Sudan oil
- Killing around oil refineries
- Continued underdevelopment of South Sudan and other parts of Sudan such as Nuba Mountains and Southern Blue Nile
- Concentration of power in the hands of only a few cliques of national Islamic fundamentalists and associated parties in Khartoum and immediate areas around it, leaving the rest of Sudan where the majority live in ruins

1983–2004 War between SPLA/SPLM and the Khartoum government was no more limited to South Sudan like that of Anya-nya. It extended up to Nuba Mountains, South Blue Nile, and to some extent Darfur. During this period more than two million African Sudanese were killed by the Islamist Army of the

Khartoum government that declared a holy Islamic Jihad war on the South Sudanese and other Sudanese Africans irrespective of whether they were even Muslims like them. Of course no Christian or animist was spared by the Jihadists in the course of their religious massacres. The Sudan government used every means at their disposal, such as Antenov military planes, to bombard civilians and even chemical weapons, apart from leaching Arab militias mixed with non-uniformed government soldiers to massacre civilians and loot all their livestock and destroy their property. The SPLA/M fought vigorously to defend itself and innocent civilians in the areas under their control. It proved an invincible force that successfully liberated a lot of towns and captured many military battalions of the Sudan government. Realising that it could not defeat SPLA/M, the Sudan government in Khartoum was obliged to participate in peace negotiations with SPLA/M, starting in Abuja of Nigeria and ending in Naivasha of Kenya. Behind these peace talks were predominantly IGGAT Countries and friends of IGGAT like Norway, Britain, and the United States.

2005–2011 Comprehensive Peace Agreement

9.1.2005 A Comprehensive Peace Agreement (CPA) was signed between the National Congress government in Khartoum and the SPLA/M, which effectively ended the twenty-two-year war.

9.1.2005–9.7.2005 Pre-interim period of the CPA during which arrangements were to be made for the SPLA/M forces and leadership to return to Khartoum and other areas controlled by the Sudan army.

9.7.2005 SPLA/M leadership returned to Khartoum led by Dr. John Garang De Mabior, amid a huge reception by millions of people. He was appointed and sworn in the next day on 7 October 2005 as the first vice president of Sudan, president of South Sudan, and commander in chief of SPLA. This marked the beginning of the six-year interim period. Sadly he (John Garang), who was so instrumental in bringing about the CPA, was to live for only twenty-one days after that.

30.7.2005 Dr. John Garang De Mabior died tragically in a mysterious helicopter disaster together with six other South Sudanese and seven Ugandan citizens. He was returning from a trip to Uganda where he went to meet with his old friend and ally, President Youweri Musseveni of Uganda. This death shocked the world and sparked wide riots all over South Sudan and Khartoum, leading sadly to loss of more lives and property. His deputy, Mr. Salva Kiir Mayardit, was promptly and unanimously elected by the SPLM leadership to fill his position, thereby avoiding any rivalry and conflict of power that might have led to a disastrous split in SPLA/M.

11.8.2005 General Salva Kiir Mayardit was sworn in as the first vice president of the Republic of Sudan and president of the government of South Sudan.

9.7.2005–9.7.2011 Interim period during which there would be a government of South Sudan (GOSS) led by Dr. Salva Kiir Mayardit with Dr. Riek Macar Teny as his deputy and the government of Sudan (GOS), spearheaded by Mr. Omer El Bashir of National Congress Party with General Salva Kiir Mayardit of SPLM as first vice president and Mr. Osman Mohamed Taha also of the National Congress Party as second vice president.

This interim period is expected to culminate in a referendum for South Sudan when South Sudanese will finally decide whether to remain part of One United Sudan or secede into an Independent South Sudan.

DECISIVE ABYEI/SOUTHERN SUDAN REFERENDUM

Nine January 2011 is the expected date for the Referendum of Southern Sudan together with that of Abyei. This should resolve the longstanding conflict once and for all and hopefully lead to permanent peace. The boundary dispute and rivalry over oil fields are potential areas of crises that can trigger future wars if adequate care is not taken to reach permanent resolutions.

Massive celebrations for South Sudan freedom if secession is the choice at the referendum should inevitably follow.

This date of 9 January 2011 is calculated as follows:

- **9 January 2005** Comprehensive Peace Agreement signed and a six-month interval began
- **9 July 2005** Six-year interim period began
- **9 July 2011** Six-year interim period ends
- **9 January 2011** The referendum should begin (six months before the end of the interim period). Registration of voters for the referendum should be done three months before. Thus the registration should begin any date in 2010 and must be completed before **9 October 2010**

Associated Conflicts

Darfur Conflict

A new rebellion in the western region of Darfur began in early 2003. The rebels accuse the central government of neglecting the Darfur region, although there is uncertainty regarding the objectives of the rebels and whether they merely seek an improved position for Darfur within Sudan or outright secession. Both the government and the rebels have been accused of atrocities in this war, although most of the blame has fallen on Arab militias (Janjaweed) allied with the government. The rebels have alleged that these militias have been engaging in ethnic cleansing in Darfur, and the fighting has displaced hundreds of thousands of people, many of them seeking refuge in neighbouring Chad. The government claimed victory over the rebels after capturing Tine, a town on the border with Chad, in early 2004, but violence continues and as of 2010 the humanitarian situation remained very poor.

Originally, the Darfurians formed two liberation movements: the Sudan Liberation Movement/Army (SLM/A), led by Abdel Wahid el Nur, followed by the Justice and Equality Movement (JEM), headed by Khalil Ibrahim.

Splintering of the initial two Darfurian movements to over twenty has not been helpful in either allowing a comprehensive peace agreement to be reached in Darfur or enabling Darfurian fighters to win the war militarily.

EXAMPLES OF DARFURIAN MOVEMENTS

In an attempt to assist the Darfurian movements to reach a common negotiating position and enhance prospects of achieving peace in Darfur, the Sudan People's Liberation Movement launched an initiative of its own. It formed an SPLM Task Force on Darfur on 31 March 2007. This task force organised a conference for Darfurian movements in Juba in 2007 and succeeded to reduce the multiple splinter groups from aver twenty to only five, namely:

1. Sudan Liberation Movement/Army (SLM/A), headed by Ahmed Abdel Shafi

2. United Resistance Front (URF), headed by Abu Garda

3. SLM/A, headed by Abel Wahid el Nur

4. SLM/A Unity, headed by Abdalla Yaha

5. Justice and Equality Movement (JEM), led by Khalil Ibrahim

Further attempts are planned by the SPLM Task Force to either forge more unification if possible or at least a common negotiation position among the five Darfurian movements.

A positive development for humanitarian purpose at least is the deployment of UN-AU hybrid force in Darfur under the name of United Nations Mission in Darfur (UNMID). This happened after many years of resistance by the National Congress component of the Sudan government. The extent to which this hybrid force will succeed to protect civilian lives in Darfur depends heavily on the strength of the mandate given to them.

Chadian-Sudanese Conflict

As widely stated in public media, the Chadian-Sudanese conflict officially started on 23 December 2005 when the government of Chad declared a state of war with Sudan and called for the citizens of Chad to mobilize themselves against the "common enemy," which the Chadian government sees as the Rally for Democracy and Liberty (RDL) militants, Chadian rebels, backed by the Sudanese government, and Sudanese militiamen. Militants have attacked villages and towns in eastern Chad, stealing cattle, murdering citizens, and burning houses. Over two hundred thousand refugees from the Darfur region of northwestern Sudan currently claim asylum in eastern Chad. Chadian President Idriss Déby accuses Sudanese President Omar Hassan Ahmad al-Bashir of trying to "destabilize our country, to drive our people into misery, to create disorder and export the war from Darfur to Chad."

An attack on the Chadian town of Adré near the Sudanese border led to the deaths of between one hundred and three hundred rebels based upon conflicting news reports. The Sudanese government was blamed for the attack, which was the second in the region in three days, but Sudanese foreign ministry spokesman Jamal Mohammed Ibrahim denies any Sudanese involvement, "We are not for any escalation with Chad. We technically deny involvement in Chadian internal affairs." This attack was the final straw that led to the declaration of war by Chad and the alleged deployment of the Chadian.

With the conclusion of Darfur Peace Agreement in 2006, these two conflicts would hopefully have been resolved. On the contrary, a major offensive was relaunched by rebels on Chad, presumably backed by Sudan army forces, in 2008, that could have captured Ndjamena had it not been successfully repulsed by Chadian army. It remains to be seen whether the subsequent peace agreement, signed in Dakar by President Omer Beshir of Sudan and President Idriss Déby of Chad, will hold.

LORD RESISTANCE ARMY

Rebel forces called Lord Resistance Army (LRA) have been battling the Ugandan army using South Sudan as their base. As a result of being located within the territory of South Sudan, they have been involved in killing South Sudanese in states of Equatoria, especially Western Equatoria. Attempts are under way to resolve this conflict, heralded by mediatory talks held between the government of Southern Sudan and the Lord Resistance Army. These talks have successfully led to an agreement which was due to be signed between the Uganda government and LRA. Unfortunately, the leadership of LRA reportedly did not turn up for the signing of that agreement. When political elders, including Desmond Tutu and US ex-President Jimmy Carter recently, visited Juba in 2007, they praised Southern Sudan for succeeding to help almost resolve the LRA-Uganda conflict that had puzzled the world for so long. The same commendation is expressed by many members of the international community including the United Nations and the African Union.

SOUTHERN BLUE NILE AND NUBA MOUNTAINS

These areas are parts of the marginalized Sudan. They participated in the SPLA war as part of New Sudan alongside South

Sudan. Along with Abyei, they constitute the other areas considered in the Comprehensive Peace Agreement.

While Abyei and South Sudan will hold their referenda, Southern Blue Nile and Nuba Mountains will also hold their Popular Consultations, respectively, as per the Comprehensive Peace Agreement.

H5 CONCLUSION OF HISTORY

The beauty of our land lies in its historical greatness and our inherent ability to sustain a long and painful struggle over a period of more than a thousand years, whatever the difficulties we encounter. It is also shown by our ability to cope irrespective of sudden tragedies such as the death of our departed leader, Dr. John Garang De Mabior.

When we become an independent state, we will strive to lead the world again as our ancestors had done in the past. Unlike others, our dream is not to dominate the world and impose our culture and religion on everybody. It is to contribute positively to the overall welfare of all people on Earth. When our ancestors first discovered writing, architecture, and cutlery, for example, they became indispensable gifts to all mankind. We may have lagged behind thereafter because of the unfortunate war dictated by rivalry from other races that envied us because of our precious resources and beautiful land. We have now stood firm in the Heart of Africa. No more shall we accept being dispersed any farther.

It makes one feel like flying in the air with one's own wings to be an offspring of such great people if not the greatest in the world. Yes, we were great people before and we shall no doubt become great people again come the year 2011and beyond.

POLITICS

A Land So Contentious

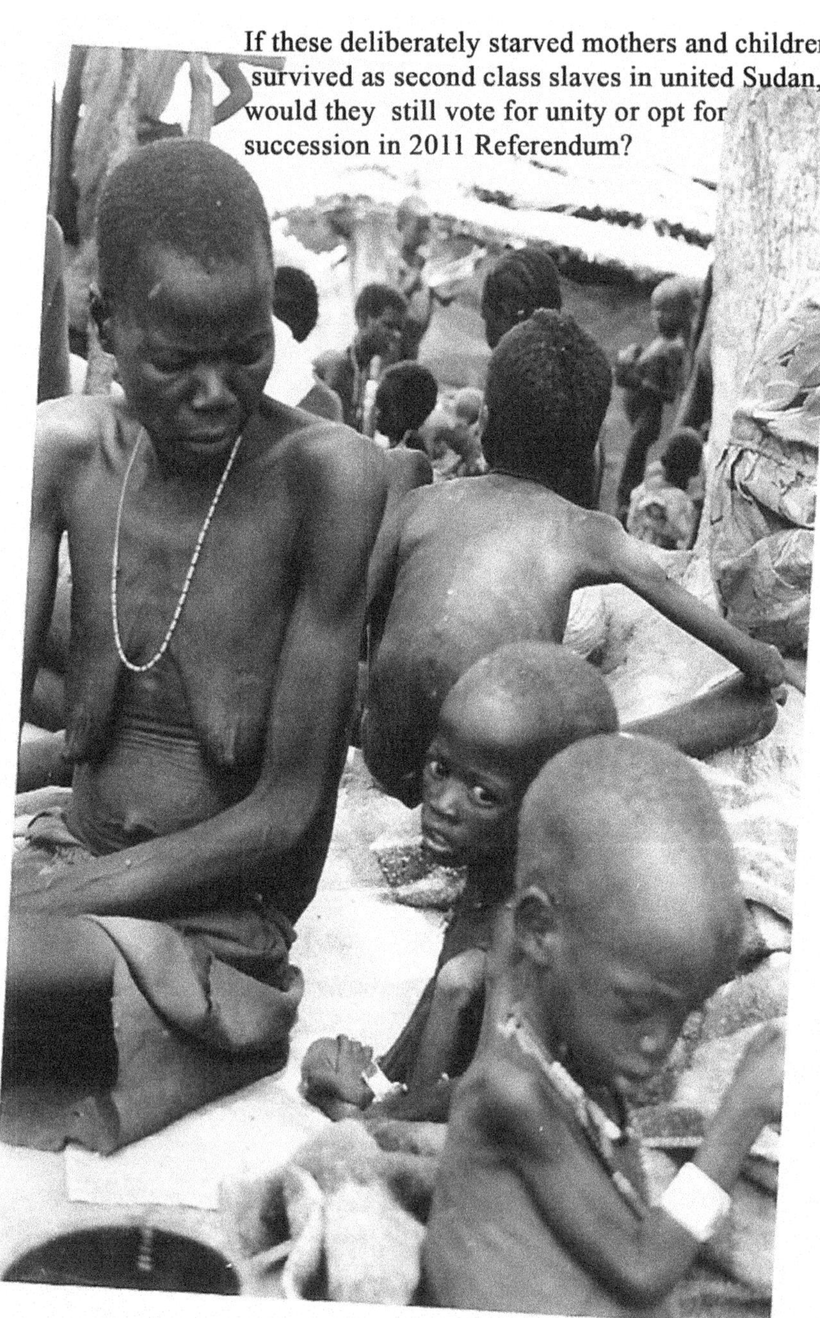

If these deliberately starved mothers and children survived as second class slaves in united Sudan, would they still vote for unity or opt for succession in 2011 Referendum?

P1 SELF-DETERMINATION

Self-determination is a free-will of people to determine their own future destiny democratically. It is an absolute right of any marginalised and oppressed people in any part of the world to decide their fate once and for all. For example, the people of the Land of South Sudan can exercise their right to self-determination to decide whether to remain part of the whole Sudan or to secede to become an independent nation.

The Land and People of South Sudan that have suffered so much and so long are also grateful to all the people, parties, organisations, and governments that helped to create a long-awaited golden opportunity for them to exercise this right in 2011.

After denying the People of South Sudan this right it is now enshrined in the Comprehensive Peace Agreement (CPA) signed in Nairobi City on 9 January 2009. Article 1.3 of Agreed Principles of the CPA clearly states that the People of South Sudan have the right to self-determination, inter alia, through a referendum to determine their future status. The same agreement empowers the people of Abyei to exercise this right to self-determination in a Simultaneous Referendum and the People of Southern Blue Nile and Nuba Mountains in form of Popular Consultations.

This Right to Self-Determination is subsequently adopted from the CPA and fully endorsed by articles in the Interim Constitution of the Republic of Sudan and Interim Constitution of Southern Sudan.

P2 Popular Consultation

A popular consultation is a process by which the opinions of all the members of a land are consulted about an issue of general concern. For example, people of a part of a country can be consulted whether an agreement made for their area is worthy or not.

As stated earlier elsewhere in this book, two areas of Sudan also have agreement made for them as per the CPA. These areas are the Nuba Mountains and Southern Blue Nile.

Indeed, the CPA gives the SPLM 45 percent of power in the two areas and resolves the problem of land, which was one of the main reasons people of the two areas took up arms. Then it provides for the right of popular consultation after four years for the people to give their views and decision on the agreement of the two areas.

Thus these Popular Consultations should take place before the referendum of Southern Sudan and Abyei that should take place at the sixth year (2011). Time-wise, these Popular Consultations should be conducted after four years of the CPA Agreement anytime between 9 July 2009 when the Fourth Year of Interim Period ends and 9 January 2011 when the referendum of Southern Sudan must take place simultaneously with that of Abyei Area.

P3 2011 REFERENDUM

Referendum is an occasion when all the people in a country can vote in order to show their opinion about a political question. For example, is South Sudan to remain a united part of Sudan or secede?

A key component of the Comprehensive Peace Agreement signed on 9 January 2005 is that a referendum will be conducted at the end of the six-year interim period. There will be one for the People of Southern Sudan to decide once and for all on permanent **UNITY** of entire Sudan or **SECESSION** of Southern Sudan. The other one that will be conducted simultaneously is that for people of Abyei Area to decide whether to be part and parcel of Northern Sudan or of Bahr-el-Ghazal State of Southern Sudan.

The articles specifying these referenda in the CPA and the options to be voted for are as follows:

Article 2.5 At the end of the six-year Interim Period there shall be an internationally monitored referendum, organised jointly by the GOS and the SPLM/A, for the People of South Sudan to: confirm the unity of the Sudan by voting to adopt the system of government established under the peace agreement; or to vote for secession.

1.3 End of Interim Period: Simultaneously with the referendum for Southern Sudan, the residents of Abyei will cast a separate ballot. The proposition voted on in the separate ballot will present the residents of Abyei with the following choices, irrespective of the results of the southern referendum:

a. That Abyei retain its special administrative status in the north;
b. That Abyei be part of Bahr el Ghazal.

The CPA also articulates for relevant **Referendum Commissions** as follows:

Article 2.10.1.5 An ad-hoc Commission shall be established to monitor and ensure accuracy, legitimacy, and transparency of the referendum as mentioned in the Machakos Protocol on Self-Determination for the people of South Sudan, which shall also include international experts.

Article 8.1 There shall be established by the presidency an Abyei Referendum Commission to conduct the Abyei referendum simultaneously with the referendum of Southern Sudan. The composition of the commission shall be determined by the presidency.

The dates relevant to the referenda are as follows:

- **9 January 2005** Comprehensive Peace Agreement signed and a six-month interval began

- **9 July 2005** Six-year interim period began

- **9 July 2011** Six-year interim period ends

- **9 July 2009** The Referendum Law should have been enacted (that is before the end of the fourth year of the Interim Period). Sadly, this date is now exceeded amid an ongoing dialogue between the SPLM and the NCP before the referendum bill is to be presented to the National Legislative Assembly. Some of the contentious issues under debate are said to include post-referendum arrangements, who is a Southern Sudanese, whether voting in the referendum should be confined within Southern Sudan or extended elsewhere, whether international observers will be needed, how many people will constitute the Referendum Commission, where the data of the referendum will be analyzed after voting, and whether the outcome of the referendum is to be determined by 75 percent (three-quarters of the voters), as advocated by the NCP, or 50+ 1 percent (simple majority of the voters), as asserted by the SPLM. Details of this dialogue may be publicized by the CPA partners sooner or later.

- **9 October 2010** The registration of voters for the Referendum should have been completed, as this should be done three months before the actual voting on the referendum is done. Thus the registration for the voters for the referendum should begin any date in 2010 and must be completed before 9 October 2010.

- **9 January 2011** The Referendum of South Sudan and Abyei should begin simultaneously (six months before the end of the interim period).

It is important to emphasize that the referendum is to be conducted six months before the end of the interim period as stated in both the CPA and Interim Constitutions of the Republic of the Sudan and of Southern Sudan, Therefore it should start on 9 January 2011. If the registration of voters for the referendum also started in January 2011, as mistyped in the schedules mentioned in the CPA, it would mean that the dates for registration of voters and for the referendum itself fell in the same month of January 2011, without allowing the three-month gap when the registration should have been completed, as speculated in the CPA. However, the voters should be registered 3 months before the referendum is conducted.

If unity has been made attractive enough during the six-year interim period, the people of Southern Sudan are expected to vote for UNITY and those of Abyei may see no need to leave from being part of Northern Sudan. On the contrary, if unity has not been made attractive enough, Southern Sudan will opt for secession and Abyei shall probably prefer to become part of the South as before.

However, for the referendum to take place smoothly, it is expected that the boundaries of both Abyei and Southern Sudan must have been determined. As highlighted by a recent petition submitted to the United Nations, Inter-Governmental Authority on Development, and some governments/organisations, the National Congress Party has been systematically violating the CPA:

To:

1. Honourable Ban Ki Moon, United Nations Secretary General, New York

2. Head of the United Nations Mission in Sudan, Khartoum

3. The Member Countries of the Inter-Governmental Authority on Development (IGAD).

4. The President of the United States of America, Washington, DC.

5. The Prime Minister of Her Majesty's Government of the United Kingdom of Great Britain, London.

6. The Royal Norwegian Government

7. The Prime Minister of the Italian Government, Rome.

8. The Chairman of the Comprehensive Peace Agreement, Assessment and Evaluation Commission

From:

1. Citizens of South Sudan

2. South Sudanese Nongovernmental Organisations, in and outside the country.

3. South Sudanese Civil Society Associations.

Subject: Breaches of the Comprehensive Peace Agreement by the Government of the Sudan

We the undersigned Sudanese citizens, NGOs, and the Civil Society Associations, inside and outside the Sudan, have been following with keen interest, events in our country since the signing of the Comprehensive Peace Agreement (CPA) between the Government of Sudan (GOS) and the Sudan People's Liberation Movement/Army (SPLM/A) on 9 January 2005. Almost three years have now elapsed, and regrettably not much progress in the implementation of the CPA is taking place. The reality on the ground is that the CPA is at the brink of collapse and the Sudan is at the risk of reverting to war.

As early as the second anniversary of the signing of the CPA marked in Juba on 9 July 2006, the first vice president of the Sudan, president of the Government of South Sudan (GOSS), and Commander in Chief of the SPLA, Lt. General Salva Kiir Mayardit, warned that the Agreement was facing crisis and there was a growing risk of the country returning to war. He repeated this message in his address to the South Sudan Legislative Assembly on 11 September 2007 in Juba, more than one year later. This time the language is terse and more alarming than before when he said, "Today—and I do not want to mince my words—I am worried and deeply concerned about the status of CPA implementation...I am worried...that it is likely that the Sudan will reverse again to war if we do not act now with our partner NCP."

As concerned South Sudanese, we view these developments in our country as a real threat to the peace that was ushered in by the CPA. This state of affairs has developed because GOS, represented by the National Congress Party (NCP) under the leadership of Lt. General Omer Hassan Ahmed El-Bashir, president of the Republic of the Sudan, continues undermining the CPA and is dragging its feet in the implementation of the peace agreement. Not only that, the NCP is engaging in acts of distrust, sabotage, and hate, acts that shake the very fabric of the CPA. The following are some of the serious breaches of the agreement that show the NCP is not interested in its implementation, which, if not rectified, can lead to what the president of South Sudan has warned will take place: the Sudan reversing to war.

1. The Sudan Armed Forces (SAF) Presence in South Sudan beyond 9 July 2007 and other Violations

According to the CPA, the Sudan armed forces should have redeployed its forces from the south by 9 July 2007. While the SPLA have withdrawn completely from the North, this has not been reciprocated by SAF. Instead, SAF has dug in and reinforced its positions in the South since the signing of the CPA as demonstrated by the following hostile acts:

1. SAF has since increased the number of its troops of the Thirty-first Brigade in the Abyei area.

2. The SAF garrison at Renk in northern Upper Nile has increased its troop numbers, and tanks had recently been moved to the area.

3. SAF continues to arm huge numbers of the nomads and these will be very difficult to disarm.

4. In late 2006, SAF established a new garrison at Wadakona, which lies a few kilometres north of Renk on the west bank of the Nile.

5. SAF has moved tanks to Bentiu and, in fact, has increased its tanks over the past year.

6. SAF was engaged in attacking civilians in and around Juba in October and November 2006. This was proved by the SPLA arresting SAF demobilized officers during these attacks.

7. All along, GOS (NCP) Military Intelligence (MI) policy and work has been to encourage and create instability in the South. The fighting in Malakal in November 2006 was a result of this policy.

8. On 6 September 2007, SPLA forces in Muglad, South Kordofan, in central Sudan, were surrounded by SAF. The SPLA had gone to the area legally at the request of the citizens there. That military standoff almost led to an armed military confrontation between the SAF and the SPLA

2. Feet-dragging on Reforms and Formation of Commissions stipulated by the CPA

The NCP has systematically stalled the formation of a number of commissions of the CPA, and maintains a complete political control over the north of the country by legal and legislative manipulations, manifested in its selective avoidance of the bodies that oversee the implementation of the CPA, such as the Constitutional Review Commission. It has successfully avoided the democratic reforms it signed on to in the CPA, while paying lip service to others. Here are some examples.

1. Although NCP claims to have enacted bills on the freedom of the press and freedom of speech and of association, these rights continue to be infringed upon in the country on a daily basis.

2. Human rights abuses are rampant in the country.

3. The NCP-dominated government has starved the Border Commission of funds, making it unable to do its work. Needless to say, without this commission completing its task, elections slated for 2009 and the 2011 referendum will not be able to take place on time.

4. The NCP practically runs the country single-handedly, while excluding the SPLM from major national decisions. Its foreign policies, as exemplified by the stand on Darfur, are totally the opposite of those of the SPLM. Recently, it expelled a number of foreign diplomats without consultation with the SPLM.

5. On 11 September 2007, heavily armed police of a supposed government of national unity raided the SPLM offices in Khartoum. No reasons or explanations were given. This act alone threatens the existence of the coalition (partnership) government, between the SPLM and the NCP. It shows the NCP's contempt for its partner in government and can do whatever it wants with impunity.

3. Lack of Transparency on the Exploitation and Sharing of the Country's Oil Wealth

After insisting on retaining the Oil and Gas ministry of the country, the NCP has so far failed to bring transparency into the Ministry of Gas and Energy. It took a lot of cajoling for the GOS to constitute the Oil Commission. In spite of that, the commission has been emasculated with no powers or access to information on contract agreements, etc. Of great concern are the following:

1. The NCP, without any explanation, deliberately recently reduced the transfer of oil revenue to the South from US$100 million to a mere US$44 million monthly, in spite of the facts that the (a) oil prices have been rising in the international market; and (b) the amount of oil being produced per day is on the increase.

2. In spite of the fact that half of the oil is said to come from the south, no efforts are being made to have southerners also employed either in the Ministry of Gas and Oil or in the upstream or downstream operations of the oil industry in the Sudan.

3. The south has no knowledge of just how much oil is being pumped in the southern oil fields, nor does it know how much money comes into the national coffer from the oil. All the south gets is the meagre US$44 million or so at the end of each month.

4. The Abyei Protocol

The NCP has so far refused to implement the Abyei Protocol. It has also refused to implement the Abyei Boundary Commission (ABC) Report, which was carefully and thoroughly researched and written by experts of impeccable credentials, endorsed from the outset by NCP itself. The refusal appears to be because the report does not favour the perceived position of the NCP.

5. The South-North Border Demarcation and the Population Census

The NCP has intentionally avoided implementing the CPA provisions on issues pertaining to the South–North border demarcation. This is a very sensitive issue in its own right, given the fact that successive northern regimes in Khartoum have encroached on the territories that have been part of the south since the colonial era, and the NCP will not want to let go of these areas. We believe the Boundary Commission is going to face the same fate as the ABC, making it a potentially dangerous flashpoint.

Delays in the border demarcation will inevitably mean delays in the population census. The NCP continues to obstruct the preparations for the implementation of the CPA provisions that deal with Population Census due early 2008. So far the commission charged with this very important task has been starved of the funds it needs, and arrangements for a pilot plan have now been postponed several times.

Given the above record of inaction and counteractions by NCP, it has become evident to us that the NCP has not, and will never develop a relationship of trust between the South and the North. Instead, it continuously engages in acts of sabotage and planting hatred, which are surely leading to the complete abrogation of the CPA. Such blatant acts by NCP seriously worry us as citizens. They imply that Sudan is entering a seriously dangerous period, which, if left unchecked, could easily turn into a full-scale war.

While the NCP is doing all this, the United Nations organisation should not be silently watching, as if tacitly approving the NCP's slow, systematic and sure abrogation of the CPA. Two years ago, the UN General Assembly agreed that it has responsibility to protect people whose governments would not safeguard their lives. We thought this declaration of shouldering the responsibility to protect such people was a breakthrough, that it would extend to protect the peace process ushered in by the CPA and to protect the People of Sudan, especially of South Sudan against rogue regimes. We are urging the UN to live up to its declaration, and not allow the NCP to kill the CPA.

It is pertinent that we remind ourselves and the international community that, when the CPA was signed on 9 January 2005, the international community undertook to back it. Now the CPA is in danger of collapse due primarily to NCP sabotage and international neglect. The international overseers of the implementation of the CPA, prominently the United Nations Mission in Sudan (UNMIS), the Inter-Governmental Authority on Development (IGAD), the United States, the United Kingdom, Norway, and Italy, appear to have dozed off, leaving the NCP to wreak havoc on the CPA. It is time they wake up from their deep slumber to make the parties, especially the NCP, live up to their responsibilities of implementing the agreement to the letter. The deathly silence from those of you who pledged to protect the CPA when it was being formulated and finally signed, has given the NCP the perfect excuse and freedom to deal with it as it pleases. The failure of the UN-led Disarmament, Demobilization and Re-integration program (DDR) is another pointer to the collapse of the CPA.

Given the situation as described above, the collapse of the CPA is imminent and the return to South–North war is real. Once war breaks out again, it will have devastating effects and consequences in the entire region. So, to save the CPA, and to prevent this imminent danger of war, we therefore urge the international community in general, and particularly the UN Mission in Sudan (UNMIS), the Inter-Governmental Authority on Development (IGAD), the United States, the United Kingdom, Norway, Italy, and the CPA Assessment and Evaluation Commission, to take whatever actions necessary to protect it.

We call on you all to:

1. Put pressure on the parties, especially the NCP to implement the agreement to the letter without excuses or delay.

2. Send a clear message to all parties, especially to the NCP, that any feet dragging, avoidance, or deviation from the CPA shall have serious consequences.

3. Pressurize the NCP to effect the democratic reforms as stipulated in the CPA.

We are certain that, as custodians of the CPA, you will appreciate the gravity of the situation and will ensure that the citizens of Sudan are protected from the dominance of the NCP government in Khartoum, and that Sudan does not slip back to war again.

Thank you all.

Signed By

Over Three Hundred People and Organisations Worldwide

The action taken by the First Lieutenant General Salva Kiir Mayardit, first vice president of the Republic of Sudan, president of the government of Southern Sudan, chairman of SPLM, and commander in chief of SPLA, to withdraw SPLM ministers from the Government of National Unity in October 2007 until Sudan President Omer el Hassen Ahmed el Beshir and his National Congress Party implements violated aspects of the CPA, is widely viewed as a vital step. Quoting from a press conference conducted in Juba by President Salva Kiir Mayardit: "The National Congress Party has been taking us, in the SPLM, for a ride. We do not intend to start another war. We intend to protect the CPA. It is the collapse of the CPA that will trigger war. We call upon the International Community, IGAD, and friends of IGAD to intervene and help protect the CPA."

Ignoring the media abuses of second vice president of Sudan Ali Osman Mohammed Tah along with similar-minded leaders of NCP, GOSS President Salva Kiir Mayardit and first vice president of Sudan stated in the press conference, "I have not come here to respond to negative media waged by others."

By simply stating the facts, in a cool and calm manner, free of insults and dirty language, President Salva Kiir Mayardit proved his personality to all. As the author knew him from early school days, he has never insulted anybody publicly. He is a fighter, but not a dirty linguist like those who have publicly exposed their malicious motives in their own-dominated media in Khartoum.

It is hoped that the NCP will see sense in joining the SPLM to uphold the CPA and resolve the political crisis that has developed and allow the SPLM to return to participate in GONU. For the government in Khartoum can no longer be referred to as a Government of National Unity stipulated in the CPA without the SPLM.

Nevertheless, it can be argued that if tactical delays continue to be imposed by the NCP to obstruct, for example, the census and the delineation of boundaries as a way of preventing the referendum from taking place, the Government of Southern Sudan will have no choice but to unilaterally draw what it believes to be the boundaries of Southern Sudan and Abyei, then conduct the census within them prior to the end of the interim period. After all, what is prohibited in the CPA is unilateral abrogation by the parties to it. I believe any unilateral decisions taken or to be taken by the SPLM in order to protect or implement the CPA are legal and constitutional.

At the end of the day, the Sudanese people along with the international community that witnessed the CPA will have to intervene to resolve the crisis in order to protect the CPA from collapsing.

Further insight to the state of affairs regarding the Comprehensive Peace Agreement and the function of the Government of Southern Sudan can be deduced from the latest speech of President Salva Kiir Mayardit prior to the publication of this book. He delivered this speech in Wau Town during the celebration of the third anniversary of this peace agreement in January 2008:

SPEECH OF GENERAL SALVA KIIR MAYARDIT, PRESIDENT OF THE GOVERNMENT OF SOUTHERN SUDAN

ON THE OCCASION OF THE THIRD ANNIVERSARY CELEBRATIONS OF THE COMPREHENSIVE PEACE AGREEMENT

14 JANUARY 2008, WAU, WESTERN BAHR EL GHAZAL STATE

- Hon. Dr. Riek Machar, Vice President of GoSS
- Hon. James Wani, Speaker of Southern Sudan Legislative Assembly (SSLA)
- *Hon. Marc Nyipoc, Governor of Western Bahr el Ghazal State*
- *All Governors Attending this Important Occasion*
- *Advisors and Ministers of the Government of National Unity and Government of Southern Sudan*
- *Heads of Commissions and Other Independent Public Institutions*
- *Hon. Members of Legislature at All Levels*
- *Leaders of the Sudanese Political Parties*
- *All Diplomatic Corps*
- *Representatives of UN and International Organisations*
- *Members of the Organising Committee for This Occasion*
- *Compatriots, Sudanese Women, Youth, and Children*

- ***Commanders and Soldiers of our Armed Forces***
- ***Distinguished Guests***
- ***Ladies and Gentlemen***

Dear Citizens:

I salute you all on this most important day in our national calendar, the day our country regained peace and tasted stability after more than two decades of protracted civil war. May I ask you to rise and observe a one-minute silence in memory of Dr. John Garang de Mabior and all our martyrs, heroes, and heroines whose selfless sacrifices during our liberation struggle shall always inspire us during peacetime. On the day of commemorating CPA, we should recall and be proud of our long and heroic struggle for justice, freedom, equality and dignity in Sudan. Having been into the New Year, I find it also an opportune occasion to wish you all a very happy and prosperous new year.

The January 9 is and will remain a significant day in the history of our country. Indeed, CPA, as eloquently described by President Bashir in Naivasha, marks "The birth of Sudan's Second Independence." We hope all Sudanese people, particularly their leaders, should indeed seize the opportunity provided for by the CPA to recreate and reposition Sudan to re-emerge as a leading nation in the region. In recognition of its importance, the Government of Southern Sudan resolved that 9 January to be a "Peace Day" and a national holiday to be celebrated in all states of Southern Sudan. Recently, the Government of National Unity made a similar decision and we have just finished the celebrations of 9 January in Khartoum. Your celebration here in Wau complements the national celebrations but it is even more colourful and more of people's celebrations.

Dear Compatriots:

The dying days of 2007 and opening of 2008 have seen a convergence of a series of happy religions and national occasions, including the Eid El Adha, Christmas, Independence Day, and now Peace Day. May this be a beginning of happier times ahead of us during 2008.

Three years have now passed since the signing of the CPA in Nairobi, Kenya, on 9 January 2005. It has not been exactly smooth sailing during those three years, but our assessment is generally encouraging and promising. The CPA has been subjected to some tough trials and shocks but it has managed to survive and remain the guiding instrument for good governance in our country. CPA shall always be the basis upon which the SPLM shall politically relate to and engage with the National Congress Party and other political parties in building new Sudan through democratic transformation.

Dear Citizens,

The CPA has been a blessing for our country. Its immediate and greatest effect has been peace that is being enjoyed by people in most parts of Sudan. Thousands of lives have been preserved since the guns went silent. Sudanese mothers recognise this fact better than others because their sons have been spared from the military conscription program that had hitherto been enforced.

Life has returned to normal in most areas formerly affected by the war. Many citizens have returned to their original homes either from exile or camps of internal displacement. Importantly, the life of an average household is changing and improving every day through its own efforts. Whenever I return to Juba I do see a lot of changes and I am seeing the same in Wau and other parts of Southern Sudan. People have taken the development into their own hands and that is an encouraging sign, as real development comes from citizens with government creating for them conducive environment.

At the national level, the economy of Sudan is now the fastest growing economy in the region. With the overall atmosphere of peace and stability ushered in by the CPA, there has been considerable economic growth and resurgence throughout the country. Whatever may be said by our detractors, the greatest peace dividend for the ordinary Sudanese citizens in both the South and the North has been the freedom and ability to move and pursue private business interests anywhere in our country.

Besides economic growth and stability, Sudan has now a new currency, Sudanese Pound, which was designed for the first time with your full participation and it now reflects the diversity of Sudan as required by the provisions of CPA and our constitution. With one currency, Sudan is now one and harmonized economic entity with one legal tender that can facilitate the effective management of our economy within national macroeconomic and monetary policies. Bank of Southern Sudan is now operational and efforts are now on the way to effect the conventional banking system in Southern Sudan.

Dear Citizens,

At the level of Southern Sudan, the GoSS has been receiving financial transfers representing its 50 percent oil revenue share from the oil produced in Southern Sudan. Since the signing of the CPA, GoSS has been receiving on average US $1 billion per year as oil revenue. There have been a lot of questions and even doubt in media and even from our key political partner, NCP, about the way we have been using the resources transferred to GoSS. Although we are not obliged to answer such question, as we have our own institutions (Southern Sudan Legislative Assembly, Southern Sudan Audit Chamber) that would provide full account of the usage of such funds, I would like to share with our citizens some basic facts.

I would like to inform our citizens that what we are receiving from GoNU as net oil revenue is only 50 percent of oil produced in Southern Sudan and we receive 0 percent from all revenues including oil revenue generated in Northern Sudan. The share of Southern Sudan from the total revenues generated by GoNU is on average 10 percent compared to its population that is estimated to be around 33 percent of the total population of Sudan. Despite the impact of war, the average citizen in Southern Sudan is paradoxically receiving on average far fewer resources than the average Sudanese citizen. Although, we do not want to blame anybody, as such allocations are as per the provisions of the CPA, we would want our citizens to know these facts.

Dear Compatriots,

Concerning the question of what have we been doing with whatever resources we have been receiving, I would like to share with you the following:

When we formed the GoSS in 2005, we inherited a corrupt system of civil service that was used as part of counterinsurgency warfare to bribe and soothe southerners not to join the SPLM but to mobilize them against the SPLM. The salaries only constitute on average more than 40 percent of our total expenditure, while development expenditures constitute on average less than 22 percent of total expenditures. This situation has been worsened by the absorption of a huge number of OAGs into the SPLA, particularly after the Juba Declaration. Although the bulk of these meagre resources go toward meeting salaries, serious efforts are being made to ensure that the ratio of salaries to development expenditures is reversed in 2008 budget.

With development expenditures, our Ministry of Education, Science, and Technology succeeded to increase enrolment of pupils by almost three times from 343,000 in 2005 to over 1 million in 2007. The enrolment of female pupils increased to over

31 percent in 2007. Also the Ministry of Health managed in 2007 to supply essential medicines to over 1000 health facilities being managed by over 1,600 health professionals, while over 60,000 treated bed nets were distributed. The Ministry of Cooperatives and Rural Development managed in 2007 to construct about 306 new boreholes and rehabilitated 231 water sources making total number of operational water sources in Southern Sudan to about 4,264. Our Ministry of Roads and Transport has de-mined and rehabilitated about 1862 kms of roads in 2007, while rehabilitation of Juba-Bor-Malakal road (769 km) is ongoing, while rehabilitation of nearly 1,937 kms of Murram roads will commence in 2008 and upgrading of 1,000 kms of roads to asphalt road will also start in 2008.

I hope these statistics will help you to judge what we have been doing with the resources that we have been receiving. As we have committed ourselves to zero tolerance to corruption and transparency in the use of public funds, we are keen to audit all accounts of our government at all levels and we will make public such audit report.

Distinguished Guests, Ladies, and Gentlemen,

While we continue to pull our efforts together to ensure smooth implementation of the CPA, I would also like to acknowledge that challenges ahead are enormous. There is need for the SPLM-NCP partnership to strengthen in order to avoid recurrence of similar crises like what we experienced recently and we should be ready to learn lessons for the future.

The recommendations of the six-person committee and the recent meetings of the presidency with the Joint Defence Board and North-South Border Committee show a renewed commitment to the full implementation of CPA but we need see in the near future how we will walk the talk, particularly in the redeployment of forces. I personally urge the chief of staff of Sudan armed forces and SPLA to fully implement the resolutions of JDB and not to reschedule again the dates agreed upon for the redeployment of forces.

Despite our renewed commitment to the full implementation of CPA, the implementation of Abyei Protocol shall remain a litmus test for our confidence building. Any further delay in the implementation of Abyei Protocol will make our partnership vulnerable to further disagreement over population census, demarcation of the North-South border, general elections, national reconciliation, referendum on the right of self-determination and role of international community, and witnesses of CPA. I recently appointed Comrade Edward Lino as SPLM chairman in Abyei Area so as to organise the returnees and prepare ground for the implementation of Abyei Protocol. It will again be a serious violation of CPA if we fail again in 2008 to implement Abyei Protocol and our conscience and moral obligations would not allow us to continue depriving the people of the Abyei area from enjoying the dividends of peace.

Besides the pending problem of Abyei Protocol, I do clearly see some critical areas that may create future conflict in the process of CPA implementation. These issues include possible disagreement on the report of the North-South Border Committee, results of the population census, results of general elections, conduct and results of popular consultation, results and outcome of the referenda (Abyei and Right of Self-determination). In order to overcome these potential challenges, there is need for SPLM and NCP to continue developing functioning mechanisms for credible CPA implementation and to proactively discuss these issues within the existing mechanisms agreed upon by the two parties.

Dear Citizens:

Our contemporary political history in the Sudan tells us that the political power of the state has been changing hands between elites without the real choice of the people. One of the biggest achievements of the CPA is the recognition that the sovereignty of the state is vested in the people and to be exercised through their elected democratic and representative institutions in free and fair elections. As provided for in the CPA, the general elections are to be conducted by 2009 and such elections will be critical impetus for true change and empowering of our people to choose their leaders and elect their democratic institutions. This will be the slimmest opportunity for Sudanese people to bring a real change through their true and free will as basis for democratic transformation and national reconciliation.

Prior to the conduct of general elections, we are to show to our people that we and our current institutions do respect and uphold the bill of rights and fundamental freedoms as enshrined in our constitutions and CPA. There is no justification, for whatever reason, to unlawfully detain innocent citizens without any legal basis. We are so delighted by the decision of President Bashir to release all political detainees and we hope that all other citizens who are illegally detained to be tried or otherwise are released immediately. It is critical to show to our citizens that we are serious, sincere and committed to rule of law and democratic transformation. The hope of our people hangs on the ability of the signatories of CPA to take a lead in maintaining rule of law and respecting basic principles of equal rights and citizenship, as we now live in a world where repression of people's rights is untenable.

As SPLM, we are committed to holding fair and transparent general elections by 2009 as provided for by the provisions of CPA and INC. I, therefore, call upon all political forces in the Sudan to take an active role in the forthcoming general elections and to ensure such elections are fair. We should avoid what happened in Kenya general elections and we should learn from such experience so as to ensure fair elections that can produce acceptable results. I am delighted that all political parties have now agreed to allocate 25 percent of all seats in general elections to women. This is affirmation to our commitment to empowering women as marginalised of marginalised but it is also recognition of their critical role in our society and during our liberation struggle.

Distinguished Guests, Ladies, and Gentlemen,

We all know that since independence in 1956, Sudan has been haunted with cumulative bitterness, wounds, hatred, mistrust, tensions, anger, and grievances either in the way our rulers have been misusing their powers and victimizing our citizens or the way our citizens have been related to each other as citizens. Our nation needs a serious and genuine process of reconciliation, healing, forgiveness, and confidence building. Now the CPA provides us with a golden opportunity to heal such wounds and grievances of the past and to start building a new Sudan based on citizenship and respect of people's basic rights.

We have now agreed in the presidency to initiate the national reconciliation process that would involve all political forces and civil society. But as leaders of political parties in Sudan, we should take the lead and courage to apologize to our people for whatever we have committed against them in the past. A commitment to national reconciliation and healing process demands us all to forgive one another and forge ahead with laying down new basis for transforming Sudan to a respectable county.

In the SPLM we have started such process immediately after the signing of CPA when our great leader, Dr. John Garang, during a conference of all chiefs and community leaders of New Sudan, apologized to chiefs and citizens for whatever crimes were committed by SPLA soldiers during the liberation struggle and asked them as well for forgiveness. During war, we initiated a people-to-people reconciliation process that resulted in the Wunlit Peace Conference that resolved the conflict between Dinka and Nuer. We have also initiated the South-South reconciliation process that resulted in the Juba Declaration and reconciliation with all other armed groups and their absorption into SPLA.

I would like to seize this opportunity as well to apologize to all Sudanese for whatever actions taken by our SPLA forces during our liberation struggle that might have affected you personally or members of your family. For us in the SPLM, we are on a higher moral ground, as we have shown to the world an exemplary spirit of forgiveness during difficult times of war as we kept and released thousands of prisoners of war who are now living freely with their families. If we can forgive and save lives of those who fought us, the SPLM is ready to forgive as well those who might have committed any crimes against its members, particularly during war.

My Dear Compatriots:

We are committed as per the provisions of the CPA and policies of the SPLM to making unity of the Sudan an attractive option and a priority on a new basis of good governance, democracy, equality, justice, respect of human rights, and equitable socioeconomic development. Despite our conditional commitment to the unity of Sudan, the SPLM is equally committed to ensuring that People of Southern Sudan exercise their constitutional right of self-determination in an internationally monitored referendum. The SPLM is committed as well to the outcome of such referendum.

Whatever the outcome of such referendum, the North and South shall remain inseparable entities and we need to invest now in national programmes that would strengthen and cement such relations, particularly in Southern Sudan and transitional areas. President Bashir has popularly stated that if the South opts for separation, we shall remain the best neighbours but let us hope that People of Southern Sudan will vote for unity. It should be obvious to all of us that greater responsibility for making unity an attractive option lies with the Government of National Unity.

Making unity attractive means convincing the ordinary citizen of Southern Sudan who will vote in the referendum of 2011 that he or she stands to enjoy more benefits in a united Sudan rather than in an independent Southern Sudan. There is no better way to achieve this than to improve the social and economic welfare of the citizens, particularly through national programmes and projects. In our last meeting of the presidency we have resolved to initiate such national programmes in Southern Sudan and to invest as well in the transitional areas along the North-South border.

Mr. President, My Dear Compatriots,

The conflict in Darfur continues to be a matter of great concern for the government and citizens of Sudan. We see peace as indivisible in the context of one country. We are unable to fully enjoy the peace that the CPA brought to us while we empathetically feel the pain and suffering of our brothers and sisters in Darfur.

The SPLM has been involved in an effort to unify the Darfurian armed movements because we feel that the chances of reaching an agreement with one movement are much higher than with a myriad of them. While we may not claim full success in that endeavour, we are gratified to declare that the numerous Darfurian movements have agreed to group themselves in three organisations. What is urgently required now is for these new groups to have a fresh go at serious and honest negotiations with the Government of National Unity. The SPLM shall work toward forging a common position with the NCP in the search for a comprehensive peace in Darfur and the SPLM will have a strong team in the next round of peace talks.

In order to facilitate the peace process and create a conducive atmosphere for the peace talks, we are for the immediate and unconditional deployment of the hybrid force in Darfur. It is crucial that the humanitarian aspect of the conflict should be seen to be given the priority that it deserves. The protection of civilians in the area will induce a relaxed atmosphere and encourage the combatants to allow their representatives to negotiate sincerely with the view to reaching a peace agreement satisfactory to all sides. I personally appeal to all the parties concerned to make 2008 the year of peace in Darfur.

Mr. President, My Dear Compatriots,

The recent spate of fighting in Northern Bahr el Ghazal and the heavy casualties that have resulted from it have been the most unfortunate development. It is regrettable to lose innocent lives when we should be enjoying the dividends of peace. I sincerely pass my condolences to all families who lost their members in this unfortunate incident.

Why did this carnage resulting in unnecessary loss of life have to be triggered at all? I suspect that sworn enemies of peace are still hard at work trying to ignite a new war. These are people who seem to enjoy chaos and have never been comfortable with the restoration of peace in Southern Sudan. Whether that strange state of mind is motivated by material gain under war conditions or by sheer sadism remains to be established. But I have this to tell such people: you are wasting your time and innocent lives. We shall not allow you to take our people back to war. If you had not physically fought in the past, then take our advice: war is bad; do not trigger it. If you had actually participated in the fighting and were lucky to survive then thank God your creator but do not overplay your hand.

While waiting for the report of the North-South Border Committee, we have agreed with President Bashir to keep the forces of SPLA in Northern Bhar el Ghazal State south of Kiir River (Bhar el Arab), while Sudan Armed Forces to remain north of Kiir River. As commander in chief of the SPLA, I have ordered the

SPLA forces to remain south of Kiir River and not to cross the river and I expect SAF have received the same directives.

For the movement of Arab nomads, many of you will have heard or read in the media my directives to the governors and traditional chiefs of the Southern States sharing borders with some Northern States to the effect that they should facilitate the movement into their areas of Arab nomads seeking pastures and water sources. The Misseiriya nomads would be among the major beneficiaries of this directive. The media campaign and alleged fighting between Misseiriya and SPLA forces are baseless and are meant to use Arab nomads again to fight war of others. The interest of Arab nomads is more in Southern Sudan and with the SPLM as party of marginalised People of Sudan.

The SPLM is a national party and is concerned with the problem of our nomads in northern Sudan. For Misseiriya, the SPLM recognises them as people who have suffered a great deal during war; that is why the SPLM stood firm to allocate them 2 percent of oil produced in Abyei area. We in the SPLM are committed to ensure for Arab nomads seasonal access to water and pastures in Southern Sudan not only now but even if the South opts for separation.

Dear Citizens,

The CPA was subjected to some serious tests about three months ago when the SPLM recalled their ministers in GoNU till tangible progress is seen in the implementation of CPA. This crisis has now been overcome amicably through long discussions between the SPLM and NCP. On our part, the intention had always been to draw attention to serious aspects of implementation of the CPA that could not afford to be ignored any further. There has never been doubt in our mind that the NCP would ultimately appreciate our concerns and move to take the necessary measures to allay those concerns. The current cordial status of relations between the CPA signatories proves that our hopes and expectations were not misplaced.

The IGAD countries, the IGAD Partners Forum, the AU, the Arab League, and the UN, all of which witnessed the signing of the CPA, should continue to monitor its implementation. I also wish to call upon all donors to scale up their development assistance so as to help us realise peace dividends for our people during the second phase of the Interim Period.

I call upon our people to take the population census seriously and cooperate with the institutions and personnel that will carry it out. We urge every adult citizen to exercise their democratic right by registering for the 2009 general elections.

My Dear Compatriots,

We in the SPLM are not oblivious to the fact that it took enormous courage for the NCP to sign the CPA with us. The political culture and attitudes prevailing in Northern Sudan at the time, hardened by two decades of a devastating civil war, intimidated many political leaders and made them shy away from such hard decisions.

I therefore wish to recognise, our great leader, Dr. John Garang, and Ustaz Ali Osman Mohd Taha as national heroes, as this agreement we celebrate today is their handiwork, not simply because it bears their signatures but because they negotiated every word that it contains. We owe them a great deal and we should one day them honour them with a special event.

For President Bashir, this is your agreement, for without your endorsement it could not have come to be. You inspired the top leadership of the NCP to endorse this agreement; otherwise, you would not have done it unilaterally. May I ask this huge audience to rise and give a huge hand of applause to our heroes and heroines of peace?

For you, the great people of the Sudan, this agreement is in the final analysis your baby. None of the individual signatories would have had the power to append his signature to this historic agreement if you had stood against it. The most telling mark of your approval was the way you in your millions welcomed to Khartoum our late hero, Dr. John Garang de Mabior.

Let us uphold the CPA and help our leadership implement it in letter and spirit.

May God Almighty bless you all and always protect our country.

Thank you.

As highlighted in the above speech of President Salva Kiir Mayardit and the preceding petition, there is no doubt that the CPA is facing a lot of serious challenges. The article below, written earlier by me, summarises how I want the SPLM to face these obstacles:

FACING TOUGH CPA CHALLENGES TOGETHER

By Dr. Achier Deng Akol

When things are tough, there is a need for all targeted people to remain united and face common challenges together. This way they are more likely to overcome the tough obstacles and emerge victorious together.

Succumbing to the tough challenges and breaking away from the group is nothing more than a cowardly act which usually leads to miserable failure. When a herd of animals are attacked by a fierce lion, it is the single animal that breaks away from the rest of the herd which becomes more vulnerable on its own.

If that single animal was asked to explain why it broke off from the herd, it could state a lot of lame excuses. For example,

"I thought I would outrun the lion," "I felt not fully protected within the herd," "I wanted to go and hide somewhere away from the lion." These could be reasonable excuses, although still lame. For the truth is that the single animal must have reacted illogically out of fear. However, if the lost prey were to say, "I broke away in order to bring about an EC (effective change) in how to best protect the herd," that would be a clear lie and pure camouflage.

Indeed, when things are tough, the true colours of people emerge. At times of hunger and starvation, those who were thought to be generous show their true mean colour by keeping the little food they have to themselves in the hope that they would be the only ones to survive. Similarly, some people who talk highly about themselves as heroes and heroines start to shiver and run away as cowards when the battle begins.

There is no doubt that Sudan People's Liberation Movement (SPLM) currently faces a lot of tough challenges during the Interim Period of the Comprehensive Peace Agreement (CPA). It is equally true that the remaining twelve months before the end of the Interim Period are critical. To improve prospects of success and achieve a common dream, there is a strong need for the SPLM to remain solidly united. Forming splinter groups such as DC (Democratic Change), FC (Freedom Change), JC (Justice Change), EC (Equality Change), SC (Secular Change), and so on as initiated by others is nothing more than a recipe for doom and gloom.

P4 UNITY OPTION

Unity is the first option offered for the referendum of South Sudan. It means Southern Sudan is to remain part and parcel of the whole Sudan under the current arrangements of a limited Government of Southern Sudan. It will not have its own full sovereignty as an independent country. It also means People of Southern Sudan will continue to remain as lower class citizens in their own country at the national level. More importantly, there may be no more desire to continue to make unity attractive and the treatment of Southern Sudanese may drastically drop back to pre-CPA status. There is no article in the CPA or the Interim Constitutions that says unity of Sudan should continue to be made attractive to Southern Sudanese after the 2011 referendum.

The following articles, speeches, and quotations touch on the aspects of this option:

The South and the Unity of Sudan: Khartoum Version

A Nuba Vision

Volume 1, Issue 4, June 2002

Sudan's Future: A Choice between Federation and Confederation

BY SULEIMAN MUSA RAHHAL

Sudan's peace process has gained some momentum following the US peace proposal initiated by former senator John Danforth, President Bush's special envoy for Peace in Sudan. John Danforth laid down four action proposals for peace and he chose the Nuba Mountains as a test case for peace building. One of the outcomes of this initiative is the six-month cease-fire agreement for the Nuba Mountains which was signed in Burgenstock on 19 January. This allowed humanitarian aid delivery into the Nuba Mountains after a decade of access denial to the area. It is hoped that this cease-fire agreement could be extended to other areas of conflict so that a comprehensive peace process could begin.

Over the past ten years several initiatives have sought to end the conflict, starting with Abuja in Nigeria 1992, then followed by Inter-Governmental Authority and Development (IGAD) in 1994 and an Egyptian/Libyan initiative in 1998. Yet all have failed to achieve peace for Sudan. However, the recent American involvement in search for peace in Sudan has brought some hope, particularly following the Swiss Cease-fire Agreement for the Nuba Mountains. We believe if this agreement is extended to include other areas of conflict then the chance to reaching a peace settlement could not be too far.

In addition to the American efforts, the British government has also become involved, and appointed a former ambassador, Alan Goulty, as special representative for peace in Sudan. There are also intensive diplomatic efforts and activities by other European countries such as Norway, Switzerland, as well as by several African countries and one hopes that all these efforts can materialise into a just and lasting peace for our country.

But what kind of peaceful solution are we contemplating? We believe that peace cannot be built on injustice just to satisfy current international concerns. For a genuine peace we need to address some of the fundamental issues that have divided the Sudanese people for generations.

Sudan is the largest state in Africa and a country of tremendous diversity in terms of religion, ethnicity, culture, and languages. In any rational nation this would be a source of pride, but for the rulers in Khartoum the fact that the majority of Sudanese are not pre Arab appears to be a source of deep shame. In order to accommodate these diversities one needs to meet the aspirations and the demands of all these people. Not a simple matter. The Sudanese people first of all need to examine and find remedies to the underlying root causes to the conflict that has divided them for so long.

One of the remedies for such a large country is that it needs restructuring and above all a genuine constitution which will embrace all the Sudanese regardless of their culture, language, religion, or ethnic origin. In addition there is a need for devolution of power and the exercise of self-determination, which are essential prerequisites to preserving the unity of the country.

The governments that ruled Sudan since independence in 1956 have tried all various forms of governance including military dictatorship and Westminster-style democracy, but all failed dismally, because power has always remained with central government, despite promises of decentralisation and federation. This obviously is due to the luck of a decentralised constitution expressing the national consensus, desires, and aspirations of all people of the Sudan. If unity is to be achieved for Sudan there is a genuine need for a unitary constitution tailored to suit a democratic environment.

More importantly, this unitary constitution needs to enshrine the ideals and aspirations of all our people. It is therefore necessary to have devolution of power from the centre to the regions to avoid marginalisation of the peripheries as it has been in the past. This is the best way to ensure that the regions obtain their share of power and equitable share of economic development and wealth of the nation.

Now there is a bright light at the end of the tunnel which is a positive signal for peace, and of course this will depend entirely on the trust and the sincerity of the warring parties.

However, before peace comes the Sudanese politicians need to learn from the bad experiences of the past, in particular from the last two interim arrangement periods of 1965 and 1985. Before we get into a referendum we need to establish a well-defined unitary constitution which should include a strong federal system of governance which should be independent from the state government except for foreign affairs, currency, army, and security. Because such a federal system is the only one that is sufficiently workable that can hold our diverse country together. In this there is a very strong guarantee on the delegation of powers to federal states. For example, large countries such as India, United States of America, and Germany have all adopted federal systems for government giving much power to federal states which has proven to be workable, because the federal structure of the constitution guarantees authority to the states.

It is important for Sudan to have a system for division of power between federal and state governments. Usually a strong federalism is based on reduced central powers except in case of national army, external security, currency, and foreign affairs, which should be left to the central governments. This will be the only important mean for providing greater self-rule for Sudanese in all parts of the country. For an effective federal system one needs to restructure the country into eleven states and these should be the nine provinces created by British and plus two new provinces which are Nuba Mountains Province, which was amalgamated in 1929, to Kordofan Province and Ingessena Hills Province to be created.

The federation which the present government has adopted recently for Sudan is not an ideal federation that can address the need for a real devolution of power. The present government has created twenty-six federal states which definitely need huge resources to run besides the fact that all the powers still remain with the federal government, namely with the president who has the right to appoint state governors and the power to dismiss them.

Finally, the current proposed solution of one country with two self-governing systems definitely will not be an ideal outcome to the complex problem of the diversity of the country. One of the problems which such system will face is the basic issue of the constitution. Is the country going to have two constitutions? What will be the situation of the two million southerners residing in the north and will the same apply to northerners living in South? In addition, what will be the solution for the marginalised people of the north Sudan, who resorted to the armed struggle for more than seventeen years, fighting for justice and freedom? What will be the situation of the nomads who seasonally travel between north and south for grazing? These are difficult questions which need answers before we think of adopting such a solution for our country.

I believe a workable solution in this case is a strong federation. A genuine federalism will take into account all these problems including the demand for internal self-determination and administrative autonomy for the marginalised people in the country in a similar manner to that adopted elsewhere, in particular in Ethiopia. I believe this is the best option for Sudan and for the unity of our country. Most Nuba are staunchly unionist and are thus calling for self-determination within a united Sudan.

DR. JOHN GARANG DE MABIOR LAST SPLM/A ANNIVERSARY SPEECH

FROM: CHAIRMAN/C-IN-C, SPLM/SPLA
TO: ALL UNITS

CHAIRMAN'S TWENTY-SECOND ANIVERSARY ADDRESS AT A MASS RALLY IN RUMBEK ON 16 MAY 2005

1. Special Anniversary Greetings. Today, 16 May 2005, is our twenty-second anniversary. This year is a special anniversary. It comes after we have signed the Comprehensive Peace Agreement (CPA) last 9 January 2005. This is therefore our last anniversary in the bush and before we become the Government of Southern Sudan (GOSS). This is a great and special day, and this is why I have come to Rumbek to celebrate with you and with the people of New Sudan. On the occasion of this twenty-second anniversary, I congratulate all officers, NCOs, men and cadres of the SPLA; I congratulate all in the SPLM and all in the CANS; I congratulate all our civil population from Nimule to Juba, Wau, Abyei, Malakal, Kadugli, and Damazine from Nimule to Halfa; Geneinna to Kassala for achieving the CPA. I congratulate all of you who are in this rally and through you and this rally I greet all our people everywhere in Sudan and in

Diaspora, and congratulate them for achieving a fair and just peace.

2. Tribute and Salute to the Martyrs. Before I make my address on this special and great occasion of our twenty-second anniversary, I first pay tribute and salute the memory and honour of all our martyrs, who have fallen in the struggle for Sudanese dignity before independence, during the Anyanya Movement and in the war that has just ended. It is because of their ultimate sacrifice that it was possible to reach the CPA. I salute the memory of these martyrs as a reminder that they did not die in vain. The legacy and spirit of their struggle and sacrifice will always guide us and all generations to come toward a better and ever better Southern Sudan and Sudan as a whole, whatever the result of the referendum on self-determination will be at the end of the six-year Interim Period. I therefore ask you to stand and observe one minute of solemn silence as a tribute and salute to our martyrs and wounded heroes to whom we dedicate this day and occasion...(after pause...). We shall hold special celebrations of the twenty-second anniversary for the founding units of the SPLA–105 and 104 Battalions, Jamus, Tiger, and Tumsah battalions and Katibat Banat. This celebration will be done in Bor as soon as conditions allow. Some veterans from 105, 104, Jamus, Tiger, Tumsah, and Katibat Banat are here today—104, 105, Tiger, Jamus, Tumsah, and Katibat Banat Oye! I greet you who are here and all your colleagues everywhere. I also greet all the other historic units and formations of the SPLA. Koryom Oye! Muormuor Oye! Zalzal Oye! Infigar Oye! Mukushasha Oye! SPLA Oye! SPLM Oye! After the celebrations of the initial four formations of the SPLA, we shall also organise get-together celebrations for all units and formations of the SPLA, so that these eventually become annual events organised and funded by the members themselves. We shall also organise occasions for Anya-nya veterans from who the SPLM/A took the torch of liberation and freedom. Yes, we must keep, remember and glorify our struggle and our history, because a

people without a history are doomed to extinction to become dinosaurs in history books.

3. Local Insecurity Must Stop Immediately. The struggle has been long, twenty-two years today, and it has been hard. There has been a great deal of suffering. More than one million people have died of war and war-related causes; more than three million have been displaced internally and as refugees, and despite our best community efforts, the vast majority of our children have lost opportunities for education. With conclusion of the CPA all this suffering must now stop, but ironically we are losing lives and property in this sub-Region through sectional and clan fighting. I here ask and here order that all sectional and clan fighting must stop forthwith. All cattle rustling and cattle thefts and the killings associated with them must stop forthwith. All stolen cattle must be returned to their owners and lives lost must be compensated according to customary law and all necessary legal measures must be taken against the culprits involved in this unnecessary fighting and unnecessary loss of lives and property. I have come to Rumbek to celebrate our last anniversary in the Bush, and also to use my presence here to work with local authorities and the SPLM-LC to bring to an immediate end the rampant insecurity that has recently afflicted the three sub-Regions of Lakes, Warrap, and Western Upper Nile. Accordingly, I have ordered all local authorities of the three sub-Regions to Rumbek, and they should already be here, so that we resolve this uncalled for situation of local insecurity. So the commissioners of all Yirol counties, all Rumbek counties, all Tonj counties, all Gogrial counties, and all bordering counties of Western Upper Nile should be here along with the military authorities of the First and Third Front. The insecurity must end immediately and everything must be done to end it and to do justice to victims. There must not be any unnecessary loss of life and property when we have achieved the CPA.

4. Looking Back at Twenty-two Years of Struggle. As we celebrate twenty-two years of our heroic struggle and this time

in peace, let us look back and rearm ourselves with the inspiration that has kept us for the last twenty-two years and has reached us this far. As I said before, the struggle has been long and hard with much causality in lives and property and lost opportunities. But as long as the land and the cause are not lost, everything else may be lost, but can and will be regained, and much more added. The struggle itself as we look back has been a miracle as it went forward and backward, but overall it went forward until we reached the CPA. The struggle will go through four phases. We have already travelled through two of these phases and two more are in front of us. These four phases are:

Four Phases of the Struggle:

- Phase 1: 1983–1991: The golden years of the revolution.

- Phase 2: 1991–2004: Years of darkness, serious struggle, negotiations.

- Phase 3: 2005–2010: We have just begun six years of the Interim Period.

- Phase 4: Beyond 2011: Post-Interim Period; depends on result of RSD.

How did we get to this peace agreement?

It is because we defined the problem we set out to solve correctly. Our vision was correct—to solve Mashkalaat al-Sudan not al-Junub. From the vision flowed our objectives, strategies, and tactics.

Our objectives were and are:

(a) New Sudan and (b) RSD.

It is because of the relentless war we fought all over the Sudan. It is because we stayed the course, we were consistent and persistent.

I pay tribute to our martyrs, wounded heroes & SPLA—they brought CPA and we will take care of the widows and orphans and disabled. I pay tribute to our civil population, who provided the logistics for the war, and the SPLM/GOSS will faithfully serve you, the people, by translating the CPA into tangible benefits of development and services.

5. Forgiveness, Reconciliation, and Unity. Now that we have signed the CPA, our next and immediate task is to ensure that it is implemented in letter and spirit, and in order to do this correctly, my main message to you is on the need for forgiveness, reconciliation, and unity of the people of New Sudan and the unity of your movement, the SPLM/SPLA, so that we are best able to face the challenges of peace that are ahead of us. In order to implement the CPA, the unity of the SPLM/A, and of the people of New Sudan, is of paramount importance, indeed, unity is a necessary condition for successful implementation of the CPA because those opposed to the CPA in both North and South will try to divide us and use some of us to derail and renege on the CPA. Those who are opposed to the CPA have no other weapon except to hope that the SPLM/A and the People of Southern Sudan will be divided as happened in 1991. This must not be allowed and everything must be done to abort such diabolic plans. Our weapon to stop such plans and ill-wishes is forgiveness, reconciliation, and unity. This was my main message in the recently held and successful South-South Dialogue and it is my main message in this anniversary celebrations. The "Covenant of the People of Southern Sudan" which was the end result of the South-South Dialogue was signed by twenty-four Southern Sudanese leaders and witnessed by former President Daniel Arap Moi. It is only the leaders of Armed Groups affiliated to the GOS that were not present at the South-South Dialogue, and this is because the government

prevented them from travelling to Nairobi. We will continue to work and I am personally in contact with them to bring them into the process of forgiveness, reconciliation, and unity, so that we implement the CPA in a stable and peaceful Southern Sudan and achieve the aspirations of our people. There is no reason why these Armed Groups should continue to be used as counterinsurgency forces because the insurgency is over and so the government will have no use for them, and we welcome them to the fold of Southern Sudan.

6. The CPA is good and it belongs to all Sudanese. As we begin the twenty-third year of our struggle, our main task, as I said before, shall be to implement the CPA and to develop new tools of struggle for this purpose. The CPA is good and it belongs to all the Sudanese people, and so I appeal to all Sudanese to support the CPA and to achieve consensus around it. It is true that the CPA was negotiated by the SPLM and NCP-GOS; however, the CPA does not belong to the SPLM nor to the NCP-GOS; it does not belong to John Garang and Ali Osman who signed it; it belongs to all Sudanese; it belongs to you, the people, and so you own it and use it for the development and provision of basic services. Although some of you have read the CPA and although it has been explained to you many times, I want to summarize in twelve points what the People of Southern Sudan, Nuba Mountains, Blue Nile, and Abyei and Sudanese in general have achieved in the CPA:

(1) CPA Ends the War. The first great achievement of the CPA is that it has ended a war that has lasted twenty-two years, and more importantly it has ended the war through a just and honourable peace with dignity. With the CPA there will be no more bombs dropping from the sky on innocent children and women. Instead of the cries of children and the wailing of women and the pain of the last twenty-two years of war, peace will bless us with prosperity and happiness. The CPA will move our people away from war, insecurity, instability and suffering to peace, security, stability, and development. This is a great achievement.

(2) Secondly, Right of Self-Determination. At the end of six years, southerners will vote in a free and internationally monitored referendum on self-determination, to choose whether to remain in a united Sudan under the "one country two systems" arrangement, or opt for an independent Southern Sudan. The challenge now for Sudan is to make unity attractive to Southern Sudanese so that they vote for it during the referendum. If unity is not made attractive, why would any Southerner vote himself or herself into second-class citizenship? If Sudan does not sufficiently and fundamentally change, why should anybody vote to become a servant instead of being a master in his/her own independent house? Clearly the Sudanese must work hard during the Interim Period to make unity attractive, if they want the Sudan to remain united as one country that accommodates all its citizens equally.

(3) Third, North/South Border Demarcation. An issue related to the right of self-determination is that of return to Southern Sudan of all areas that were annexed to Northern Sudan after 1956 by various Khartoum regimes. This will be determined by a North/South Boundary Commission, as provided for in the CPA. These areas are in Bahr el Ghazal and Upper Nile, and include Kafia Kingi and Hofret Nahas in Western Bahr el Ghazal and Chali al-Fil in North Eastern Upper Nile. Even Higlig is reported to have been recently annexed to a newly created province in Kordofan called Keilak. The CPA clearly states that the boundaries of Southern Sudan are as they stood on 1 January 1956 and any areas that were part of Southern Sudan by this date must be returned to the administration of the GOSS.

(4) Real Power in the South within the context of a "One Country Two Systems Model." Southern Sudan shall have its own Government of Southern Sudan (GOSS). It will be an SPLM-based government, and for the first time in its history, Southern Sudan shall have genuine political power that does not depend on the goodwill of the central government, but that depends on the will of the People of Southern Sudan. This power will be

exercised in the context of a "one country two systems" model, which the SPLM has advocated since the Abuja talks in 1993 and during the IGAD talks. The GOSS will exercise extensive, exclusive, and concurrent political powers including the power to initiate and conclude international agreements in social, cultural, educational, and economic fields with foreign countries and international organisations and to have offices abroad for these purposes.

(5) Fifth, Significant and Real Power in the Center. The SPLM and Southern Sudan shall also have significant and real power in the central government, as we shall have up to ten full ministers, eleven state ministers, and the office of the first vice president, with powers as well as at least 25 percent of posts in the national civil service as well as in the administration of the national capital. The SPLM and Southern Sudan's presence in Khartoum will not be token representation as happened before. In the CPA we have grouped the ministries into three clusters: (a) nine Sovereignty Ministries from which we shall have three, (b) ten Economy Ministries from which we shall have three, and (c) eleven Services Ministries from which we shall have four. We shall also have at least eleven state ministers also similarly clustered. We will put our best people in these ministries and we shall assert ourselves; nobody will push us aside or marginalise us in any way in the cabinet to which we shall belong by right not by invitation or someone else's goodwill. Our presence in the central government at all levels will be real and effective and it shall be by the authority of the CPA and the Interim National Constitution.

(6) Sixth, an independent SPLA during the Interim Period. The SPLA shall remain a standing army under its own command and shall be considered and treated equally with SAF as part of Sudan's National Armed Forces. Meanwhile, a forty-thousand-strong Joint Integrated Unit (JIU) is to be created of equal numbers from the two armed forces to be deployed in Southern Sudan, the two areas, the national capital and Abyei. At the end of six years if the result of the referendum on self-determination

is unity, the two armies will merge to become one national army; otherwise, if the result is in favour of independence, the SPLA would be transformed into the national army of Southern Sudan. The Security Arrangements Agreement and the existence of two armies during the Interim Period are the most important guarantees for stability and implementation of the peace agreement, in addition, of course, to the goodwill of the parties and international guarantees.

(7) Seventh, Wealth Sharing and Sources of Revenue for the GOSS. Unlike the Addis Ababa Agreement, the CPA provides Southern Sudan with its own organic sources of revenue that do not depend on Khartoum. There are four such sources of revenue, namely: (a) 50 percent of oil revenues, (b) 50 percent of non-oil central government revenues generated in Southern Sudan, (c) revenues generated by the GOSS by virtue of its taxing powers; and (d) international assistance to Southern Sudan, which will come directly to Southern Sudan through the Bank of Southern Sudan (BOSS). And as you might have followed in the news, the Oslo Donors Conference generated more than four billion US dollars in pledges. At least 50 percent of these pledges shall accrue to Southern Sudan and the rest for other war-affected areas in the North, i.e., of Nuba Mountains, Southern Blue Nile, Abyei, Eastern Sudan, and Darfur as well as other neglected areas of the North.

(8) Eighth, Own Banking System for Southern Sudan. Southern Sudan will also have its own secular banking system within the context of a "one country two systems" model. We have agreed that there will be one Central Bank of Sudan, but it will have two windows, one window for Islamic banking for the North, and one window for conventional banking for the South. The secular window of the CBS will be operated by the Bank of Southern Sudan (BOSS), which shall have the power to open correspondent accounts with foreign banks of its choice. This means that BOSS will operate with international banks directly and only keep the mother CBS informed. Moreover there will

be one currency for the country, which shall be agreed upon by the parties, but in the meantime the currencies circulating in Southern Sudan are recognised; that is why the Sudanese pound is operating in our areas as legal tender until when we jointly issue the new agreed currency. Unlike the case of the Addis Ababa Agreement, Southern Sudan and GOSS shall make their financial transactions with the CBS and with the international community through the BOSS.

The currency just issued in Rumbek is not a new currency; it is old notes of the Sudan pound, which was circulating before, that has been reissued as happens in any economy since notes get worn out; that is why the exchange value is the same. I understand that the quality of the paper of the currency is poor and that there are other technical problems. These will be solved and the notes improved to standard quality, and the new Sudan pound at the same market value as the old notes will continue to circulate until when both the new Sudan pound and the dinar are replaced by a new joint currency agreed to by the parties as came in the CPA.

(9) Ninth, Resolution of the Problem of Abyei. As you all know, the problem of Abyei is even older, as that of the south as Abyei was annexed to Kordofan in 1905, one hundred years ago, while Southern Sudan was formally amalgamated with the North in 1947 by the colonial regime and Darfur in 1916. The CPA grants Abyei the right of self-determination, whereby the people of Abyei will conduct a separate referendum but the same day as Southerners to choose whether to remain in the North or return to the South. The oil of Abyei is also split six ways: 2 percent for Ngok Dinka, 2 percent for Missiriya, 2 percent for Western Kodorfan State, 2 percent for Bahr el Ghazal, 42 percent for GOSS and 50 percent for the GONU. And during the six years of the Interim Period Abyei will be under a special administration under the supervision of the presidency, and one battalion of JIUs for security in addition to international monitors and observers. This is a major achievement and we congratulate

the people of Abyei and wish them well in their new political dispensation.

(10) Tenth, the Two Areas Agreement. The two areas (Nuba Mountains and Southern Blue Nile) also have a good agreement as part of the CPA. The CPA gives the SPLM 45 percent of power in the two areas, resolves the problem of land, which was one of the main reasons people of the two areas took up arms, and provides for the right of popular consultation after four years for the people to give their views and decision on the agreement of the two areas. I want to assure the people of the two areas that the SPLM will never abandon them as some agitators say in their propaganda. Firstly, the SPLA will remain in the two areas in the form of JIUs; secondly, excess forces above those required for the JIUs will be deployed in the South together with other SPLA units and they shall be under SPLA GHQ, and thirdly, it is the same SPLM that shall form the GOSS and the 45 percent share in the state governments of Nuba Mountains and Southern Blue Nile. As you can see, both the SPLM and the SPLA will remain united and the two areas are inseparable components.

(11) Eleventh, the SPLM shall remain a national political Movement. The CPA enables the SPLM to retain its national character and to expand all over the Sudan. The SPLM shall consolidate itself in Southern Sudan where we shall have 70 percent of power and in the Nuba Mountains and Southern Blue Nile where we shall have 45 percent of power. The SPLM shall also have 10 percent of power in all the remaining fifteen states of the North. With the consolidation of the SPLM in Southern Sudan and its expansion and consolidation in the Nuba Mountains, Southern Blue Nile, and the other states of the North, the SPLM clearly has the potential to become the majority party in the coming national elections at all levels—local, state and national. I therefore on the occasion of this twenty-second anniversary celebrations appeal to all Sudanese everywhere—in the South, Nuba Mountains, Blue Nile, Eastern Sudan, Northern

Kordofan, Khartoum, Central Sudan, and the far North—to join the SPLM and rally behind so that we complete the project of New Sudan and build a Great Sudan.

(12) Finally, the CPA is also good for all others. The CPA is not only good for the SPLM, Southern Sudan, Nuba Mountains, Blue Nile, and Abyei; it is also good for the NCP and for all other political forces in the North and for all of Sudan. For the NCP they become our partners for at least six years, and for the other political forces in the North the CPA achieves all the objectives they have struggled for including democracy and elections, Interim Government, Interim Constitution, and human rights. The CPA can also be adapted and applied to bring peace in other parts of the country such as Darfur and Eastern Sudan. The CPA represent a true and genuine paradigm shift for the democratic transformation of the Sudan, if implemented, and for the renewal of Sudan to achieve prosperity and happiness for all Sudanese in our lifetime and for all future generations to come.

As you can see in the twelve points that I have just presented, the CPA contains all the objectives we have struggled to achieve over the last twenty-two years. When you combine (a) real power in the GOSS, (b) an independent SPLA, (c) organic sources of revenue for the GOSS, and (d) a separate banking system, then one can say that we truly have an autonomous Southern Sudan. And as I said before, the CPA is also good for everybody else in the Sudan, for all the political forces, and for all the Sudanese people. The SPLM and the NCP brought the CPA, but it now belongs to all the Sudanese people and it is a win-win agreement for all. There are no losers in the CPA, as it gives everyone his or her rights. In general, the "one country two systems model" shall be reflected in all structures and relationships. The connection between Khartoum and Juba shall only be nominal at the topmost macro levels such as the national constitutional court, the office of the first vice president, the dual banking system, the JIUs and JDB, and so on. Some people have argued that the CPA presents separatist arrangements, but I disagree; the CPA is actually good for the unity of the country, for unity can be based only on freedom, equality, and confidence. Only if, or rather when, Southerners and the marginalised People of Sudan in general are assured of their rights, of equality, of justice, can they voluntarily choose to remain in a united and new Sudan, not out of coercion but because they want to.

7. SPLM Program during the Interim Period. The CPA is clearly a good agreement. What are left are its implementation and its translation into tangible benefits for the People of southern Sudan, the two areas, Abyei and the whole of Sudan. I have summarized the SPLM post-war programmes and priorities in the following six points. These are programmes that will fundamentally change the lives of the people of New Sudan. The peace dividend that they expect as individuals and as communities and for which they have fought for the last fifty years since August 1955 will be provided by these programmes, and I ask all the people of new Sudan to build consensus around these programmes and to own them; these are:

(1) The Wounds of War and Healing. I believe that our first and task and priority is to heal, to forgive, to reconcile, and to unite around the CPA and its implementation so that we face the challenges of the Interim Period with a unified purpose, will and cohesion. This is what we did recently in the South-South dialogue, and I have called a conference of all the counties involved in instability of the last few months in Lakes, Warrap, and Western Upper Nile. The peace, reconciliation, and stability must begin here where we have our Interim SPLM administration.

(2) Governance Infrastructure. Our second priority is the establishment of a good governance infrastructure and the rule of law and order to ensure justice and stability all over Southern Sudan. This governance must be inclusive of all ethnic groups in all aspects of politics, power, and the economy, and must be completely transparent and fight nepotism and corruption.

(3) Physical Infrastructure. Our third priority shall be physical Infrastructure—roads, railways, river transport, telecommunications, and electric power generation, and we are starting literally from scratch. Since creation, there has never been a single tarmac road in Southern Sudan, an area the size of Kenya and Uganda put together. We shall concentrate our energies on the construction of thirteen key roads, these are: (1) Juba-Nimule, (2) Juba-Kapoeta-Lokichoggio, (3) Wau-Rumbek-Maridi-Yei-Kaya, (4) Juba-Yei-Lasu, (5) Juba-Malakal-Renk, (6) Wau-Tambura-Yambio-Maridi, (7) Rumbek-Yirol-Bor-Pochalla, (8) Wau-Warrap-Abyei-Kadugli, (9) Melut-Adar-Ulu-Kurmuk-Damazine, (10) Malakal-Nasir-Jekou, and (11) Wau-Aweil-Babanusa,

(12) Wau-Raga-Nyala to Darfur and Shambe-Yirol-Bentiu-Pariang-Jaw-Kadugli. In addition to the roads, two railway linkages are important: the rehabilitation of the Wau-Aweil-Babanusa railway and a railway connecting Juba to Mombasa, either through Uganda or Kenya. We are also discussing with DR Congo linking of Juba-Yei-Lasu with Kisangani by railway to have access to the Atlantic Ocean and open up DR Congo markets to Southern Sudan. Opening up of River Nile transport is also urgent. Finally, construction of a major dam for hydroelectric generation at Fulla rapids or Bedden Falls south of Juba is critical to overall development of Southern Sudan. This transport network will link Southern Sudan with Northern Sudan and with the Greater Horn of Africa and the Great Lakes Area, and create a major market of some three hundred million people. It is a win-win strategy for all stakeholders in the Sudan, in the Region and the rest of the world. I ask the people of New Sudan to be forward looking in having bigger economic and political entities in the Region.

(4) Economic Development and Financial Infrastructure. On the economic front our goal is clearly set; within the context of the CPA, and in conformity with the millennium development goals, both the Government of National Unity and Government of Southern Sudan (GOSS) shall adopt poverty eradication as

the ultimate objective of socioeconomic development. To this end, of poverty eradication, the SPLM shall adopt an economic development vision and program that emphasizes economic growth through rural development and transformation of traditional agriculture that is integrated with agro-industries. We aim to transform the present subsistence traditional agriculture in Southern Sudan and other areas through technological innovations, and make agriculture the engine of growth. The SPLM vision is encapsulated in two slogans to "use the oil revenues to fuel agriculture" and to "take towns to people in the countryside rather than people to towns" and more than 90 percent of the population of New Sudan live in rural areas. For any meaningful development to take place we must have a functioning a viable market including financial institutions of different times and encourage a vibrant market economy.

(5) Provision of Social or Public Services. Our fifth priority is the provision of basic social services—education, health, sanitation, and clean water, etc to our people, and the facilitation of the return, reintegration and rehabilitation of some three million IDPs and refuges that are expected to return to their homes following the CPA. It is estimated that more than one million people have returned to their homes over the last six months, and the internationally community has done nothing in this grave situation. I appeal to the UN and the international community to urgently come to the assistance of the People of Southern Sudan, the Two Areas, and Abyei.

(6) Youth, Women, and the Diaspora. Finally, I want to briefly mention and appeal to three important constituencies of our people; these are the youth, women, and the Diaspora. We need the Diaspora to return and contribute to the building of the nation or if they cannot return to assist where they are. Our children have been deprived of the vitality of youth! From the day of birth our children have seen no peace, and we must concentrate on the development of youth in the next phase. Women, the "marginalised of the marginalised," must be given

special attention in development of skills and income generating activities. Women will be effectively empowered through girl child education, pro-women government policies, and, above all, income-generating opportunities. Only when women are able to bring home a respectable income alongside their husbands will they become fully empowered and respected. Civil society groups will also need to be empowered to participate effectively in all these initiatives and activities.

(7) Emphasis on Human Resource Development. In general, the SPLM shall give priority to human resource development as the most effective strategy for poverty eradication and economic development. The SPLM has already announced its policy of free universal primary school education so that by 2015 all girls and boys of school going age do go to school, and by that time we should also have free secondary school education. Other initiatives shall also be introduced for those beyond primary school age, including adult and functional education and vocational training to develop skills.

CONCLUSION: I want in closing to assure you all once more that there shall be enough room for all Southern Sudanese who wish to participate, and by way this assurance I often have quoted the Gospel of John 14 V 1-2. "Do not be worried and upset," Jesus told them. "Believe in God and believe also in me. There are many rooms in my Father's house, and I am going to prepare a place for you. I would not tell you this if it were not true." So, I say to all Southerners that there will be many rooms in the GOSS and GONU, and all are welcome. In the legislature, for example, we shall have 135 members in the Central Parliament, 170 in the Southern Parliament, and about 400 in the Parliaments of the ten Southern States; that alone is more than 700 legislators. In the Executive, Southerners will have 10 full Ministers and at least 10 state ministers in the GONU and about 20 ministers in the GOSS and some 40 Ministers in the state governments; these are more than 70 ministers. Then you have the judiciary and civil service. And with the massive development we shall launch the private sector will be very lucrative and full of jobs. As you can see, there will be enough room for everyone; our problem will actually be lack of manpower.

I want to conclude by assuring you that the SPLM will continue to be steadfast, that the SPLM will continue to be a movement of the people and for the people; the SPLM shall not betray your cause and trust as we have not betrayed you over the last twenty-two years of struggle. The SPLM shall continue its vision and ideals that it has sacrificed for over the last twenty-one years and for which we have shed tears and blood. Again, on the occasion of this special twenty-second anniversary celebration, I once more congratulate you for the CPA and salute our martyrs to whom this day belongs. I greet and congratulate all the People of Sudan wherever you may be this anniversary day. I assure you all that the Movement will be faithful and loyal to the objectives of the struggle. The SPLM/SPLA will never betray the cause of our people, and our track record is known to all. I wish you well as we begin the twenty-third year of our struggle. God bless you all. SPLM Oye! SPLA Oye! New Sudan Oye! Victory to the SPLM/SPLA and to the people of New Sudan!

STATEMENT OF GENERAL SALVA KIIR MAYARDIT ON UNITY OF SUDAN:

"Making unity attractive means convincing the ordinary citizen of Southern Sudan who will vote in the referendum of 2011 that he or she stands to enjoy more benefits in a united Sudan rather than in an independent Southern Sudan," Salva Kiir Mayardit, on 14 January 2008 at his speech during the celebration of the Third Anniversary of the CPA in Wau Town

Thus if the citizens of Southern Sudan feel that unity has not been made attractive enough, they can vote for independence. If they feel it has been made attractive enough, they would vote for unity of Sudan.

P5 SECESSION OPTION

This is the second option for the referendum of Southern Sudan. It means the land and people of Southern Sudan that have suffered for so long as oppressed and marginalised people become fully independent. The long word of Southern Sudan will probably be shortened to South Sudan, unless another better name is agreed upon. The other long phrase of president of the Government of Southern Sudan will be sweetly shortened to president of South Sudan. South Sudan shall have total sovereignty over its own territory. The People of South Sudan will enjoy absolute rights over their revenue without being compelled to give away 50 percent. Most importantly, they will no longer be lower class citizens in their own country

The following speech and subsequent quotation explore this option too including a detailed discussion on why this may become the choice for the people of Southern Sudan.

UNIVERSITY OF PENNSYLVANIA—AFRICAN STUDIES CENTER

South Sudan: A History of Political Domination—A Case of Self-Determination (Riek Machar)

SOUTH SUDAN: A HISTORY OF POLITICAL DOMINATION—A CASE OF SELF-DETERMINATION

By Dr. Riek Machar Teny-Dhurgon

Chairman and Commander in Chief, SSIM/A.

Since the historic Nasir Declaration of 28 August 1991, the demand of the People of South Sudan for the right of self-determination, as a peaceful political resolution of the forty year war in the Sudan, has been a real challenging problem to Sudanese political forces and parties. The SSIM/A (formerly the SPLM/A-United) had been engaged in many peace initiatives with this present regime of the National Islamic Front (NIF) to find a solution to the conflict. Among these initiatives are: the Frankfurt Talks of 25 January 1992; the Nigerian mediated Abuja Peace Talks of May/June 1992; the Nairobi May-June 1993 Talks and the Inter-Governmental Authority on Drought and Development (IGADD) mediated Peace Talks, 6 January 1994 through 19 September 1994. In these talks, the SSIM/A had demonstrated its commitment to the search for lasting and just peace in South Sudan and above all the SSIM/A had specifically underlined the right of self-determination for the People of South Sudan as the cornerstone for settlement that would meet their legitimate aspirations.

The People of South Sudan have been denied this right by the different regimes that ruled the Sudan since its constitution as a state. However, it is now imperative that peace shall prevail only when the People of South Sudan are acceded their inalienable right to self-determination.

On the other hand, although it is generally accepted that there is racial, religious, cultural, linguistic, and historical diversity in the Sudan, these diversities have not been used to help enrich and consolidate the unity of the new state, but rather were used by the ruling Arab elites in the North to oppress, subjugate and exploit the People of South Sudan resulting in conflicts and wars.

HISTORICAL PERSPECTIVE

To clarify the objective of the struggle of the People of South Sudan, it is important to go quickly over the colonial history of the South Sudan—the territorial unit claiming the right of self-determination.

Before the Turko-Egyptian invasion of 1821, the Sudan consisted of Kingdoms and tribal communities without modern forms of government as we have today. In other words, Sudan in its present boundaries did not exist.

The Turko-Egyptian occupation of 1821 was promoted by the expansionist ambitions of the Ottoman empire and its craving for wealth and markets. The main commodities of interest were slaves, gold, ivory, and timber. South Sudan and her people became the main source of these commodities. The Turko-Egyptian and the North Sudanese collaborated in their raids against the South Sudan for slaves resulting in millions of South Sudanese people being taken into slavery in the Arab and New World.

Although the Turko-Egyptian rule lasted for a period of sixty years, it did not control all the Sudan. South Sudan in particular was not fully brought under the administration of the invading alien power. Similarly, the Mahdist administration of 1883–1898 did not succeed to impose its full authority on the whole of South Sudan.

The Belgians in 1892, advancing from the former Belgian Congo (now Zaire), captured Western Equatoria up to Mongalla and established the Lado Enclave as part of the Belgian Congo. During the same period (1892) the French, led by Major Marchand, occupied large parts of South Sudan (Bahr el Ghazal, Western Upper Nile up to Fashoda) and by 1896 they had established a firm administration in these areas. Another French expedition which started off in 1897 from Djibouti moving through Ethiopia and along the Baro and Sobat Rivers failed to link up with Fashoda expedition. The French had wanted to annex South Sudan to the French territories in West Africa. However, an international conflict developed between the British and the French over South Sudan, commonly known as the Fashoda Incident.

Again, in 1898, the Sudan was reconquered by a joint British and Egyptian forces resulting in the signing of the Condominium Agreement between the British and the Egyptian to administer the Sudan in its present boundaries.

In 1899, the British and the French concluded an agreement in Europe which made the French pull out of South Sudan handing over its portion of South Sudan to the same authorities who were already in control of North Sudan. A similar incident took place in 1910 when the Belgians withdrew from the Lado Enclave after an agreement was concluded in 1896 stipulating that the Enclave was to be handed over to the British after the death of King Leopold. The king died in 1910. The withdrawal of the French and Belgians from South Sudan ceded the territory to the British.

THE BRITISH SEPARATE ADMINISTRATION POLICY (1898–1947)

Owing to the geographical, political, historical, and cultural differences between North and South Sudan, the British devised a system of a separate administration for the two countries. To guarantee the effectiveness of the separate administration policy the British passed the Closed Districts Ordinances of 1920s. In consolidation of this policy, the Passports and Permits Ordinance was promulgated in 1922. This ordinance required the use of passports and permits for travellers shuttling between the two countries of North and South Sudan. The permits were to specify the conditions and purposes of the visits. The immigration policy was further strengthened by the permits and trade order enacted in 1925. This law required North Sudanese to obtain permits to conduct trade in South Sudan. Finally, a language policy was developed and enforced in South Sudan in 1928. This policy adopted English as the official language for South Sudan and approved the use of the following local languages: Dinka, Bari, Nuer, Latuko, Shilluk, and Zande. Arabic was categorically rejected as a language in South Sudan. The cumulative effect of the immigration and trade laws coupled with the language policy was to maintain South Sudan as a separate country from North Sudan. In fact, colonial governors from South Sudan used to attend regular administrative conferences in East Africa instead of Khartoum.

After the establishment of the Condominium rule, the British continued to consolidate its position in North Sudan by creating the necessary administrative and political structures for the state of North Sudan. In an effort to prepare the North Sudan for self-rule, the North Sudan Advisory Council Ordinance was enacted in 1943. The ordinance covered all the six North Sudan provinces, comprising of: Khartoum, Kordofan, Darfur, Eastern, and Northern and Blue Nile provinces. This council was empowered to advise the condominium authority on how to administer North Sudan in certain specific areas. Members of the advisory council were all North Sudanese. The ordinance had no application or relevance to the territory of South Sudan. Thus far, North and South Sudan were regarded as two separate countries colonised by the British and Egyptians.

COLONIAL BRITAIN HANDS OVER SOUTH SUDAN TO THE NORTH

Instead of establishing an advisory council for South Sudan similar to that of North Sudan, the resolutions of the Administrative Conference held in Khartoum in 1946 surprisingly advocated the colonisation of South by North Sudan. It must, however, be pointed out that the conference took the decision at the back of the People of South Sudan as they were not represented and because the conference was meant for administrators in North Sudan only, the British administrators in South Sudan did not attend. Consequently, this unexpected outcome revealed the conspiracy between the British and the North Sudanese supported by Egypt to hand over South Sudan to North Sudan as a colonial territory. Certainly, this plan provoked bitter reaction from the South Sudanese and their sympathisers.

The betrayal of South Sudan by the British was finally concluded in the infamous Juba conference of 1947. Precisely the conference was convened to inform the chiefs of South Sudan of the irreversible decision to hand over South Sudan to the new colonial masters from North Sudan. This unpalatable decision was crowned by the promulgation and establishment of the Sudan

Legislative Assembly in 1948. Thirteen delegates from South Sudan were handpicked and forced to represent South Sudan in the Assembly. The Cairo Agreement of 1953 was no exception to the rule. Once again, the colonial masters from Britain and North Sudan masquerading as representatives of national political parties with tacit support of the Egyptian government conspired to grant self-determination to the Sudan without the participation of South Sudan. The People of South Sudan were deliberately excluded on the pretext that they had no political parties or organisations. This was yet another ploy made by political parties of North Sudan to claim representation of South Sudan with the erroneous and unjustifiable assumption that the Sudan is one country. Nevertheless, the People of South Sudan regard themselves as "internally colonised people." The deliberate handover of South Sudan to North Sudan by the British was one of the greatest blunders ever made in the diplomacy of the British colonial history. If the British had felt that South Sudan was not yet ready to become an independent state by itself then, they should have either handed over its administration to an international body like the UN instead of North Sudan or should have left North Sudan get independence separately as they did with North Rhodesia. It is now up to the British to correct this serious error of judgement, that has cost millions of lives of the People of South Sudan, by supporting the call of the People of South Sudan for full independence.

POST COLONIAL ERA: North-South Relations

Independence for Sudan meant nothing for South Sudan but a change of masters as the North Sudanese took over the colonial state. The North Sudanese elites failed to evolve policies that would have consolidated national unity and stability. As a result, the Sudan has been plunged into continuous state of political, constitutional, economic and military crisis till today. Various governments and regimes in Khartoum waged war and denied the South Sudanese equality, social justice, freedom, and effective participation in the running of the State.

In brief, North-South relations since independence until now has been characterised by the following:

–Political marginalisation of the South through underrepresentation, discrimination, and other restrictions that did not permit South Sudanese to occupy certain important constitutional posts.

–Deliberate retardation and neglect of socioeconomic development of South Sudan as all socioeconomic development projects are concentrated in North Sudan.

–Cultural subjugation through imposition of Arabic culture and Islamic values on the People of South Sudan in a deliberate attempt to destroy their African culture and heritage. The declaration of Sudan as an Islamic state by the present regime has relegated South Sudanese to third class citizens. This imposition of cultural and religious laws—Islamic sharia—is a negation of common citizenship which could be the basis of national unity, equality and social justice in a heterogeneous state such as the Sudan.

–The crisis of national identity is a creation of North Sudan which defines the Sudanese identity in Arab and Islamic terms. The North political elites consider the Sudanese citizenship as a transition to full integration into the Arab identity. This undermines the right of the vast African majority to whose identity should be fully embodied in the character of the state.

–Abuse of fundamental human rights of South Sudanese people through the following practises:

a. Decimation of the population of South Sudan through prosecution of war and perpetrating large scale massacres of innocent people by various North regimes:

–Yei, Maridi and Kodok Massacres in 1964 were carried out by the regime of Abboud.

–Juba, Wau, Torit, Warajwok, Bor, Akobo Massacres in 1965 were carried out by Mohammed Ahmed Mahgoub government.

–Dhaein Massacre 1987/88 in which three thousand South Sudanese were killed by government militias and police.

–Wau Massacre in 1987 in which more than one hundred people were killed by government army.

–Jebelien Massacre in 1989/90 in which more than two thousand South Sudanese were killed by government militia.

b. Indiscriminate bombing and raiding of civil population centres leading to massive displacement of people from their homes. Already there are over three million South Sudanese in the North living under subhuman conditions in the outskirts of Khartoum and other major cities in the North.

c. Denial of basic human needs and use of food as a weapon for conversion into Islamic religion.

d. Forced Islamization and Arabization of the educational system in the South with the aim to kill indigenous languages and cultures to accentuate Islamic and Arabic dominance.

e. Political executions, detentions without trials, and disappearance of South Sudanese in the government-controlled towns.

f. Reviving of slavery and slave trade during this war.

The enumerated violations and practises are true evidences of the failure of the two parts to co-exist and live harmoniously as a nation. As matter of fact, it is the people of the South who are the victims of this tragic situation. Attempts made in the past with the successive regimes that came to power in Khartoum to find a durable solution to the problem of South Sudan all ended in failure. Even the Addis Ababa Agreement of 1972, which brought relative peace and stability to the South, was unilaterally abrogated by General Numeiri in 1983 returning the Sudan to war.

PRINCIPLES FOR THE RESOLUTION OF THE CONFLICT IN THE SUDAN: THE RIGHT OF SELF-DETERMINATION

On the basis of the facts stated above, it is obvious that the Sudan has been at war with itself for the last forty years. This state of affairs if allowed to continue would work to the detriment of the people of the Sudan in both North and South, and could have negative consequences on regional peace and stability. It is our strong belief that the only way forward in the resolution of this conflict and the attainment of just and lasting peace is to allow the People of South Sudan to freely exercise their inalienable and democratic right to self-determination through an internationally supervised referendum.

THE SUDANESE POLITICAL PARTIES AND THE RIGHT OF SELF-DETERMINATION

In this connection, it would be recalled that a major breakthrough was made between the SSIM/A (formerly SPLM/A-United) and the NIF government, particularly in the Frankfurt Talks of 25 January 1995 and in the Nairobi Talks of May 1993, where the NIF regime conceded referendum to People of South Sudan. Yet, we are concerned by the fact that the same NIF regime has respected neither the agreed issues in the Frankfurt nor Nairobi Talks. This intransigent attitude, if maintained by the regime, will not bring to an end this tragic chapter of war, suffering and hopelessness in the Sudan.

Historically, the other Sudanese political parties, namely: the Umma Party, the Sudan People's Liberation Movement/Army, the Democratic Unionist Party (DUP), the National Islamic Front, and the Communist Party have been against acceding to the People of South Sudan their inalienable right to self-determination. However, since the historic Nasir Declaration of 28 August 1991 some of these parties started to make public pronouncement about self-determination. Since 1983, the Sudan People's Liberation Movement/Army (SPLM/A) has been fighting South Sudanese groups that called for the right of self-determination for the People of South Sudan. This was epitomised in the bitter wars the SPLM/A waged against the Anya-nya II "separatist" from 1983 to 1991 and against the Nasir faction of the SPLM/A since 1991. Despite the hostility of the SPLM/A against SSIM/A, the SPLM/A reluctantly recognised the right of self-determination in Abuja I Peace Talks, the Washington Declaration and Common Agenda for IGADD Peace Talks. The Communist Party of the Sudan has been discussing the principle for sometime but with no commitment to its implementation. The Umma Party has made a move to recognising self-determination as stated in Sayyed Sadiq el Mahdi Discussion Paper of 10 November 1993 and reinforced in the Chukudum Agreement between the Umma and the SPLM/SPLA. In addition, all the Sudanese opposition political parties that met in Bonn recognised this principle, except the DUP which inserted a reservation. Although, the DUP has consistently stood against the right of self-determination for People of South Sudan, it recognised the principle at subsequent meetings in Asmara.

Internationally, the right of self-determination for People of South Sudan has gained credence and has been recognised as a basic human right as well as a democratic principle for resolving conflicts by Pan-African Seventh Congress in Kampala, 3–9 April 1994 and IGADD in its Declaration of Principles (DOP). It is now imperative that the demand of the People of South Sudan for exercise of their inalienable right to self-determination has gain substantial grounds in the Sudan, regionally in Africa as well as internationally and therefore cannot be anymore ignored.

Thus, should the NIF government and the other North Sudanese political forces concede to the People of South Sudan the exercise of the right to self-determination in an internationally supervised referendum then the following issues could be discussed:

A. Cessation of hostilities and cease-fire;

B. Details of the conduct of the referendum;

C. The length of the interim period;

d. The status of the South during the interim period; and

e. Security arrangements during the interim period.

DR. JOHN GARANG DE MABIOR ADVICE ON REFERENDUM

"I and those who joined me in the bush and fought for more than twenty years have brought to you CPA in a golden plate. Our mission is accomplished. It is now your turn, especially those who did not have a chance to experience bush life. When time comes to vote at referendum, it is your golden choice to determine your fate? Would you like to vote to be second-class citizens in your own country? It is absolutely your choice."

John Garang De Mabior

P6 ENORMOUS SUFFERING: Points for secession or independence of South Sudan

To help one decide whether to vote for Unity or Secession in the case of South Sudan, or to join Bahr-el-Ghazal or remain in Kordofan in the case of Abyei, it is essential to reflect on the extent of suffering that had been inflicted and endured over fifty years of contemporary war.

To begin with, the picture at the beginning of this chapter on politics, of a fellow South Sudanese child deliberately starved in a united Sudan; with vultures waiting to eat him or her as soon as he or she dies, gives a glimpse of the extent of our suffering as marginalised People of South Sudan in the hands of successive governments in Kar-tuom (misnamed Khartoum) since 1956. Would this child like eligible voters to vote for unity in 2011 referendum?

Indeed, a lot of pain has been inflicted on various ethnic populations worldwide. All are bad and should not have been allowed to happen. None of them equate in magnitude and severity to that inflicted on the land and People of South Sudan. Indeed, what the world recently witnessed and rightfully rallied against in Darfur is a small fraction of the worst disaster that had occurred repeatedly in South Sudan. This is not a statement to underestimate the genocide that unfolded in Darfur. It is to assert a historical fact for everybody on this planet to know.

It is also a fact to clarify to anyone who is not aware that South Sudan and Darfur are parts and parcel of the wider and larger Sudanese Black African populations equally targeted to be exterminated by Arab Jihadists along with the Nubian remnants in the far North near Egypt, the Nuba Mountains, and the Southern Blue Nile, including Hadendewa and Agassana.

I call these Black African populations in Sudan the lucky ones as a lot of other similar ethnic populations have indeed been wiped off the face of this Earth all along the Nile from the Mediterranean Ocean to the Heart of Africa by the same enemy. Sadly of course a lot of the ones that perished are not even mentioned in historical books so that they can at least be remembered.

Think for a moment now of any pain that can be inflicted by a merciless and ruthless foe on a people targeted. Multiply that a million times and you will have a clue of what has been happening to us.

Here are some of the cruelties and casualties that has been inflicted on the People of South Sudan over the years in sustained genocide leading to a loss of over two and half million lives so far. Every child of this land who does not know about these pains, especially those born abroad must read and remember them. Every foreigner that wonders why secession is an option of a referendum in South Sudan should also glance at them. They are reasons for secession, unless of course miraculously nullified by the healing process of making unity attractive. They include the following ones:

1. Slavery
2. Sharia
3. Marginalisation
4. Oppression
5. Discrimination
6. Torture
7. Humiliation
8. Deprivation
9. Barbarism
10. Massacre
11. Assassination
12. Antagonisation
13. Starvation
14. Bombing
15. Falsification
16. Arabisation
17. Islamisation
18. Opposition
19. Rejection
20. Obligation
21. Non-attraction

P6.1. SLAVERY

Slavery is the condition of being forced to work for somebody else for nothing or being completely dominated by another. It has been abolished worldwide except in South Sudan not withstanding other areas I may not know. It was magnified, masterminded and spearheaded by Arab traders during the colonial era all over the Sudan Belt that stretched from Somalia in the Horn of Africa up to Sierra Leone and beyond in West Africa. It is not a surprise to see that those who are continuing this inhuman practise are the very ascendants of the historical slave traders.

They target mostly weak children and women who are unable to defend themselves or escape the frequent raids conducted by the Arab Militias called Mirihaleen. Of course teenagers, overpowered by the raiders, are also taken for slavery.

Once taken, they usually have their Achilles tendon severed to ensure that they do not easily escape. They are also continuously tortured to submit and forced to labour in farms and such others lest they are killed. Some of the children are sold on to Saudia and other Arab countries.

Stories narrated by some previous slaves who managed to escape or were retrieved through some humanitarian organisations are very touching and have been produced and circulated as films.

All other Black African people in Sudan, of course, irrespective of what positions they hold or professions they acquired, are looked at and commonly insulted as slaves by those who consider themselves Arabs in Sudan.

So slavery is a primary and constant agony in the hearts and nerves of every South Sudanese inflicted on them by fellow Sudanese who believe they are first-class Arabs.

P6.2 SHARIA

Sharia is defined in Encarta as an Islamic, religious law, based on the Koran. The indiscriminate imposition of this law in Sudan by the then Sudan President Jaafar Mohammed el Numeiry was the main trigger of SPLM/A in 1983. It continued to be the principal obstacle to peace even up to the last hour of talks in Naivasha that culminated in the current Comprehensive Peace Agreement. Even so, if South Sudan will vote to secede in 2011, it will primarily be because of these Sharia Laws. Therefore, I would like to encourage every reader of this book, particularly those who would like to understand what exactly Sharia is and why some women worldwide and most marginalised Sudanese are against it, to read the details that follow below.

So that I am not seen to be biased, I have simply reproduced below excerpts of articles written by experts on Islam that provides essential background information about Sharia Law. I am grateful to the writers of those articles.

What is Sharia?

Literally, it means "path," or "path to water," says Clark Lombardi, an expert on Islamic law at the University of Washington's School of Law. In its religious sense, it means God's law, the body of commands that, if followed, will provide the path to salvation. According to Islamic teaching, *Sharia* is revealed in divine signs that must be interpreted by humans. The law is derived from four main sources:

- the Quran, Islam's holy book, considered the literal word of God;
- the *hadith*, or record of the actions and sayings of the Prophet Mohammed, whose life is to be emulated;
- *ijma*, the consensus of Islamic scholars; and
- *Qiyas*, a kind of reasoning that uses analogies to apply precedents established by the holy texts to problems not covered by them, for example, a ban

on narcotics based on the Quranic injunction against wine-drinking.

Does Sharia apply only to religious matters?

No. *Sharia* governs all aspects of life, from relations between men and women to ethics in business and banking. Some aspects of *Sharia* have become part of modern legal codes and are enforced by national judicial systems, while others are a matter of personal conscience. Entirely secular law is not an option under a classical interpretation of Islam, experts say. "In Islam, there is no separation between the secular and the sacred. The law is suffused with religion," says David Powers, a professor of Islamic law and history at Cornell University.

How is sharia applied to banking and finance laws?

Islamic banking and finance is a rapidly expanding industry that seeks to harmonize modern business practises and traditional religious norms. Classical *sharia* prohibits riba, the charging of interest. It also condemns excessive profits and requires Muslims to invest only in ventures that are consistent with Islamic principles; for example, investing in a brewery or casino is forbidden.

For which crimes does the Quran mandate specific punishment?

Five crimes known as the Hadd offenses, Lombardi says. Because these offenses are mentioned in the Quran, committing them is considered an affront to God. They are:

- Wine-drinking and, by extension, alcohol-drinking, punishable by flogging

- Unlawful sexual intercourse, punishable by flogging for unmarried offenders and stoning to death for adulterers

- False accusation of unlawful sexual intercourse, punishable by flogging

- Theft, punishable by the amputation of a hand

- Highway robbery, punishable by amputation, or execution if the crime results in a homicide

What happens in the case of apostasy?

The traditional punishment for Islamic apostasy—leaving Islam for another religion or otherwise abandoning the Islamic faith—is death. The best-known modern case involved author Salman Rushdie, whose 1988 novel, *The Satanic Verses*, offended many devout Muslims. Ayatollah Ruhollah Khomeini, the supreme leader of Iran, declared Rushdie an apostate and condemned him to death. In 1993, an Egyptian court ruled that the writings of Nasr Abu Zayd, a professor, were evidence of apostasy. The court ordered that Zayd be divorced from his Muslim wife (Zayd now lives with his wife in the Netherlands). The vast majority of Muslim nations no longer prescribe death for apostates. On the other hand, says Powers, "Many modern Islamic nations say they guarantee freedom of religion. But this does not necessarily include the right to speak openly against Islam and act on those ideas." Conversions from Islam to other religions are generally not permitted in Muslim countries.

What are the traditional sharia laws governing personal status issues?

- **Marriage:** Islamic marriage is a contract between a man and a woman. In the broadest of terms, the husband pledges to support his wife in exchange for her obedience, Brown says. Women can demand certain rights by writing them into the marriage contract, but the man is the head of the family, and traditionally, a wife may not act against her husband's wishes. (The Quran permits men to use physical force against disobedient wives in some circumstances, Powers says.) Traditional practises still have significant impact on modern law: in Yemen and other nations, a woman cannot work if her husband expressly forbids it. In Syria, a wife can work without her husband's consent, if she renounces her claim on him for financial support. Under *sharia*, a Muslim woman cannot be married legally to a non-Muslim man, but a Muslim man can be married to a non-Muslim woman. Marriages can traditionally take place at young ages—in Iran, the age of consent is thirteen for females and fifteen for males, and younger with a court's permission. In Yemen, the minimum marriage age is fifteen.

- **Divorce:** Under *sharia*, the husband has the unilateral right to divorce his wife without cause. He can accomplish this by uttering the phrase "I divorce you" three times over the course of three months. If he does divorce her, he must pay her a sum of money agreed to before the wedding in the marriage contract and permit her to keep her dowry, Powers says. Classical *sharia* lays out very limited conditions under which a woman can divorce a man—he must be infertile at the time of marriage, insane, or have leprosy or another contagious skin disease. Most Islamic nations, including Egypt and Iran, now allow women to sue for divorce for many other reasons, including the failure to provide financial support.

- **Polygamy:** The Quran gives men the right to have up to four wives. There are some traditional limitations: a man must treat all co-wives equitably, provide them with separate dwellings, and acknowledge in a marriage contract his other spouses, if any. A woman cannot forbid the practise, but can insist on a divorce if her husband takes a second wife. Polygamy remains on the books in most Islamic countries, but some countries limit it through legislation. It is banned in Tunisia and Turkey, though reportedly it is still practised in some areas of Turkey.

- **Custody:** In a divorce, the children traditionally belong to the father, but the mother has the right to care for them while they are young, Powers says. The age at which a mother loses custody differs from nation to nation. In Iran, the mother's custody ends at seven for boys and girls; in Pakistan, it's seven for boys and puberty for girls. Many nations, however, allow courts to extend the mother's custody if it is deemed in the child's interest.

- **Inheritance:** Mothers, wives, and daughters are guaranteed an inheritance in the case of a man's death. In the seventh century A.D., when the law was developed, this was a major step forward for women, Powers says. However, *sharia* also dictates that men inherit twice the share of women because, traditionally, men were responsible for women, Powers says.

Are non-Muslims bound by personal status sharia courts?

- Generally speaking, no minorities in Muslim nations are generally governed under separate personal-status laws reflecting their own traditions, experts say. In Egypt, for example, Coptic Christians marry under Christian law, and foreigners marry under the laws of their countries of origin, Brown says. Criminal law, which is generally no longer based on *sharia*, applies to both foreigners and citizens.

— By Sharon Otterman, associate director, cfr.org

EXAMPLES OF SOME SHARIA LAWS

1. A Muslim cannot be put to death for the murder of an unbeliever.

2. A Muslim man is allowed to beat his wife or wives.

3. A Muslim man is allowed to have four wives at one time.

4. A Muslim man can divorce his wife or wives instantaneously. Then he can marry a new set of wives and continue the cycle.

5. A Muslim woman must pay money to the husband by court orders to have the marriage dissolved.

6. If a divorced couple wants to remarry each other, the wife must marry another person, must have complete sex with him, and must be divorced by him willingly.

7. The evidence required in a case of adultery is that of four Muslim adult men

8. Women's testimony is not accepted in cases of adultery or in any capital offence.

9. Evidence of a female singer and slave (male or female) is not admissible.

10. Testimony of a non-Muslim that has been punished for false accusation is inadmissible. If s/he later becomes a Muslim, her/his evidence is then admissible.

11. The judge of the court shall be a Muslim. The judge may be a non-Muslim only if the accused is a non-Muslim.

12. Adoption is not allowed in Sharia.

13. Custody of children goes to mother as long as the children need care, normally nine years for boys and seven for girls, after which the father takes over. But if the mother does not pray or gets married, the children immediately go to the father.

14. Women inherit half of men.

15. Women's witness is half of men's in business transactions.

16. If a woman is killed, the blood money (the money a killer has to pay to the family of the killed on demand to get acquitted) is half of that of a Muslim man.

17. Apostates (Muslims who leave Islam) automatically get death penalty. If not available for killing, their marriage is dissolved and they cannot inherit from Muslim parents or children.

18. Muslim men can marry Christian and Jews women but Muslim women can marry only a Muslim man.

19. A Muslim virgin cannot marry without permission of her male guardian.

20. A man can marry a woman for a fixed time, from few hours to several years.

AUTHOR'S POINT OF VIEW

There may be people in Southern Sudan and Abyei that love Sharia Laws and would like them not to be cancelled. They are free to vote for unity or remain in an Islamic Sudan in the 2011 referendum.

Likewise those that fear Sharia Law and do not want to continue as part of an Islamic Sudan, can opt to vote for secession of Southern Sudan and join Bahr-el-Ghazal in the case of Abyei.

With due respect to Islam as a religion, I totally disagree and hereby put on records for everybody to note that Sharia, however good it might be to others, is a law that should not be applied to my land and People of South Sudan. As indicated in extracts above, it is viewed by many women as unfair to them. It is also incompatible with aspects of customary law practised by Africans in Sudan and considered by many as too severe.

I also deplore those who argue that it will help stop alcoholism, prostitution, AIDS, and other things by sharing with everybody the following facts:

A lot of us in South Sudan never tasted alcohol or illicit drugs since we were born and that is not because of Sharia. I was born in 1950s to parents who never heard any law called Sharia until they died. Yet they brought me up as a teetotaller and I have continued to be so as a refugee in UK where alcohol is in abundance and there was no Sharia there to stop me. And I am just one example among so many South Sudanese worldwide

While I agree that any law which limits promiscuity could reduce incidence of HIV/AIDS, I feel it is just a simple search for additional reasons to justify the imposition of Sharia to assert these as its advantages. After all, Sharia laws were invented long before the advent of HIV and AIDS. Billions of people worldwide are also free of HIV and AIDS when they have nothing to do with Sharia.

Of course, in any legal system, human error can occur in the course of its application. That is why some people were legally hanged to death in the past in some parts of the world only to discover later that they were actually innocent. Similarly, there are people whose limbs had been amputated as thieves in Sudan under Sharia Law and could be innocent. To these amputees, especially those who are not Muslims and to whom Sharia had been forcibly applied, I say this:

You do not need both hands to vote in a referendum. You do not even need a single finger to do so if both your hands are amputated. Yes, forced amputation will continue to traumatise you psychologically for the rest of your life time; but you will be consoled to a great extent when you ultimately walk proudly to a polling station, pick up a vote with the other hand or even with a stump or mouth and fingerprint or toe-print (if fingerless) against your choice. If you still like to continue to live as a non-Muslim in one Sudan where Sharia Law could still be enforced on you, you are free to do so by voting for unity in the Referendum. If you feel enough is enough and you want to spend the remaining years of your life in a fresh air of secularism and absolute freedom, you can opt for secession. The choice will absolutely be yours.

As for the true Muslims that were rightfully punished by amputation for stealing, what can I say to you, more than the fact that Islam is your religion and Sharia is your law and I guess you are bound to accept the punishment, lament, and reform yourself.

To everybody else, I would like to add that no Muslim ruler in Khartoum will put his or her neck forward to abrogate Sharia laws in Sudan. Everything else can potentially be altered radically to make unity of entire Sudan attractive to South Sudanese except Sharia. Therefore, the outcome of the referendum might already have been predetermined, not by us South Sudanese; but by the leaders who imposed Sharia Law all over the Sudan.

Indeed we maybe a minority in terms of Islam in Sudan. But, we are a religious minority who did not invite other different majorities to force us to follow their ways of life. Unless Sharia Law in Sudan is miraculously cancelled, we will be obliged to vote to have a land of our own where we will be free and contented to continue to live in our own ways.

P6.3. MARGINALISATION

Marginalisation in a nutshell, is prevention from having attention or power. In other words, it is the taking or keeping somebody or something away from the centre of attention, influence, or power.

As Dr. John Garang de Mabior frequently stated, there are many types of majorities in Sudan. Islam could be one and Black Africans is another. Both the large number of Muslims in Sudan and the entire rural Black African majority in Sudan are sadly marginalised in their own country.

In fact, the root causes of extreme poverty in Southern Sudan, Abyei, Eastern Sudan, Nuba Mountains, Darfur, and even the far North of Nubia is nothing else than deliberate economic marginalisation. Just visit these areas and compare them to Khartoum and its vicinity in terms of relative level of development. You will be astonished.

Sudan as a whole may be classified as a developing nation. Nevertheless, if the little resources it has were equitably shared all over the country, no part of Sudan would have felt marginalised and most of the wars could have been avoided.

Unless equitable development is done convincingly during the interim period, it simply means it cannot take place in a united Sudan. Therefore, the answer for non-marginalisation probably lies more in a separate than united Sudan.

P6.4 OPPRESSION

Oppression is subjecting a person or a people to a harsh or cruel form of domination.

Since the so-called independence of Sudan from 1956, Sudan had been ruled by a succession of oppressive regimes based in Khartoum. Almost all people in Sudan from the South to the far North and from the East to the West have been subjected by these regimes to harsh or cruel form of domination. No one, for example, from the Nubians in the far North, the Nuba

Mountains, Darfur, Southern Blue Nile, not to mention Southern Sudan, has ever been allowed to rule Sudan since then.

The top leadership of Sudan only rotated among the clique in the centre of Sudan around Khartoum. Sometimes pseudo-elections were conducted to mislead the world that some democracy existed in Sudan. The reality was that power was changed by simply moving to and fro between civilian Jalabias to military kakis.

In the eyes of the oppressive dictatorial regimes, people are classified in Sudan into four classes: male Arab Muslim is the top class followed by female Arab Muslim, male and female African Muslim, down to all non-Muslims. Thus the non-Muslims in Sudan are actually less in value than second-class citizens; they are fourth class citizens. Indeed, the large majority of Black Africans constitute the lower classes while the Arabs make up the first class.

In their eyes and minds too. A Black African, Muslim or not is nothing more than a slave. As slaves, they deserve no treatment other than the harsh one normally rendered to slaves.

Any reaction against mistreatment was met with even harsher oppressive or suppressive actions aimed at silencing slaves or subduing them permanently.

People oppressed usually prefer to go their own way if they have a chance to exercise their right for self-determination in a referendum. Thus People of Southern Sudan are more likely to vote for secession than unity unless they decide to forgive their oppressors and are sure that they will not be oppressed again in a united Sudan.

P6.5 DISCRIMINATION

Discrimination is unfair treatment of one person or group, usually because of prejudice about race, ethnic group, age group, religion, or gender.

Yes, there was apartheid in South Africa. It was definitely bad and we are pleased it is gone. But, let it be known that it was nothing compared to the apartheid in Sudan.

Watch the film of Steve Biko and also read the book called *Cry My Beloved Country*. You will need to be brave enough not to be moved emotionally and even weep in sympathy to the suffering inflicted to our African brothers and sisters in South Africa during their apartheid system.

Now multiply that in your mind a thousand times to have an idea of the amount of suffering inflicted by Sudanese apartheid system on Black Africans.

Imagine people being rounded up in their thousands in what is supposed to be a national capital city and gathered in a large open square during the burning heat and horrible dust. Then, shoot water at them in tubes like the ones use to quench fire, as a way of giving them water to drink. Imagine too hot food being thrown to them like dogs and bitches from a distance to feed them. Even animals are at least taken to a river or pond to drink; they are not told to open their mouths and have water sprayed into the air for them to catch and drink. But, to them who did that, Sudanese Africans are worse than animals.

That was what happened during the inhuman" Kasha" or massive arrest inflicted indiscriminately on our people in Khartoum in the 1970s for committing the crime of going to their national capital city Khartoum. I witnessed this myself when I was a student at the University of Khartoum.

Apart from difference in magnitude, Sudanese apartheid unlike what was in South Africa is irresolvable. Our Nelson Mandelas are not allowed to occupy the top seat of the president of Sudan under any circumstances just to give one example. Many nations like South Africa learnt a lot from previous mistakes and moved on. I wonder whether Sudan can do the same. I believe those that cannot succeed in a united Sudan will have no choice than to curve their own top seats for their Nelson Mandelas as a last and final resort in a separate nation.

P6.6 TORTURE

Torture is the inflicting of severe physical pain on somebody, for example, as punishment or to persuade somebody to confess or recant something.

Almost every South Sudanese I know has been tortured physically or psychologically over the course of the last fifty years of our protracted struggle. Existing scars, amputated limbs, damaged eyesight, extensive depression, suicides, and reported murders in prison cells or torturing units speak for themselves.

LIVING EXAMPLES OF EXTREME TORTURE OF SOUTH SUDANESE

This was the most difficult part of this book for me to write because I started weeping the moment I typed the above heading of extreme torture of our people in South Sudan. It is so painful to have either been tortured or witnessed torture, a cruelty beyond imagination that must not be allowed to happen.

Volumes up on volumes of books can be written about this for years and yet not all would be documented. I do not need to go beyond my immediate family Deng Akol Ayay to find examples of fellow South Sudanese who have suffered from the torturous and murderous hands of military or security or militia units of Sudan government. I will take the courage to painfully share some of these examples as evidence for records:

AYAY DENG AKOL: THE MAN WHO REFUSED TO CRY

My own elder brother, called Ayay Deng Akol, popularly nicknamed as Ayay Majok, was well known for his unlimited bravery in Kuac Area where we originate in South Sudan. In one of the tribal battles at Lukluk, all people at his side ran away except him. He would not accept being labelled a coward, so he continued fighting the crowd on his own at the other side of the battle. He had no chance to defeat hundreds of his opponents on his own using simply a shield and spears and could have been killed when he refused to run. Fortunately, his opponents admired his extensive bravery and courage and decided to spare his life.

This information was known to "Arab" security forces and national defence agents in Kuajok.

One day, information leaked out to these forces and agents that Ayay Majok could be meeting with Anya-naya soldiers at his house. He was also marked as a general suspect anyway because a lot of his relatives had joined the Anya-nya forces then and were considered to be assisting the rebellion war in the area in 1963. So they decided to send a squad to his house at TokTong at Jur Riverside about three miles away from Kuajok in a deliberate attempt to catch him red-handed.

Ayay did not know how to read and write and he was handed a letter to deliver as a favour to link up two families separated by war. He knew the content of the letter was purely humanitarian but it could be risky if it reached the hands of enemy security forces. It could be used to justify that he was indeed assisting the Anya nya, which was a crime punishable by death in the hands of Sudan army, police, or militia called National Defence Forces (Haress el Wathan) at that time. So he decided to hold tight to the letter with a plan to deliver it as soon as possible before anybody discovered it.

Those who handed him the letter to deliver had just left and before he could set off to forward it, he suddenly noticed the enemy security forces approaching about one hundred yards away. He was still holding the letter in his hand and had to think in a split of second about how to hide it to save his own life. If he ran, they would shoot him; so he walked quickly toward the river with the intention to throw it into the water. Suddenly, he felt if he did so, it would be seen floating and retrieved.

The security forces predicted from the distance that Ayay Majok was up to something. They wondered why he was hurrying toward the river and decided to double their steps to catch up with him.

Glancing over his shoulder, he spotted those forces advancing speedily toward him. He barely had any time and he could be seen throwing the paper away. Therefore, he quickly dipped it in water to soak or wet it and he pushed it down his throat and almost choked.

"What are you doing? What was that white thing you were swallowing?" the head of the squad asked him as they caught up with him.

"Nothing, just some white edible beet," Ayay replied.

"Why did you have to hurry to the river when you saw us and why did you have to come all the way to the river just to swallow a beet?" they continued to interrogate him while smacking him heavily in his face.

He noticed they were carrying rifles, flogging items, and heavy sticks. They could shoot or slaughter him instantly if he hit back the commander of the squad that smacked him. Therefore, he opted to remain calm and continue to respond to their inquiry.

"Why did you smack me? I came to the river just to soak the beet and not to run away from you. I would have run off and rowed away in my boat that you can see there at the bank of the river."

"How dare you question why I smacked you, you filthy dog!" the military corporal remarked and started to flog Ayay Majok. "We do not believe you and we will beat the man out of you today until you cry in the name of your mother. You who is known to be exceptionally brave, we will prove to everybody else that you are not brave at all. We will show that you are just a coward by flogging you in front of everybody around until you cry 'Ma Oh!' Only then shall we stop flogging you and released you to spend the rest of your life as a coward instead of a hero people think you are."

It is very humiliating and an indication of absolute cowardice for an adult to issue a hue and cry of Ma OH! In the local African culture, you would be ostracised in the society as a pure coward forever and insulted by others every time you attempt to raise your voice in the future in protest.

Suddenly he was manhandled and overpowered by all the members of the squad and had his hands firmly tied behind his back. Then they started flogging him by hitting all parts of his body while dragging him publicly from his house at Toktong area up to Kuajok Police Station.

He was not taken into a police cell to continue to beat him there away from any crowd to avoid humiliation. Instead, in an attempt to humiliate him while inflicting pain on him, they continued to flog him severely and openly in front of the station. Of course, more police and militia had to be called in to stand by ready to shoot anybody just in case there is a rescue attempt for him.

The air was still and the atmosphere tense. People were allowed to watch as long as they stood a distance away. Anybody else who dared to echo a word in defence was almost shot.

"All they want is to humiliate me and insult my land and my people," he felt. "For my land and my people, if not for my own dignity, I will not echo that cry. I will prefer to die than to live in humiliation and be known as a coward who defamed his land and his People of South Sudan." Ayay decided never to cry, however painfully he was flogged. The saying that it is a coward who runs or gives in to live for another day was shameful in his culture and was never an option in his mind. He would echo instead a heroic song or phrase of bravery in the name of his land every time they hit him hard. Not a drop of tears was noticed down his face. All that flowed briskly from his body was blood of endless torture.

His skin was swelling up, bruised and cut in various places, especially on his back that was lashed more often. For hours and hours the flogging went on till sunset and continued deep into the night. The floggers had to take it on in turn, as they were getting tired themselves.

"Cry, man," some of the floggers who were also used to flogging him as a double humiliation begged him in sympathy as a way to spare him from further agony possible death.

"If I did that, I will let you yourself and everybody else down. Just pick one of their guns and finish me off to spare me from continuing humiliation. The pain of flogging would go after whenever the torture stops. But the agony of public humiliation will remain to torment me forever. Just pick the gun and shoot me."

"What is he saying to you?" the head of the security squad asked.

"Nothing" He was just moaning and murmuring words I could not understand"

The floggers started hitting striking him on his head, arms, belly and some of the harsher "Arabs" went for his scrota hoping that would work.

"Carry on with the flogging. And don't just hit him on his back or bumps. Hit him hard elsewhere that is more painful too. Perhaps that will get him to cry. It is a positive sign that he has started to moan. Soon we will hear him cry Ma Oh!" he ordered.

They complied. But, no stroke, however painful, worked. Ultimately, the floggers had to give up and seek alternative orders from the head of the unit as to what to do since Away absolutely refused to cry.

"What shall we do now, sir?" they asked. "This man is not going to cry whatsoever."

"Let him go. He is a stupid dog," he shouted angrily. "We will deal away with him another day."

Both the physical and psychological scars on my elder brother remained as a living proof of that severe torture inflicted on him by the very government security forces that were meant to protect him as a civilian.

"They thought I was a coward who would ashamed of my land and I proved them wrong. Our ultimate freedom will take these scars away," he would tell anyone who asked. Sadly, he did not live to see the day when we would cast a decisive vote against ruthless tortures and lift our flag of that freedom.

THE WOMEN WHO USED AIDS TO FIGHT FOR THEIR LAND AND PEOPLE (KATIBA HIV)

Widespread raping of women was another very sad method of torturing our people. It was done by Sudan army or their militia to inflict pain in the women themselves and all South Sudanese in general.

The women raped were not necessarily relatives or wives of the freedom fighters. Most of them were even those who had remained in the towns and cities still controlled by the Sudan army.

Others were those found in as innocent civilians living in the countryside by the raiding militia or regular army forces commanded by Khartoum.

One of them is a lady who made an anonymous phone call to me and refused to reveal her name. She said she was just a young fourteen-year-old virgin who simply left their home, at the instructions of her mother, to purchase an onion at the market for cooking. Her menstrual period had just begun, but sex did not still cross her mind. She had no idea about a horrendous disastrous experience that was going to happen to her that day.

On her way to the market she spotted an army jeep approaching behind her full of uniformed soldiers of Sudan army. To her that was a common normal scene. She thought they were just protective soldiers patrolling the town and she never worried until the jeep pulled off and stood beside her on the road.

She knew there was no reason at all for the jeep to stop by her and she attempted to run away frightened. But, the soldiers caught up with her and quickly grasped and dragged her into the jeep. Then they drove swiftly away toward the army barracks. She was screaming and they had to smack her and forced her to be silent while they drove off.

When they reached near the barracks, they drove into the surrounding bush and pushed her to lie flat on the ground.

"Some of the men held me firmly down by pushing on my forehead, shoulders and legs," she remarked. "One of them pushed painfully on my mouth so that nobody can hear me if I screamed. I thought they were going to cut my throat to death. I did not know that they were going to do the worse thing to me. Sincerely, I wished they had killed me instead.

"The first dress that was ripped apart was my skirt followed by my underpants. One of them then jumped and laid heavily on me pushing my thighs apart and forced her penis inside my vagina. Only then did realise I was being raped."

"Leave, please, I tried to plead, and only a groaning sound was coming out, as my mouth was tightly held closed.

"Painfully he thrust me and I wished it had at least ended with one man. Unfortunately, they took their turns on me one by one. They did not care at all about blood that was tricking down my thighs nor the enormous pain they were inflicting on me. Not even my tears that were trickling down my face bothered them and I wonder now if they even took any notice of them.

"The next dress that one soldier holding my forehead ripped off was my top blouse while I was being raped by another. Then he started to traumatically squeeze both my breasts and pull on my hair. He was the last person I remember who ultimately jumped on me and raped me too.

"'Shall we kill her or leave her?' one of the soldiers asked as they were about to leave. 'Let us leave her,' another replied. 'Nobody would touch us even if she told anybody and we might need to fuck her another day. If we killed her, we would not be able to go to her grave and fuck her there.'

"Then they all drove away in their jeep. I was left alone in the bush and could not spot anybody to hold my hands as I was too weak to even stand up. I was not also sure that they had actually gone far away from me. So, I decided to lie quietly there for few minutes listening intensively for the sound of their car to fade away. That way, I would confirm that they had definitely gone.

"Finally, I managed to get up and stroll all the way back to our house in the town while avoiding the main road, just in case they or other soldiers in a different car might spot and snatch me too.

"My mother was anxious why I delayed and knew something sinister might have happened. I was not a child who would drift away to do other things and disappoint my mother whenever she sent me anywhere. Everything became clear to her when I arrived and told her what happened. Like the soldiers said, there was nothing in her powers to do short of committing suicide by going to the army barracks with me in attempt to identify and report the culprits to their senior officers. She knew other mothers who did that before ended up being also raped, tortured, and killed.

"My father was among those massacred by militia forces when I was only three years old, my mother told me. He was not there to fight for me and I believe he might not have been in exactly the same weak position like my mother.

"The words 'there is nothing they can do to us even if they heard' kept ringing all the time in my mind and I decided that I will try to do whatever I can as revenge. I believe I am not the only victim of their brutality and I might team with others in the future to serve them a heavy blow.

"Luckily I escaped pregnancy. However, a confidential test I did later revealed that I had HIV. I never had intercourse with anybody else before or after and there is no way I could have acquired from someone else.

"HIV on top of rape hit me hard emotionally and made me even more determined to do something as a revenge and continuation of the struggle that took away the life of my father and left me an early orphan.

"I decided to make myself available to Sudan army soldiers and militia wherever they are in order to give back to them their virus. My hope was to infect as many of them as possible before the virus kills me. This way, I hope that a lot of them would die of AIDS as a bullet they had shot me with in the first place.

"Bit by bit I discovered other few South Sudanese ladies that were doing exactly the same. Of course, there could have been other women who were forced to sell themselves as a way to survive or feed their children at very difficult times.

"Three of us decided to hold a secret meeting under the pretext of a birthday occasion. In the meeting we made the following resolutions.

- We should keep this mission a secret, especially during the war.
- We must reject any sexual intercourse with any of our own people so that we do not infect them too.
- If few trusted ones insisted to know why, we can just tell them we do not like them. It is difficult to know who to trust and it is safer not to tell them the truth about our HIV status and what we are doing with the virus as a genuine reason. Who knows—one of them might accuse us to the enemy.
- We called ourselves KATIBA HIV and only used the secret code KH to identify ourselves.

"As regards the clients, we were not short of them. After all they thought we were either simply interested in them or their money. They also knew we had no direct links with SPLA/M.

"Later on we learnt that some Eritrean women used to sell themselves for sex to obtain money to sponsor their movement and help in the liberation of their land. We wished we had done the same too," she asserted.

"Of course, as decent people of South Sudan, we do not deliberately spread a dangerous disease to harm others. Our culture is against such a practise. However, if enemy forces throw a dynamo to you with the intention of eliminating you and you catch it before it explodes, would it be wrong to throw it back to them in order to protect yourselves?" she argued.

"My only prayer now is for the virus not to take my life before I cast my decisive vote in 2011 against the inhuman rapists," she continued. "I strongly believe that people prefer to get out of the cell (One Sudan) where they were tortured rather than continue to stay there lest they are reminded now and then about the pains and agonies they suffered. Worst of all, their children and future generations will continue to suffer the same cycle of rape, torture, and such others indefinitely in the dangerous cell if their parents now spoil the chance of exiting in 2011 referendum."

P6.7 HUMILIATION

Humiliation is the act of damaging somebody's dignity or pride. Many examples can be given and indeed I have already touched on this above. Our African culture is considered to be inferior and jeered upon. Our languages are referred to as simple dialects. Whatever the level of education, one is approached in streets of Khartoum for example, and asked whether you might be interested to work as a domestic servant.

I remember when I was practising as a medical doctor in Omdurman Hospital, some pseudo-superiors would knock the door of the office where I was waiting to see patients and ask me where the doctor was. To them, a Black man cannot qualify to be a medical doctor, engineer, lawyer or any other professional.

I believe all of them are silently shocked to find out that a Nuba woman, not even a Nuba man has become a national minister of health with a PhD qualification when to them a Nuba is only a latrine bucket carrier. And, of course, every South Sudanese in their eyes is a slave whatever post he holds in Sudan.

Of course, humiliation can be healed by apology, compensatory good treatment, and full recognition of dignity of others. If these wounds are completely healed in 2011, there will be no excuse to vote for secession later—but, will they?

P6.8 DEPRIVATION

Deprivation is the act of taking something away from somebody or preventing somebody from having something. Ask which schools and hospitals are the worst if we have any at all in terms of lack of facilities. Ask if there had been any big successful developmental industries established in marginalised areas. You will arrive at one common answer. South Sudan is the most deprived area in Sudan even though it is now the riches part of the country in terms of oil revenue.

Glance too at the list of people that ever ruled Sudan as presidents or prime ministers since the so-called independence of Sudan. You will find the Mohammed Mahjoub, Ibrahim Aboud, Sadig el Mahdi, Jaafar Mohammed el Numeiry, Sowar el Dhab and Omar el Hassan. Not a single person from the larger rural African Population of Western, Eastern and South Sudan, for example.

No Black African Sudanese is eligible to rule Sudan as a president or prime minister. We had to fight for fifty years and lose over four and half million lives before we could occupy the second seat of the first vice president.

Are we prepared to sacrifice four and half more millions of lives over a period of another fifty years to move up one more step and become the top leader? Would it even help our cause if it is now offered as a last-minute manoeuvre to stop the South from secession?

Probably, the answer to both questions is NO.

P6.9. BARBARISM

Barbarism is a cruel or brutal act. Sudan was one of the few countries where very barbaric acts of the past were continued. Decapitation and public exhibition of human heads is long abandoned wherever it was practised worldwide. Yet, my own classmate called Ngeny Anei was decapitated by Sudan army as an Anya-nya freedom fighter in the 1960s and his head was put on the top of a long wooden bar and displayed publicly in Gogrial Area of South Sudan. This barbaric exhibition was celebrated with victorious songs and laughter at the same time.

More recently (1983–2005), determined to leave no soul alive, attacking soldiers or militia would not only kill pregnant women. They would also perforate their wombs many times to ensure that the foetus inside stood no chance of survival. Where else in the world would that happen in modern times even as a part of war? Nowhere else, as far as I know, has such terrible barbarism persisted!

How would men that were decapitated and pregnant women whose wombs were perforated vote in 2011 referendum if they had a chance to do so? I doubt whether they would vote for unity nor would their own children unless, of course, unity is made so attractive up to a level of forgiveness!

P6.10 MASSACRE

Massacre is the vicious killing of large numbers of people or animals. Recently, a journalist referred to the genocide in Darfur and Rwanda as the worst humanitarian disasters in the world. Definitely they are examples of horrible genocide. But, the massive indiscriminate killings that had been inflicted in almost every corner of South Sudan are beyond any description. In fact, if all skulls of people killed in this area from 1955 to 2005 were gathered and heaped up, they would be more than those in Darfur and Rwanda combined. Examples of these massacres are stated in the preceding section on history.

"Never again," echoed in the voices of singers of Rwanda, is a very touching phrase that clearly say that such horrible genocide as happened in Rwanda should never be repeated anywhere in the world. One wishes the world would listen and respond positively.

Massacres or genocide has one intention: extermination of a group of people. Obviously if people of Southern Sudan felt threatened with a risk of extermination, they are more likely to vote for secession in 2011 as a protective measure for existence, unless of course that threat has been completely removed from their minds as a way of making unity attractive during the interim period.

P6.11 ASSASSINATION

Assassination is the killing of a political or other public figure by a sudden violent attack.

"Memories that are strongly imparted in the minds of children at an early age never die away."

We were in the train with my own father Deng Akol Ayay in Wau Station on the day William Deng Nhial was assassinated. My father was unwell and I was accompanying him on a journey to Khartoum for further treatment.

"Thugs!" my father burst out loudly in anger, while we were waiting for the train to start to move. "They had killed Father Saturnino and now William Deng Nhial."

"Don't shout," whispered a fellow Southern Sudanese who was sitting nearby. "They will kill you too, old man, if they hear what you are saying."

"Let them kill me too," my father replied. "How worthy is my life without those who care for our welfare?"

My feelings were deeply struck and I began to wonder who these two people were that my father so valued to the extent that he was ready to die in protest. I heard about William Deng Nhial before; but that was the first time I heard of Father Saturnino Ohure and I decided to find out more information about both of them.

If my father was alive when Dr. John Garang De Mabior met his fate in the tragic plane crash, I believe he could have reacted likewise unless there are convincing reasons beyond doubt that only the bad weather and mountain are the ones to blame in this case.

FATHER SATURNINO OHURE 1938-1967

Father Saturnino Ohure was a Catholic, Lotuho priest. He was born of Xillange and Ixonom about 1921 and was baptized at Torit in 1931. Soon he asked to enter Okaru Seminary, where he passed to Gulu in 1938. On 21 December 1946 he was ordained a priest, together with Father Avellino Wani at Gulu. Some years later he was given responsibilities with the same father at Lirya mission until 1955, when the existing Sudanese priests were transferred to the new vicariate of Rumbek under Bishop Irenaeus Dud. At the first general parliamentary elections he stood for Torit and was elected. He soon became a leader of Southern MPs in the Constituent Assembly. When the Assembly was dissolved by the military government in November 1958, Father Saturnino retired to Yei and Porkele. In 1961, informed of his imminent arrest he fled to Uganda together with other ex-parliamentarians where he helped and counselled Sudanese refugees. In one of his travels in this connection he was killed by a Ugandan soldier near Kitgum on 22 January 1967

WILLIAM DENG NHIAL

William Deng Nhial, was a prominent Southern icon, who founded a political party called Sudan African National Union (SANU) together with Father Saturnino Ohure and Joseph Uduho. Like Dr. John Garang De Mabior, he was a Charismatic leader who also preached about unity in Sudan until he met his death in similar mysterious fashion while on his way to his hometown of Tonj in 1968. Their deaths are similar in a sense that they were unexpected and they occurred at time their presence in the Sudanese political arena was needed the most. They both died in such moments for being the voice of voiceless.

It was always alleged by Khartoum governments that fellow Southerners assassinated William Deng (a scheme orchestrated to downplay the true assassins in the stratagem). But his death was a weird conspiracy against his being tall in issues regarding the injustice and dishonesty of Sadiq's government. It was also to stop him from reaching Khartoum and becoming the ruler of Sudan, following his triumph in the elections when Sadig el Mahdi lost in the same elections. It was until thirty-five years later that his true assassins were revealed as admitted on BBC by Sadig Al Mahadi who then was Sudan Prime Minister that William was assassinated by the Sudanese military. Indeed, a special task force of Sudan army was designated to waylay him between Rumbek and Tonj.

DR. JOHN GARANG DE MABIOR (23 June 1945–30 July 2005)

Only history will tell whether the death of Dr. John Garang De Mabior was simply due to faulty weather and mountains.

He was the first vice president of Sudan and former leader of the revolutionary Sudan People's Liberation Army.

EARLY LIFE

John Garang, whose full name is John Garang de Mabior Atem Arwei Akur Ayen Arwei de Dhiop, was born to Aulian clan at Wankulei Village in Northern Bor—Konggor County of Upper Nile Region of South Sudan on 23 June 1945. He is a member of the (Dinka) ethnic group, born into a poor family, and orphaned by the age of ten. Had his uncle, who was working at Malek Dairy then, not taken care of him and put him to school, he might not have become educated. His uncle was transferred to Tonj Diary in the early fifties where John Garang started his education at Bongo Elementary School. He completed his primary school and was accepted at Bussere North Intermediate School. Before John could finish his intermediate education, he lost his uncle in Tonj. This was a big loss to him, as his uncle played both roles as a father and uncle. Equally, determined as he is, Garang successfully finished his intermediate school and was accepted at Rumbek Secondary School.

In 1962, John, like the rest of the youth from Southern Sudan, who were unhappy about the ways the North was handling the political situations in the South, joined the first Sudanese civil war, but because he was so young, the leaders encouraged him and others his age to seek an education. He then fled to Ethiopia as a refugee. In Ethiopia, John could not fit in as the political ideology there was bourgeois in nature. He wanted a country, where he could freely exercise his political ideas. Therefore, he moved to Tanzania where he met Musevenni of Uganda.

Because of the ongoing fighting, Garang was forced to attend his secondary education in Tanzania. After winning a missionary scholarship, he went on to earn a Bachelor of Arts Degree in Economics in 1969 from Grinnell College in Iowa in the United States. He was known there for his bookishness. He was subsequently offered another scholarship to pursue postgraduate studies at the University of California at Berkeley, but chose to return to Tanzania and study East African agricultural economics as a Thomas J. Watson Fellow at the University of

Dar es Salaam. As a member of the University Students' African Revolutionary Front, a student group at the university, he made the acquaintance of Yoweri Museveni, who would go on to become president of Uganda and a close ally. However, Garang soon decided to return to Sudan and join the rebels. This was the era when the ideology of "Pan-Africanism" was spreading through the entire African continent.

ANYA-NYA ONE

Upon graduation in 1969, he joined Anya Nya one. Joseph Lagu, who had taken over the Southern Sudan Liberation Movement (SSLM), appointed John Garang as his Adjutant. Early 1970, John went to Israel for a military training. When he came back from Israel, he was commissioned as Captain. In the 1970, there were lots of activities about the negotiations between May Regime and SSLM. John disagreed with his boss (Lagu) over terms of negotiations. So Lagu fired him as adjutant and appointed Allison Moggaya as his adjutant. Equally, agreement was reached in February 1972 between May Regime and SSLM.

ADDIS ABABA AGREEMENT

The Anya-nya civil war ended with the Addis Ababa agreement of 1972 and Garang, like many rebels, was absorbed into the Sudanese military. John, being at odd with leaders in Upper Nile, was absorbed in Bahr el Ghazal, as captain and based in Bussere, this time as adjutant of Joseph Kuol Ammuom. This was the golden chance for John to start the activities for the next liberation movement. While absorption was in process, John wrote a strongly worded letter to Marshall Jaafer el Numeiry, opposing the integration. As a result, John was transferred to Malakal.

He did not spend two months in Malakal. He was called at HQ in Kh artoum and was sent to the United States for a company course. John was being exiled. One year later, he was back to

Sudan after the course. Again, the Khartoum regime arranged another scholarship and sent him back to do a master's degree in agriculture. Two years later, he was back with a master of science degree. Still Khartoum was uncomfortable with his presence and talked to CCI, the company that was digging the Jonglei Canal to send him abroad on a further scholarship. Hence, he was back to Iowa State University for his PhD in economics at Iowa State University, after writing a thesis on the agricultural development of Southern Sudan.

For eleven years, he was a career soldier and rose from the rank of captain to colonel after taking the Infantry Officers' Advanced Course at Fort Benning, Georgia. By 1983, Col. Garang was the head of the Staff College in Omdurman and a lecturer in University of Khartoum. Along with other officers he was involved in a political campaign within the army.

Though John was the most active organiser and member of South Sudan Free Officers Movement (SSFFM), he was not the leader as the members lined themselves up according to their ranks. Albino Akol Akol was the overall chairman, Gordon Mayen was deputy, and Paterno was the general secretary. The list is long. But very important to mention is that John seemed to have established his leadership base among the junior officers. It was through his efforts that SSFOM was able to recruit Southern Sudanese officers, who originally were from the Sudanese military college; good examples are Arok Thon Arok, Taher Bior Ajak, Nichnora Magar Aciek, Chol Ayauak, Martin Manyiel Ayuel, Faustino Atem Gualdit, Abulgashim Hussein, plus a number of junior officers.

The SSFFM agreed that the first bullet was to be fired at Ariel were the situation was tensed. The Anya-nya one soldiers refused transfer to the North. Albino Akol Akol, the Chairman of SSFFM was coxed in by Numeiry, against his will, to convince those forces in Aweil to accept transfer, which he did very well. This had angered a number of SSFFM members and preparation was on the way to replace Albino from the SSFFM leadership.

Fortunately, thinks worked out in favour of John Garang. One of his group members, within SSFFM volunteered to take advantage of Bor crisis... Kerubino Kuanyin Bol, who was the commander of Paschalla garrison, took the responsibility. John took leave and went to Bor.

John Garang remained the chairman of SPLM and C-in-C of the SPLA since 1983 until 30 July 2005 when he met his death in mysterious circumstances.

SPLA/M WAR

On 12 May 1983, when the situation in Bor was beyond control, Numeiry, having the hangover of Albino success in Aweil, wanted to use Garang to squash the Bor's mutiny. Of course, it did not work, as John was a party to Kerubino's activities.

Garang went to Bor, ostensibly to mediate with about five hundred southern government soldiers in battalion 105 who were resisting being rotated to posts in the north. However, as stated above, he was already part of a conspiracy among some officers in the Southern Command arranging for the defection of battalion 105 to the antigovernment rebels. When the government attacked Bor on 16 May 1983 and the battalion pulled out, Garang left Bor on 18 May 1983 and went by an alternate route to join them in the rebel stronghold in Ethiopia.

In Bilpam, Akuot Atem and Gai Tut had established their power based with Anya-nya Two. When John arrived on 24 May 1983, the tension was high as Gai and Akuot wanted to absorb John and his group to Anya-nya Two. The negotiations to form one movement took five months. Gai and Akuot fled to South Sudan and John and his group announced the formation of SPLM/A.

John was chairman of SPLM and commander and chief of the SPLA, with Kerubino his deputy.

By the end of July, Garang had brought over three thousand rebel soldiers under his control through the newly-created Sudan People's Liberation Army/Movement (SPLA/M), which was opposed to military rule and Islamic dominance of the country, and encouraged other army garrisons to mutiny against the Islamic law imposed on the country by the government.[1] This action marked the commonly agreed upon beginning of the Second Sudanese Civil War, which resulted in one and half million deaths over twenty years of conflict. Although Garang was Christian and most of southern Sudan is non-Muslim (mostly animist), he did not initially focus on the religious aspects of the war.

The SPLA gained the backing of Libya, Uganda, and Ethiopia. Garang and his army controlled a large part of the southern regions of the country, named New Sudan. He claimed his troops' courage came from "the conviction that we are fighting a just cause. That is something North Sudan and its people don't have." Critics attributed financial motivations to his rebellion, noting that much of Sudan's oil wealth lies in the south of the country.

Garang refused to participate in the 1985 interim government or 1986 elections, remaining a rebel leader. However, the SPLA and government signed a peace agreement on 9 January 2005.

On 9 July 2005, Garang returned to Khartoum, after twenty-one years of SPLA/M war and was received by millions of people. He was sworn in the next day of arrival as first vice president, the second-most powerful person in the country, following a ceremony in which he and President Omar al-Bashir signed a power-sharing constitution. He also became the president of the Government of Southern Sudan with limited autonomy for the six years before a scheduled decisive referendum of possible secession. He also remained the commander in chief of SPLA.

No Christian or Southerner had ever held a government post as high as first vice president. Commenting after the ceremony, Garang stated, "I congratulate the Sudanese people, this is not my peace or the peace of al-Bashir, it is the peace of the Sudanese people."

TRAGIC DEATH

In late July 2005, Garang died after the Ugandan presidential Mi-172 helicopter he was riding in crashed. He had been returning from a meeting in Rwakitura with longtime ally President Yoweri Museveni of Uganda. Sudanese state television initially reported that Garang's craft had landed safely, but Abdel Basset Sabdarat, the country's information minister, went on TV hours later to deny the report. Soon afterward, a statement released by the office of Sudanese President Omar el-Bashir confirmed that a Ugandan presidential helicopter, crashed into "a mountain range in southern Sudan because of poor visibility and this resulted in the death of Dr. John Garang De Mabior, six of his colleagues and seven Ugandan crew members."

His body was flown to New Site, a Southern Sudanese settlement near the scene of the crash, where former SPLA fighters and civilian supporters have gathered to pay their respects to Garang. His body was then taken around parts of the homeland before the funeral took place on 3 August in Juba.

QUESTIONS ABOUT DEATH

The Sudanese government and the head of the SPLA both blamed the weather for the accident. There are, however, doubts, especially among the basis of the SPLA, as to the truth of this. Yoweri Museveni, the Ugandan president claims that the possibility of "external factors" having played a role could not be eliminated. An investigation committee was formed and early reports are said to suggest pilot error. Yet a lot of questions will continue to remain unanswered.

CONSEQUENCES OF DEATH

Others might have expected the SPLA/M to split and collapse following the tragic death. On the contrary, SPLA/M acted swiftly and unanimously to appoint Salva Kiir Mayardit, his long-term deputy in his position.

Considered instrumental in ending the civil war, the effect of Garang's death upon the peace deal is uncertain. The government declared three days of national mourning, which did not stop large-scale rioting in Khartoum which killed at least twenty-four as youth from south Sudan attacked Arabs and clashed with security forces. After three days of violence, the death toll had risen to eighty-four[4]. Unrest was also reported in other parts of the country. Leading members of the SPLM, including Garang's successor Salva Kiir Mayardit, stated that the peace process would continue. Analysts suggested that the death could result in anything from a new democratic openness in the SPLA, which some have criticized for being overly dominated by Garang, to an outbreak of open warfare between the various southern factions that Garang had brought together.

The United States State Department argued that Garang's presence in the government would have helped solve the Darfur conflict in western Sudan, but others consider these claims "excessively optimistic."

SURVIVED FAMILY

John Garang de Mabior had five brothers and two sisters. Four of them are dead. They include Akuol Mabior Atem who died in Kartoum in 1970, survived by only one son called Kwer Marwual after sadly losing seven children in war; Aruei Mabior Atem killed in late '50s during a tribal fight in Buk Village; Areng Mabior who died in a car accident in Gadarif in 2000 while she was trying to cross to Ethiopia in order to join the movement (also survived by only one son called Emanuel Atem); and Akoi Mabior Atem killed at the beginning of the war in 1983.

Surviving siblings of John Garang are Atem Mabior Atem, Deng Mabior Atem of Gel-weng Forces, and Commander Malual de Mabior Atem of 104/105 Division.

Marriage-wise, John Garang de Mabior fell in love and married a girl called Rebecca Nyandeng Chol Atem in December 1975 while he was a commander of 104/105 armed forces in Bor. Dr. Garang is now survived by his wife Mrs. Rebecca Nyandeng de Mabior, and six children, two sons and four daughters namely Mabior, Chol, Gak, Akuol, Nyanker, and Atong, from first to last borne.

During his funeral, his wife stated, "I will not weep now just because my husband is dead. I will wait and weep later if his vision is not implemented." Now she is an active member of Government of Southern Sudan (GOSS) where she served first as a minister of Transport and Communications and next as a presidential adviser on gender.

ADVICE ON REFERENDUM

His advice on how people would vote in the 2011 referendum is best reflected in a statement he made when he addressed an audience few months before his death saying: "I and those who joined me in the bush and fought for more than twenty years have brought to you CPA in a golden plate. Our mission is accomplished. It is now your turn, especially those who did not have a chance to experience bush life. When time comes to vote at referendum, it is your golden choice to determine your fate? Would you like to vote to be second-class citizens in your own country? It is absolutely your choice."

While continuing to mourn the departure of Dr. John Garang De Mabior, let eligible voters digest his advice properly and choose to liberate themselves once and for all from longstanding slavery and oppression if no other better choice is offered to them by the end of the interim period.

P6.12 ANTAGONISATION

Antagonisation is the act of causing a person or animal to be hostile.

The enemies of peace understand clearly that our strength as Southern Sudanese lies in our total unity. They have also learnt from the previous colonial strategy of divide and rule. Therefore differences among us are initiated, masterminded, encouraged, and maintained by them as a successful way of weakening us.

Lots of examples can be given during the long course of our liberation struggle. The 1947 Juba Conference is said to have been influenced negatively through the enemy's efforts to split the delegates over a period of twenty-four hours. During the first seventeen years of war (1955–1972) the enemy established a task force called the National Defence Force, referred to earlier in order to foil that war. The South did not remain under one region as speculated in the Addis Ababa Agreement before President Numeiry abrogated it. Many more militia were formed subsequently with the event of SPLA/M in the second phase of the war (1983–1985). Internal splits were always vigorously encouraged by our enemy whether or not they were purely initiated by us. The fires that burnt recently at the start of the six-year interim period in Yambio and Wau, for example, could have been fuelled if not also ignited with the help of our opponents.

Sadly, a lot of precious lives were previously lost as a direct result of these splits. Late Joseph Uduho is a more recent example along with thousands of civilians. The enemy always gained grounds whenever we were weakened by the splits.

I remember at this juncture my own friend called Peter Wek Kuanyin and how he died. He was an SPLA captain who was commanding forces around the Gogrial area. When he heard the news of the split of SPLA/M in 1991, he was deeply disappointed and affected. So he rallied all forces in his command to stand in a circle around him. Then he addressed them saying: "As you have heard, our movement has sadly split. This is a bad sign. We may no more succeed to win the war and liberate ourselves and our land. I called you to tell you that I am not going to wait and see the day when our movement collapses and the enemy overcomes us all." Then he saluted his forces and suddenly pulled out his pistol and shot himself in the head.

His forces, who had not anticipated that he was going to shoot himself, dashed in to catch and hold him before he fell on the ground. But it was too late to rescue him. Peter died instantly in their arms.

His death showed the extent to which some of us deplore our disunity and the advantage that it gives to our enemy. Conversely, it proves our enormous desire to remain united and strong in order to achieve our common goal of full liberation.

In fact, the negative propaganda against us worldwide is that we are a people who can be so hostile to one another and should not be allowed to become independent lest we end up killing and finishing ourselves. In other words we are projected as people that cannot succeed to govern ourselves.

The choice rests with all of us as a people of South Sudan: to throw away our bitter differences, political or tribal, and stand strongly as one nation or continue to antagonise ourselves with or without the encouragement of our opponents and remain slaves forever.

P6.13 STARVATION

Starvation is the state of suffering or dying through lack of food. This is one of the consequences of economic deprivation and marginalisation. It is also a mechanism for genocide.

The following story gives some insight about severe famine and our indigenous strategies for survival.

GIVE ME MILK, MUMMY

During the severe famine of 1998, a mother was determined to save her baby from starvation in South Sudan. She herself was also starving. Hence her breasts were virtually dry. Yet she persisted to force her baby to continue to suckle hoping that they may still produce some milk. As they were unresponsive to further stimulation, her infant repeatedly rejected the breast. Ultimately, she was obliged to resort to alternative and unconventional means of survival in an attempt to rescue her baby, as there was no food at all available to give. She tried to feed her with all sorts of things including leaves from trees, bitter root juices, mud soaked with saliva and even her own urine but the baby rejected them all. Finally, she picked up a sharp piece of wood and pricked both her nipples many times in order to bleed hoping that her baby would mistake blood for breast milk and accept to suckle but the baby turned its mouth away. When relief workers later arrived they found her dead under a tree still holding her baby tightly between her arms and her nipples, which had stopped bleeding, still continued to show multiple puncture wounds.

Of course the baby in question would be thirteen years old in 2011 and will not vote in the referendum. However, there are similar survivors of the severe famines inflicted in Southern Sudan by a combination of draught and deliberate destruction of means of life, that would be old enough to cast their votes in that referendum. They will be free to decide whether to remain united with those militia and forces that burnt their crops and looted their means of survival or secede.

P6.14 BOMBING

Bombing is the act of or process of dropping bombs from aircraft. This is could be another reason for secession, trivial though it might appear to others. For, people who had no heart to spare at least innocent children that are starving in internal refugee camps or schooling under trees and instead used air force to persistently bombard them to death are probably unforgivable.

P6.15 FALSIFICATION

Falsification is deliberate misrepresentation of the truth or facts.

Ever since I was born in the early 1950s, all I have been hearing on Omdurman television and radio, especially about us in South Sudan, are lies, lies, and lies. The entire world is persistently fed with nothing else but lies about us. Even the existence of a seventeen-year civil war from 1955 to 1972 in the country was denied internationally by Khartoum.

Every time President Salva Kiir Mayardit pays a visit abroad, lies are created out of the blue to misinform the world that he has died in a plane crash like Dr. John Garang De Mabior. So far, by the time this book was being published, Dr. Salva Kiir Mayardit has been reported dead four times, especially when he pays an official trip to Kampala. This is a clear example of continuing falsification. It also reflects the malicious intentions and ominous wishes in the minds of the rumour perpetrators and rumourmongers.

What is equally worrying are explanations given by my colleagues who are experts, some of whom hold doctorates of philosophy (PhDs) in Islamic studies. They say Jihadists are advised to concede agreements when they are relatively weak and unable to win a war. Then use the peace interval to build more power and then overcome their opponents. They even cite examples of wars in the past where such advice was successfully followed.

We already know how the Addis Ababa Agreement was described as not a Bible or Koran by President Jaafar Mohammed el Numeiry before he threw it into the dustbin. The current Comprehensive Peace Agreement might be thicker and stronger than the Addis Ababa Agreement. Yet we should remain vigilant and be prepared for the worst possible scenario just in case history repeats itself.

P6.16 ARABISATION

Arabisation is making something conform to Arab customs or culture. ISLAMISATION is conversion of people into or countries to Islam or cause people, institutions, or countries to follow Islamic Law.

In the context of Sudan, both go hand in hand. They are the two goals that successive governments in Khartoum aimed to achieve. That is to Arabise and Islamise everybody in Sudan by hooks and screws.

Having succeeded, so they think, to label Sudan as an Arab Middle-East country, the next mission is to force all the citizens to adopt Arabism as their culture and Islam as religion.

Forcing of Arabic to be the national language and compulsory medium of instruction in schools and universities, the violent suppression of Christianity and aggressive promotion of Islam, imposition of Sharia Laws, stigmatisation of African cultures and projection of Arab culture as superior and many more all point toward these dual dream objectives.

One can be a Muslim without being forced. One can also be a Muslim and remain an African without necessarily considering oneself as a charcoal-skin Arab. Melanocyte cells that constantly produce black skin pigment cannot also be eradicated by any topical dyes nor are they killed inside black couples through intermarriage to light-skinned Arabians.

I lived for three years in Nigeria and did not come across a Hausa Muslim that regarded himself or herself as an Arab simply because of the ability to speak Arabic and professing to Islam.

The additional allegation is that below the ebony skin of a Sudanese Muslim that speaks Arabic is a trait of Arabic blood as an additional justification for Arab identity is nothing more than a specialist fabrication already discussed above.

These are issues where we will never concur. The choice therefore remains twofold. Accept to be a Black Arab and vote for unity or remain an African and opt for secession. This applies wherever a referendum would be held in Sudan, South, West, East, or elsewhere.

It is worth remembering that identity is a primary cause of conflict in Sudan.

It will be resolved only in the ballot boxes of the 2011 Referendum.

P6.17 ISLAMISATION

Forcing or coercing people to become Muslims, as practised by successive Khartoum-based governments is a cardinal reason that will leave South Sudan with no alternative than to go. If more people become Christians in the South, it is not because they hate Islam; but, because Christianity is not forced on them. There are no Christianists that threaten to kill South Sudanese when they reject or abandon Christianity, unlike Jihadists who implement the death penalty on anyone that does not accept or abandon Islam (Islamic apostasy).

I also believe that even if the whole of South Sudan were to be 100 percent Islamised, it would still opt to become independent. This is because the issue is not religion itself; it is the use of religion as a tool to oppress and marginalise others. That explains why the people of Darfur, Nuba Mountains, Eastern Sudan, and Nubia in the far North continue to be oppressed and treated as second-class citizens along with "Southern" Sudanese, despite the fact that they are currently overwhelmingly Muslims.

P6.18 OPPOSITION

For ages and ages, the marginalised and oppressed people of the South have always been forced to the back bench of politics and leadership as an opposition group without seeing any light ahead to become forerunners. Whether in the judiciary, legislature, and executive components of the government, or in the army or civilian units of the nation of Sudan, they played only the back roles. If anything, a good number have ended up walking to their graves like William Deng Nhial and Philip Abbas Gabush.

Things were continued to be engineered by the forerunners and it was up to the followers to accept or oppose. As most of the things engineered by the top leaders were adverse to the marginalised people; they had no choice than to oppose and oppose. God knows how many times the Black Africans walked out of the National Assembly in Khartoum in protest to one harmful decision after another since the so-called independence of 1956, just to give one example. A lot also were arrested and imprisoned many times for peacefully opposing negative policies of oppressive regimes to the extent that the prisons became almost like their own homes. None of them had any chance of walking out from a prison to the seat of the president of Sudan like Nelson Mandela of South Africa.

It took South Sudan fifty years to rise to the level of the first vice president and that is even a secondary position. Should it wait another fifty years to become a national top runner? Even if the South had the patience to wait another half a century, what is the guarantee that they will not remain second-class runners forever? Do people of the South and Abyei want to remain in opposition forever?

I guess these are questions that will undoubtedly influence the direction of voting in the referendum.

P6.19 REJECTION

Rejection is the rejecting of something or somebody, or the act of being rejected. If South Sudan secedes, it is basically because it has been rejected by the rest of Sudan. The people and land of South Sudan have been pleading for five mandatory things in one package and they have been denied. These five things are DEMOCRACY, FREEDOM, EQUALTY, JUSTICE, and SECULARISM in absolute terms. Instead they are offered other packages that have continued to harm them severely for a very long time, as elaborated above.

DEMOCRACY is a system of government based on the principle of majority decision making. The Black African majority who predominantly reside in rural Sudan are undermined.

FREEDOM is a state in which somebody is able to act and live as he or she chooses, without being subjected to any undue restraints and restrictions. In a system where discriminatory Sharia laws, slavery, and social marginalisation are norms, just to give three examples, absolute freedom is nonexistent.

EQUALITY is a state in which rights, treatment, quantity, or values are equal to all others in a given group. Full equality under the law cannot exist where women and Black Africans are regarded and treated as inferior compared to "Arab" males. For example, a Black African non-Muslim is not eligible to become the president of Sudan. It took fifty years of contemporary warfare for a Black African non-Muslim to achieve a position of the first vice president, with precautions put in place to ensure that he does not inherit the presidency for a second if the president dies; it must be inherited by another "Arab" Muslim temporarily or permanently.

JUSTICE is fairness or reasonableness, especially in the way people are treated or decisions are made. Instead of justice, the large indigenous majority of Sudan is subjected to oppression, torture and enslavement, as elaborated above. There can be no justice where the law itself is discriminatory and where inhuman practises happen in the face of the law.

SECULARISM is the belief that religion and religious bodies should have no part in political or civic affairs or in running public institutions, especially schools. To others, Islam as a religion cannot be separated from the state or governance. Likewise, there is no compromise that can be reached with those who cannot accept to be governed under Islamic religion.

"Give me five," South Sudan cried for over fifty years or more. "No!" all successive governments based in Khartoum since independence refused. Six years of interim period is enough for this long cry to be met in total in order to give unity a chance. Otherwise, rejected South Sudan will have no option but to go in 2011.

P6.20 OBLIGATION

Obligation is something that must be done because of legal or moral duty.

The people of South Sudan are obliged to their promised land of South Sudan to defend and own it. They have tried over the years to share it with the rest of Sudan through unity and that only brought destruction, exploitation, and suffering to say the least.

They are also obliged and grateful to all millions of their martyrs and the Almighty God without whom no referendum would have been agreed to at all. The least that can be done to them is to honour that referendum letter by letter and make a decisive vote for permanent peace and stability in 2011.

P6.21 NON-ATTRACTION

A golden opportunity was provided to make Unity attractive to the land and people of Southern Sudan during the six-year interim period (2005-2011). If this is done effectively, it will encourage people of Southern Sudan to vote for unity in the 2011 referendum.

At the time this book was published, at the fourth year of the Interim Period, not much had been done to make unity attractive. Not a single national project has been revived or implemented in South Sudan by the Government of National Unity in order to make unity attractive. Instead a negative attitude has been developed that the South is already going whatever the North does and there is no need to waste resources of the North on it. These are just lame excuses to continue to justify their long-term strategy of marginalisation and economic deprivation. If the South refuses to vote for Unity later, it is simply because the opportunity to make it attractive was lost.

The above-mentioned twenty-one reasons for secession may appear too many. Yet they are just few of my own and I believe there are more justifications in the minds of other fellow marginalised people of Sudan.

P7 POINTS AGAINST SECESSION OR INDEPENDENCE OF SOUTH SUDAN

There are arguments put forth by others as their points against secession of South Sudan. They include some of the following:

P7.1 LOW EDUCATION LEVEL They assert that the level of education of people of South Sudan is too low to enable them to effectively run their own country. Apparently, this was the same argument used in the past, as far back as 1947 to deny the people and the land of South Sudan the right of self-determination. Not even federation was offered for similar reasons.

It is true that the level of education could have been very low in the past compared to those in Central Sudan. However things have now moved on many years later to the extent that the people of South Sudan now hold more degrees and certificates on their shelves. Furthermore, South Sudan, like other marginalised areas of Sudan, is deliberately deprived of education in order to continue to be oppressed and marginalised. The best way to increase the level of literacy in South Sudan is actually to allow secession to avoid suppression of education as a weapon of oppression. Furthermore, with the little education we the people of South Sudan have, we have managed to prove to the world that we can manage our own affairs, during the period of the High Executive Council (1972–1982) and the current era of the Government of Southern Sudan (2005–2011). It is also possible that the number of people of South Sudan that are literate at the moment exceed those of other countries at the time of their independences, putting into consideration all those that continued to learn internally and in Diaspora during the war (1983–2008).

There is also no threshold of a level of education that is specified to be reached before any group of people are allowed to exercise their right to self-determination, as far as I know.

P7.2 LANDLOCKED Some believe South Sudan cannot succeed to manage its economy if it becomes independent because it is landlocked. This is also an archaic argument. There are a lot of land-locked countries that gained their total freedom and are now thriving in all the continents of the world. Neighbouring ports can be shared with amicable agreements. The world has also moved on to the extent that there are huge aircraft carriers that can be used to airlift essential goods to any destination. These can be used in lieu of ships apart from trains that can carry goods from one country to another without necessarily crossing a sea or an ocean. There are ways around landlocking and this should not continue to be used to deny the land and people of South their right to secede if they want to.

P7.3 PROTECTION OF WATER OF THE NILE Some think that if people of South Sudan are allowed to become independent, they will block the water of the Nile not to flow to North Sudan and Egypt, thereby jeopardizing the lives of People in those areas. For the last 1,549 years that the People of Kush and New Kush have been struggling (460–2009), there is not a single report that they ever deliberately interfered with the natural flow of the water of the Nile in any direction. The opposition waged against the digging of Jonglei Canal was not based on depriving Egypt with water. It was because of the serious hazardous consequences of that canal on the local inhabitants.

The people of South Sudan will respect the Nile Agreements as long as they do not risk their own livelihood and survival. Therefore, neither North Sudan nor Egypt should fear that South Sudan will interfere with the natural flow of water to their areas.

P7.4 INSECURITY Others say the ongoing insecurity in South Sudan may spill to the regions if it becomes independent. It is true that there is a widespread level of insecurity currently in South Sudan. There are clashes over cattle raiding. The Lord Resistance Army (LRA) and Ombororo are inflicting disastrous damage on civil populations in many parts of South Sudan. However, most of this insecurity is deliberately engineered by those who want to use as a reason to project people of South Sudan as those that cannot succeed to rule themselves. They arm the civilians, establish, and use militias or members of their organised armed forces.

Indeed South Sudan will never become secured until it delinks from the Central Clique of Sudan. It will then independently use its legal organs to establish law and order without interference of malicious rivals. This way, it can contribute to overall regional security.

P7.5 UNLEASHING TERRORISTS Interestingly, there are few, especially in some parts of Europe that feel that if South Sudan becomes independent, terrorists they are blocking in North Sudan will be unleashed and can hit the rest of the world. They prefer that the people of South Sudan should continue to be used as an internal human shield to contain these terrorists inside the boundary of a united Sudan.

Surely, the proponents of this strategy have got it totally wrong. The world generally and the rest of Africa behind South Sudan is better protected by a strong independent South Sudan than a weak, oppressed South Sudan. The responsibility of combating international terrorism should be a shared one by all nations opposed to it. Besides, it is unfair and inhuman to allow the people of South Sudan to be exterminated internally by terrorists in a united Sudan as human shields for others. It is equally inconsiderate to consider them as mere human shields for others. It is better to allow South Sudan to become independent and provide it with effective defensive mechanism to contribute to the overall safety of the rest of Africa and the world at large.

P7.6 POVERTY Other circles argue that South Sudan is too poor to succeed to survive as an independent country. In fact, the South is poor simply because it is robbed of its resources in a united Sudan. It will be better of economically when it becomes independent to manage its own definitive resources. For example, it will not be bound to continue to allow 50 percent of its oil to be compulsorily taken by the Central Government of Sudan.

The reason why South Sudan was not allowed to become independent for many years is not because it is poor. On the contrary, it is because it is rich with a lot of natural resources. If it was poor, the rest of Sudan would not have seen the need to hang on to it all these years. It could have gained its full freedom a long time ago.

Those who think the South is too poor to become independent should try to understand why the ruling National Congress Party in Sudan insists nowadays to engage the Sudan People's Liberation Movement in discussions about post-referendum arrangements They want the South to go with some of the debts incurred without its consent from the International Monetary Fund. They also want the rich South to agree to concede some of its oilfields or continue to allow some percentage of its oil to go to the Government of North Sudan afterward. If the South was a poor weakling that could not stand on its own feet, all this talk about post-referendum arrangements would not arise.

Furthermore, many independent nations in Asia and Africa, for example, are described as poor developing countries. They are pushing forward to enjoy fruits of their independence without being asked to give up their sovereignty and emerge totally with other countries for reasons of extreme poverty. Economic alliances like the ones forged by the American and European Countries for mutual economic survival. An independent South Sudan can join IGAD Countries and mutually survive.

Poverty that arises from long-term economic marginalisation and deprivation in a united Sudan, in addition to continuous failure to make unity attractive, can best be resolved by secession.

P7.7 UNSTABLE CONTINENT

Creation of new states is not encouraged by some African and European countries in light of the overall instability of the African continent. However, a main contributing factor to this instability in Africa is a long-standing war involving South

Sudan and Abyei Area. Resolving these conflicts permanently through exercises of self-determination is the best way to bring about stability in the continent whether or not this leads to creation of new states. Both Africa and Europe would be more unstable now if the previous wars for independence and territorial control were continued till now and not resolved through creation of sovereign states.

P7.8 UNSTABLE ECONOMY

Any country that has just emerged from war will start with a nonexistent, poor, and unstable economy. Furthermore, continuation of economic deprivation by Khartoum underpaying oil money and marginalisation by not starting at least one national project in South Sudan and Abyei are major causes of economic instability in these areas. Unless economic deprivation and marginalisation are nipped in the bud and the weeds that cause them are permanently pushed aside via secession, South Sudan will remain forever underdeveloped.

P7.9 POLITICAL FRAGILITY

As long as some circles of Northern Sudan continue to destabilize South Sudan politically through encouragement of dissidents and saboteurs and as long as they continue to compromise its security via militias, it will remain politically fragile. Despite these obstacles, the Government of Southern Sudan has managed to contribute to the improvement of the political situation as stated by President Salva Kiir Mayardit below:

"Let me state it in no certain terms that the Government of Southern Sudan has come a long way since the signing of the CPA and we have been able not only to start building Southern Sudan from scratch but we have been able politically to contribute toward transforming and shaping Sudan for better."

If the CPA is fully implemented, these fruits that are beginning to emerge will increase and the longstanding political conflict involving South Sudan and Abyei will be permanently resolved. The reverse would be to return to war and cause more political fragility and economic instability in these areas.

P8 SUCCESS OF REFERENDUM OR POPULAR CONSULTATION: Prepare well and Beware our people!

For the referendum or popular consultation to succeed, adequate preparation and prevention of pitfalls are vital.

P8.1 PREPARATION FOR 2011 REFERENDUM AND POPULAR CONSULTATIONS

- Appropriate referendum and popular consultation laws must be passed with internal regulations
- Existing laws that inhibit democracy must be repealed
- Respective commissions, observers or monitors must be appointed in time and empowered
- Adequate funding should be budgeted for and timely availed with operational plan and timelines
- Various units of law enforcement agencies should be trained to protect the people and maintain law and order during the voting
- The population that will vote should be properly registered and adequately educated on how to practically participate in these exercises of self-determination
- Prospective pitfalls must be anticipated and prevented as discussed fully below.

P8.02 PREVENTION OF PITFALLS

Below are some things that can go wrong and affect the process and outcome of the referendum or popular consultation in Sudan in the year 2011 unless they are anticipated and prevented:

P8.1 SLEEPING

If people sleep before, during or after a referendum or Popular Consultation, or become complacent and overconfident, they can lose its outcome. There is a need to beware and remain continuously vigilant because anything can go wrong in the process. The reason why some succeed and others fail in life is because while those that succeed work hard day and night, the ones that fail remain asleep at that time.

P8.2 LEGISLATION-DELAYING (LAWS AND REGULATIONS)

The Referendum Bill should have been presented and enacted into law before the end of the Fourth Year of the Interim Period i.e., 9 July 2009 as per the Comprehensive Peace Agreement (CPA). Feet-dragging by the National Congress Party to delay the passing of this law well beyond the time limit is a tactic intended to block the referendum or provoke Southern Sudanese and People of Abyei to start war and use that as a pretext to cancel the CPA completely.

The same delay tactic is aimed at pushing the enactment of this bill till after the forthcoming elections in 2010 when the proportion of SPLM representatives will dwindle to a level that cannot protect the CPA as a whole and the referendum in particular. Then the provisions pertaining to the CPA and the referendum in the Interim Constitution of Republic of Sudan can be scrubbed against the will of the SPLM.

All the existing weight of the SPLM was thrown behind the process of ensuring that the 2011 referendum law should be enacted satisfactorily by the National Assembly before the 2010 elections, preferably by December 2009. This succeeded. The referendum law was at last passed; but the referendum commission was yet to be established up to the time this book was published. Nevertheless, an exceptional level of patience should continue to be exercised by the SPLM to avoid being provoked by the NCP to restart the war. However, peaceful methods like the recent walkout of the SPLM members from the Sudan National Assembly in Khartoum in protest of the delay in the presentation of the Referendum Bill is a necessary, heroic, and commendable move.

I would like to commend the SPLM leadership for continuing to exercise an exceptional level of restrain in the face of ongoing serious intimidation by the NCP. The arbitrary arrest of SPLM Secretary General Pagan Amum, Deputy Secretary General Yasir Araman, and associated political leaders in early December 2009 is an example of severe provocation that could trigger widespread unrest and possible war. Fortunately, the SPLM top leadership opted to do everything possible to avoid dragging the country back to a disastrous war and call instead for the vital laws to be enacted by the current Legislative Assembly, including the referendum and popular consultation Laws:

Press Release: SPLM Chairman's Address to the Nation

08 December 2009

07 December 2009

Current Political Situation

Fellow Sudanese citizens and friends, I take this opportunity to address the nation on the current political situation in our country. You are all aware that this morning the political situation in the country has taken yet another shocking direction.

Members of the SPLM leadership, constitutional post holders, and members of national legislature in Khartoum have been illegally arrested and this prompted us to call for an emergency meeting of the SPLM Leadership where it was resolved that the situation must be contained. The SPLM leadership also resolved to use all the necessary means to ensure that the country does not reverse to war. These arrests are not only provocative but unjustified because the Interim National Constitution of the Sudan (INC) and the CPA allow for peaceful and democratic procession to express political opinion.

In this regard, the SPLM and other political parties countrywide have been pressurizing the NCP to repeal those laws that inhibit the democratic process and for the current National Assembly to pass the necessary laws that foster full democratic transformation of the country. Unfortunately, the NCP leadership has been resisting constitutional obligations by using their mechanical majority in both organs of government to pursue their own political agenda. This implicitly maintains the status quo and old mentality of doing business contrary to the letter and spirit of the CPA. In order to normally proceed with the implementation of the CPA, I call upon the NCP leadership to extend the life span of this current assembly to enable it to pass all the necessary laws required for smooth transition to democracy.

Fellow citizens, the SPLM is committed to peace and stability in the country and accept such procession as an expression of the free will of the people. We therefore call upon the NCP leadership to unconditionally release all detainees who include the SPLM secretary general, his deputy, and other comrades and any other Sudanese who were arrested this morning. We also hope that these citizens of the country have not been mishandled during the period of detention. Those officers who arrested our members should be brought to books. It should be noted that any continuation in the arbitrary detention of people will only worsen matters and will not serve the peace and stability of the country.

Finally, we call upon all Sudanese people to remain calm and to exercise ultimate restraint and exercise their constitutional rights of expression within the law. The SPLM and the NCP should jointly move quickly to work together to resolve the outstanding issues of CPA in order to allow the democratic transformation process to ensue. I have just spoken with President Al Bashir and we both have agreed to maintain calm and restraint during this critical moment of our history. President Bashir has reassured me that all detainees will be released. We have also discussed the need to urgently pass the Southern Sudan Referendum Law, Abyei Referendum Law, and the Popular Consultation Law, National Security Law, the Criminal Procedure Act, the Penal Code, and the Repeal of Public Order Act, Popular Police Act, and Popular Defence Act by the current assembly.

P8.3 NON-BOUNDARY DRAWING

The reason why the NCP is also dragging their feet in allowing the Southern Sudan Boundary to be drawn as well as implementing The Hague ruling for the Abyei Boundary is similarly linked to attempts to interfere with the referendum in those areas. This is apart from issues related to oil-sharing.

Of course the referendum can still be conducted, especially now that it is agreed to be conducted in specified centers all over the Sudan and abroad! However, the exact area where the outcome of the referendum will be implemented if it is recession of Southern Sudan or becoming part of Bahr-el-Ghazal in the case of Abyei will remain ambiguous without mapping out the North-South or North-Abyei Boundaries. This ambiguity can be a potential source of future conflict at contested sites of those boundaries in the near future. Therefore, these boundaries should be drawn without further delay in the interest of all to avoid an irresolvable Kashmir-like war erupting later in Sudan.

P8.4 POSTPONING

The date agreed for the referendum to take place should not be exceeded lest it can be deferred indefinitely. Besides, postponement may trigger conflict and war that can lead to cancellation of the referendum.

Another factor that can interfere with any elections and referenda is the rainy season. Luckily, the month of January when the referendum is planned to take place falls outside the rainy season.

P8.5 CANCELLING

Cancelling an agreed referendum or popular consultation by anyone is a recipe for trouble. An example is the abrogation of the 1972 Addis Ababa Agreement by Sudan President Jaafar Mohammed Nemeiry, which triggered the SPLA War.

P8.6 RIGGING

A Referendum can be rigged, especially be those opposed to it. This can be done by allowing staff at polling stations to tick options on behalf of the voters under the pretext that they are helping. Wrong options can be ticked against the wish of the voters or many votes can be ticked secretly by individuals in order to negatively influence the outcome.

P8.7 BRIBING

Money can be used to bribe voters to vote otherwise, contrary to their desire. Therefore voters should be educated to either reject the dirty money or accept it and still vote secretly the way they actually desire. They can also report the bribers so that they can be dealt with by law.

P8.8 INTIMIDATING

Voters maybe threatened and intimidated to vote against their wish. They should be educated that they are protected by law and should not be frightened. Such legal protection must be visibly provided in every polling station.

P8.9 ABSTAINING

Where the outcome of the referendum depends on proportion of votes cast and ultimate percentage obtained, it becomes absolutely necessary that every voter is encouraged to attend and vote in time. Misinforming voters that the referendum is cancelled or deferred when it is not can lead to many abstentions. Besides, they can be deliberately frightened off not to attend and vote. These must not be allowed to happen through positive and massive voter education, apart from putting adequate protective measures in place.

In the case of the South Sudan referendum in 2011, if two-thirds of the registered voters fail to cast their votes, its result will not be recognised even if it is 100 percent. Besides, unless at least 50 percent+1 vote for secession, the opportunity for South Sudan to become independent through the ballot will have slipped off indefinitely. Therefore, every Southern Sudanese that is registered and bears and does not want to remain a slave in a united Sudan forever, must attend the referendum in 2011 and cast the vote.

P8.10 MISTAKING

Making mistakes during voting can prove very costly. For example, ticking or thumbing the wrong side of the vote. Or thumbing the correct side and failing to insert the vote into the ballot box. Even conceding to ticking as the procedure of voting as opposed to thumbing when most of the expected voters of South Sudan are illiterate. Such mistakes should be avoided by all means.

P8.11 DELAYED COUNTING

If counting is delayed after a ballot box is filled and sealed, a number of things can happen. Ballot boxes can disappear or be replaced with wrong ones however scrupulous their protection is through deliberate human bias or uncovered loopholes. Unfilled ballot boxes can be opened, stacked with false votes and resealed. Therefore, counting of ballot boxes should run concurrently with voting.

P8.12 UNDER-RESOURCING

Limiting resources required to efficiently conduct the referendum can be used to fail it. Human resources in terms of conducting, supervising, monitoring, and protecting voting and voters for example, may be overwhelmed if inadequate. Financial resources may be restricted to under-fund the referendum and de-motivate the staff. Material resources required for carrying it out such as ballot boxes and actual paper votes may not be provided sufficiently or in time.

Learning from the recent census, conducted in Sudan, a lot of centers in Southern Sudan did not receive census forms in time. As a result, many areas were under-counted. Nevertheless, the census in Southern Sudan would have been a lot worse if the Government of Southern Sudan did not rescue the situation by injecting some of its own money. The same may have to be done for the referendum to succeed.

P8.13 UNDERCOUNTING

Cast votes may be undercounted where the leading result is not the one desired by staff at a polling station. Learning again from the recent census in Sudan, the number of Southern Sudanese in states of Northern Sudan was deliberately undercounted. Likewise, the number of votes cast in those Northern states for secession of Southern Sudan can be undercounted unless extra precautions are taken to prevent that.

P8.14 INFLATING

Other than undercounting undesired votes, desired ones can be inflated. In Darfur, for instance, the proportion of Arab tribes was overinflated in contrast to African ethnic groups during the recent Sudan census. Thus the proportion of those opting to remain in Kordufan under special arrangements can be overinflated well above those preferring to join Bahr-el-Ghazal in the case of the Abyei referendum. Similarly, those opting for unity of Sudan can be overinflated in the referendum of Southern Sudan at centers located in the states of Northern Sudan or Arab countries that are opposed to secession of Southern Sudan. Effective counteractive measures, proven to have worked elsewhere in the world must be agreed up on and put in place to avoid this malice.

P8.15 SOUTHERNIZING

Non-Southern Sudanese may be made to falsely claim and register as Southern Sudanese in order to become eligible voters in the Southern Sudan referendum. The same can happen in the case of the Abyei referendum and Popular Consultations where nonresidents or noncitizens can falsely legitimize their voting status. Southernizing, Abyei-nizing, Nuba-nizing, and Southern Blue Niling is a real risk that cannot be ignored. For example, during the war, a lot people in Northern Sudan are reported to have falsely claimed as Southern Sudanese using forged birth or age assessment certificates in order to occupy positions earmarked for Southern Sudanese there. The simple use of such certificates to justify being a Southern Sudanese, for example, should no longer be allowed. Besides, definition of eligible voters in the referenda and Popular Consultations should be crystal clear and strictly adhered to.

P8.16 VOTE DIVERTING

Counting actual votes wrongly is a common way of altering results of a referendum. In the case of the Southern Sudan referendum, for instance, votes for secession may be diverted and counted as those for unity. Therefore manual counting must be done transparently in front of observers, monitors, and representatives to avoid any falsification and misinterpretation.

P8.17 MISTIMING

If voters do not exactly remember the exact period of polling, they may turn up only after the voting is over. They should constantly be reminded of the deadline for voting and encouraged to attend and vote before then. In fact, the voting register can be scrutinized daily to identify those that have not yet cast their votes as potential defaulters to be targeted and reminded.

P8.18 IMPERSONATING

If a meticulous identification procedure is not followed, other people can impersonate actual voters and cast votes as ineligible voters. By the time the actual voters arrive, they will be told they had already voted when they had not. This can lead to clashes and crises in the polling stations, apart from producing a negative, unexpected outcome.

P8-19 VOTERS CARD BUYING

As seen in recent voter registration, voters' identity cards are bought by saboteurs who want to destroy them or those who intend to use them later to cast illegal votes to their interest. The same can happen in the case of referendum and popular consultations. For example, those who want to vote for unity of Sudan may buy these cards and use them to their advantage.

This can be prevented by educating people not to sell their cards whatever the amount of money paid. Selling them would mean they have sold the Land and People, including themselves, to permanent slavery and misery and no amount of money on Earth can justify that.

P8-20 GHOST-NAMING

Ghost names can be included in the voting register and used negatively. This can be prevented by correctly identifying eligible voters and issuing them with voting identification cards before the referendum.

P8.21 DISRUPTING

Voting can be deliberately disrupted by saboteurs and antagonists. For example, opposing voters can be provoked to fight. Polling stations can be attacked militarily to disrupt and stop the voting. They can also be burned down or bombed deliberately.

Another simpler way of disrupting and distorting the referendum or popular consultations is the stealing or robbing of voters' registers for destruction or malicious use.

The level of security must be raised to its maximum and every step possible should be taken by protective forces to avert any form of disruption.

P8.22 BODY-MASKING

Covering the entire face and body with opaque veils can be used to mask ineligible voters under the cover of Islamic dress. For example, men can be dressed as women with Islamic veils by criminals that want to abuse the true faith of Islam and use it to negatively influence the outcome of a referendum.

Reliable security women that are genuine Southern Sudanese must be involved to check any voters that come with all bodies including faces covered to ensure they are not masked ineligible voters.

This now an acceptable practise in places like airports for public safety and security as long as a female is searched by another female. There is no reason why the same procedure of checking is not applied in a referendum.

P8.23 BOYCOTTING

Boycotting an exercise of self-determination like a referendum by genuine eligible voters in order to fail it is probably academic, as it would be a senseless and unwise error. People who fought for so long and sacrificed many lives and vital body parts are unlikely to boycott a process of exercising their right to self-determination. However, those that forged eligibility to vote can do so if they believe they constitute two-thirds of the registered voters in order to nullify the result in the case of the Southern Sudan referendum where at least two-thirds is required to validate the outcome. Nevertheless, why would they do so when they can simply use their perceived majority to obtain the result they want through the ballot box?

P8.24 OVERRELYING

It is good to be confident and not overconfident. It is also good to rely on one another as one people with a common fate. However, if we simply over-rely on ourselves and remain complacent without doing more to ensure that the forthcoming referenda and Popular Consultations are conducted fair and free, we will lose.

P8.25 BIASED DATA PROGRAMMING

The machine used to analyze data of votes may be programmed with a bias to produce a predetermined outcome. For example, it may be programmed by those who desire the option of unity in the Southern Sudan referendum to give an ultimate result of unity, even though the actual choice that won is secession. This can be done if the machine is obtained or purchased from a country that is opposed to independence of Southern Sudan, or a country that has been influenced by political leaders in or outside the government of Sudan that are prepared to do anything humanly possible to block the separation of Southern Sudan.

In fact, what happened in Florida during the elections of George Bush and Al Gore illustrates that reliance on machines for voting can lead to huge problems and serious election disputes even in very advanced nations, not to speak of underdeveloped countries like Sudan.

To prevent this bias or mechanical faults, the SPLM and the Government of Southern Sudan should object to use of a machine for analysis of votes in the referendum and Popular Consultations, especially if it is provided by a country that was opposed to the SPLA/M during the war. The data should first be counted and analyzed manually in front of all observers and representatives and, if need be, subsequent mechanical analysis can follow for simple verification and confirmation. A rumour that a programmable machine is planned to be purchased from France by the government of the Republic of Sudan and used to predetermine the outcome of 2011 referendum of Southern Sudan and Abyei should not be dismissed simply as a smoke without fire. Allowing such a machine to be used and later complaining after the result is out will be nothing more than a step too late.

P8.26 RESULT FORGING

Apart from falsifying votes and voting eligibility as stated above, the entire result of a referendum or popular consultation can be forged and declared different from the real one. This can be done by the leadership of a relevant commission. Therefore it is of utmost importance that trusted members of the SPLM occupy the leadership positions of the referendum commission or popular consultation commissions or committees in order to safeguard against such last-minute disastrous alterations or forgeries.

P8.27 RESULT DENYING

Even though the voting goes on well and all observers are satisfied with the correct procedure, the defeated side can still reject the outcome of a referendum in a last and desperate attempt to foil it and block its implementation. Should this happen, the positive outcome must be immediately declared and implemented with regional and international support. For example, if the result of the referendum of South Sudan is secession by over 50 percent+1, and it is not publicly declared within the agreed period, it can prove a disastrous error. It will give its antagonists opportunity to sabotage or reverse it.

P8.28 LEADERS ELIMINATING

When they fail to defeat leaders, losers sometimes resort to assassination. What happened to William Deng Nhial after winning elections, as stated earlier in this book, is a relevant example. Kennedy, Ghandi, and Bhouto are examples of leaders eliminated in other parts of the world before or after successful elections. Therefore, it is of utmost importance that maximum protection must be accorded to all our leaders as they are obvious targets of opponents of self-determination. What happened recently in Kampala, when the tyre of plane carrying our leader Salva Kiir Mayardit burst into pieces just before takeoff is a serious warning sign that cannot and should not be ignored. All rumours poured into the air by evil-wishers about his death whenever he visits a place like Uganda should not be viewed as simple smoke without fire.

So, if we win the referendum, let us celebrate while we watch our backs!

These are just few examples that come to mind of things to watch out for. There are probably more than that which others can elaborate on. The important thing to remember is that anything can go wrong with voting in a referendum or popular consultation. Therefore, the land and people of South Sudan and Abyei must take all precautions to ensure that their will is not distorted or averted in the referenda. The same applies to the Nuba Mountains and Southern Blue Nile in terms of their popular consultations.

The opportunity for these areas to achieve their right to exercise self-determination through referendum or popular consultation came after long bloodshed and huge suffering and sacrifice. Such an opportunity should not be foiled or allowed to slip away.

As they say, opportunity does not knock twice. If this opportunity of exercising self-determination is missed or misused, it will never arise again. To exercise it properly and successfully, the following practical suggestions should be considered:

ONE PRIORITY: We who will exercise it should look at referendum or popular consultation as our number one priority, if not the only one as we approach the year 2011.

ONE LEADERSHIP: We who share a common fate as one people should all rally behind one leader irrespective of any differences or political parties if only for the purpose of letting self-determination succeed. If the children of Israel did not rally all behind Joshua, he would not have delivered them to their Promised Land and our Joshua is Salva Kiir Mayardit.

ONE TEAM: Learning from sports, we should also exercise our will as one well organised and cooperative team in order to win the vital matches.

ONE CHOICE: Having failed to make unity attractive, there is only one crystal clear choice and that is secession for South

Sudan and Bahr-el-Ghazal for Abyei; the alternative is permanent slavery and second-class citizenship. Therefore, we must bear one choice in all our minds and avoid wavering.

ONE TONGUE: With one choice in mind, we must talk in one tongue as we approach 9 January 2011. The only words to be transcribed from the tip to the base of our tongues are two: ultimate freedom. Then we will guarantee that we shall not by mistake pronounce other ambiguous words that can confuse our people at the crucial time when they need to focus and determine their rightful future.

ONE VOTE: If we have one choice in mind and we speak in the same tongue, we are likely to cast one vote as a team under one leadership with exercise of self-determination as the top priority. We cannot risk casting different votes when we intend to liberate our land and ourselves from misery and slavery. Let us march in our millions to the polling stations, throw in the same vote, and walk out proud and free.

P9 POST-REFERENDUM ARRANGEMENTS

As stated earlier, the debate on post-referendum arrangements is underway. This has necessitated a symposium to be organised by the Government of Southern Sudan in Juba on 5–6 of December 2009 at Southern Sudan Legislative Assembly, under the forum entitled: Public Forum Southern: Preparing for 2011 and Beyond.

This symposium was opened by General Salva Kiir Mayardit, first vice president of the Republic of Sudan and president of Government of Southern Sudan (GOSS) with the following remarks:

Opening Remarks
By
H.E General Salva Kiir Mayardit,

First Vice President of the Republic, and President of the Government of Southern Sudan
Symposium on "Southern Sudan: Preparing for 2011 and Beyond"
Southern Sudan Legislative Assembly
5 December 2009

- **H. E Dry. Riek Machar Teny**—Vice President of the Government of Southern Sudan
- **Hon. Peter Gbandi**—Acting Speaker of Southern Sudan Legislative Assembly
- **Justice John Wol Makkec**—President of the Supreme Court
- **Presidential Advisors**
- **Representatives of Political Parties**
- **Ministers at All Levels of Government**
- **Members of the Various Legislatures**
- **Representatives of the Diplomatic Missions**
- **Religious Leaders**
- **Ladies and Gentlemen**

I feel honoured to address the opening session of this symposium, which in my view represents our total determination and commitment to fully implement the CPA. I thank you all for sparing time from your busy schedules to come and participate in this important event.

Before I proceed with my remarks, may we all stand up to observe a minute of silence to remember our fallen brothers and sisters who sacrificed their lives for the sake of our peace and freedom? Addressing post-referendum issues is critical to the full implementation of the CPA and the future of our country. This symposium provides a vital opportunity for the people of the Sudan to discuss the post-referendum challenges and come up with practical solution in order to ensure lasting peace and stability in the country.

As we are all aware, the people of Southern Sudan and Abyei Area will exercise their rights of self-determination in the next thirteen months. In this referendum, the people of Southern Sudan will choose between a united Sudan or opt for a separate state. In a similar manner the people of Abyei Area can choose to either remain in the North or join the South.

The right to self-determination of the people of Southern Sudan is not something anyone who is concerned about the future of this country should downplay. The 2011 referendum is a historical opportunity for the people of the Sudan to peacefully determine the political destiny of the country. I think whatever strong views or opinions we hold as political parties, politicians, or individuals, it is important that we all prepare ourselves for both scenarios of either a vote for independence or vote for continued unity.

I know that the CPA has been a very bumpy ride since its signing in 2005, but the right of the people of Southern Sudan in 2011 to choose their political destiny survived this bumpy ride. Should the road toward 2011 referendum be deliberately made impossible by any person, political party or group then it will be the responsibility of the peace loving people of the Sudan to make it possible. As stated by our late Chairman Dr. John Garang that in order to fully implement the CPA, we should make the cost of non-implementation of CPA more than the cost of its implementation. This symposium is an attempt to increase the cost of non-implementation of CPA and to make the implementation of CPA peaceful and attractive.

The 2011 referendum must be fully a free and fair process in which the people not the politicians can make their own judgment on either unity or separation. This process must be totally free from any manipulation or intimidation. For those who will be campaigning for either the two options, it must be a battle to win hearts and minds and to accept the outcome in a humble manner. In this game, the people and not the politicians will be the only players.

For those who still think they can impose their own political views on the people of Southern Sudan during the referendum, I think it is in the interest of all political parties in the country to respect the free will of the people. Gone are the days in which politicians were capable of patronizing the people's minds. We are today living in a free world in which even the people in rural areas have a clue about their political rights.

We will work with all political parties in the country to push for the passage of laws that can facilitate the peaceful conduct of the referendum for the people of Southern Sudan in 2011. We will not allow any form of intimidation or disruption of what has to be a truly valid representation of the will of the people.

We are all aware of efforts by certain circles to frustrate the 2011 referendum. Various prophets of doom and gloom have already gone further to claim that if Southern Sudan was to become independent it would be a failed state. Let me state it in no certain terms that the Government of Southern Sudan has come a long way since the signing of the CPA. We have been able not only to start building Southern Sudan from scratch but we have been able politically to contribute toward transforming and shaping Sudan for better.

The limited space of freedom that we enjoy today in Sudan is because of the CPA which came as a result of the enormous sacrifices of the marginalised people of Sudan, particularly the people of Southern Sudan. Our people have suffered a great deal, and the minimum we can do is to protect their achievements in the CPA, particularly the exercise of the right of self-determination and popular consultation. As president of GOSS, I can tell you now that this government is not going to let the people of Southern Sudan fail to realise their political aspirations.

Morally and legally, I am personally bound to ensure full implementation of the CPA including the exercise of the right of self-determination. If the people vote for unity, we will ensure that Southern Sudan continuous its development into strong and vibrant entity within the wider framework of a viable and democratic united Sudan. Likewise, if the people vote to fulfil their right to self-determination and opt for secession, we will build on the foundation of the GOSS institutions and become a state that is strong, viable, prosperous, democratic politically inclusive, accountable, and able to live in peace with all its neighbours.

If we are to be equally well prepared for both of the possible referendum outcomes, then all of us have a lot of work to do in anticipation of January 2011. We need to ensure a peaceful and fair process with a high level on information particularly by citizens. We need to prepare ourselves to accept the outcome of the referendum. We need to develop mechanism for a smooth transition and implementation of the referendum outcome. Sadly, there are some who want, or at least expect us, to fail in this process—but I see no reason why we should.

We all know that January 2011 referendum will not by itself resolve the entire political issues pertaining to Sudan's historical problems. We therefore sincerely hope that a framework for a permanent resolution to the Darfur conflict, and the need of other marginalised areas within northern Sudan, can be found over the coming year—to enable the post-2011 period to be one of genuine peace and prosperity for all the peoples of the Sudan. I am confident that the people of the Sudan will come together and collectively determine the best outcome for their long-term future. Whichever of the two outcomes this may be, I urge our African neighbours and international community to abide by the choice of the people and support us to implement it.

I hope that this symposium will critically address key post-referendum issues and come up with practical recommendations to overcome any of the challenges during the post referendum period. Finally, my special thanks go to the Ministry of Presidential Affairs in the office of the president and the Southern Sudan Legislative Assembly for collaboratively organising this symposium. I also thank our development partners for contributing to the success of this historic event: The Public International Law and Public Group (PILPG), the World Bank, UNDP, Humanity United, and Chatham House.

I wish you success and May God Bless you all!

Post-referendum arrangements cover the following areas:

- **Declaration of Result**

  The first post-referendum arrangement is to declare the result without delay. Other post-referendum arrangements should not be used as strings attached to either prevent the referendum from taking place or block the pronouncement of the result. The referendum itself cannot be post until its outcome is declared.

  If the outcome is secession, the following text can be improved upon by political, legal, language and other experts and used for the declaration:

  Having won the vote to secede from the Republic of Sudan in an internationally supervised Referendum conducted from Ninth Day of the Month of January in the Year of our Lord 2011, I, General Salva Kiir Mayardit, in my capacity as the president of the Government of Southern Sudan, Chairman of the Sudan People's Liberation Movement and Commander in Chief of Sudan People's Liberation Army, hereby make the following declaration:

  The Land, People, and Spirits of Southern Sudan are now fully independent with effect from the ninth of January

2011. Their new Republic shall be called in short South Sudan till confirmed or altered through a popular or parliamentary consultation.

I equally direct for this will of the People to be implemented forthwith and call up on all nations and people of goodwill to support this newly born independent country to start to stand and walk. Likewise, on behalf of all the people of South Sudan, I would like to use this opportunity to wish the remaining Republic of Sudan good luck in its future as a sisterly neighbouring country.

Long Live the New Republic of South Sudan!

Long Live its Martyrs that sacrificed their lives for its liberty and its Survivors!

If the result is Unity of Sudan, the above draft can be altered and used to declare it.

- **Implementation of Result**

Similarly, the referendum cannot be considered as post until its outcome is implemented. Therefore the next post-referendum arrangement, in my view, is implementation of the result of that referendum.

Having been declared an independent country, for example, its president should be sworn in, a care-taking government appointed and sworn in, and people allowed to at least celebrate their real independence before other post-referendum arrangements are made.

- **Declaration of Permanent Principles (DOPP)**

While the result is being implemented, permanent principles will need to be formulated and declared. These will be used to govern the areas that conducted the referendum permanently depending on the outcome of the referendum.

Of course if the outcome is unity of Sudan, the principles will simply be those of the Government of Southern Sudan under the overall sovereignty of Sudan. Acceptance of second-class citizenship as a permanent standard will have been endorsed as a matter of principle.

On the other hand, should the choice be secession, the following draft can kick-start a more detailed and appropriate Declaration of Permanent Principles (DOPP):

The Land, People, and Spirits of South Sudan, having suffered so much for so long from segregate, racial, and religious oppression and slavery, which forced them ultimately to secede in a referendum conducted from the Ninth Day of the Month of January in the Year 2011, hereby make the following permanent declaration:

That at no time now and in the future must the People of this Land ever again be subjected to another segregate, racial, and religious oppression and/or condone any form of human slavery. The Land of South Sudan shall remain a racial free and secular country forever.

This can be expanded to incorporate the important overall principles of democracy, freedom, equality, and justice, all of which constituted the bases for the long and costly struggle from the year 640 AC.

- **Dispute Arbitration**

If the result of the referendum is contested, it can lead to serious military confrontation unless managed well. One way of managing it safely is to immediately involve regional and international arbitration. For example, if the result of the referendum of Southern Sudan is secession, this can be declared and an arbitration process simultaneously triggered in case of dispute over the result. The declaration can later be reviewed, depending on the ruling of arbitration. The same should apply in the case of the unity option.

- **Compensation**

  South Sudan can demand compensations for slavery and losses during the Anya-nya and SPLA/M wars from 1955.

- **Refunding**

  Funds owed to South Sudan and Abyei, from oil revenue since the beginning of its exploitation and shares of these areas from National Budgets that had been underpaid or unpaid since independence was imposed in Sudan in 1955 should be repaid to the people of South Sudan and Abyei.

- **Protective Shields**

  Measures to ensure that a secular African culture prevails forever in South Sudan should be put in place. International laws governing sovereignty and conventional international relationships must be complied with. South Sudan would be free to establish protective military allies.

- **Citizenship Rights**

  South Sudanese citizenship should be established as defined in interim constitution of South Sudan if the vote is recession. Other Sudanese will continue with Sudanese citizenship. Dual citizenship should be avoided initially.

- **Civil Service**

  Priority for civil service in South Sudan should go to South Sudanese and vice versa for North Sudan if the choice is secession.

- **Internally Displaced Persons (IDPs)**

  IDPs on either side should be allowed safe passage without any repercussions in the case of secession. They can opt to live anywhere in Sudan if the choice is unity of one Sudan.

- **Refugees**

  The Geneva Conventions should be used to govern how to deal with genuine refugees.

- **Transboundary Populations**

  Once the boundaries are clearly established, transboundary populations should be allowed to cross over and reside in areas where their citizenship definitely falls. After that, conventional international laws will guide interactions across borders.

- **Security Arrangements**

  These will be implemented as agreed in the Comprehensive Peace Agreement, depending on outcome of the referendum. For example, the SPLA component of the Joint Integrated Unit (JIU) will form the Army of South Sudan along with the rest of the SPLA outside the JIU.

International law prohibiting invasion of an independent country by another will be automatically invoked to ensure that peace and stability prevail between Old Sudan and South Sudan in case of secession.

- **International Arrangements**

South Sudan is expected to become a new member state of United Nations and it is more likely to exit from membership of the Arab League when it becomes an independent country. As stated above, conventional laws governing member states of the UN will be adopted and complied with.

- **Natural Resources: Land, Water, and Oil**

Once the boundaries are specified, sovereignty over respective land, water, and oil resources will be established. South Sudan will not prevent the natural flow of Nile water to benefit life beyond its boundary when it becomes independent. Likewise, other countries along the River Nile will not be expected to prevent South Sudan from using water of the Nile within its boundary to support and sustain life.

Ethnic groups like Misseriya will be encouraged to establish grazing areas and water sources within their defined localities in Northern Sudan. This will avoid unnecessary long migration southward and cross-border clashes. Should it become vital for these ethnic groups to gain access temporarily to water and grazing areas inside Southern Sudan, this can be allowed provided they leave behind any weapons and adhere to immigration requirements across neighbouring countries.

Oil fields must be strictly defined according to the boundaries of 1-1-1956. Thereafter, absolute ownership of the oil fields will be established automatically, depending on where they fall. South Sudan will have a 100 percent share of the oil that falls inside its map if it becomes independent. Terms will have to be negotiated and agreed up on if it opts to continue to use pipelines and refineries in Northern Sudan. It will consider the possibility of using any port and any company it prefers, depending on the extent of favourability of new terms. Of course, if relations continue to be cordial, prices of oil can be discounted between neighbouring countries without breaking international laws governing the sale of oil, if any.

- **Currency**

Northern Sudan can continue with the current Sudanese pound if it wants to while South Sudan can develop its own unique currency using its share of reserves deposited with the International Monetary Fund or World Bank. It can call its currency the South Sudan pound (SSD) or weng, as previously proposed, just to give two examples.

- **Division of Debts**

A third of the debts can be inherited by South Sudan provided that the Government of Southern Sudan was involved in acquiring them for debts after July 2005 and previous Southern Sudan Regional governments for debts from 1972–2005. South Sudan, however, will not be bound to inherit any debts that were obtained without its consent or for uses that did not in any way benefit it unless one-third of the current value of that loan is transferred in cash to the Bank of Southern Sudan

- **Division of Assets**

National assets will have to be shared in such a way that South Sudan takes a third of them. The ones based in the South can be automatically taken over by the South and the same applies to the North. However, as the value of the assets located in the South falls short of a third of the overall national assets, some of the assets in the North will have to be owned by the South and used as an embassy or business centres.

- **Economic Cooperation**

  Independent countries survive through regional and international economic cooperation. Therefore, South Sudan and North Sudan will follow suit if they become separate countries from 2011. Specific areas of such cooperation will be determined. For example, they can become members of IGAD.

- **Mutual Recognition**

If all goes well, it is expected that the two emerging independent countries will mutually recognise each other should the result of the referendum become secession. This way they will have started to sow seeds of future coexistence as friendly neighbours in peace and prosperity. For even bitter enemies can become great friends, after all, especially when they know each other so well!

The above-mentioned comments on post-referendum arrangements were made before resolutions or recommendations of the symposium on the 2011 referendum held in Juba on 5–6 December 2009 were obtained. If there are better arrangements than the ones suggested in this book, they will be welcome as long as they do not adversely affect South Sudan. South Sudan will not move from second-class citizenship to second class nationhood! The mentality and stratification of second-class must vanish instantly if the choice is secession.

P10 IS SOUTH SUDAN INDEPENDENCE INEVITABLE?

Salva Kiir: North Sudan "failed" to make unity attractive

Wednesday, 04 November 2009 09:18 Sudan Miraya FM

The first vice president and president of the Government of Southern Sudan, Salva Kiir Mayardit, said he cannot call on southerners to vote for unity in the absence of development in the south. He said the north has failed to make unity attractive for southerners. In the same context, Mr Salva Kiir urged southern Sudanese citizens to go to registration centres in high turnout areas in order to be able to elect their representatives in the upcoming general elections. His call came during a visit he paid to voter registration centres in Juba.

SPLM leading member, Deng Alor, called for what he described a "peaceful divorce" between Northern and Southern Sudan. Alor said the remaining time for the South Sudan referendum is insufficient to make unity attractive, pointing that the Government of National Unity did not make any developmental projects in the south. Alor's criticism came during a symposium on Unity and Self-Determination in Sudan, organised by the UN Mission in Sudan on Tuesday in Khartoum. Meanwhile, a member in the National Congress Party, Ghazi Salaheddine, accused SPLM of failing to govern the south, adding that "not holding elections on time would be a betrayal of the peace deal." He went on to say that South Sudan referendum "will not take place unless through an elected government."

Salva Kiir sells independence to Southern Sudanese

Sunday, 01 November 2009 15:51 Sudan Miraya FM

The president of Sudan's semi-autonomous south has urged southern Sudanese to vote for separation in the 2011 referendum.

Salva Kiir said, "Sudan remaining united will render the southern Sudanese second-class citizens, whereas separation will grant freedom."

Kiir spoke at the end of a mass at Saint Theresa's Cathedral in Juba on Saturday.

Is an independent South Sudan now inevitable?

4 NOVEMBER 2009 03:22 EST REUTER

http://blogs.reuters.com/africanews/files/2009/11/sudan.jpg

So, is it now inevitable that Sudan's oil-producing south will decide to split away from the north as an independent country in a looming secession referendum in 2011?

That was the conclusion of some observers of a bluntly worded exchange of views between two leading lights from the north and the south at a symposium in Khartoum on Tuesday.

Sudan's Muslim north fought a two-decade civil war with southerners, most of them Christians and followers of traditional beliefs. The 2005 peace deal that ended that conflict set up a north/south coalition government and promised a referendum on southern secession.

Sudan's foreign minister, Deng Alor, told journalists at the symposium most of his fellow southerners, embittered by decades of northern oppression and imposed Islamic values, "overwhelmingly" wanted independence. Only a miracle would change their minds, he said, going on to appeal for a "peaceful divorce" should the south choose to split.

Two days earlier, southern president Salva Kiir shocked many when he openly told a cathedral congregation they should choose independence if they wanted to be free and unity if they wanted to be "second class" in their own country.

Powerful northern presidential advisor Ghazi Salaheddin countered on Tuesday by accusing southerners of paranoia, "living in victimhood" and mismanaging their own semi-autonomous region. The comments were unusually blunt and personal for such a public venue. To many, their tone was a bitter reminder of the rhetoric routinely thrown around before the signing of the 2005 Comprehensive Peace Agreement (CPA).

Sudan commentator Alex de Waal wrote on his blog that many of the comments echoed what had been said in earlier closed sessions in the U.N. sponsored conference.

"During the earlier sessions of the symposium, the same theme was repeatedly made: Sudan is entering its last days as a single nation. Among the northerners, there was immense regret, but also acceptance of the inevitability of the split. One well-known Islamist said that secession was coming and the important thing was to make it smooth."

Managing a smooth secession would be a huge task for northerners and southerners weighed down by decades of mistrust and bitter grievance, poisoned by ethnic and religious divisions.

There are many good reasons for them to want a peaceful divorce, beyond avoiding another bloody conflict.

The biggest factor is that they both need each other when it comes to oil — the south has most of the country's proven oil reserves while the north currently has the refineries and the pipeline routes to the sea.

But any managed separation needs planning, and plenty of it. So far there has been no sign that the two sides have got together for any kind of strategising on the implications of separation after the referendum.

The head of the U.N. in Sudan, Ashraf Qazi, tried to accentuate the positive when he summed up Tuesday's discussions, saying both sides remained committed to the ideal of unity.

But there was a telling slip as he finished his summation.

"We are still at a moment of hope. And I believe that the leadership of the two *countries* which have ensured that the peace is maintained, that the ceasefire has not broken down, during the period of the CPA, they have already shown that responsibility. They can rise to the challenge even now."

RELATED PUBLIC COMMENTS

9 November 2009
5:47 am EST
They have tried, but with the glaring differences that have appeared, the north and the south look like an odd couple. Indeed, how can they reconcile things like sharia? With regard to resources, oil and water will be indeed major challenges as they need each other for efficient resource management. What will Egypt do? It depends on the south for its water supply. Will there be a rapprochement with Juba or will it back Khartoum? How about Kenya, also be key for the south, and other neighbours? The future will of course depend on great and middle powers policy: United States, Russia, China, France but also Iran. StrategiCo. currently rates Sudan 12/14 (14 = maximum risk).

Posted by Lydie Boka

10 November 2009
10:21 pm EST
Unfortunately it is highly likely that Sudan will split. Both new countries will suffer enormously. They will both have

their micro-civil war. It won't be North against South, but it will be perceived as marginalised minorities against the new central governments. The South will be worse since it has much more disgruntled jobless youth. If both parts of Sudan believe they want better future, they should look around them and learn from countries trying to unify in order to face global problems. Sudan should be aspiring to African unity, not splitting nations. Both parts should stop criticising each other. Yes, the Northern government was involved in militant Islam in the past and were keen on Sharia law. But, this is history. Southern government is partially corrupt. But they have done significant good deeds trying to build their region from scratch. Yes, money was blundered in the South. But as we know, the blunderers and facilitators are Ugandans, Kenyans, and Ethiopians. The North should admire what the SPLM done during the past few years. The South should also acknowledge the good deeds that Northern government has done, including partnering in peace. I hope the South can have an option of voting for extending the transitional period. A longer peaceful period may build trust and pave the way to keep the country unified.

Posted by Kuku Abdul Rassa

13 November 2009
2:33 pm EST
I would like to comment to let South Sudan look themselves as new state if we want peace, or if want another war, let the ruling parties of Sudan talking about the unity Sudan.There is no chance for unity of Sudan to be maintained as it had not been made attractive, Let the south declare their independence as new country. South and north are reality different for everything to live together with Araba north. Thanks to God to bring the CPA by west ministers' ideologies of saving life of all worlds

Posted by Raannaath

15 November 2009
10:17 am EST
I advocate the idea to divide the Sudan in two parts. That's a good idea. The African countries are bigger; that's why they have failed to govern the entire continent. Let the south Sudan split from the north where the Arabs ruled in evil ways of discrimination against African people.

Posted by fidele

19 November 2009
11:55 pm EST
Is Nigeria the next one to split? They too have a major Islam-Christian divide and plenty of oil to share.

Posted by Hmmmm

24 November 2009
10:15 pm EST
Arab countries historically wanted always to be united as long as long as one country rules the other(s). In Sudan, union with the South has always been with the North ruling the South. With such a difference in cultures and so much distrust, it will do no harm for them to separate. Thereafter, if they still need each other, cooperation could carry on for instance with the export of oil from the South and the refining in the North and hopefully other sectors. As for Sharia law, the North could be freer to apply it if they so wish and the South would not feel threatened by it anymore. And maybe one day, like in Europe, African countries may find a common ground to unite including the North and the South of Sudan whilst maintaining still that sense of independence.

Nafie Ali Nafie: NCP would accept 2011 referendum results

Sunday, 15 November 2009 18:00 Sudan Miraya FM

The deputy chairman of the National Congress Party, Nafie Ali Nafie, said that his party will accept results of the 2011 referendum on self-determination for the people of southern Sudan. He said the referendum results should express the will of the people of southern Sudan and "not the will of SPLM or other southern parties," as he puts it.

U.S. Says Sudan's 2010 Elections in Doubt

Sudan may be unable to hold credible elections in coming months because the ruling party and opposition cannot agree on ground rules for the polls, the U.S. State Department said on Friday.

28 November 2009

WASHINGTON, 27 Nov 2009 (Reuters)–At the end of a trip to Sudan by President Barack Obama's special envoy Scott Gration, the State Department said it saw little movement on issues such as voter registration and border delineation between Khartoum and the semi-autonomous South—endangering plans for national elections in April 2010 and a referendum on southern succession in 2011.

"Without immediate resolution of these disputes, we are concerned about the chances for conducting credible elections and referenda," it said in a statement.

"Unfortunately, the parties have not yet demonstrated the political will necessary to achieve resolution on these difficult and sensitive issues."

Gration's trip to Sudan was his first since Washington announced in October it would keep economic sanctions on Sudan but would also offer Khartoum new incentives to end violence in Darfur and the South.

The Sudan People's Liberation Movement (SPLM), former southern rebels who are now junior partners in the governing coalition under the terms of a 2005 peace deal, have accused the North of stalling on a democratic transformation and undermining plans for free elections.

The SPLM and other parties said on Wednesday they would delay a decision on whether to boycott April's elections in part due to a week-long extension of the voter registration period.

The strains have raised fears the north-south civil war—fueled by issues including religion, ethnicity, oil, and ideology between mostly Christian southern rebels and the Islamist Khartoum government—could reignite.

South Sudan leaders arrested
By Barney Jopson in Nairobi

Published: 8 December 2009 02:22 Last updated: 8 December 2009 02:22

Police in Khartoum arrested three senior members of south Sudan's main political party on Monday in the latest sign of worsening relations between the ruling regime and former rebels from the south.

Fears of a renewed **conflict** have surged in recent months as tempers frayed over the faltering implementation of a 2005 peace deal. This landmark agreement ended the latest phase of a civil war between north and south which began in the 1950s.

Pagan Amum, the secretary general of the Sudan People's Liberation Movement, a former rebel group that now rules the semi-autonomous south, was arrested during a protest in Khartoum, along with his deputy and an SPLM minister.

They were released later in the day and received a rapturous welcome. The men had been leading a banned pro-democracy demonstration outside parliament.

The civil war between the Arab-led north and rebels from south Sudan was one of Africa's longest and bloodiest conflicts, claiming perhaps 2m lives between 1983 and 2005.

If this conflict restarts, it could trigger a new **humanitarian crisis** and threaten Sudan's oil industry, whose resources are mainly in the south.

Tensions between the National Congress Party of President Omar al-Bashir and the SPLM have been rising due to the approach of two crucial events mapped out in the 2005 peace deal.

One is a national election that was originally scheduled for this year but has been pushed back to 2010. The other is a referendum on independence for south Sudan, due in January 2011. If it goes ahead, this poll is likely to result in a majority vote for secession.

But diplomats and analysts say there are doubts about whether Mr Bashir's regime will allow either to happen in a free and fair way. Khartoum is concerned about its access to oil wealth and has limited tolerance for dissent.

The SPLM and northern opposition parties had called Monday's rally to demand democratic reforms ahead of the election. It was a rare public challenge to Mr Bashir and the Sudanese authorities announced on Sunday that the demonstration was banned.

Police beat protesters and onlookers outside parliament with batons as Mr Amum, was driven away with other SPLM officials, according to Reuters.

Salva Kiir, the SPLM leader and the president of south Sudan, said in a statement that the arrests were "provocative and unjustified" and denounced the National Congress Party's "old mentality of doing business contrary to the letter and spirit of the [peace deal]."

Louise Roland-Gosselin, the director of Waging Peace, a human rights group, said: "This latest crackdown also reveals the dangers involved in showing dissent in Sudan, even when the Khartoum government is eager to demonstrate its democratic credentials by holding an election. It is clear to all those working in and around Sudan that there is a real possibility that relations between the NCP and the SPLM could completely break down."

P11 Unilateral Declaration of Independence (UDI)

Unilateral Declaration of Independence (UDI) is an option where a top leader of a part of a country declares the independence of that part of the country without a prior consent of the overall leader of the country; as was done successfully by United States of America, Sudan and Eritrea.

There are people who believe that UDI will be the only option left for the leadership of Sudan People's Liberation Movement and the presidency of the Government of Southern Sudan if the Comprehensive Peace Agreement (CPA) is abrogated or cancelled and the South Sudan referendum is blocked by force. However, it would be best for all concerned parties to allow the CPA to be fully implemented smoothly including the referendum. This will be the best way of preventing South Sudan from breaking away if unity has been made attractive enough. It will avoid ignition of a referendum war that can be more difficult and very disastrous on both sides. It is also the best way of guaranteeing a future peaceful relationship between neighbouring North Sudan and South Sudan should the latter opt to secede and become a fully independent country. As Sadig Mahdi has said during his recent visit to Juba, it may be too late to make unity attractive to the people of Southern Sudan and it is better for Northern Sudan to concentrate on building future cordial relationship with a potentially independent South Sudan. This may not be far from the truth.

Some analysts argue that UDI may be a preferred choice of some members of the National Congress Party (NCP) so that the North will not blame them in the future that they were the ones who allowed the South to break away. However, all political parties in Northern Sudan are allowed to assist in making unity attractive to Southern Sudan and if secession still becomes the choice of the people of South Sudan in 2011 referendum, they should not blame the NCP afterward. The blame, if any, would go to the collective failure by all to make the unity option more attractive than the secession option.

If UDI is to be used at all, it will really have to be the last resort!

DEDICATIONS

A Land So Momentous

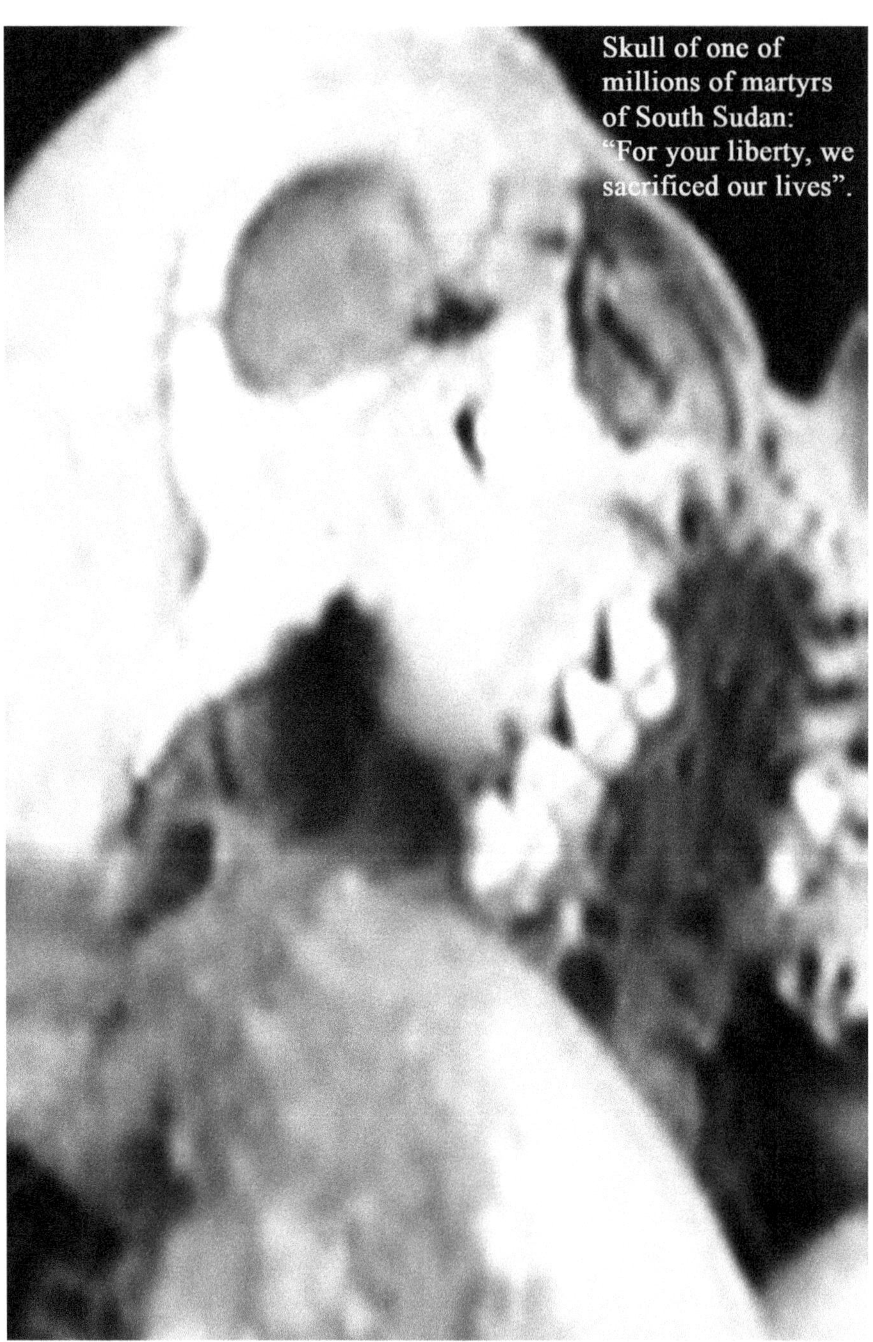

Skull of one of millions of martyrs of South Sudan: "For your liberty, we sacrificed our lives".

D1 ULTIMATE SACRIFICE

One of the signs which proves beyond doubt that we love and cherish our land of South Sudan so much is the fact that millions of our people readily sacrificed their lives and vital parts of their bodies for it. Furthermore, we would have given it up a long time ago if we do not value it extremely instead of continuing to fight for it for 1,369 years so far, since the year 640 AC and suffer enormous pain and suffering. At the beginning of this chapter is a true picture of a skull of one of the millions of martyrs that sacrificed their lives for the liberty of the land and people of South Sudan. May the Almighty God rest his or her soul in peace along with all fellow martyrs.

Remembering Martyrs

The least those of us who survived can do is to remember the millions of our martyrs that died for our liberty. Below are few examples of how we can remember them forever:

Minutes of Silence

Holding at least a minute of silence before starting a meeting or other event to remember our martyrs should be maintained. This accords them the respect they deserve and keeps their memory alight.

Liberty Statues

Having paid their lives for our liberty, it is incumbent upon us to erect liberty statues where their names can be transcribed, as is done in most countries, as an absolute honour for their heroism and sacrifice.

Freedom Squares

The same applies to establishment of freedom squares where important rallies can be staged with our martyrs in mind.

Memorial Days

At least one day a year should be dedicated as A South Sudan National War Memorial Day. This can be done specifically to remember all the martyrs. Alternatively it can be combined with SPLA Anniversary, Torit Anniversary, or Dr. John Garang Memorial.

Before this book was printed, this request has been met. The thirtieth of July, when Dr. John Garang died, has been dedicated as the Martyrs' Day.

Few Seconds Stop Every Day for Our Martyrs

Whenever I pass by the shrine of Dr. John Garang de Mabior in Juba first time in a day, I always stop my car for few seconds. I have done this every day since I returned to Juba from October 2006. I will continue to do so as long as I am alive, not only for the departed leader buried in that shrine; but for all the millions of our martyrs that sacrificed their lives for our liberty.

Continuing Struggle

A number of our heroes and heroines who had little time to leave us a message prior to their death whispered words like SPLA OYEE while gasping or scribbled down powerful abbreviations like "SC" with shaking fingers, where SC stands for Struggle Continues. Commanders Martin Manyiel and Ager Gum are two examples among so many heroes and heroines who did that.

All our martyrs therefore expect us to continue the struggle for which they paid ultimate sacrifice. The worst thing we can do is to let them down and abandon the struggle.

D2 SENSITIVE STATEMENTS

Apart from ultimate sacrifice and suffering, the extreme love and dedication we hold in our hearts for our land is reflected in our statements, actions, plans, songs, and poetry. Here are some of the words I refer to as sensitive statements, mostly my own, given as examples.

Oh! My navel, from my cradle, Remember!

Oh! My navel
From my cradle
Remember!
You are a black seed
Of Mid-African fruit
Not a strange breed
Of Mid-Eastern brute

A Prayer for Marginalised Sudan

God deliver us   from slavery
And rescue us   from misery

When they were thirsty

When they were thirsty   they drank urine
When they were hungry   they ate leaves
They did all that   for our liberty

When you hear the word south

When you hear the word south or the phrase Heart of Africa anywhere in the world, it means South Sudan.

When we differ

When we differ, let the common love and dedication we hold deeply in our hearts for our land and people of South Sudan continue to unite us. Let us not instead slaughter one another and make others think that we are unable to live safely together or rule ourselves independently.

If you were naturally allowed

When a person loves his or her own land so much, it rises above everything else. If you were naturally allowed, would you marry the land called South Sudan?

As for me, I unreservedly would.

The desire that burns in our hearts

The desire that burns in our hearts like fire is South Sudan Freedom. Let us all work hard to make this burning desire a reality in 2011.

When you vote at the referendum

When you vote at the referendum in 2011, remember all the millions of our martyrs and living heroes and heroines who sacrificed their lives or vital parts of their bodies for our freedom.

If the sun rises without our freedom in 2012

If the sun rises without our freedom on 1 January 2012, declare it Joshua or I bid this world farewell!

Survival of children

Survival of children lies in the hands of leaders who own the land

D3 SENSATIONAL ACTIONS

They say actions speak louder than words. The sensational actions described below are mere examples of my own and I believe they are the tip of an iceberg of things our people did in South Sudan in dedication to their Land.

The mad things I do for my land, Free us God

Wearing a single pair of shoes in UK for a year

"Daddy, why don't you change these black shoes you have been wearing all the time"? My little son inquired. "They have even developed a big hole under them," he added.

"I have decided to wear this single pair of shoes for a complete year without changing them with other ones in total dedication to my land of South Sudan and in full empathy to our heroic soldiers of SPLA who are fighting the war barefooted," I replied.

That was in the year 1995 when my son was only five years old. Indeed, for the whole of that year I wore only that single black pair of shoes which I am still keeping in UK. I did that for my land and my people, as a little gesture of love and dedication.

The good things about shoes are that when holes develop in them, they usually do so in the soles, away from the sight of most people; except of course inquisitive and intimate small children with sharp eyes. None of my colleagues and patients spotted the hole my son saw—or did some of them and they were too shy to tell me?

Fasting twenty-four hours every Friday in UK for four years. Resumed Fasting July 2008

It was July 2002 when the peace talks between SPLA/M and Sudan government almost broke down in Machakos-Kenya.

"These vital peace talks should not break down," I told myself silently. "What can I do to help than simply pray?" I went on talking to myself alone like a madman. At that juncture an idea flashed into my mind to be fasting once a week with a prayer for the peace negotiations to hold.

"Which day of the week?" I asked myself. Hoping to be joined by others who share the same feeling with me, I chose a day that would be agreeable to both Christians and Muslims that are both involved fighting the common enemy side by side, irrespective of different religious entities. My choice fell to Friday, being a day that Muslims regard as holy as Sunday is to Christians and also the day Christians call Good Friday.

"The fasting I am going to do is a sacrifice, however little it is, and I should remember Our Lord Jesus Christ sacrificed his life for us on Friday," I went on murmuring to myself.

"How differently should I conduct my fasting not to resemble that of some pretentious hypocrites I know?" Madly I continued to whisper to and fro. "Remember, others fast only from sunrise to sunset, which lasts simply twelve hours and still some of them run to the bathrooms, pretending to take a bath and thereby steal a drink. You can absolutely fast the whole day lasting twenty-four hours from midnight to midnight without running to a bathroom" I concluded.

Thus, from July 2002 till our prayer was answered with the signing of the peace agreement in January 2005, I continued fasting twenty-four hours every Friday. You cannot imagine the enormous joy I felt when the peace was signed. Indeed, the man whose picture was flashed to all media visibly weeping the day peace was signed in Naivasha, was not the only person who shed tears of joy that day. A lot of our people that bear the love of our land in their hearts and souls must have joined him that day. Similarly, I strongly believe that I was not the only one who fasted and obviously not the only one who prayed for our peace to come.

"When did I break the fast?" I did not break it on any Friday. I had to wait several months after the peace was signed to do so on the Good Friday itself 25 March 2005 during a ceremony staged specifically for that in Birmingham, UK.

With the Comprehensive Peace agreement threatened by series of violations, I was obliged to resume fasting every Friday since July 2008. Every Friday, fasting is ended with a prayer to the Almighty God to protect the peace and prevent our people from another disastrous war and suffering. This second phase of fasting will continue until the 2011 referendum is fully exercised and implemented.

The hardest times of the fasting are the last few hours leading to midnight. The lips and throat become dry from thirst and the body starts to become generally weak. My wife Victoria Awit (Anok) tends to hold my hands whenever she notices I have become very weak. This gives me a lot of encouragement and helps me to sail through the remaining few hours. I do not know how much I can thank her for that.

The only other person I know that used to fast on Fridays during the SPLA war is our current president of Southern Sudan, Salva Kiir Mayardit. I believe there are a lot of others who fasted voluntarily likewise; for, birds of the same feathers flock together.

Lighting candles continuously till referendum day

I was extremely anxious about the safety of our leadership when our departed leader Dr. John Garang de Mabior went to Khartoum on 9 July 2005 to the extent that I was shaking restlessly that day.

"Did our leader arrive?" I asked a medical student in Khartoum over the phone while pacing up and down in my room in UK. "Yes, we are at this moment looking at his plane that has just landed and is being parked," she replied in excitement. I could hear a lot of cheers in the background of people who were ecstatic with the arrival of the leadership in Khartoum.

"How safe is he there?" I continued to inquire. "What we were all worried about is what might happen to him while flying in the air," she answered. "Now that he has safely landed, our millions who have flocked out, if nothing else, will protect him," she concluded.

I was relieved and reassured by those powerful comments, not knowing that they would remain as statements that would continue to vibrate in my mind afterward following the tragic helicopter accident that robbed us of his life. "What we were worried about is what might happen to him while flying in the air," and indeed in the air did our leader succumb.

The next day when I watched the swearing-in ceremony of Dr. John Garang de Mabior, as first vice president of Sudan and president of South Sudan, I felt happy and confirmed that the real interim period has begun. The same day I rushed to the shops in London, UK, to buy two items, namely a stop clock that I would use to count down the six years of the interim period and candles to light from now until the flag of our full independence is raised for the first time after the referendum. The countdown watch is to remind me and whoever visits my sitting room about the period of time left to the day of the referendum. The candles were to be lit in my sitting room and kept visibly beside the clock. To ensure that I do not run out of the candles before the referendum takes place I had to buy hundreds of them initially from Ikea Superstore located in a part of London called Brent and I subsequently put aside an amount of money in a little private account as a separate budget to continue to sponsor the referendum candle vigil.

Under no circumstances would I allow the candle to be put out before we vote in the referendum as long as I am alive. Looking even further, I had dreamt of taking this lit candle from one part of South Sudan to another at least during the twelve months immediately preceding the voting in the referendum, as we conclude our vigorous campaign for a unanimous vote for our ultimate freedom.

"A unanimous vote for succession, you are dreaming," remarked a friend I secretly leaked my plan to. "Don't you know that some of our people have changed during this long period?"

"Well, is that not why we will be campaigning, to target and persuade those people of ours, if any who are converted away from us?" I asserted. "They might have been adapting to survival."

Sadly, the lighting of the candles had to be delayed. I was in the process of quietly arranging to invite a number of dedicated elders and other people of my land with supporting friends to have the candle lit for the first time by one of the elders in my sitting room in London, when our leader tragically died. Tears of joy suddenly turned into tears of sadness and those hundreds of candles still lie on the spot where I had placed them in my house when I first bought them on 10 July 2005, together with the countdown clock. When the tears of sadness stopped flowing, I arranged to have the candle lit in Malakal on 16 May 2007 by SPLM Chairman Salva Kiir Mayardit during the celebration of the SPLA/M anniversary in order to start the referendum vigil. This candle was immediately transported to Juba and placed by a poster labelled as the **Light of Hope** near the shrine of our departed leader Dr. John Garang de Mabior.

STOPPING WORK FOR A YEAR TO MOURN OUR DEPARTED LEADER DR. JOHN GARANG DE MABIOR

I FEEL MY STRENGTH COMING BACK BIT BY BIT. THANK YOU, GOD.

I thought the weekend including Saturday, 30 July 2005, was a normal one apart from my participation then in a hectic all-weekend workshop at the Royal College of Obstetricians and Gynaecologists in London. Never did I know that it would mark the beginning of the worst shock of my life.

The medical workshop ran from 0900 that Saturday and ended at 1900 the following Sunday, during which all mobile phones had to be switched off to avoid any interruption.

After emerging from that teaching, the first thing I did was to switch on my mobile phone and check for messages. My heart jumped when I noticed an unimaginable number of missed calls, some of which were repeated many times.

"Who are these people ringing me a lot of times? I have never received such numerous phone calls before in my life—could something be wrong?" I wondered.

Little did I know then, that I was perhaps the only Sudanese in the world who had not heard yet about the serious tragedy that befell our land.

I chose to ring back one of the repeated numbers and it turned out to be that of Josephine Lagu Yanga. "What is up, Josephine?" I asked. "Is everything all right?"

"Haven't you heard what happened?" she answered

My heart jumped immediately. I knew straightaway something sinister and serious must have occurred. "Oh! My God, What is it again in this land of ours where deaths never stop?" I talked to myself quietly.

"No, Josephine. I haven't heard anything," I replied. "I have just come out from a workshop."

"Then you better come to my house. I cannot tell you this on the phone," she advised.

That compounded my anxiety and fear for the worst. I am not sure whether I was then driving the car or just moving with an instinct in the busy city traffic of London. Surely, I could have had a serious accident speeding nervously that time.

It was only then that the whole story about the disappearance of the helicopter carrying Dr. John Garang De Mabior and other passengers was unfolded to me late Sunday evening. Thus, I could have been the only South Sudanese in the UK if not the world who never heard of the lost plane till then.

Of course, the rest of the story, I guess, is the same for everybody else: numerous phone calls, tuning every news channel, misleading tidings before midnight about their safety followed by the real truth after midnight UK time.

"Why am I the last South Sudanese in the so-called advanced world to be so distant from the affairs of my land that weekend to the extent that I could not even hear that the life of my revolutionary leader was at stake and probably ended up as the last person to know?" is a question that never left my mind. "Why is this medical job I am doing in UK so important that I am too dragged into it to be aware in time of serious developments pertaining to my land? How is this job contributing anyway to the liberation of my land and people of South Sudan? Now that my top leader is gone do I still need to go on working in UK or should I follow his footsteps and give up everything and devote whatever period left in my life entirely to our struggle?" All are just few examples of queries raised in my mind following the tragic departure of our leader Dr. John Garang De Mabior.

With tears in my eyes and shocked nerves, I could not continue to operate and treat patients safely as a medical doctor. From a top specialist doctor that some patients in Birmingham, UK, described as "an angel on Earth," I suddenly crashed down to rock bottom beneath the level of a "beggar" in the streets of London. The high salary of nearly £70,000 per annum and a top

E-Class Mercedes car were immediately sacrificed with the job. The house too could have gone if others had not intervened to advise me not to give it up on the basis that it could be a useful asset to our land in the future. It hung by a thread of a suspended repossession court order. In the end, however, it was repossessed and I lost it.

Certainly the car had to go. For, every time I looked at it, before even driving it, I instantly recalled the time I offered my own car to be used by our leader and his accompanying delegation when they passed via London few months before his tragic death. All I would do then instead of driving it was to continue to weep or take the risk of driving while weeping. There was no way I could have afforded its monthly instalments without a salary, having abandoned the job, even if I were to decide to keep it in his memory.

Instead of running up and down in UK hospitals and royal colleges day and night, I have been consoling myself since then by sitting in a tiny room by my computer in London fighting for my land with the tips of my fingers most of the times clicking relentlessly on the keyboard…Writing one poem after another about my land and people and ensuring that it reaches every forum I can access… Drafting one petition or letter to UN, GOSS, IGGAD, and so on after another…Linking up with my people elsewhere on the Internet, phone, Skype, campaigning for our land...Establishing and running with others a think tank organisation called South Sudan Freedom…All of them may be nothing more than mere self-consolation scratches on the enemy skin.

The candlelight vigil I had lit for our referendum continued then to shine beside our liberation flag on the left side of my table. Both the candle and flag continued to encourage me to get on. The actual soil of our land of South Sudan that was sent to me all the way from my birthplace of Kuajok to London lay in our traditional calabash on the right side of the same table for me to touch every time I wept for my land in order to console and save myself from insanity or suicide.

Perhaps because of these motivating items on my table, apart from encouraging words that have continued to flock in from all my friends, relatives, and many more, I am now beginning to feel my strength coming back bit by bit. Thank you, God; with your help, who knows, I will eventually get back on my feet and operate again.

IF ONLY DREAMS WERE TRUE

I Was Visited By John Garang Last Night (12.09.05)

Soon after suggesting to our Internet discussion forum after midnight by UK time, in a reply to Arkangelo Gaudensio Wol Acueil, that we can present our urgent petition on 13 September 2005, I went to sleep briefly. Suddenly, I had a visit from our departed leader Dr. John Garang De Mabior.

"Achier," he called me. "Have you forgotten that thirteen is an unlucky number? Did you ever see me presenting an important document or holding a great occasion on the thirteenth of any month?" he asked.

"On matters of great importance in relation to our land and our people, I advise you not to take any chances," he continued.

Finally, he waved to me saying, "Bye-bye, Achier," and vanished from my sight. Then, my eyes opened instantly before I could say to him "Don't go away, my leader," or "Bye-bye, my leader"

On one hand, I am happy that our departed leader paid me a visit last night. On the other hand, I am disappointed that I did not have a chance then to speak to him too.

This indeed is the second time since he died that Dr. John Garang De Mabior paid me a visit in a dream.

The first time was when I was dreaming myself of writing a book about him to be entitled "Bye-bye, My Leader, A Farewell to Dr. John Garang De Mabior." I was asleep too that night. He promptly visited me in that dream and I could see him clearly waving to me and saying, in reply, "Bye-bye, Achier," which is the same statement he repeated to me last night.

If dreams were things one could invite to oneself, I would request my departed leader or any of our other martyrs for that matter, to visit me every night. That however, is something outside my own ability to do. What is within my ability though is to promise our departed leader now that our URGENT PETITION FROM SOUTHERN SUDANESE TO US AND THE UN will no more be presented on thirteen today. It will be presented instead on fourteen tomorrow.

If only dreams were true.

This nevertheless, is not a fiction. It is a true story in the name of the Almighty God.

And when I dedicate this book to our martyrs, I am not playing politics. I mean it deep in my heart.

RAISING SPLA FLAG IN THE UNITED STATES: AN EVENT SO MOVING SO TOUCHING

We arrived as guests of honour in Charlotte, North Carolina, to participate in the celebration of twenty-third anniversary of SPLA/M, courtesy of the SPLM Chapter in North Carolina, South Sudan Community Association, and Angelos Agok. The head of delegation of Darfur in Abuja talks, a representative of Darfur in New York and of Nuba Mountains in Washington, DC, were accompanied by me as an SPLM member from London, UK.

The hall where the occasion was being held was a large one. Between the audience and the stage was a wide space where three flags were hoisted on long erected poles. Two flags, namely the federal flag of the United States and the state flag of North Carolina, were released and flying. The third flag, that of SPLA/M, now adopted as the one of South Sudan, was rolled up and tied on top of the mast. I first wondered why it was the only flag tied and assumed may be the laws of America did not allow foreign flags to be released in their land other than via diplomatic missions. I was wrong.

After the minute silence for our departed martyrs to mark the beginning of the celebration, the master of ceremony announced that young members of the previous Red Brigade of SPLA had a performance to stage.

Then I heard heroic SPLA songs being sung from outside the hall and suddenly I saw the SPLA army marching into the hall. They were dressed in real SPLA uniforms and they were not people faking the march and mixing their legs. They were the previous SPLA soldiers who were marching professionally and singing our noble war and liberation songs.

Toward their flag they marched. Near it they halted. Then they started to display wonderful military turning manoeuvres before one of them advanced forward. He stopped at the bottom of the South Sudan Flag and saluted it first.

The hall was silent. Not even a child screamed or echoed any sound like they usually do in an occasion, and there were children of various ages there in the hall. Everybody was stunned by the occasion or remained silent in respect.

Slowly, the soldier untied the flag and released it to fly in the air along with the USA and North Carolina counterparts. It was my first time to witness our South Sudan Flag being raised publicly in a foreign land.

I was moved to see our people, our own heroes, brave children of our marginalised land perform the Duty of the Guard of Honour, to raise our flag far away in a foreign land. I could not hold back my tears.

When my turn came to speak, I refused to stand on the stage above and behind the flags, nor use the stand for delivering speeches. Instead, I plucked off the microphone near that stand and walked back to stand below our flag.

"What you have done today has moved me," I started my short speech. "I believe Almighty God was watching you when you raised our flag far away from home few minutes ago. The Almighty will help us to implement the referendum and if the choice would be secession, you will yourself raise our flag on our precious soil over our own independent land."

"As I do in London, UK, when I am happy, I read poems. Today, I will not read only one poem but several ones. After reciting the first ones alone, I will invite all of you to join me and stand around our flag and read the last poem with me. I would like the very SPLA heroes that raised the flag to join in."

After reciting few poems such as "How Else Shall We Replace Our Martyrs," in which I wish there was a machine invented that I could run day and night to produce children to replace millions lost, I then invited the entire audience and they came and stood around the flag. There were hundreds of them.

"This last poem is called "**Tears of Esplees**," I said. "Esplees is a French term adopted by English which means 'People that love their land.' Therefore tears of esplees means **tears of people that love their land**.

"When one loves one's land so much, one usually weeps for it, especially when it is so traumatised by war and long struggle. When we read this poem, I want every participant to do so with the full knowledge that land does not invariably refer to South Sudan alone. It refers to any land belonging to anyone around here. Therefore, it could be Nuba Mountains, Darfur, Southern Blue Nile, or North Carolina, as I can see residents of these places standing here. So let us all recite this poem and refer in our hearts to our respective lands that we adore and cherish."

Then we all read "Tears of Esplees" with deep universal emotions after which **I held the flag itself and kissed it** in conclusion. The hugs of appreciation I received that day in that occasion were countless and touching. They all added to the fact that it was a day I will never forget and only God knows what will happen to me should we ultimately and officially raise our own flag in our own independent land.

Tears of Esplees
A Poem to All Who Weep For Their Land

By Achier Deng Akol

Why do we weep?
For our motherland
When we think deep
About our destined trend
If you are tears of escapees
Now stop spilling over
If you are tears of esplees
Continue to flow forever

Why do we cry?
For our ultimate freedom
When we just try
Dreaming of future kingdom
If you are tears of hopelessness
Now stop spilling over
If you are tears of steadfastness
Continue to flow forever

Why do you drop?
Even when we are standing
On a beautiful hilltop
In New Sudan pondering
If you are tears of depression
Now stop spilling over
If you are tears of motivation
Continue to flow forever

Why do you flow?
Down our ecstatic face
When SPLA heroes blow
Enemy soldiers off space
If you are tears of endless slavery
Now stop spilling over
If you are tears of SPLA victory
Continue to flow forever

Why do we weep?
For our motherland
When we think deep
About our destined trend
If you are tears of escapees
Now stop spilling over
If you are tears of esplees
Continue to flow forever

CANDLES FOR SOUTH SUDAN THAT REFUSED TO LIGHT IN WASHINGTON, DC

"What is that white statue, that tall one standing there?" I asked Madam Atem Akol, the wife of my nephew Achier Ayay Deng as we drove through downtown Washington during my visit to the United States in June 2006.

"It is called Liberty and the Eagle," she replied.

"Oh! That is nice. It looks wonderful with flags all around it. I guess they are the flags of all the states that constitute the Union, the United States of America."

"Yes they are," Atem said.

The moment I learnt it was a statue called Liberty and the Eagle within the visible vicinity of the White House where the president of United States resides and serves, my mind started to consider it an important landmark worldwide.

"This is the spot where I can arrange for a candlelight vigil and photograph to be taken. Members of our organisations based in Washington, DC, and nearby areas can stand with me beneath that statue. We will light candles and request a photographer to take our join picture while holding them. We will stand shoulder to shoulder during the vigil and photograph. This will serve several purposes:

- It will be a prayer that our land and people of South Sudan will also one day become free like the United States.

- Our Promised Land, once free, will strive to become as powerful if not more as the United States.

- Our powerbase in the United States is a key to maintaining cordial links with the United States and allies to continue to solicit their support for the CPA and referendum. Therefore our own solidarity there is vital."

"Will they allow people to light candles near the White House in view of the security changes following September 11 tragedy?" Madam Atem wondered, as I began to sell my idea to others.

"We will have to inquire about that. I suppose it is allowed," I responded.

The first approach was for a meeting to be organised between various organisations of our people in Washington, DC, and nearby states. In the meeting we would emphasize the need for us to remain united to be able to wage effective campaign abroad. After the meeting, we would then proceed to perform the candlelight vigil and take the photograph.

A list of all the organisations in Washington, DC, and nearby was drawn up along with at least their respective executive members. Saturday 17 June 2006 was fixed as the date for that meeting, one day before I was to return to London, UK, at the end of my visit to the United States.

Phone calls were made to most members. Somewhere directly approached and informed during a cultural celebration of Shilluk Pashoda in Virginia and twenty-third SPLA Anniversary in North Carolina.

Lily A. Akol was invited from New Jersey to come and chair the meeting and participate in the vigil and photograph.

On Friday 15 June 2006, it became apparent that most invited members would not succeed to attend the meeting. It was also apparent that the following day would be taken over by the long-awaited Miss South Sudan Beauty Contest.

After a brief substitute meeting in Washington involving several chairpersons of organisations there, including the SPLM Chapter the night before, we first headed to the Miss South Sudan Beauty Contest in Virginia as planned. Amid the cheers of that exciting celebration, I approached Manut Bol and others to go with me to the centre of Washington, DC, for the vigil and photograph. Most, including the tall man Manut Bol, declined as they were committed elsewhere that time.

However, Mr. Deng Deng Nhial, the chair of SPLM Chapter in Washington; Miss Apuol Maduot Parek; Mrs. Ateem Wol, the wife of the chairperson of South Sudan Community Association in Washington and her three little children; and a youth member, Mr. Akok Madut Deng, kindly offered to join me.

When we reached the statue, we chose a spot that would bring most of the statue and surrounding flags in view. We took out the six candles reflecting the colours of our liberation flag: yellow, blue, black, red, green, and white and held them in the gourd. Then we tried to light the candles. Then we discovered that that the heavy wind blowing at that time would not allow any candles to remain lit. It blew them off instantly. All attempts we could think of to shield the candles from the wind ended in failure.

We looked up and around and noticed all flags fully stretched by the strong wind and opted to just hold unlit candles while taking the pictures. We had no idea how long the winds would have taken to settle down if we waited. We also spotted a crowd of spectators gazing at us probably wondering about a group of dedicated people struggling to light candles openly in a windy atmosphere. I wonder if they were asking themselves about our country of origin. A couple of them even offered to help out, including taking a shot of all of us.

Apart from the candles that could not be lit, we felt contented with the strategic picture anyway with all the sentiments associated with it. If anyone examined our throbbing hearts then, one same message would have appeared: **"Our beloved land will one day become free and powerful like the United States or even more."**

The candles for South Sudan refused to light in Washington that day; but its camera didn't. On another day, I believe they will!

FOUR TIMES UNLUCKY

1963 The Khartoum government decided to close down all schools in South Sudan in reaction to the Anya-nya War. I was in Kuajok Intermediate School then together with the current president of Southern Sudan, Salva Kiir Mayardit, among others. I walked to the nearby Anya-nya Camp under the local command of an officer called Ajiek Amet where I declared my intention to join the Anya-nya Warriors. Unfortunately, I was rejected on the basis that I was too young to be a guerrilla fighter. Tears flowed then in hopes I would be allowed to join, but they did not help.

1983 Within few weeks of the start of the SPLA War, I flew to Addis-Ababa, Ethiopia, on a scholarship offered by German Leprosy Relief Association under pretext of attending a leprology/dermatology course at Alert Centre. The real intention was to join the movement at the time when it was emerging. Unfortunately I could not link up with emerging leadership of the SPLA/M and was forced to fly back voluntarily to avoid humiliating deportation. The fact that the scholarship was offered to me through the Sudan government instead of directly was construed to mean that I could have been an agent of the Sudan government.

1987 Went to Nairobi where I met the late Commander Martin Manyiel and declared my intention to join the movement then. Unfortunately, he urged me instead to take up a British Council scholarship that had just been offered to me in Sudan to go and do a master's degree course in community health in United Kingdom of Britain.

1990 Responded to an advertisement of International Rescue Committee (IRC) based in Nairobi for a doctor to train medical assistants in Torit which was then under SPLA control. Despite the fact that the application was done through the SPLM Office of London as an opportunity for me to join the frontline and contribute medically, it was declined. The reason given was that SPLA/M policy would not allow any Sudanese to serve in the SPLA-controlled areas then unless trained militarily by SPLA.

FIGHTING FROM A DISTANCE

1959 Top of Catchiest Class, Kuajok Parish

1968 President Legion of Mary, Wau Parish

1969 Leader Boy Scouts, Bahr-el-Ghazal Region

1970 Leading student activist in Wau against Jonglei Canal

1978 Founding chairperson, African Cultural Society, University of Khartoum

1988 Intensified Poetry in Diaspora as an international weapon for liberation

1998 Founding chairperson, Beyond Tears Charity, London, UK

1997 Founding chairperson, SPLM Chapter, Birmingham, UK

1999 Editor-in-chief, New Sudan Herald Magazine, UK

1999 Author of a book called *A Mother's Millennium Dream*

2005 Founding Chairperson, South Sudan Freedom Think Tank

Apart from holding those positions and using their platforms to campaign for freedom, democracy, equality and justice for all in Sudan, I was a leading participant in a series of protests and petitions against oppression, genocide, etc. in London, UK, and beyond.

There are those who had the chance to struggle in the frontline in the bush and others like me who only ended up simply scratching the oppressor from the distance. Below are few recent examples of petitions submitted to UN and US agencies where I was involved among thousands of others worldwide:

Urgent Petition from Southern Sudanese to US and UN Envoys

Wednesday, 14 September 2005.

CC. Mr. Jan Pronk, UN Peace Envoy in Sudan, UK Prime Minister Tony Blair, All Leaders of IGGAD and Friends of IGGAD Countries,

Leaders of TROIKA Countries, President of Canada and Australia, AU Countries, Arab League Nations and Lt. Gen. Lazaro K Sumbeiyo (Rtd.) former Chairman of the Sudan Peace Talks.

CC. Chairman of SPLM, Sudan. Various MPs and Senators, Peace Organisations.

Dated 14 September 2005

Mr. Roger Winter
US Envoy in Sudan
State Department
Washington, DC

Dear Mr. Winter:

Subject: Violations of Sudan Peace Agreement Such As Article 2.5.3 of Power Sharing

We would like to draw the attention of the United States administration through you to a serious dispute that has developed between Mr. Omar Bashir, the president of Sudan and Mr. Salva Kiir Mayardit, the first vice president of Sudan. This dispute is created by the fact that President Omar Bashir would like his own party of Sudan National Congress to take both the top economic ministerial positions namely the Ministry of Energy and Mining and also the Ministry of Finance. He, Mr. Bashir does not want to allow Sudan People's Liberation Movement under the leadership of Mr. Salva Kiir Mayardit to hold one of these two vital economic ministries. This crisis is unexpected and must be resolved swiftly and fairly for a number of reasons:

- OPPRESSION OF SOUTHERN SUDANESE: One of the reasons for the long war in Sudan has been the deliberate treatment of people of Southern Sudan as second class citizens who do not for example, deserve to be offered certain key ministerial positions. Regretfully, almost all few ministries that have been promised to Southerners will have essential components subtracted to make them incomplete. Ministry of Foreign Affairs is offered minus Foreign Trade, Higher Education is without Science and Technology and Ministry of Transport with no Communication. In other words, Southern Sudanese do not deserve full ministries. This is undoubtedly a continuation of the same mistreatment.

- VIOLATION OF PEACE AGREEMENT: Article 2.5.3 of the Comprehensive Peace Agreement in Sudan (CPA) signed between the two parties brokered mainly by United States, Britain, Norway, and IGAD countries and witnessed by the United Nations in January this year reads, "Cabinet posts and portfolios in all clusters, including the National Sovereignty Ministries shall be shared equitably and qualitatively by the two parties. The parties agree to cluster the National Ministries under the implementation modalities." Among the clusters agreed on are economic ministries the most important of which are the two ministries of Energy & Mining and Finance. Therefore, equitable and qualitative share of economic ministries should be that each of the two parties take one and not both. For the National Congress Party to insist in taking both the top economic ministries of Energy and Mining and Finance is a total violation of the CPA. This would mean President Omar Bashir was not telling the truth when he was recently promising the whole world openly that he will honour the agreement following the tragic death of Dr. John Garang De Mabior.

- ECONOMIC IMPLICATIONS: We see no harm in allowing a Southern Sudanese to hold the ministry of energy and mining for example, especially when over 90 percent of the oil is after all located in Southern Sudan. The economic development of Southern Sudan during the six years of the interim period would be almost entirely dependent on the oil revenues as the budget of Government of Southern Sudan (GOSS) will depend by 90 percent on oil revenue. The quest for exploitation of oil in the South has brought untold sufferings on the people of South Sudan in terms of forced displacement and killing. More over our Southerner's share of employment and training in this oil sector is very poor and, hence, it can be reliably corrected when one of us is at the one holding the top management of the sector. Such injustices can be fairly redressed by GOSS. These vital facts alone will motivate a Southern Sudanese to run that ministerial post even more effectively to the benefit of the whole Sudan. Hence depriving a Southern Sudanese from holding a top economic ministry is a de-motivating factor. Most importantly, money is power and to control it and its main source is to ensure that others like us in Southern Sudan continue to be deprived and oppressed forever, which is utterly unacceptable.

- PRESIDENTIAL ROLES: A president of any country is expected to exercise fairness in ministerial allocations and to maintain the overall unity of that country. It is clearly unfair for President Omar Bashir to insist that his own party is to take both top economic ministries we wonder how he will make unity of the whole Sudan attractive to Southern Sudanese by depriving them of key ministerial positions.

- DELAY OF GOSS FORMATION: As part of the Comprehensive Peace Agreement, a Government for South Sudan (GOSS) should have come into effect from July 2005. But so far that has not happened as a result of the current obstructive policies of the National Congress Government that has made any agreement with SPLM on how to share power as stipulated in CPA impossible. While playing these delaying tactics, the National Congress Government has been reluctant to release funds due to the Government of South Sudan under the pretext that such a government does not exist. And without funds, the SPLM cannot transform itself from a guerrilla movement to a government that is able to provide services to those who need them such as those who are returning to the South after the signing of peace agreement in January.

- DELAY OF PEACE COMMISIONS: The National Islamic Front (NIF) is playing tactics to delay the formation of committees/commissions to execute some of the immediate programs of the CPA such as the Cease Fire Commission, CPA Monitoring Commission, Resettlement Commissions, etc. This is done by the NIF deliberately in order to create a vacuum in which to operate freely and continue to violate the CPA.

- NEGLIGENCE OF SPLA FORCES: In a further ruthless display of bad faith, the National Congress Government has refused to finance the maintenance of the SPLA forces deployed in Khartoum last week as part of Joint Command Forces that were to be formed as a nucleus of new Sudan army should Sudan remained a united country after six-year transition period. These forces, according to CPA, are the responsibility of the national government in all aspects including funding, training, and equipment provision. This negligence compounds the dispute on power sharing.

- OTHER SERIOUS IMPLICATIONS: Dear Mr. Winter, if President Omar Bashir and his National Congress party have started to violate the CPA now at this early stage of the implementation, what is the guarantee that they will honour the result of the referendum later, if it should take place as scheduled at all? The signal they are sending is that they are not prepared to honour the agreement they have entered into with Sudan People's Liberation Movement before the international community, and are planning to sabotage the referendum from taking place in six years' time. This ought to be a cause for concern for all, including your administration pivotal in brokering a successful conclusion of the CPA. The dispute over ministerial positions and reluctance to release funds due to the government of South Sudan are merely symptoms of deep-seated intentions to completely dishonour the implementation of the agreement with the implication that the country will slide back to war.

- DISRESPECT TO THE DEAD: We feel that Omar Bashir should not have sparked this dispute so soon after the tragic death of Dr. John Garang De Mabior who was instrumental in bringing about this peace and who worked hard to ensure that such a conflict would not develop in the future as reflected by articles in the CPA of fair power sharing. It is as if the death of John Garang does not matter to President Omar Bashir and his party for them to allow a conflict like this to develop so soon after his death.

- WAR-TRIGGERING FACTORS: Given the bitter hatred that has developed over more than fifty years of war in Sudan, all it needs is a little dispute, such as disagreements over Abyei Boundary or lack of proper power sharing, to trigger another war. The last war that lasted for twenty-two years was merely triggered by a simple attempt to forcibly transfer a battalion of Southern Sudanese Soldiers from the South to the North. Therefore any violation of the CPA must not be permitted, as it can be a sufficient triggering factor for another war.

- FOUNDATION OF DISTRUST: Even if an early violation of the CPA like inequitable share of ministries does not lead to immediate return to war, it is a bad beginning which will have laid a foundation of distrust between the two major political parties and affect their future working relationships with direct negative bearings on the implementation of the comprehensive peace agreement in Sudan.

- LACK OF MUTUAL PARTNERSHIP: From the above actions, it appears that the National Congress Party is continuing to delude itself that it is still the sole master of Sudanese politics and that SPLM, which is its principal partner in the CPA does not matter. This is obviously contrary to a spirit of mutual respect expected to exist between two main political parties that are partners of any national government.

Given all the above-mentioned reasons, we would like to appeal to you, Mr. Winter, as the US Peace Envoy in Sudan and the other international observers to immediately intervene in order to fairly resolve the dispute over strategic ministerial positions as well as putting the pressure on the Presidency of Omar Bashir and his National Congress Party to honour all that has been stipulated in the CPA and to be seen to do so regarding all outstanding issues such as immediate release of the share of funds to GOSS. As this is an urgent matter, we would like you to act promptly so that the partners to January peace agreement can move to the next stage of implementing the agreement and making it a reality.

Dear Mr. Winter, your experience in Sudan and your personal involvement to see that war stops and peace is achieved in Sudan have been apparent to us. With more than twenty-five years' experience in Sudan, no one is better placed to successfully resolve even the most intractable problems. It is time you intervene and give the CPA's implementation a push forward and overcome any possibility of its early derailment. Your help is badly needed especially now that the Commission which was planned to be formed in order to monitor our Comprehensive Peace Agreement is still sadly nonexistent. We request this important Monitoring Commission to be instituted as soon as possible in order to stop all these early and any other subsequent CPA violations that maybe in the pipeline. By copy of this letter, we would also like to extent our request for urgent supportive intervention on this matter to the United Nations, all the other Leaders of the World and International Organisations stated above.

It is better to stop the fire when it is still a smoke than to later attempt to do so when it is fully burning.

Dr. Achier Deng Akol
Postal SPLA OYEE
Address 21 Francis Road
Harrow
HA1 2QY
United Kingdom
Tel. 44 (0) 2084276804

Fax: 44 (0) 2084276804

Email: thinkers@splaoyee.com

Web site: www.splaoyee.com

Signed by 1693 people worldwide, and 21 organisations

Published Wednesday 4 January 2006

URGENT PETITION FROM SOUTH SUDANESE TO UNITED NATIONS AND GOVERNMET OF SOUTHERN SUDAN (GOSS)

Date: 3 January 2006

Kofi A. Annan
United Nations Secretary-General
United Nations Headquarters
New York, USA

Cc: A. Government of South Sudan

- Salva Kiir Mayardit, President of South Sudan Juba, South Sudan

- The SPLM Party Leadership

- All Other Sudanese Parties and MPs

B. World Leaders and Human Rights Organisations

- US President George Bush
- UK Prime Minister Tony Blair
- Presidents of Canada and Australia
- AU, EU and Arab League Leaders
- Other World Leaders and Legislators
- Amnesty International and Human Rights Watch
- International Committee for Red Cross
- All Other Human Rights Organisations

Ref: Condemnation of Egypt over 30 December 2005 Cairo Massacre of Refugees and Appeal for Immediate Humanitarian Intervention

We, South Sudanese and friends worldwide are outraged and shocked by the barbaric massacre of over 265 Sudanese refugees, according to our representatives, by the Egyptian police forces in Cairo on 30 December 2005 and completely agree with your recent statement that the massacre is a "terrible tragedy that cannot be justified," plus the statement by UN High Commissioner for Refugees Mr. Antonio Gutierrez, that "there was no justification for the violence and loss of life." Similarly, we concur with Human Rights Watch deputy director Joe Stork for stating that "a police force acting responsibly would never have allowed such a tragedy to occur" before correctly asserting that "the high loss of life suggests the police acted with extreme brutality." Nevertheless, these words alone are not enough unless accompanied by practical and legal measures to save our vulnerable people in Egypt and ensure non-repetition of such tragedies elsewhere in the world.

Indeed, the Egyptian government's use of excessive force on the Sudanese refugees with rising number of deaths is an outright serious violation of the 1951 UN Convention on Refugees and their right to life and liberty and asylum as per 1948 UN Declaration on Human rights. Such brutal massacre is barbaric, callous, inhuman and absolutely illegal. It is also undiplomatic act of a supposedly highly valued government in the Middle East against unarmed and defenceless refugees and asylum seekers whose only crime they committed was to stage a three-month nonviolent sit-in protest in front of a UNHCR office in Cairo.

Sadly, the fact that this massacre happened with UNHCR simply watching terribly reminds us of massive Srebrenica and Rwanda Massacres. Over the years Egypt collaborated with the oppressive regimes in Khartoum to exploit continuous silence of the international community and treat the marginalised people of "New Sudan" as animals and massacre them. They should not be allowed to get away anymore with their barbaric and brutal acts. They must be universally condemned and held accountable for their crimes.

The "coincidence" of the visit of Foreign Affairs state minister, Mr. El Kerti, and the Egyptian army declaration of war against a peaceful sit-in protest that had continued for over two months, leaves much to be desired. Sudan National Congress Government is on record for excessive use of force against innocent citizens as happened at Soba Aradhi last June/July and following the riots after the death of first SPLM Chairman Dr John Garang. The minister's departure on the day of the killings shows no concern for the citizens at best or complete disregard for their lives and wellbeing. When the minister adds that there was no "excuse for seeking asylum" in the first place, it implicitly implies no sympathy for their condition and fate. We request an international investigation commission when formed to probe the relationship between the minister's visit and the timing of the massacre as this may reveal a significant link such as masterminding of the brutality.

Of utmost urgency is the need to care for the wounded, protect the detainees and stop deportations. We understand that over two thousand detainees with the wounded and unknown number of missing including thirty children are taken to undisclosed locations and we are alarmed by the news that UNHCR have been denied access to them by the Egyptian government. We genuinely fear that their safety and welfare is seriously compromised. Over six hundred who run the risk of being arrested, tortured or killed by Sudan army are now being deported to Khartoum. The first one hundred of them are expected in Khartoum shortly and more will follow without UN intervention.

We are also concerned about possible disrespect and mishandling of the dead. Some of us who studied and lived in Egypt are well aware of the fact that South Sudanese who are killed by Egyptians are later found in most cases without internal organs. This is because our dead people in Egypt are treated as an open source for organ donations for their sick relatives. The looting of internal organs may be happening at the moment to the bodies of our people massacred in Cairo within various mortuaries in Cairo while awaiting postmortem.

Last but not least we would like to briefly explore the original dispute that triggered these tragic crises, namely the UNHCR resolution of June 2004 to stop registering all Sudanese asylum seekers for refugee status determination (RSD) interviews in light of the current Sudan Peace Agreement. We feel that this UNHCR resolution is defective in the following ways:

- It is premature as the peace agreement is yet to be fully implemented
- No prior arrangements are made for the security, safety and well-being of returnees

- It is generalized considering continuing hostility in Eastern and Western Sudan

- It aggravated the suffering of Sudanese refugees and asylum seekers in Egypt

- Sudan Human Rights Organisation Cairo Office petitioned against it to UN Human High Commissioner for Refugees Antonio Gutierrez and recommended its suspension

- It encouraged Egyptians to mistreat Sudanese refugees culminating in this massacre

Mr. Secretary General, these acts of killing, looting of internal organs, and illegal deportations of Sudanese refugees from Egypt in eyes of the whole world are a great scandal and mockery of all the international human right laws and values. They represent a sharp fall in the moral standards of leading world nations such as Egypt and are in dire contrast to the better way South Sudan has hosted and treated refugees from various countries like Eritrea, Somalia, Ethiopia, Zaire, and Uganda plus Egyptian citizens over the years. It comes as a shame to all humanity that such barbaric and mindless acts still happen in our supposedly civilized and progressive twenty-first century world. Therefore, we the authors of this petition condemn Egypt in the strongest possible terms and appeal to you to intervene on behalf of UN and the world community to:

1. Call for the immediate release of detainees and stop forceful deportations of Sudanese refugees from Egypt to Sudan

2. Allow access to the detainees and wounded by reliable humanitarian or human right organisations for care and safety as well as allow counselling of bereaved relatives

3. Ensure the identification of all the dead and postmortem to be conducted by an international team of doctors from nonpartisan organisations or involving South Sudanese doctors

before transportation of the bodies for burial in their own soil in South Sudan

4. Order an international investigation into the circumstances surrounding the Cairo massacre including the role of Egyptian police and Sudan government in it and not allowing Egyptian authority to single-handedly investigate the cover-up.

5. Demand that all those responsible for the crime are held accountable and brought to justice including full payment of compensation to affected victims and bereaved relatives following competent assessment by a team of international experts

6. Dismiss UNHCR staff who collaborated with Egyptian police

7. Revoke the June 2004 UNHCR resolution and replace the Egyptians with international interviewers

8. Call for interviewing of all new applicants and expedition of resettlement procedures to third countries

9. Ensure provision of legal protection and humanitarian support for all the refugees in Egypt

10. Order suspension of Egypt's membership in UN and peacekeeping in Sudan pending full explanation for mistreatment and massacre of Sudanese refugees and asylum seekers

By copy of this letter we would also like to appeal to our Government of South Sudan. While we condemn Egypt, we also view that the Sudan's state minister on foreign relations statement on the incident and the Sudan's ambassador in Cairo inaction to protect the refugees, warrant they be immediate relieved from their positions by the Sudan Government of National Unity (GONU). If no action is taken against the above officials then the Government of National Unity is nothing but the shadow government of the previous NIF regime.

We are also dismayed with the initial deafening silence of the Government of South Sudan (GOSS) and above all, one of our own who is at the helm of the foreign ministry for not condemning these unwarranted and unjustified killing of our people but was able to defend the position of NIF toward Chad. This to us is very sad indeed as the welfare and security of all South Sudanese anywhere is the responsibility of the Government of South Sudan, if not the Government of Sudan. We do not think it is fair for either government to simply watch their people neglected, humiliated and now massacred without stepping in to at least give them necessary advice and guidance if not full protection in Egypt. However, the Government of South Sudan subsequent condemnation of Egypt is relieving and we would like to use the opportunity of this letter to appeal to South Sudan President Salva Kiir Mayardit to ensure that the following further steps are taken or implemented:

- Urging of Sudan foreign minister or President Omer el Beshir to also condemn Egypt

- Dispatching of an urgent delegation from South Sudan to Egypt to support the bereaved and wounded, facilitate funeral arrangements and protect our people there in liaison with humanitarian organisations and helpful nations

- Calling for Sudan GONU to take full responsibility to safely repatriate and accommodate refugees who are willing directly to their home areas in Sudan, not dumped in Khartoum

Mr. Anan, we appeal to your proven understanding of complex and intractable international issues, exceptional leadership skills, and supportive spirit and authority, together with those of all other world leaders and institutions of good will by copy of this petition to urgently intervene in order to save and protect basic human rights of all the Sudanese refugees and asylum seekers in Egypt whose lives and security have all been seriously jeopardized and compromised by recent tragic events in Cairo.

Without your immediate intervention, Sudanese refugees and asylum seekers will continue to languish in the den of murderous brutality in Egypt and end up like the Tutsis in Rwanda and Bosnians in Serbia if not worse. Please save our people now.

Signed on Behalf of South Sudanese and Friends Worldwide by:

Dr. Achier Deng Akol

Address: South Sudan Freedom, 21Francis Road - Harrow - HA1 2QY - UK

THOUSANDS OF PEOPLE ENDORSING

Letter to UN Secretary-General on UN Forces in Sudan

Tuesday, 11 April 2006.

Honourable Kofi Annan
The Secretary-General
United Nations
304 E 45th Street
New York, NY 10017
USA

Cc: Ambassador Wang Guangya
President of Security Council and
China Permanent UN Representative

E-mail: chinamission_un@fmprc.gov.cn

Ambassador John R. Bolton
US Permanent UN Representative

140 East 45th Street
New York, NY 10017

Ambassador Sir Emyr Jones Parry
UK Permanent UN Representative
One Dag Hammarskjöld
28th Floor, 885 Second Avenue
New York, NY 10017

Ambassador M. Jean-Marc de LA Sabliere
France Permanent UN Representative
One Dag Hammarskjöld Plaza
245 East 47th Street, 44th Floor
New York, NY 10017

Ambassador Mr. Sergey Lavrov
Russian Permanent UN Representative
136 East 67th Street
New York, NY 10017

Mr. Jan Pronk
Special UN Representative of the Secretary-General
United Nations Mission in Sudan (UNMIS)
P O Box 5013, Grand Central Station
New York, NY 10163-5013

Lt. General Salva Kiir Mayardit
President of Southern Sudan and
Commander in Chief of SPLA
Juba, Southern Sudan

Monday April 10, 2006

Dear Mr. Secretary-General,

Subject: **REQUEST FOR STRONGER MANDATE, POWERFUL BACK UP AND ROBUST UN FORCES IN SUDAN**

WE the undersigned Sudanese and friends are grateful to the Security Council for resolving unanimously to maintain United Nations Mission in Sudan (UNMIS) and send a new force to Darfur this year. While planning to implement this resolution, we would like you to recommend to the Security Council to **strongly mandate, powerfully backup and send robust UN forces to Darfur NOW**.

We note existing mandate of UNMIS which specifies that **acting under Chapter VII of the UN Charter, UNMIS is authorized to take the necessary action, in the areas of deployment of its forces, and as it deems within its capabilities, to protect United Nations personnel and to ensure their security and freedom of movement, as well as, without prejudice to the responsibility of the Sudanese government, to protect civilians under imminent threat of physical violence**. Please re-examine this mandate since Sudan government masterminds and backs militia genocide atrocities so that UNMIS protective actions are not limited by the phrase "Without prejudice to the responsibility of the Sudanese government." Besides, UNMIS military capabilities should be powerfully backed up to remain superior to that of Sudan government so that they are unhindered.

The African Union (AU) forces currently in Darfur cannot protect lives there against **Janjaweed** genocide atrocities as they lack necessary mandate and resources to do so. The same applies in South Sudan where the **Lord Resistance Army (LRA)** in Equatoria and other militia elsewhere are also killing innocent people now in the presence of incompletely mandated UN forces and staff whose lives are also at risk as sadly testified by the death of UN Staff **Nabil Bahjat Abdulla** following his shooting in Yei Town. We deeply regret his tragic death while trying to help our suffering people.

Apart from militia, **the continuing presence of Sudan army in Southern Sudan in locations where they are not supposed to be according to the CPA**, poises real threat to civilians and potential clashes with SPLA forces. This can easily ignite a re-start of war in Southern Sudan which further justifies the need for robust UN forces there to effectively monitor and protect the CPA.

Your Excellency, we strongly denounce the Sudan government and Egypt-driven Arab League for rejecting deployment of UN forces in Darfur in preference for ailing AU forces. Their position is totally inconsiderate and genocidal. Sudan government has already accepted the presence of international monitors by signing the CPA and Arab League driven by **refugees-murdering Egypt** is biased in favour of fellow Arabs. Besides, since they say they want to implement existing CPA and reach a new agreement in Darfur, the presence of UN forces will assist them in doing so. On the other hand, the fact that the Sudan government is opposed because they fear UN soldiers would be able to arrest anyone charged by ICC for war crimes indicates that they are simply putting their own interest over and above overall safety of the people they claim to govern. Therefore, **please urge the Sudan government and Arab League to reconsider and ignore them if they insist**. After all, the UN mandate is for protection of people's interest, not those of governments or leagues and we believe those indicted with war crimes in Darfur must be arrested and brought to justice anyway.

Latest news of prevention of your own UN Under-Secretary General for Humanitarian Affairs Mr. **Jan Egeland** from visiting Darfur by Sudan government under pretext of the Cartoon Row is a defiant and deliberate act to conceal renewed attacks on civilian population by Janjaweed Militia from the eyes of international community. **Please take unprecedented step to also recommend tougher sanctions on Sudan for continuing to defy the international community, exempting marginalised areas**.

The serial genocides in South Sudan where over two and half million lives have been lost so far and the ongoing one in Darfur with two hundred thousand people now killed and millions displaced can only be stopped by effective UN intervention. Indeed, before Darfur, **numerous generations of families were wiped out** in Dongla, Nuba Mountains, Southern Blue Nile, Abyei, Bahr-el-Ghazal, Upper Nile, and Equatoria **by the same Khartoum-backed Janjaweed called Murahilin, Mujahedeen and Ambororo. These innocent families could have been saved by UN intervention**.

Honourable Secretary-General, a precedent has long been set for UN peacekeeping forces when NATO forces under UN mandate, stepped into the Balkans to stop genocide. Whether in the Balkans or Sudan, we concur with you that genocide is evil. Moreover human life in Darfur is as valuable as that in the Balkans or elsewhere. Therefore, **immediate deployment of robust UN forces, backed by stronger NATO involvement is needed in Sudan as it was in the Balkans**.

Vital UN intervention should not be deferred till peace is reached in Darfur as demanded by Sudan government. UN forces cannot be expected to compile statistics of deaths in Darfur; they need to prevent the deaths. The suffering Darfur people, indeed the majority of peace-loving Sudanese people worldwide, **expect and demand** the UN intervention **NOW**; not following a **hypothetical and elusive peace deal**.

The money pledged in Khartoum by Arab League to African Union forces in Darfur from October 2006 is indeed **medicine after death** as described by **Baba Gana Kingibe**, Head of AU Mission in Sudan. It is also a ploy to seduce AU not to hand off to a United Nations force. **Please disregard this pledge**.

Mr. Annan, we are encouraged by the recent statement of **US President George W. Bush** that: "**There is no time to waste when there are people suffering and dying every day**." We hope Mr. Bush will follow his strong words with powerful actions.

Your own Special UN Envoy for Sudan **Mr. Jan Pronk** emphasizes that Sudan is in trouble and the international community is still not acting fast. **We believe the United Nations Security Council should not unleash a defiant government and its murderous militias to wipe out innocent civilians.**

Please consider our request and stop genocide in Sudan NOW.

Thank You.

Dr. Achier Deng Akol

For:

Organisations Endorsing:

- Abdellatife Ismail, Executive Director, Darfur Centre for Human Rights and Development, P. O. Box 48299, London W2 7YG, UK. Phones in UK (44) 207 607 2309, 07850380180, 07930691575. Phone in USA 001 312 786 1514 E-mail dcfhr@dcfhr.org Web site www.dcfhr.org

- Fr. Alex L. Kenyi, Executive Director, Assistance, Minnesota, 120 8th Street South, P. O. Box 956, Moorhead, MN 56560

- Jimmy Mulla, Southern Sudan Voice for Freedom, 1925 K Street, NW # 400, Washington, D.C. 20006, Telephone (202) 737 7200 Extension 245

- Joseph Emmanuel, Senior Program Director, Integrated Living Services, Administration and Training Centre, 655 West Smith Street, Suite #207, Kent, WA 98032, Telephone (253) 8138706

- Luka Drane Logoye, Chairman, Human Moral Care (HMC)

- Lula Rizig, President, Southern Sudan Women Empowerment Network (SSWEN), P. O. Box 64322, Phoenix, Arizona, USA

- Mayen Wol, Sudanese Community Refugee Services in Michigan, P. O. Box 2672, Grand Rapids, Michigan, 49501, USA

- Ngor Kolong Ngor, Rise Development Organisation

- Sisto Olur, Peace With Neighbours, Hjellplassen 35, N-9750 Honningsvag, Norway, Telephone 0047 9321 9832

- Dr. Achier Deng Akol, South Sudan Freedom (SSF), 21 Francis Road, Harrow, Middlesex, HA1 2QY, UK, Telephone 0044 2084276804 Silvestro Akara Bakheit, President, New Sudan Generation, 548 Carter Street, Suite 404C, San Francisco, CA 94134, USA

  People Endorsing: over 120

TOUCHING AND KISSING OUR SOIL ABROAD

Touching Our Precious Soil for the First Time in Our Life

By my son Ayay Achier Deng Akol, London, UK

I was born in London in 1990 and have never seen our homeland of South Sudan.

When I was seven years old, my parents, who are refugees in the UK, showed me and my elder brother Deng soil brought by Aunty Lucia Tambura from our homeland. It looked ebony and creamy and I could have mistaken it for a chocolate had I not been told what it was.

When I touched that soil for the first time in my life, I had mixed feelings. In the first instance, I felt excited to touch our soil the first time thousands of miles away from home. Soon after, I was sad to have been deprived of an opportunity of being born in and even just seeing our fatherland. My brother felt the same.

I shared that information with my other fellow children from the South who were born like me abroad and we decided to call ourselves "**Children of New Sudan**" and read a poem together in front of many aunties, uncles, and our parents while touching and kissing our precious soil. That was in 1998 during a celebration for Torit Anniversary staged in Arlington Hall within Central London. The leader of our team was a niece of Dr. Tabita Butrous el Shokai, the current minister of Health in Sudan. We were all five in number and every one recited his or her own part of the poem under the common theme of: **Touching Our Precious Poem for the First Time in Our Life.**

The part of the poem I read myself is still vivid in my mind and it goes like this:

This is our precious soil
We are proud to touch it
And excited to hold it
For first time in our life

Allow us to kiss it now
In front of you our elders
With a solemn promise
To cherish it forever

We will continue to fight
For our land like you

Then we handed the soil in a traditional calabash to our elder, Dr. Zachariah Bol Deng, who said moving words before passing it to Uncle Gordon Muortat Mayen who finally sprayed it onto hundreds of our people attending the celebration.

I could see most of our people weeping that day irrespective of age when they heard our poem and were being sprayed with the soil. Then we felt and knew how very precious our motherland is.

Now I am sixteen and my dream is to visit our precious homeland and vote for secession in 2011 so that no more children like me are deprived again of a chance of growing up and living happily in their own land.

DAILY TOUCHING AND KISSING OUR SOIL ABROAD

"What gift shall I bring for you from home?" inquired Mr. Mayen Wol Jong over a long-distance telephone call from Khartoum to London. "We are going to hold a prayer at our home village of Kuajok in South Sudan to celebrate the advent of CPA."

"First greet everybody at home for me. Then please collect a piece of our soil from my birthplace and despatch it to me." I responded.

Mayen Wol complied. He despatched the requested soil to his wife Ajok Majok Dut who forwarded it to me in London via Miss Abei Deng. It was like a dream for me to receive, touch, and feel the soil from my home after twenty years abroad. I felt a huge sigh of relief with a sense of joy as if I had practically got back home.

Precious as it was, I decided to place the soil in a traditional calabash that I kept constantly on the table in my computer room for easy access and visibility. Every time I felt low and homesick, I made sure I touched and kissed the soil. I did the same every night before going to sleep and first thing in the morning when I woke up.

Every touch and kiss of the soil had a special and peculiar effect on me. I felt waves of love and dedication for my land of South Sudan vibrating in me. My heart rate went up and unless I succeeded to fight back the tears, I ended up weeping. Even though I was thousands of miles away in Europe, every touch and kiss made me feel as if I was sitting there at my birthplace in my homeland, the Heart of Africa.

So daily I went on doing the ritual of touching and kissing the precious soil of my Promised Land for a long time while I was abroad until the day I boarded the plane back home following my call to service as stated below.

CALLED FOR SERVICE BY JOSHUA

Whilst on the verge of resuming work in UK as a specialist, after regaining my strength, I was called to render service in my homeland of Southern Sudan. This was a call I could not turn down despite a gross discrepancy in the salaries and other job-related benefits. This decision obviously put my house at risk in London as I could no longer afford the high mortgage payments. Eventually, it was repossessed by the bank. Likewise, I gave up my Mercedes car and other valuables in the UK.

I am only mentioning those losses of property and possessions, not because I regret the decision I made to go back home and assist my people; but, to illustrate that others also made some sacrifices even though these do not equate to those paid by our heroes and heroines in the frontline of the war.

Furthermore, no car, no possession, no house, however luxurious it may be, can exceed the extreme sweetness of one's own homeland! In those cars I drove and in those houses I lived without feeling the joy I felt when I was heading back home from Europe, even before the plane landed there.

Dr. ACHIER KISSES HIS HOMELAND AFTER TWENTY-THREE YEARS

By Mr. Alphonse Akol Thiik

A man was spotted to lie down barely on the ground and kiss the land at Juba Airport soon after stepping off from a plane at 10.35 a.m. on Monday, 2 October 2006.

Those in the crowd at the airport who did not know him before wondered if he might be a madman. Some thought he was an actor. This is because, after kissing the land he sat down on the ground touched the soil with his right hand and kissed it. He repeated that sequence of touching and kissing twenty-three times and spectators also wondered what that number exactly represented.

Soon it became apparent that the man was a child who had missed to see his homeland of South Sudan for twenty-two years from 1984 to 2006 against his own will due to circumstances of war. Indeed, he was stepping on his precious soil for the first time after those years and every touch and kiss he made represented every year he had been away from home.

His journey back home is said to have started all the way from Europe where he had been shedding miserable tears for missing his beloved homeland so much for so long.

"Missing one's own homeland after so many years is the most painful thing to happen to anyone that cherishes it," he stated. "It is even more painful emotionally than death," he added, while struggling to hold back his tears amid the crowd at the airport.

Whilst on transit for forty-eight hours in Khartoum on his way to the South he is also reported to have refused absolutely to drink water or eat food there despite extremely hot weather. He even declined meals in the plane and the first drop of mineral water offered to him on arrival in Juba, saying the following:

"The first sip of water or bite of food to go down my throat in Sudan after twenty-three years of absence should be originally from and take place in my own homeland. I can consume any other food and water from anywhere else thereafter if need be."

Asked by an observer what his name was he replied: "I am simply a lover of South Sudan that has been away for so long." He declined to specify his name, adding, "I did not touch and kiss my land in order to promote my name; I did so entirely out of pure love and dedication for my land and people of South Sudan."

However, a reliable source who knew him from childhood later revealed his name as Dr. Achier Deng Akol.

Touching the Land Every Time before Flying Abroad

After returning home, before I embark onto a plane to fly abroad on any trip, I bow and touch our precious land while I recite the following prayer:

"Our Land, I am not leaving you again for a long time. I am only going on a short trip and I will return as soon as possible if all goes on well."

Naming my Son Dhukbaai (Returning Home)

When my little son was born in Juba on 16 April 2009, I decided to name him as Deng Dhukbaai and sang a song called Methee yin acəl Dhukbaai together with my wife. Deng being the name of my father and Dhukbaai is a Jieng word that means returning home. The song literally means "Oh! Child! You are called Returning Home."

I called my son Dhukbaai in order to mark the fact that a lot of the children of Southern Sudan that had been scattered to the bush and foreign lands have returned home with the advent of the Comprehensive Peace Agreement. More will do so if 2011 referendum goes well.

D4 APPRECIATION OF DEDICATIONS

The beauty of our Land of Southern Sudan is reflected more in the endless dedications and sacrifices we its children make collectively or individually. It is similarly shown by the amount of acknowledgement and appreciation received from fellow Southerners and others for efforts exerted.

One of the Southerners who openly expressed his appreciation for our martyrs is Mr. Luk Kuth Dak as shown in his published article below:

Is South Self-determination a Gift by NCP/NIF?

The CPA and South Sudan self-determination is a victory, not a gift from NCP/NIF.

08 December 2009

By Luk Kuth Dak

I failed to understand the preposterous notion that somehow the Comprehensive Peace Agreement CPA and the right for self-determination were a gift from National Congress Party (NCP) and its radical wing the National Islamic Front (NIF) to the people of South Sudan, and therefore, they (Southerners) should be grateful and simply go along with the NCP/NIF violations of the accord, is absolutely disingenuous and a misconception, to say the least.

However, it wasn't much of a surprise for me to hear that nonsensical claim from the NCP and NIF. Unfortunately, sadly so, there have been some vocal and suspicious political voices in South Sudan who still live under the misconception that the CPA can be implemented without fighting for it, and vehemently berated the Sudan Peoples' Liberation Movement (SPLM) and the Government of South Sudan (GoSS), for taking a stand against the NCP/NIF's tangible violations of the CPA and unwillingness to honour their obligations in moving forward with its implementation, on the timely manner which was clearly spelled out and stipulated in the agreement and the constitution.

It's crystal clear, no doubt, that those people do not really know anything about the mentality of the Northern Sudanese, in general, and the NCP/NIF in particular. Truth is: if you have lived long enough among them, like I have, you must undoubtedly come to a conclusion that the only way, literally so, to get anything done with the NCP/NIF, unfortunately, is to give them the taste of their own medicine, which is confrontation and engagement. That's the only language they seem to understand better.

President Salva Kiir Mayardit should be commended for committing himself to our just cause for self-determination and self-worth after half a century long and counting of the Arabs' oppression. I cheered him when he told Southerners that their right for self-determination cannot be downplayed. (Sudan Tribune, 6 December 2009).

Yet, it's tragic, really, that we could have some people in our society who are actually content with notion of being the second-class citizens in their own land. They seem to believe that things are just going too well, and cannot fathom why the rest of us are making all this (fuss) with the NCP, which—in their ill-thinking—has given us what no other northern government has ever done. In their short-sighted judgment, the struggle has ended the moment the CPA was signed into law in 2005.

Dead wrong!

"The SPLM is increasingly becoming more and more problematic to the partnership instead of being grateful to the NCP, for allowing it the full control of the affairs of the South," screeched one member of the notorious Jallaba Southern Golden Boys' Club.

That's as treacherous as it gets. Indeed, that sentiment is nothing but a direct insult to the struggle and the sacrifices made by the brave people of South Sudan, who have given it all they have for a little over a half a century of heroism against the forces of evil and bigotry.

However, one of the bright spots in this debate is the fact that, apart from those (sellout) traitors, (all of whom we know), the whole world flat out knew that the NCP and NIF were bitterly defeated and have only adhered to the reality of the situation, after it became abundantly clear that the war was soon going to be fought not only in jungles of the South, but in their own peaceful neighbourhoods and backyards.

Therefore, if you're a South Sudanese, you should not allow anybody telling you that it wasn't a victory or a small victory. Because it was a historical and a monumental victory, and a great achievement—we should be proud of—by our brave warriors, alive and fallen.

Final Thought:

"We must learn to live together as brothers, or perish together as fools."

Dr. Martin Luther King, Jr.

I quite agree with my brother in arms, Luk Kuth Dak. The least we can all do is to continue to appreciate, particularly the ultimate sacrifices made by millions of our martyrs over the long years of our struggle for liberty. Let us remember them during the 2011 referendum and vote the way they would wish us to.

Of course if any Southern Sudanese feels so dedicated to a united Sudan, he or she will equally have an opportunity to vote for unity in that referendum.

As for my own little sacrifices and dedications stated in this book, do not ask me whether I did them for unity or secession. Of course, I did them for unity provided that it is made attractive during the interim period!

PHOTOS

A Land So Conspicuous

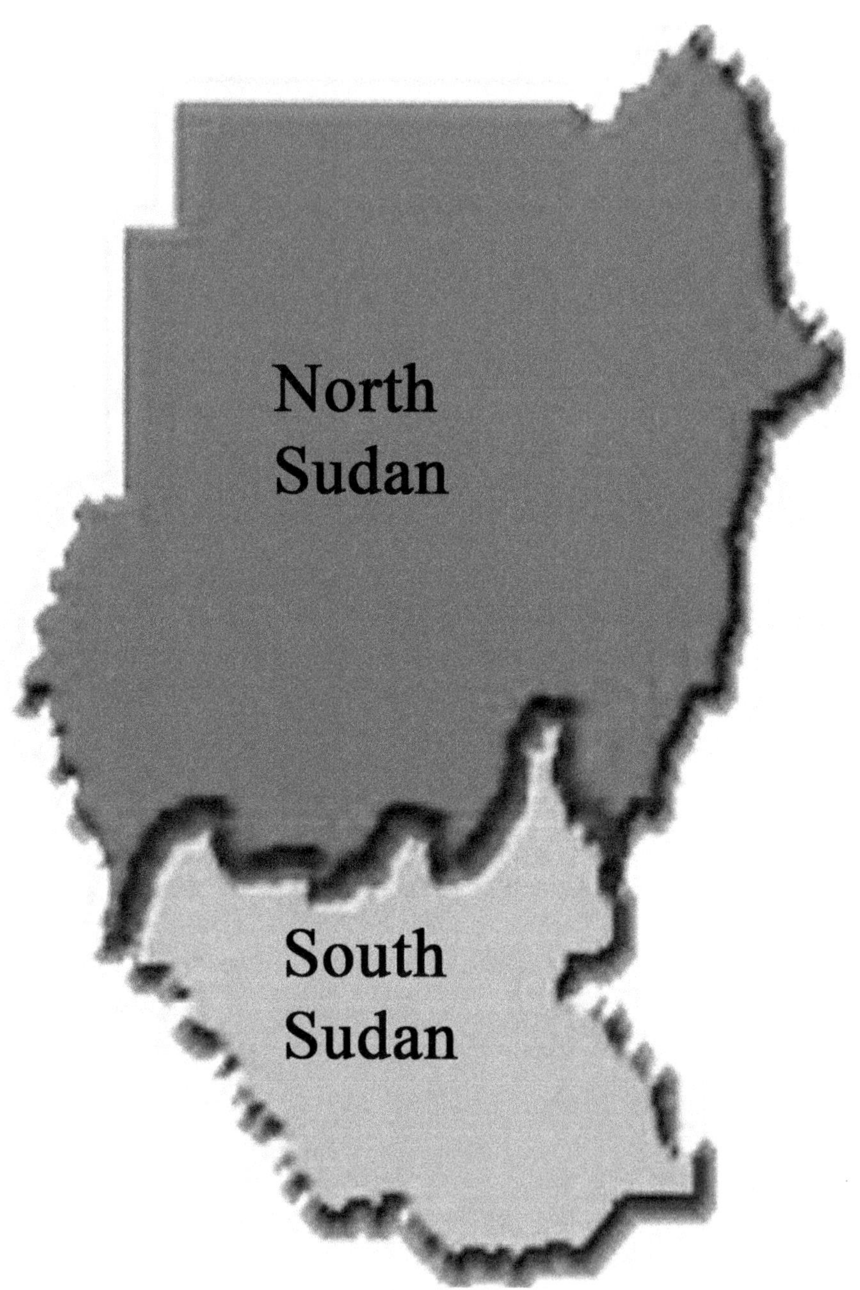
North
Sudan
South
Sudan

Flag of South Sudan

Dr. John Garang De Mabior
"Would you like to vote to be second-class citizens in your own country? It is absolutely your choice"

General Salva
Kiir Mayardit

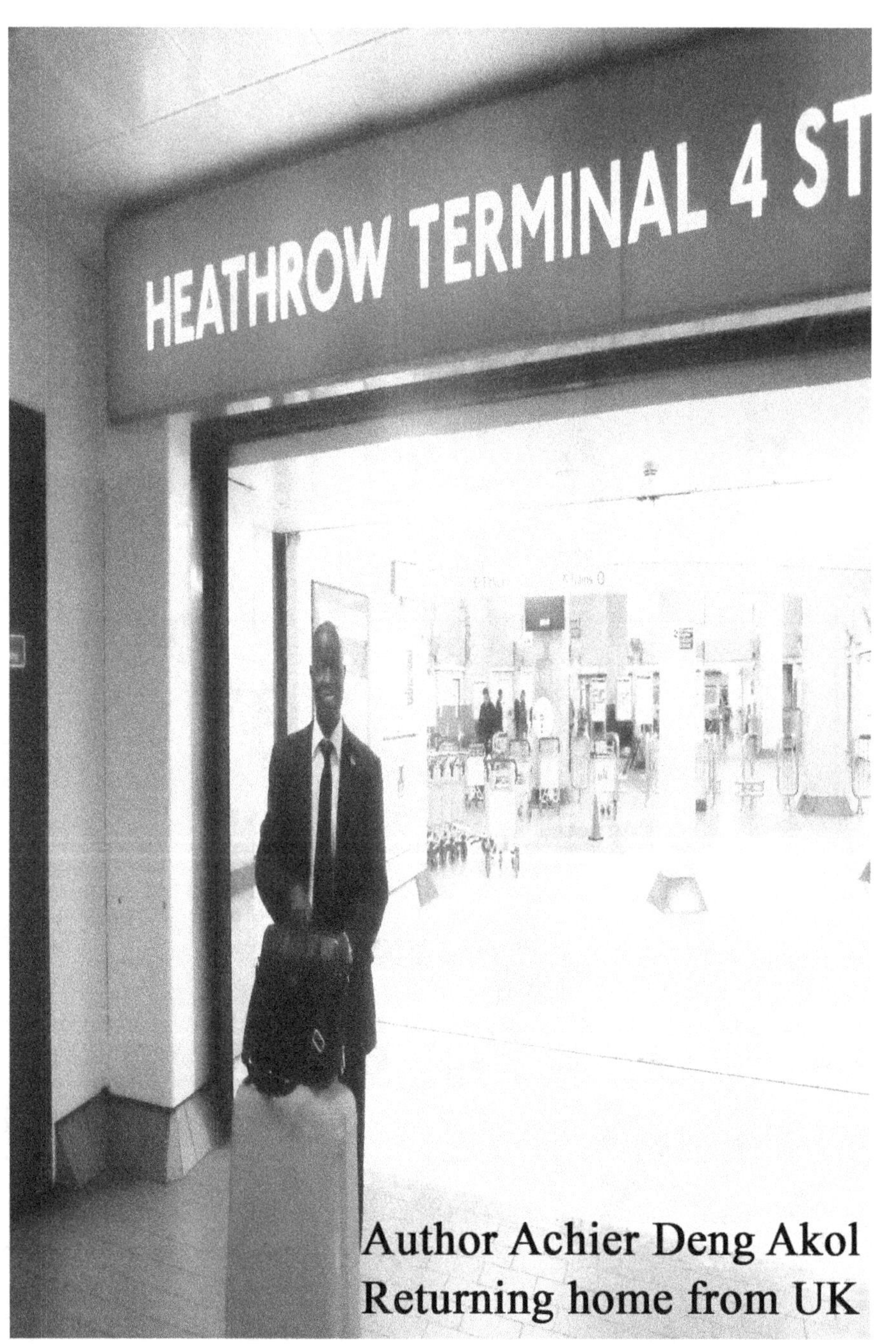

Author Achier Deng Akol
Returning home from UK

Author kissing the precious soil of his homeland on arrival after missing it for decades

Close to him, I will continue to stand,
till a new sun rises in 2011 and beyond.

Daughter Nyibol happily married to Amet after meeting and seeing her father after the war for the first

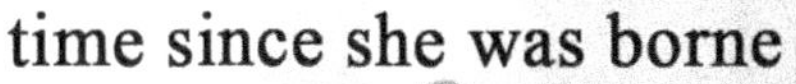

time since she was borne

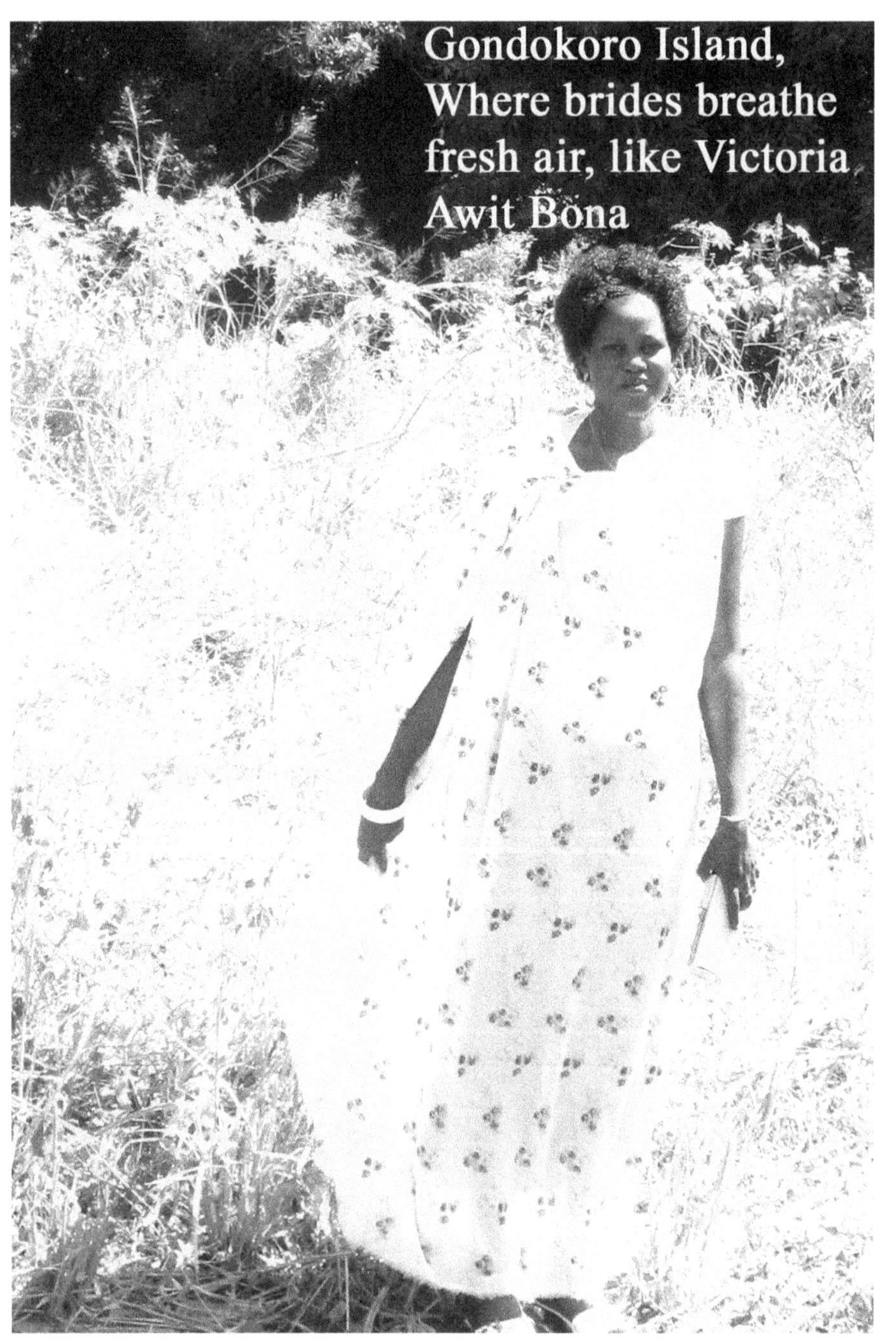

Gondokoro Island,
Where brides breathe
fresh air, like Victoria
Awit Bona

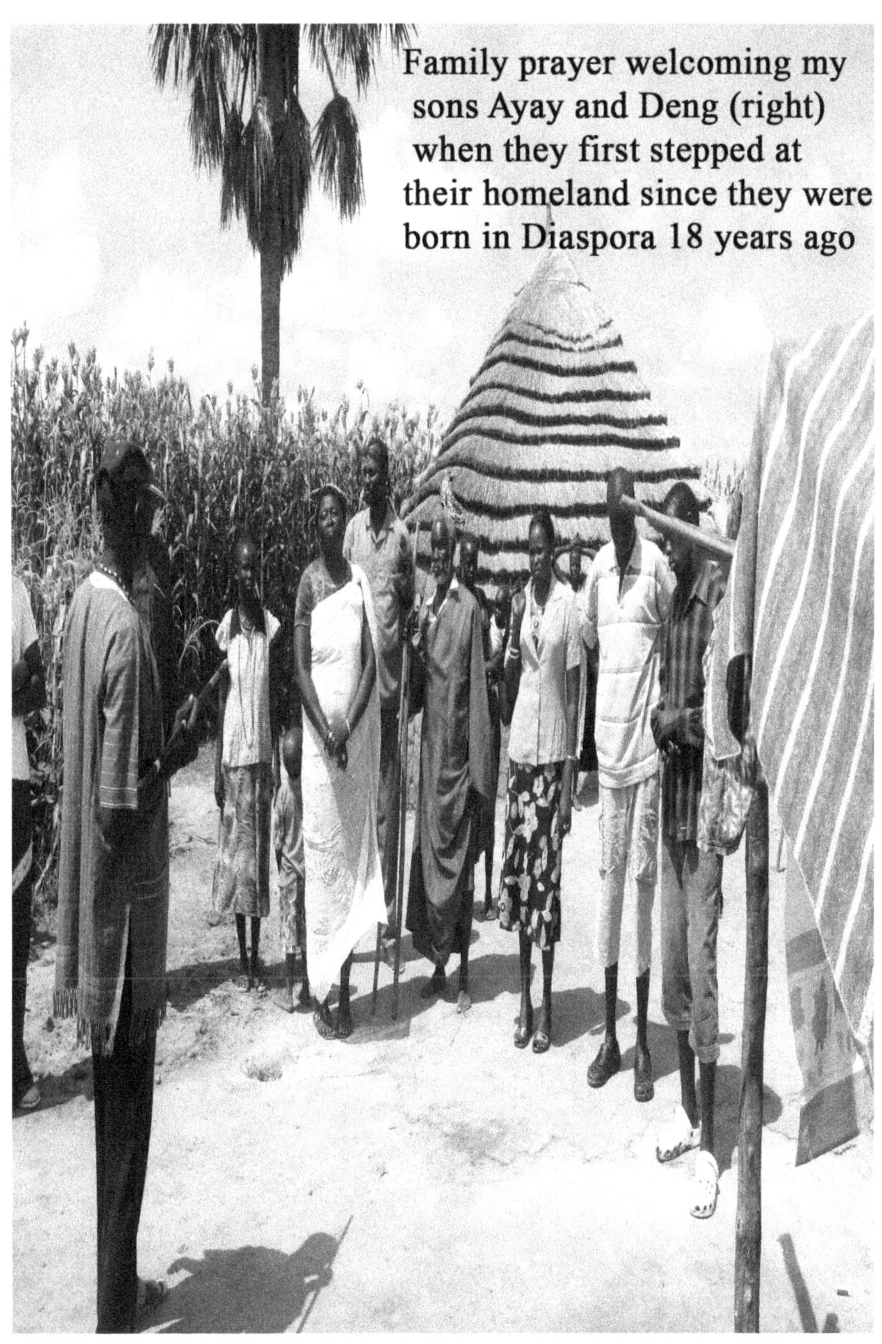

Family prayer welcoming my sons Ayay and Deng (right) when they first stepped at their homeland since they were born in Diaspora 18 years ago

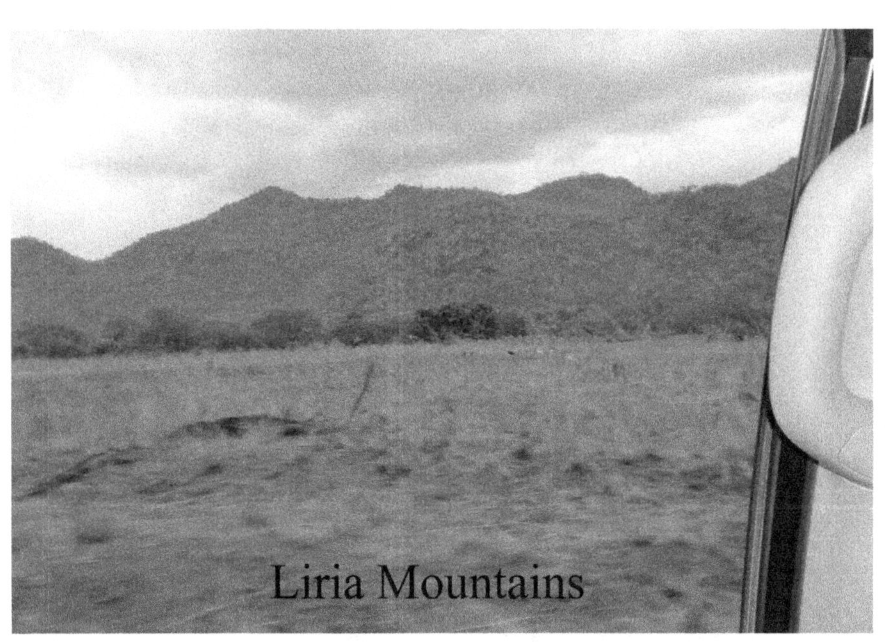

Liria Mountains

Cirlces of huts at Renk

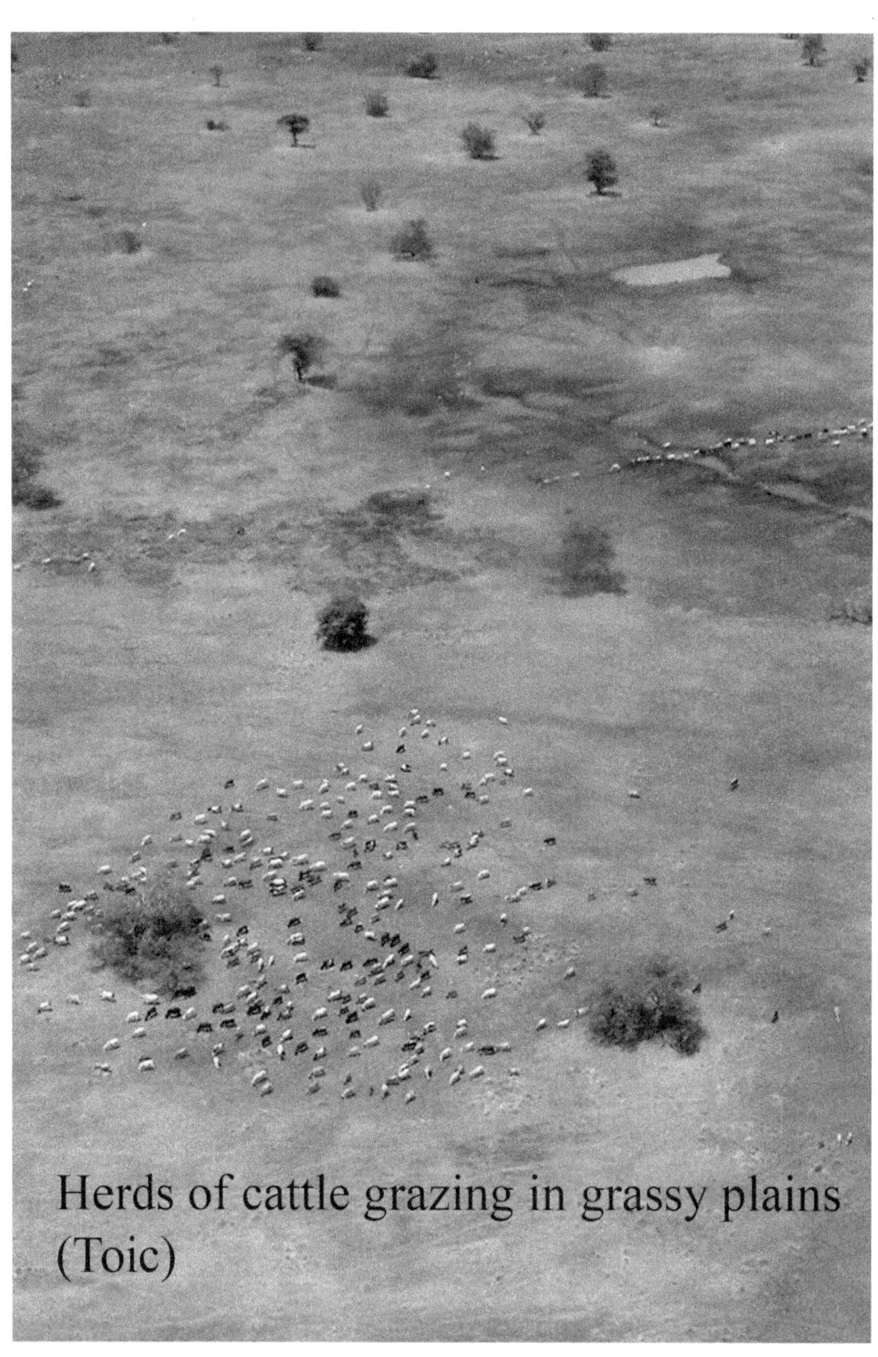

Herds of cattle grazing in grassy plains (Toic)

Beautiful Bentiu

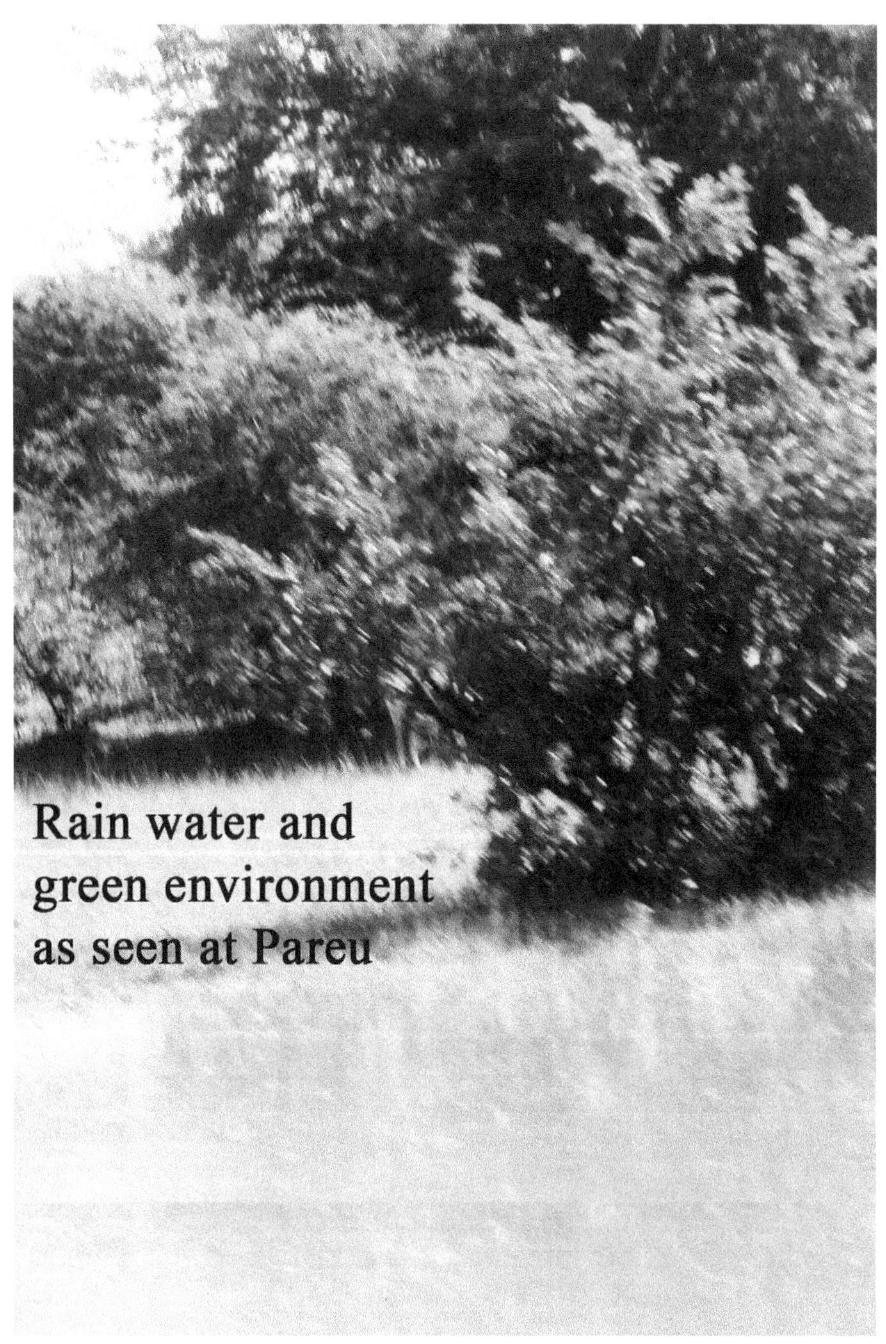

Rain water and green environment as seen at Pareu

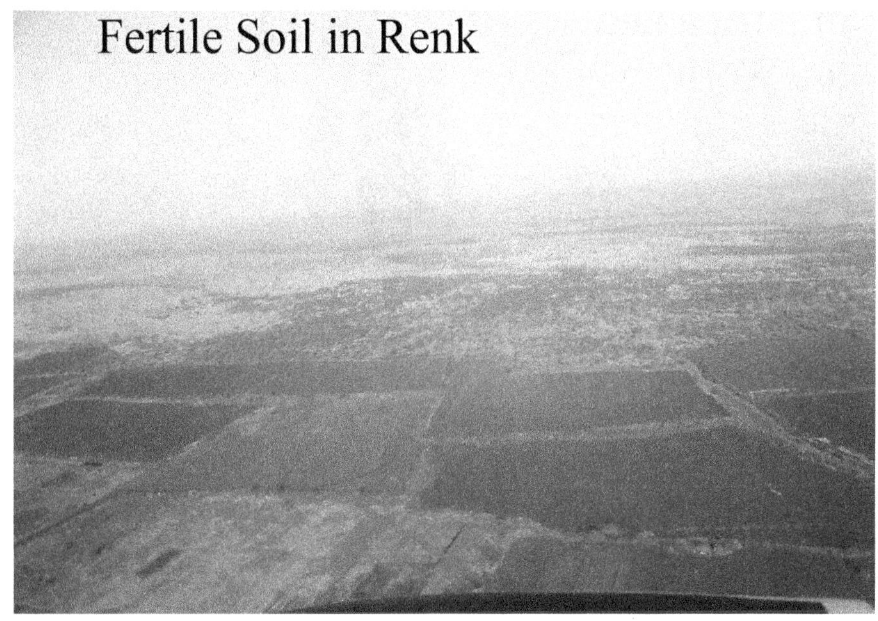

Fertile Soil in Renk

Tropical sunshine,
abundant rain and
fertile soil:
South Sudan is
a potential
bread basket
of Africa and
the World

Future seeds of maize

Future crops (koth) tugged away in the ceiling

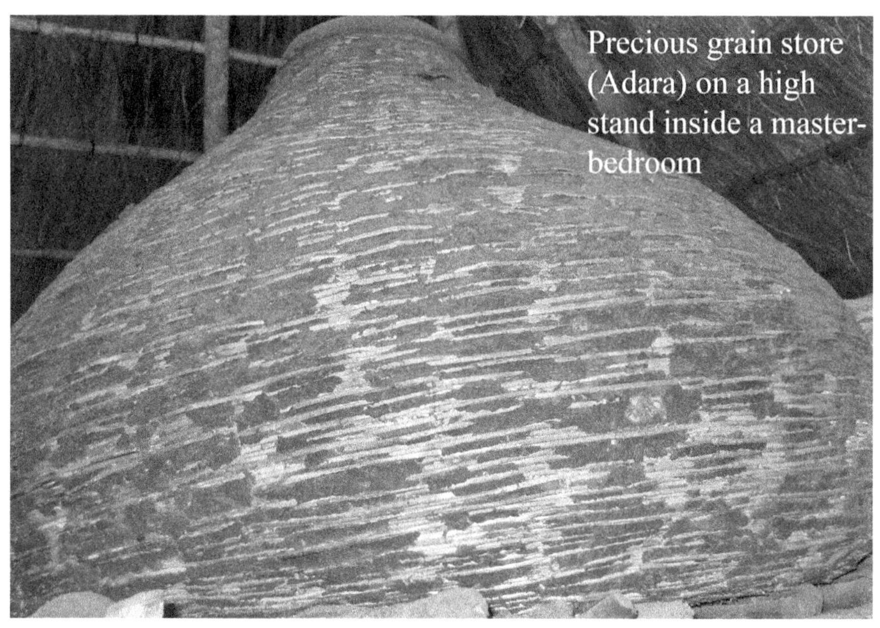
Precious grain store (Adara) on a high stand inside a master-bedroom

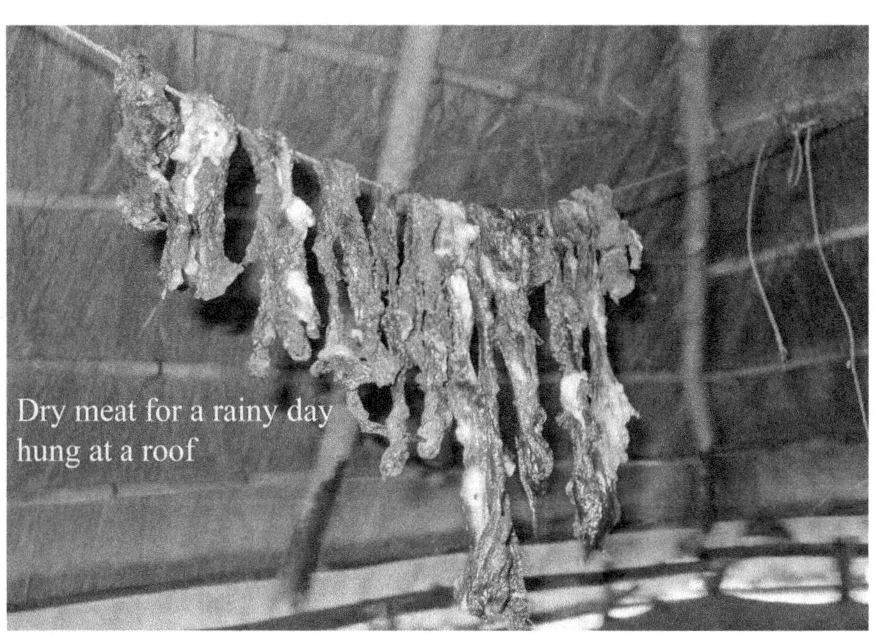

Dry meat for a rainy day hung at a roof

Grain Pounder
(Dong)

Traditional Dish (Adwok)

Shell Spoons (Thiet)

Serving Pot
(Gulung)

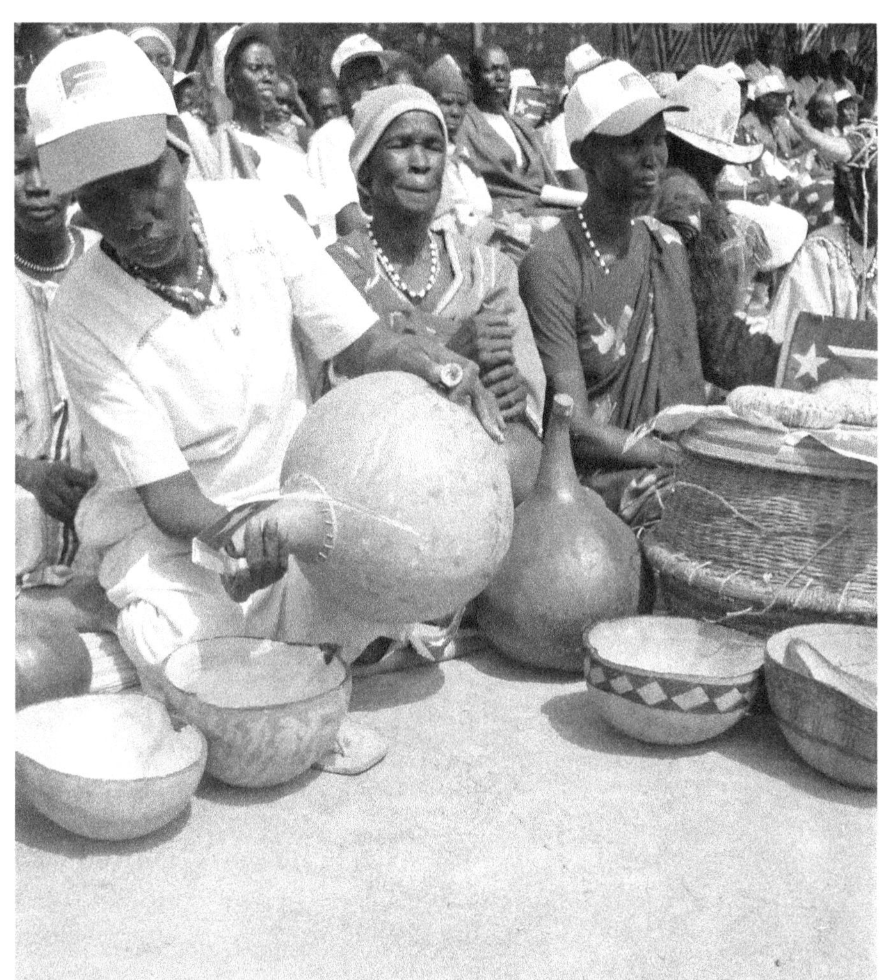

Women proudly displaying milk guords (ajiep), basket (gac) and utensils (aduk) during a presidential reception at Gong Machar. "We are the mothers that bear, deliver and care for generations".

Delicious Meals in Renk

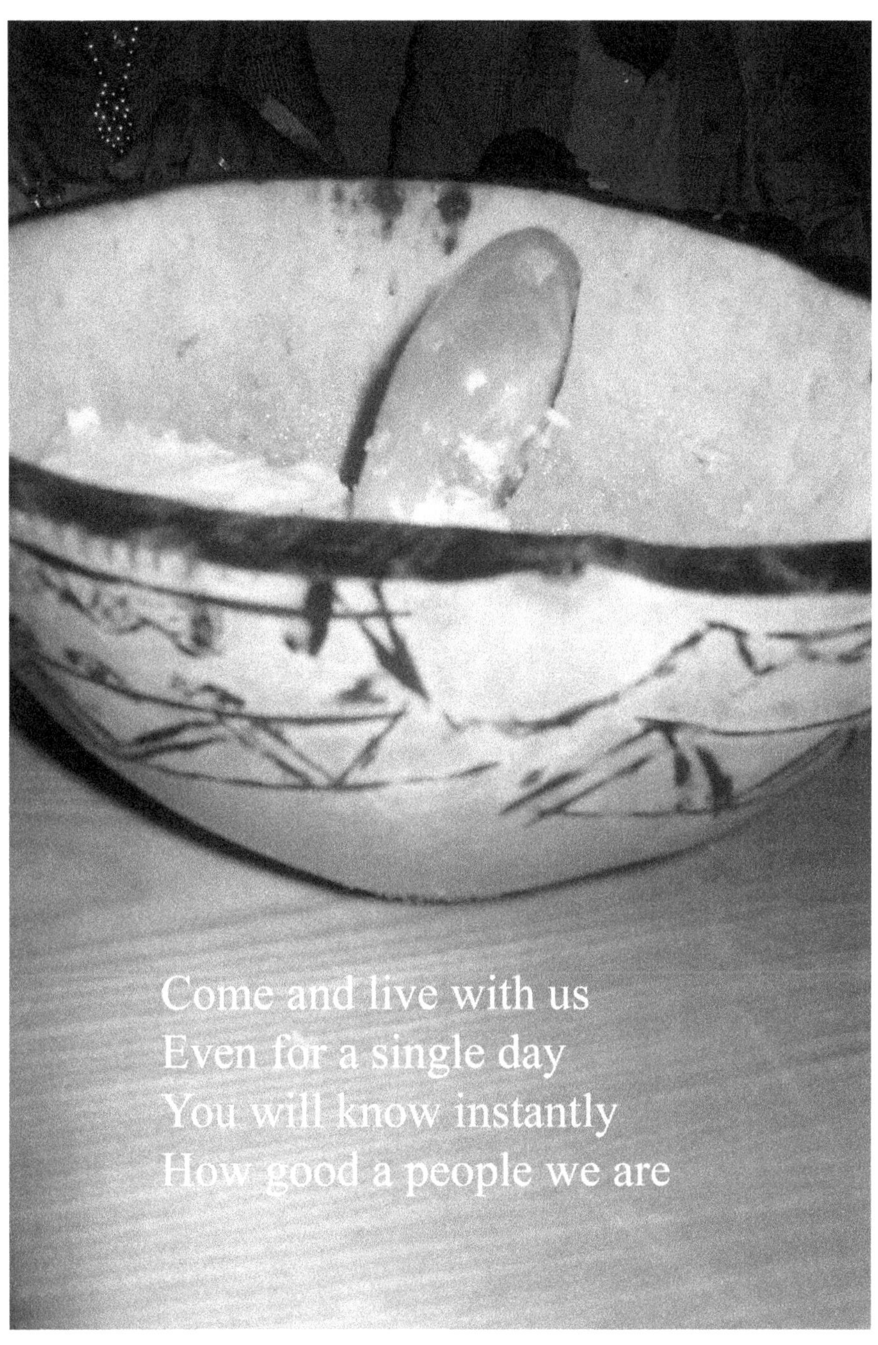
Come and live with us
Even for a single day
You will know instantly
How good a people we are

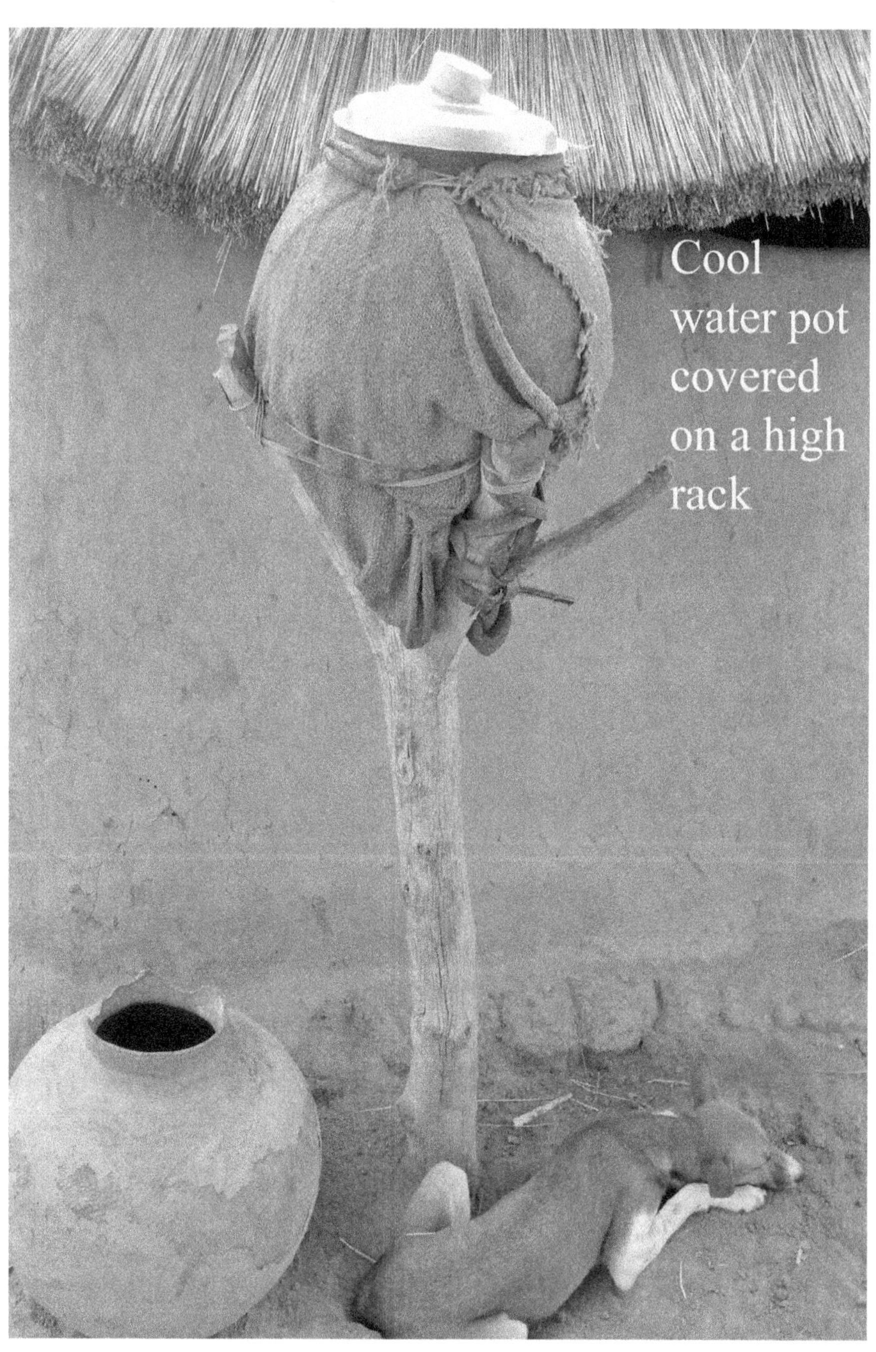
Cool water pot covered on a high rack

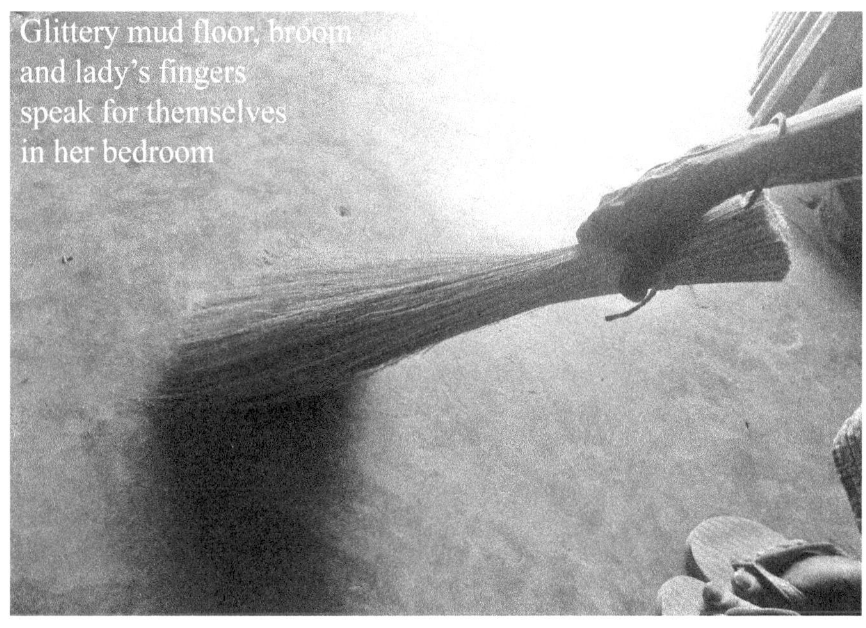
Glittery mud floor, broom
and lady's fingers
speak for themselves
in her bedroom

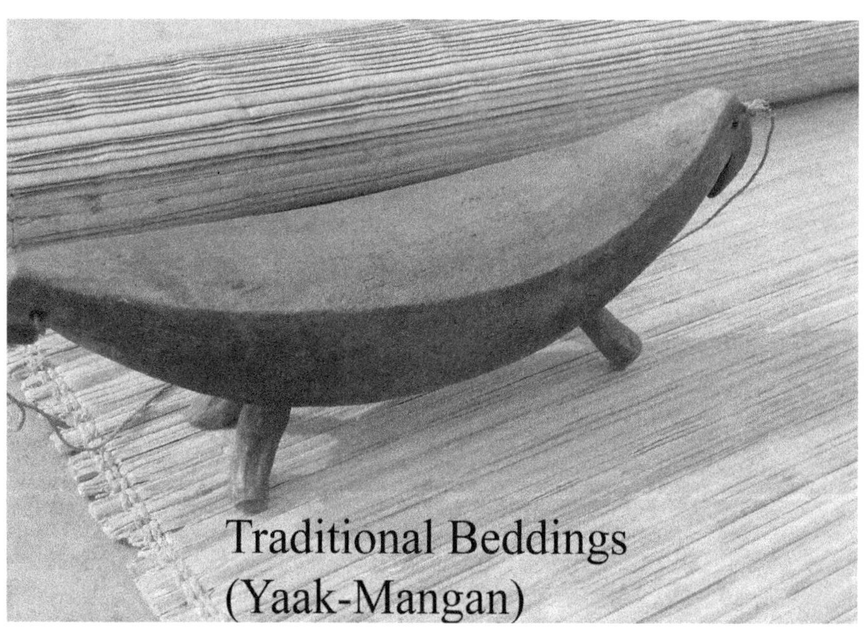

Traditional Beddings (Yaak-Mangan)

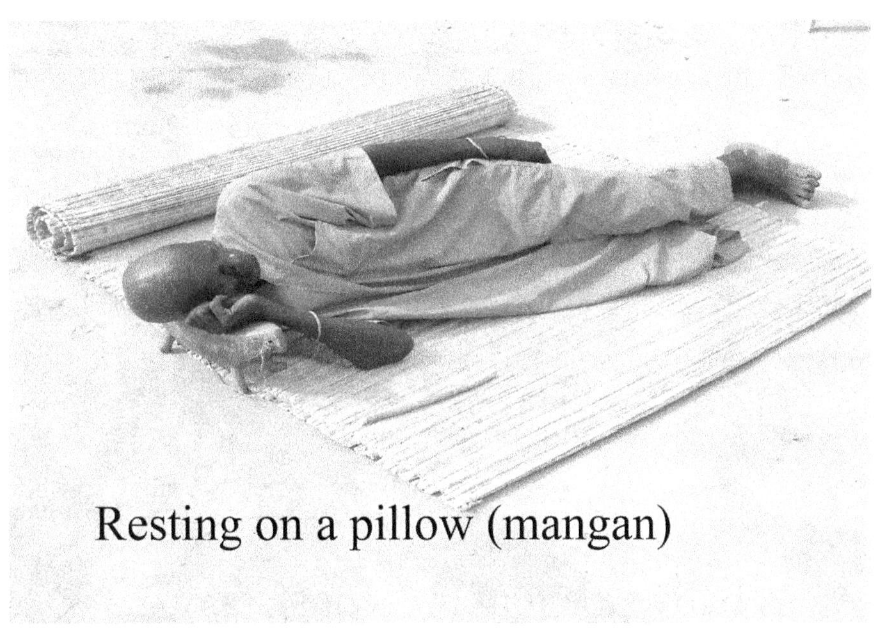

Resting on a pillow (mangan)

A baby sleeping in a cot (Diany)

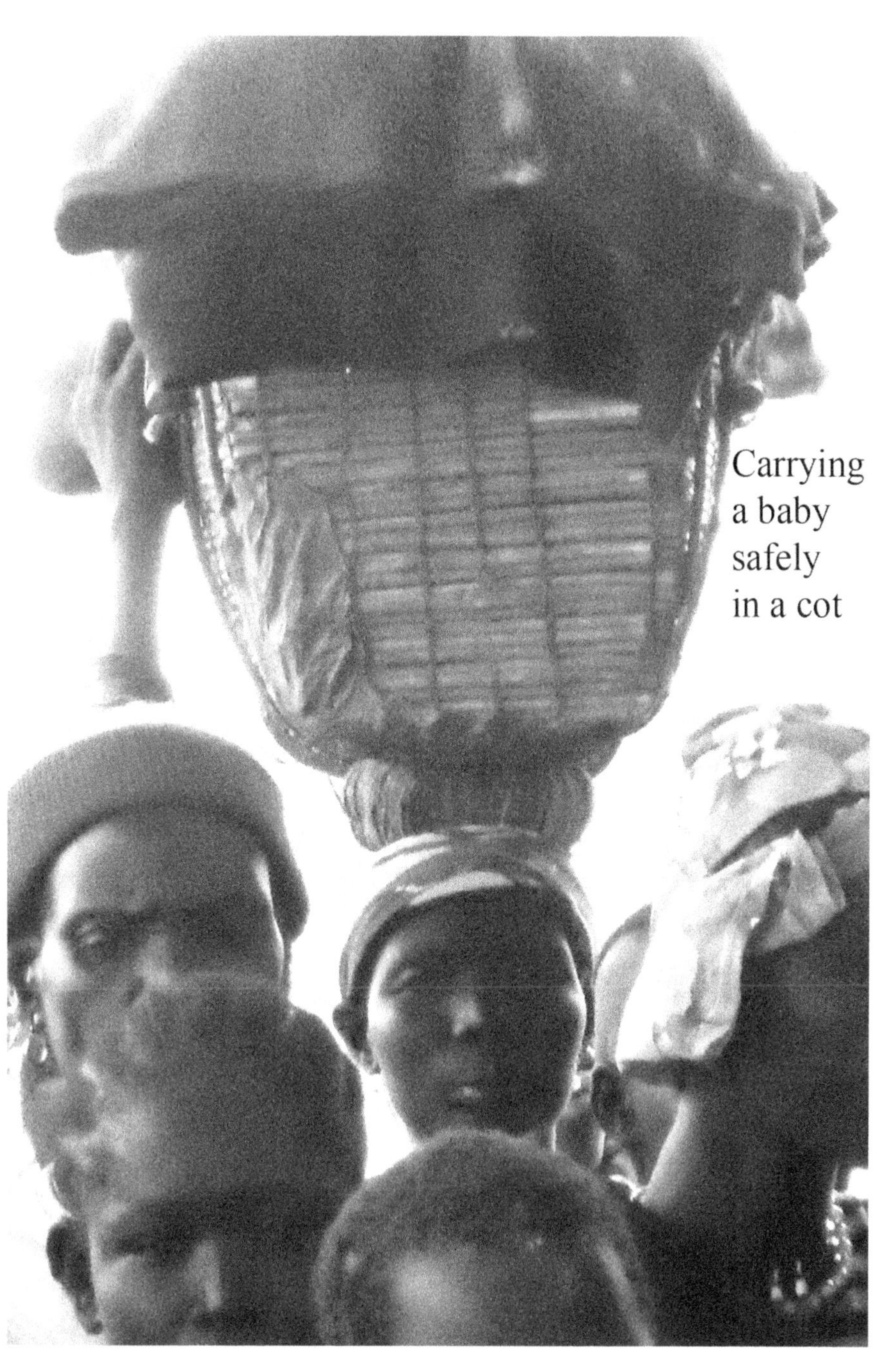

Carrying a baby safely in a cot

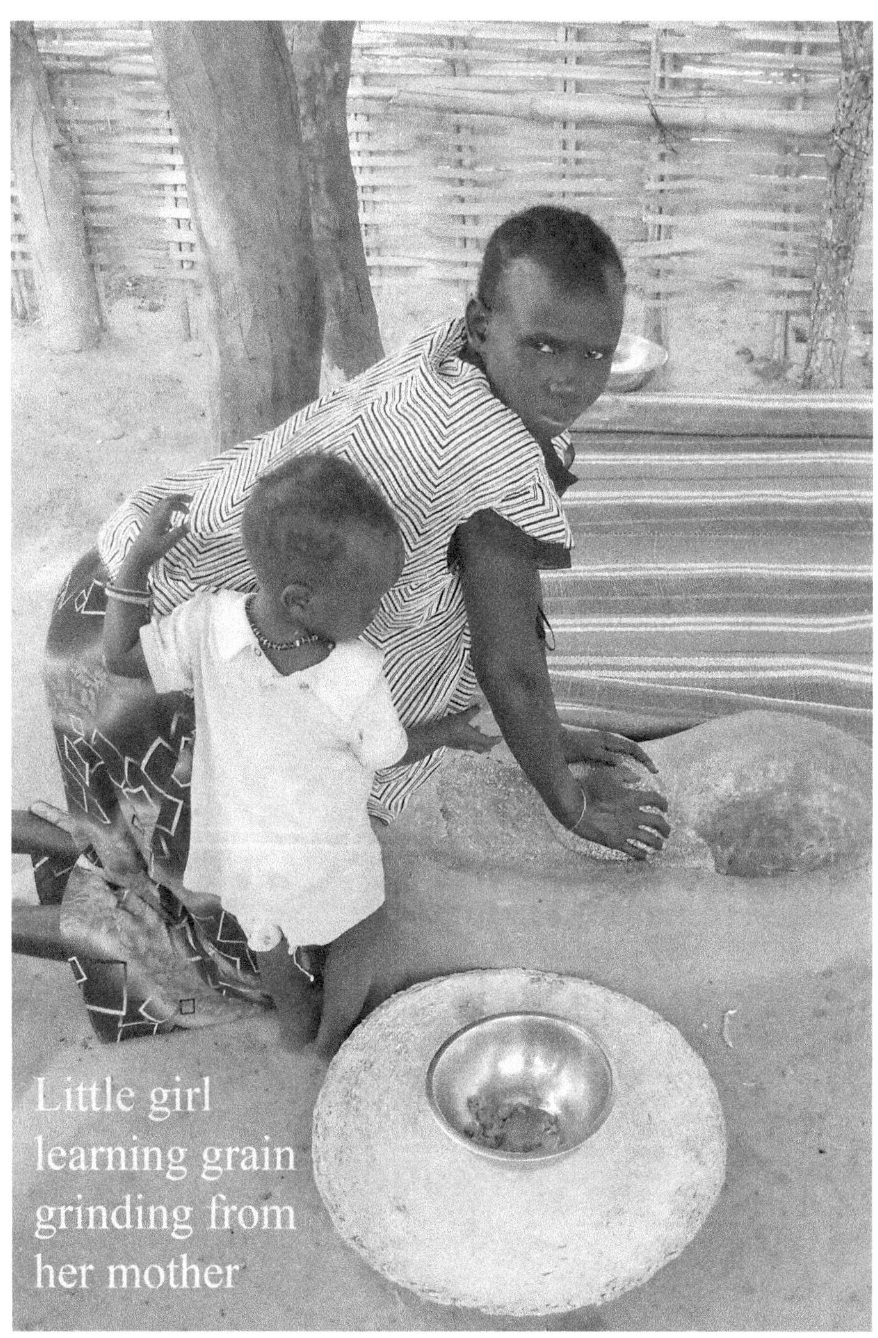

Little girl learning grain grinding from her mother

Play time at Kuajok

Akon Elementary School where President Salva Kiir Mayardit started education

Juba Airport evolving

Our bridges may be few and crude like this one in Wau. More superb ones will be developed.

Our market has re-started with selling charcoal on roads as seen near Wau; but it will surely overtake Dubai.

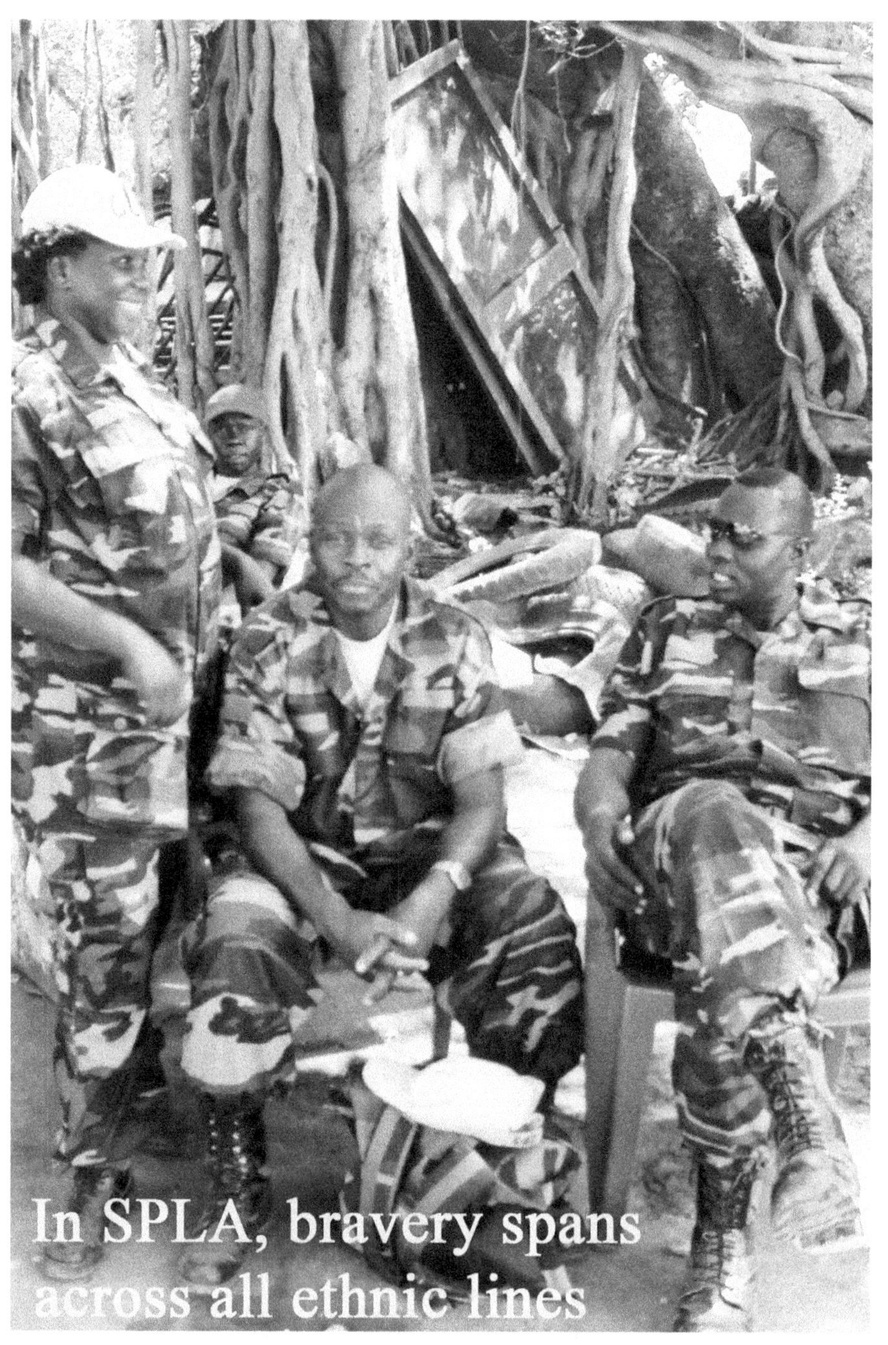

In SPLA, bravery spans across all ethnic lines

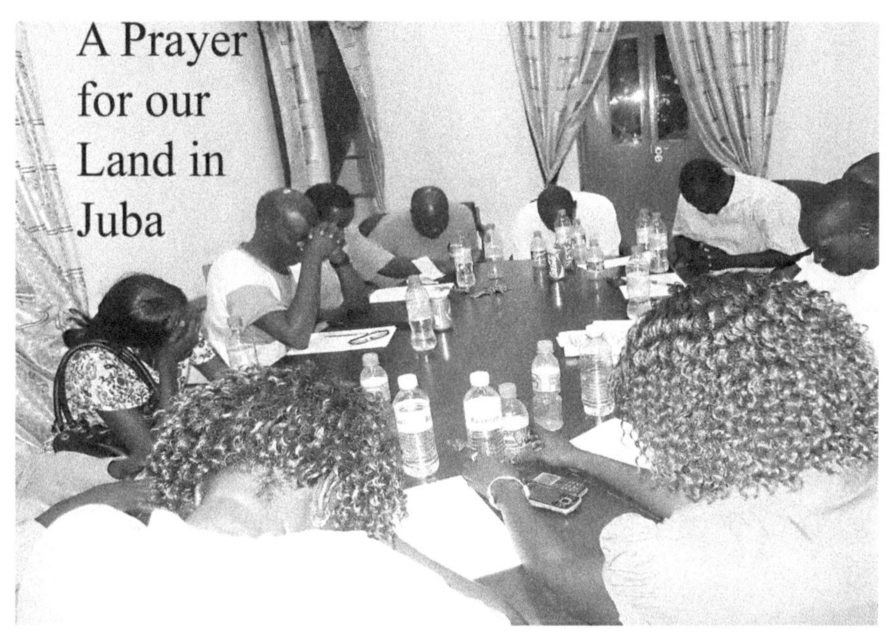
A Prayer
for our
Land in
Juba

South Sudan President Salva Kiir Mayrdit, Vice President Dr. Riek Machar Teny, Western Equatoria Governor Jema Nunu Kumba and the Medical Team for Presidential Campaign led by the Author at a campaign phase in Yambio.

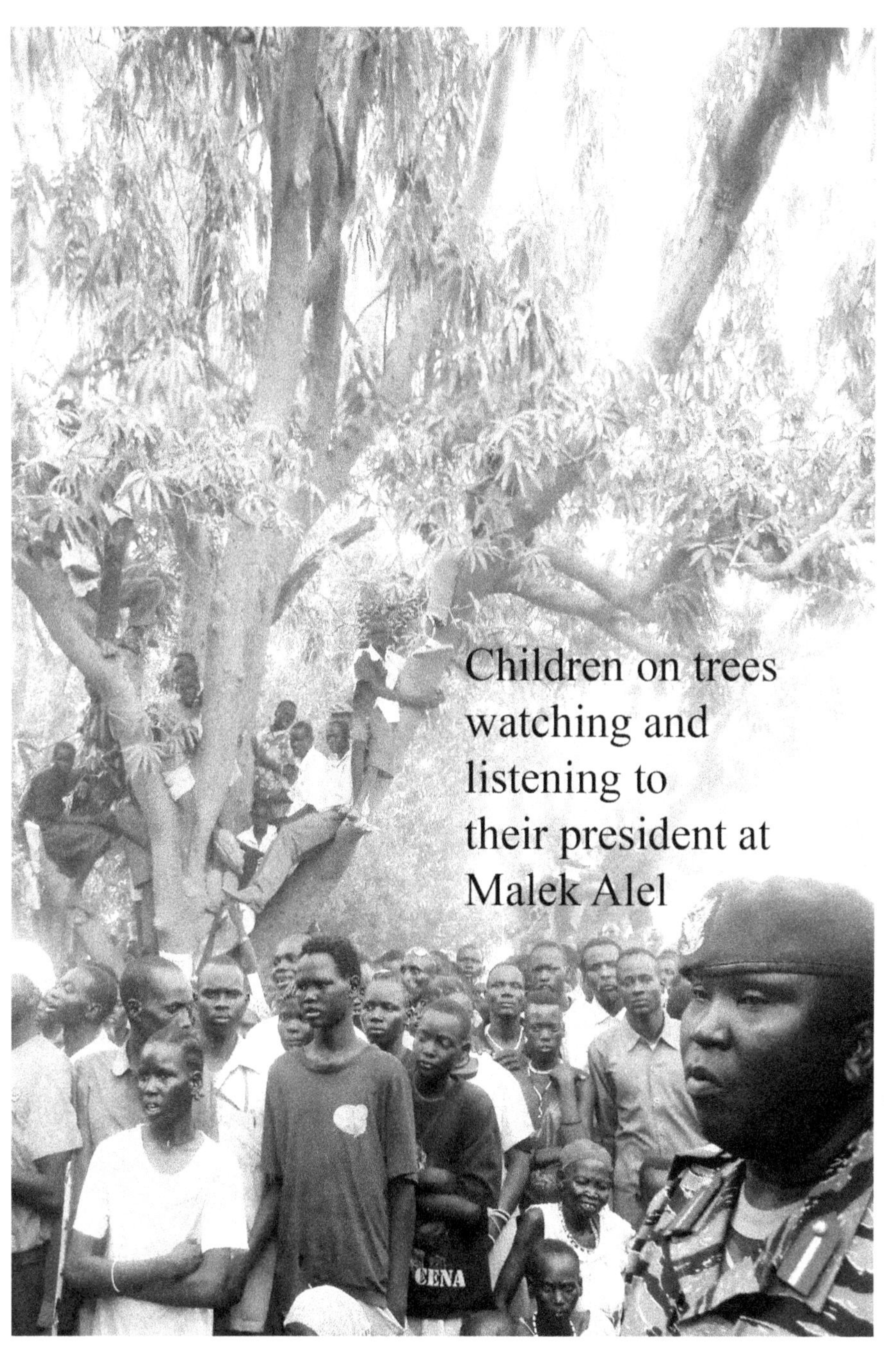

Children on trees watching and listening to their president at Malek Alel

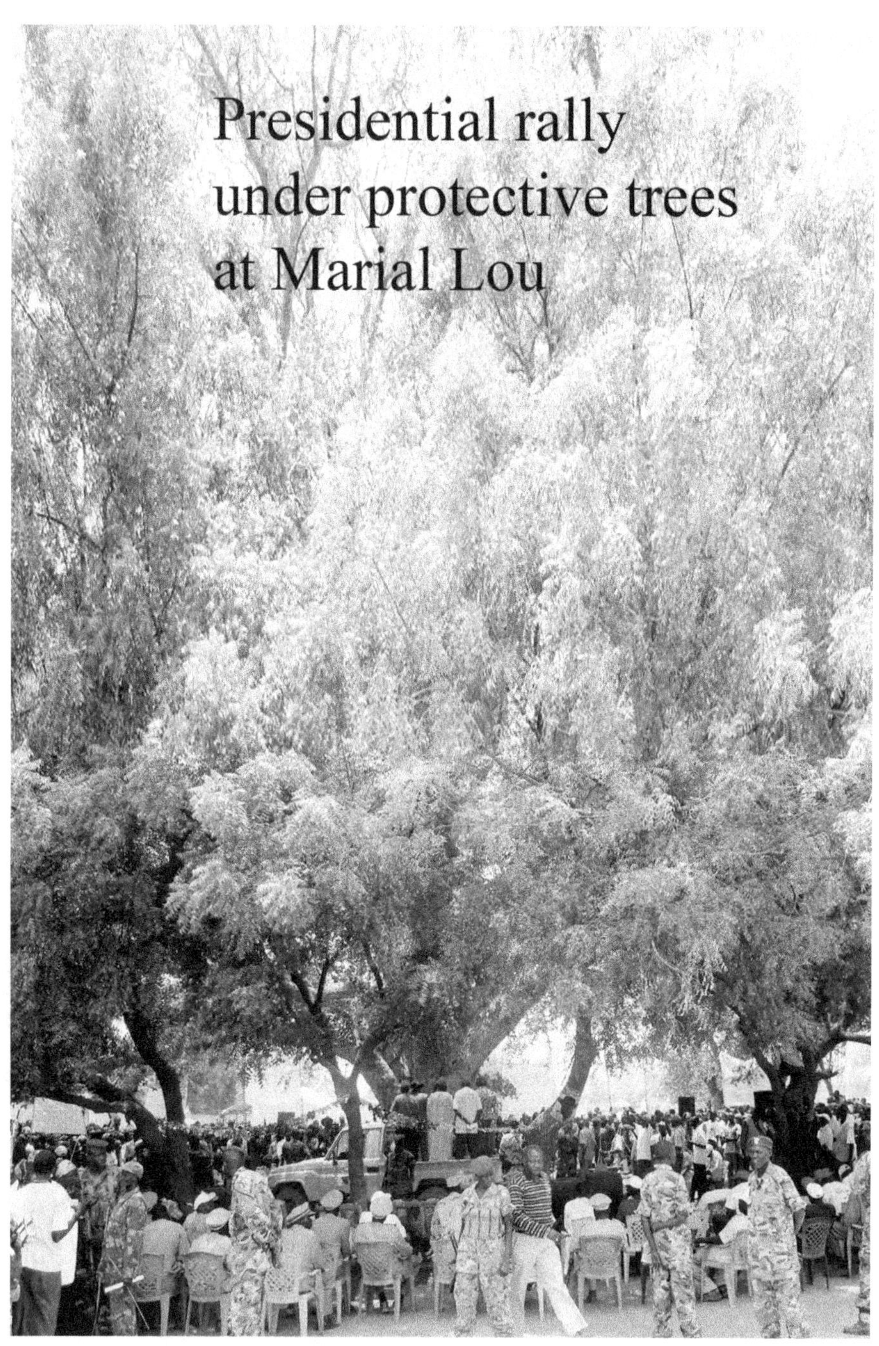
Presidential rally under protective trees at Marial Lou

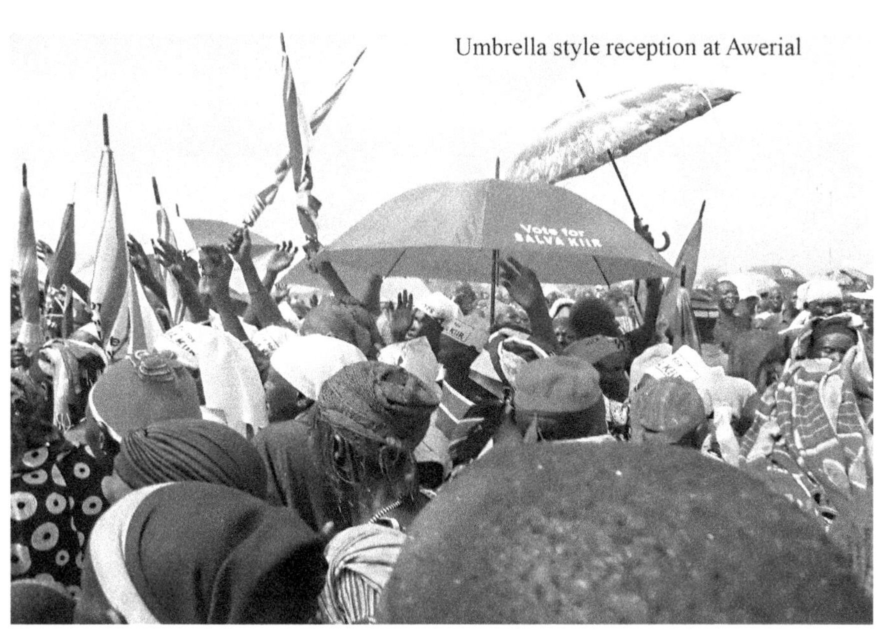

Umbrella style reception at Awerial

Pyramid reception at Mauit

SPLM has grown from founding five in 1983
to millions of members
as seen in Bentiu in 2010

Cultural dancers at Kapoeta

Lotuka cultural display in Torit

Kapoeta girls

Dho-Luo (Jur Chol) cultural display at Mapel

Zande women in Yambio

Tuic girls at Turalei

Abiliang Girls

Shilluk Girls in Malakal

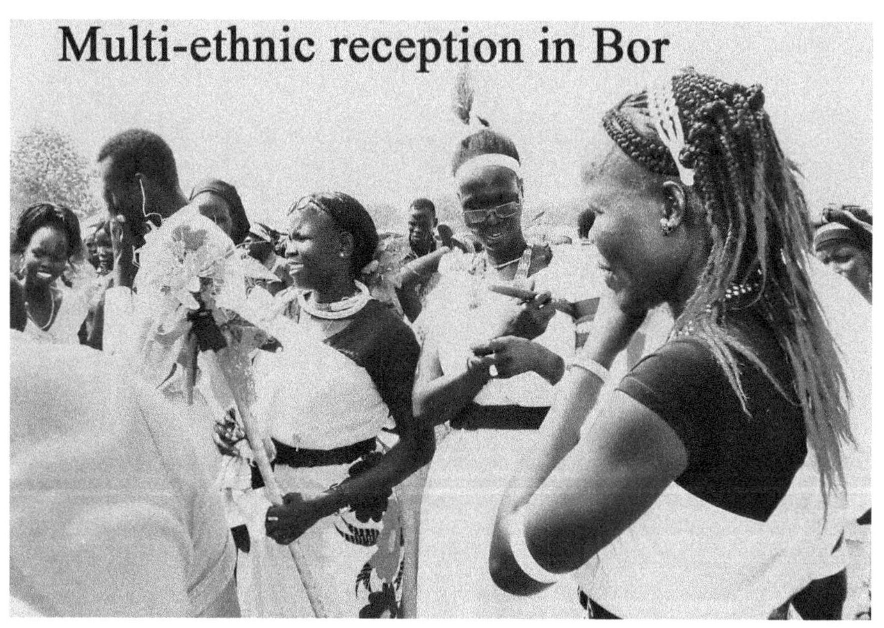

Multi-ethnic reception in Bor

Shilluk dance in Malakal

Nuer Dance
in Malkal

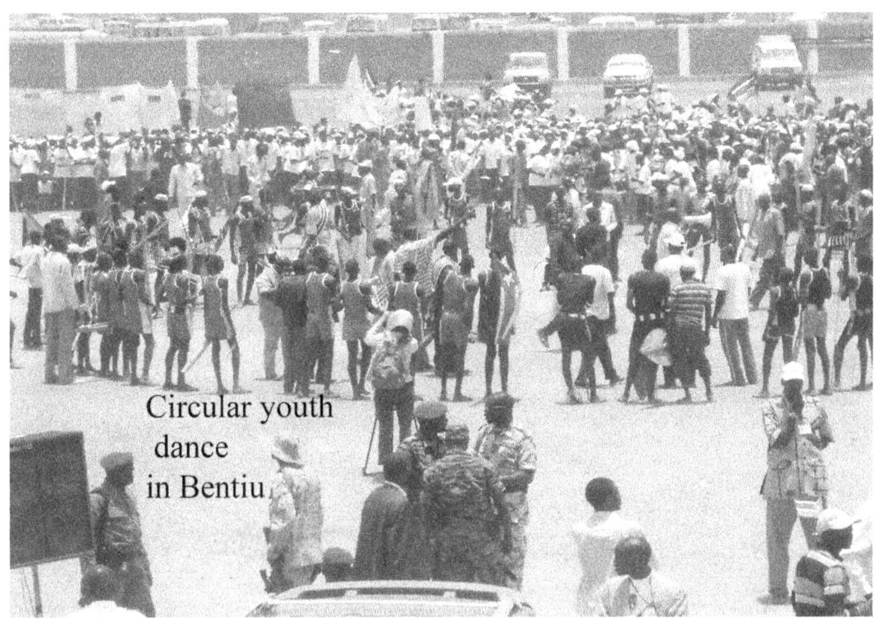

Circular youth dance in Bentiu

Abiliang Dance at Paloc

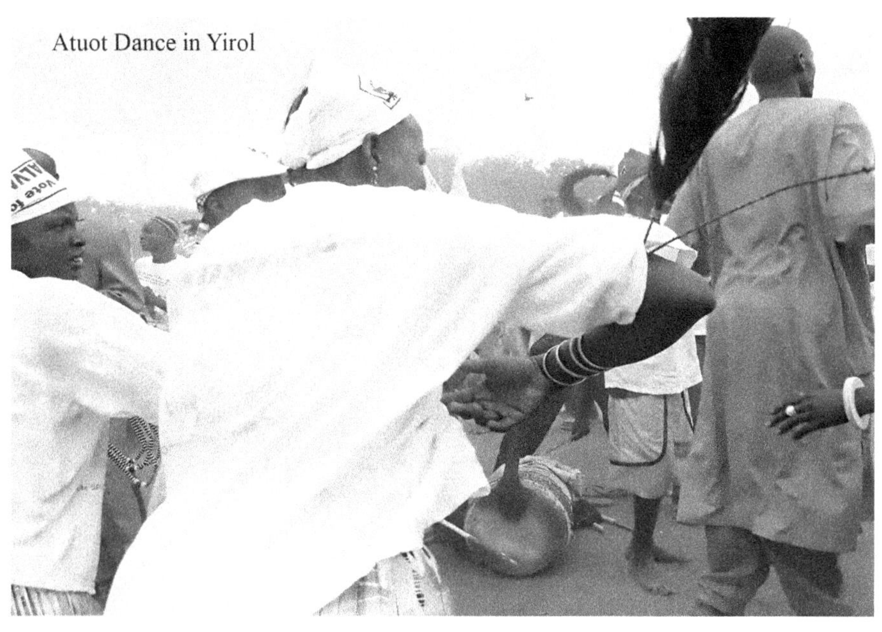

Atuot Dance in Yirol

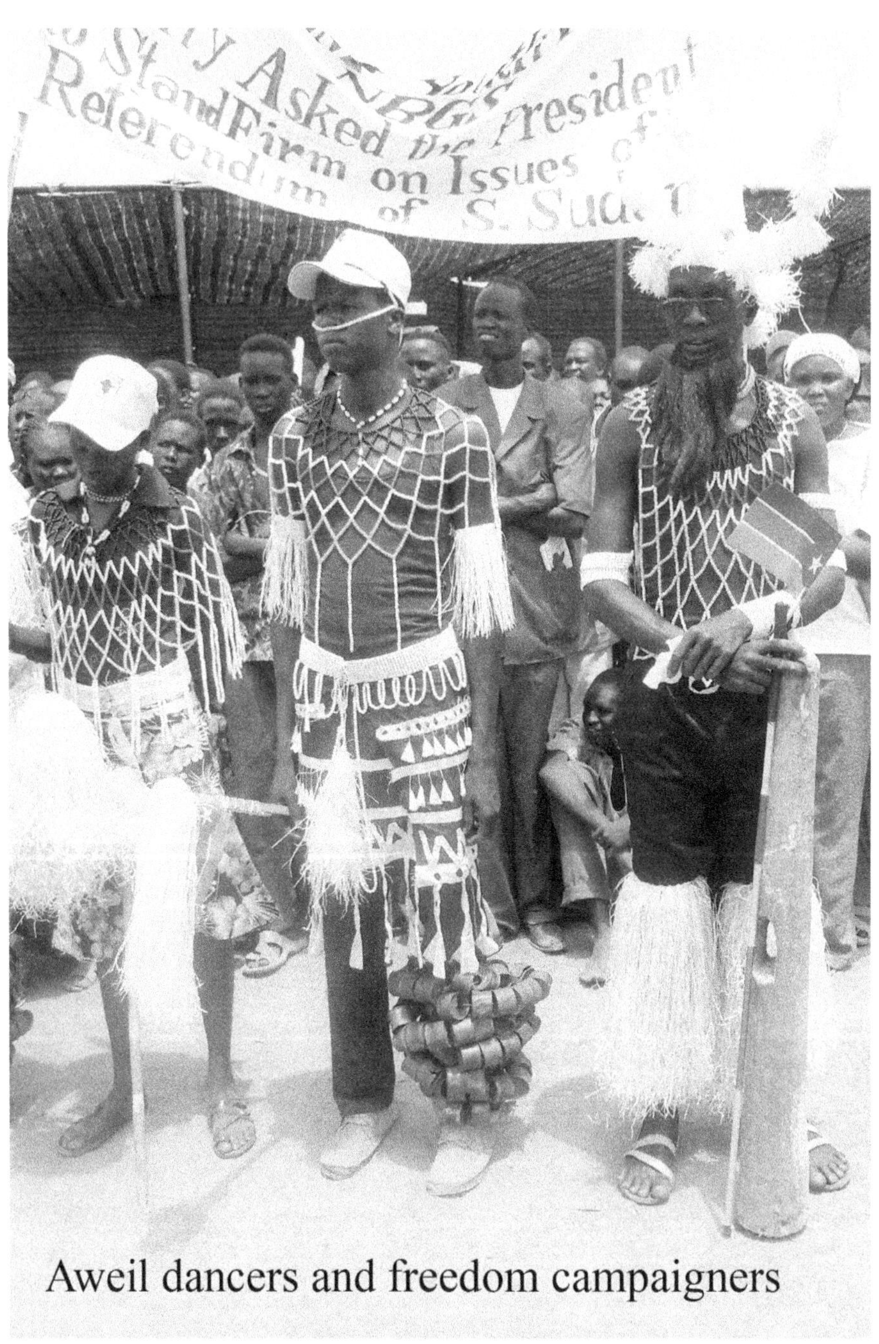

Aweil dancers and freedom campaigners

Surge for freedom at Malual Kon

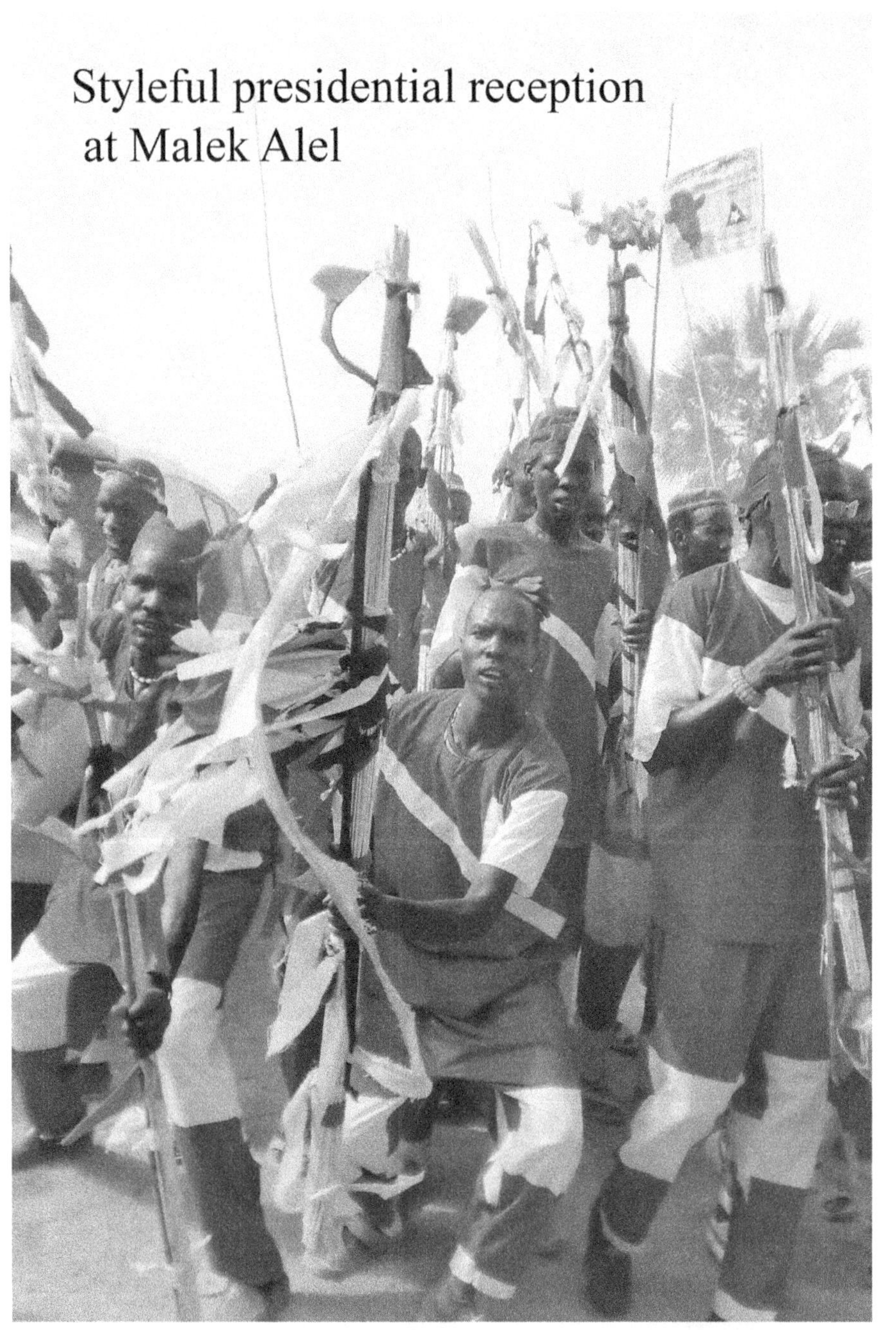

Styleful presidential reception at Malek Alel

A war disable
and veteran jumping in style
(ngan) at a reception in Tonj

Miss Nyibol Dut of Akon and team welcoming VIP guests in style in Tonj

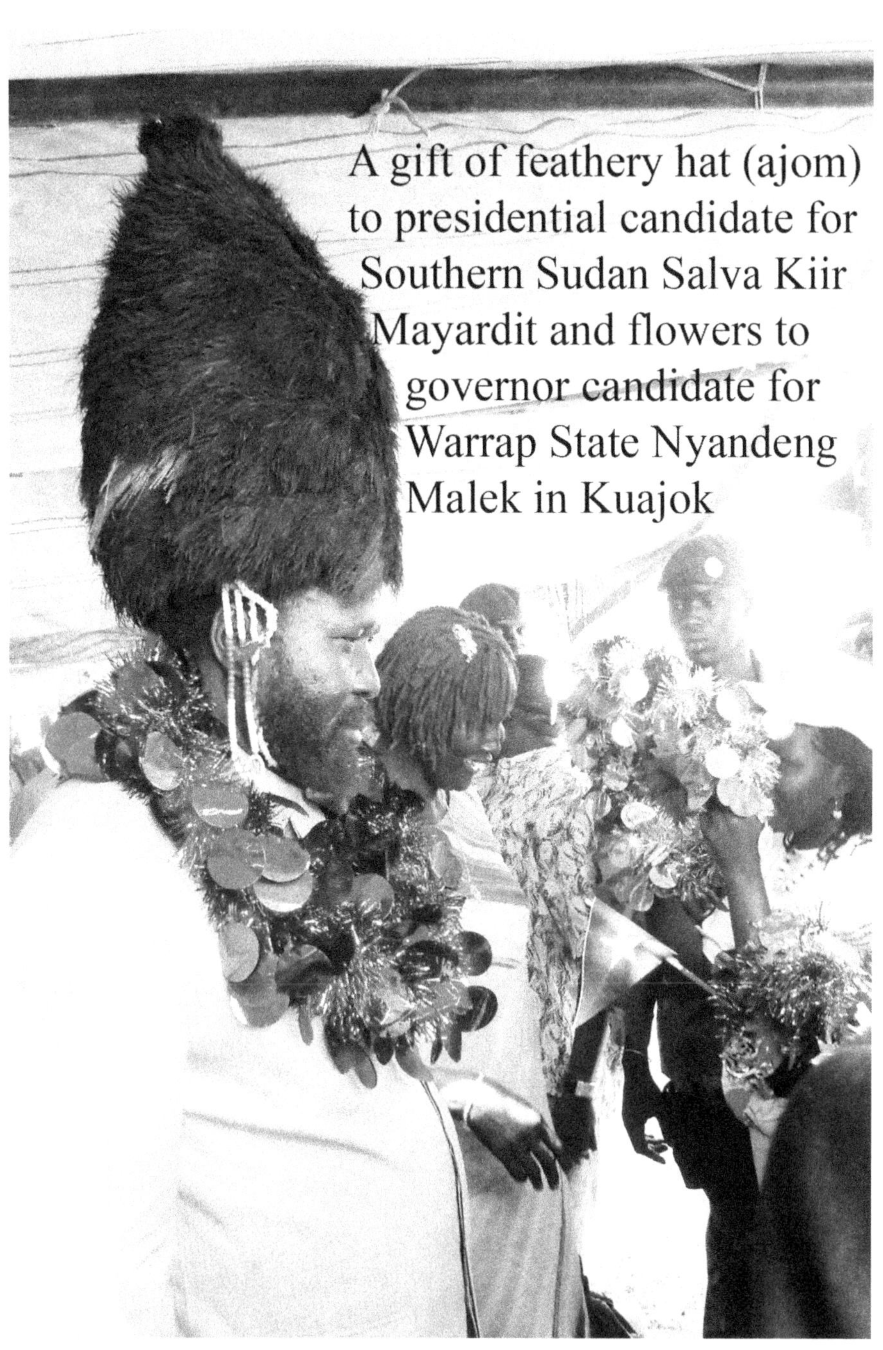
A gift of feathery hat (ajom) to presidential candidate for Southern Sudan Salva Kiir Mayardit and flowers to governor candidate for Warrap State Nyandeng Malek in Kuajok

A gift of beaded hat

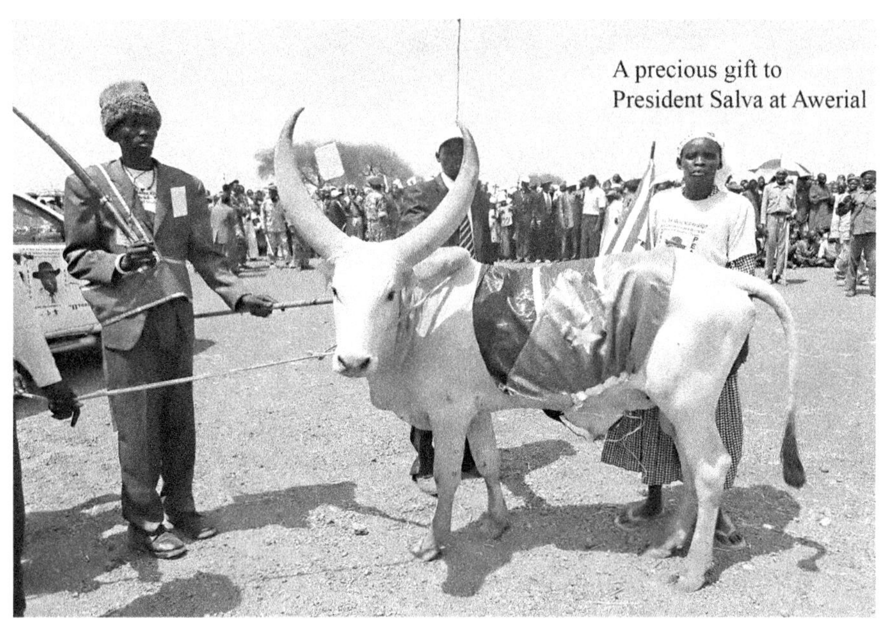
A precious gift to President Salva at Awerial

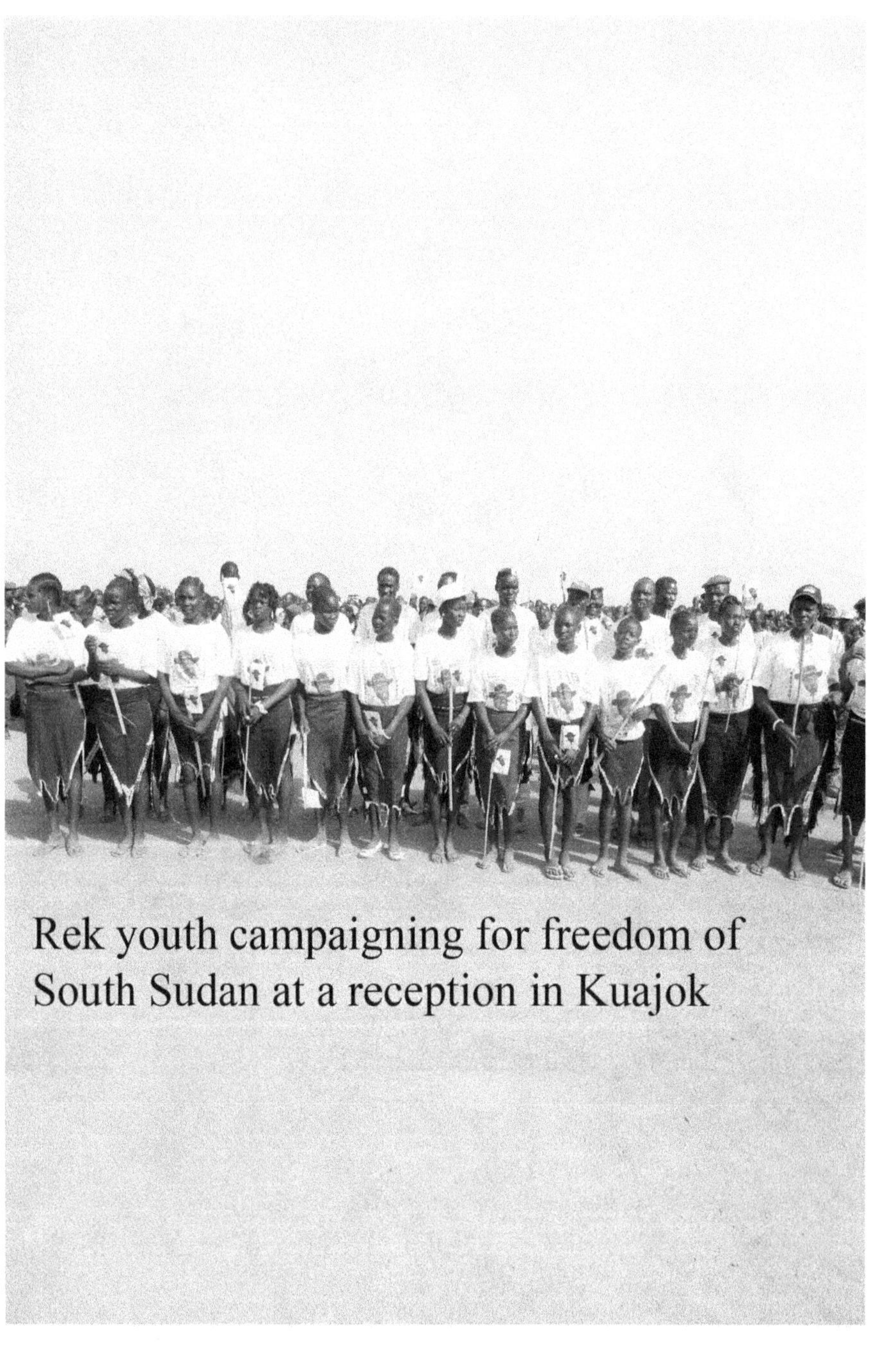

Rek youth campaigning for freedom of South Sudan at a reception in Kuajok

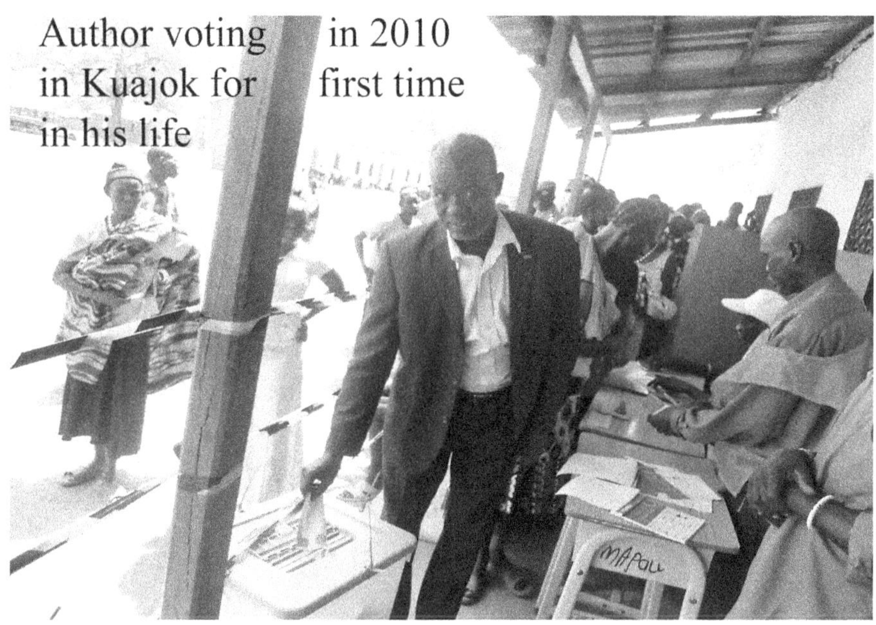

Author voting in 2010 in Kuajok for first time in his life

Baby and mum voting together in Kuajok

Horny hats campaign

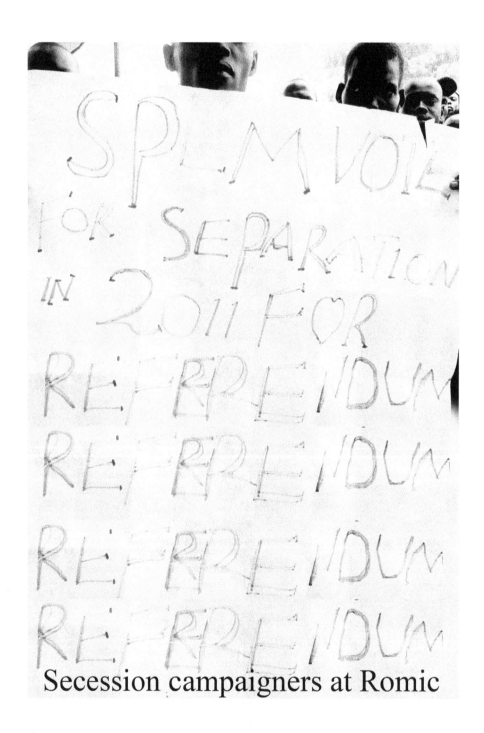

Secession campaigners at Romic

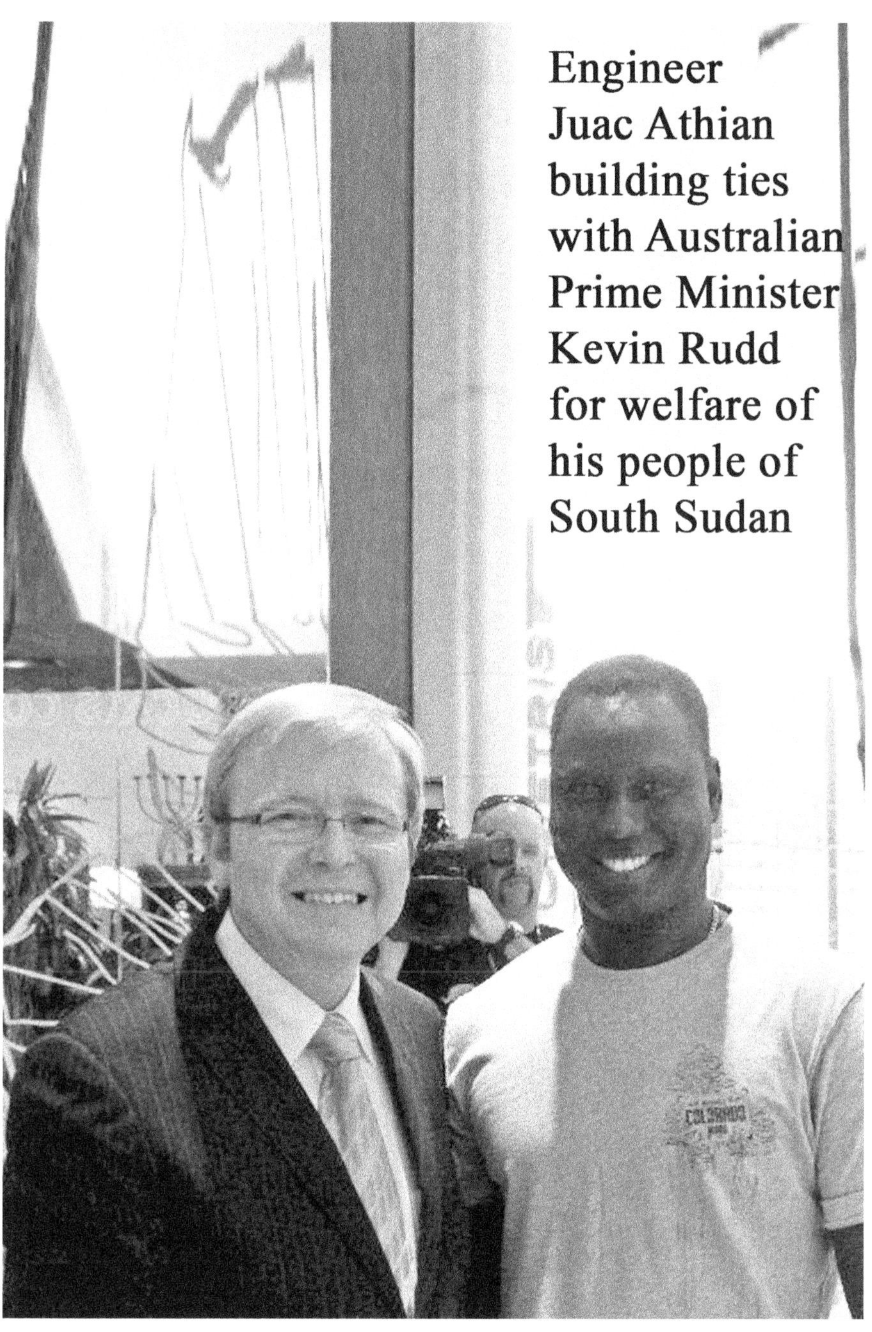

Engineer Juac Athian building ties with Australian Prime Minister Kevin Rudd for welfare of his people of South Sudan

Miss Martha Ahok, Madam Atem Deng and Dr. Akec Khoc warming up the spot in the UN Headquarters in New York, where South Sudan may be declared as a new UN Member State in 2011.

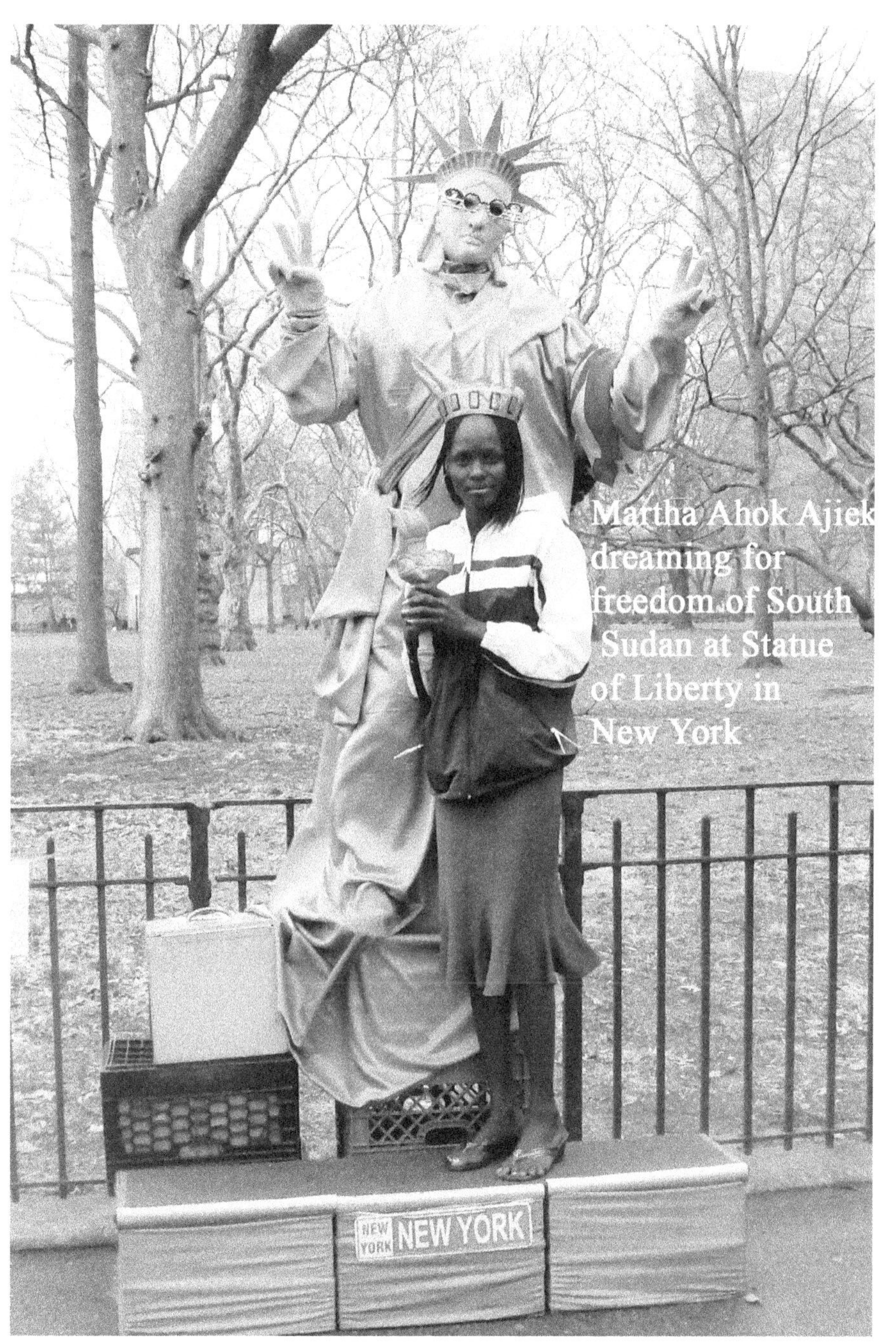

Martha Ahok Ajiek dreaming for freedom of South Sudan at Statue of Liberty in New York

SONGS

A Land So Sensuous

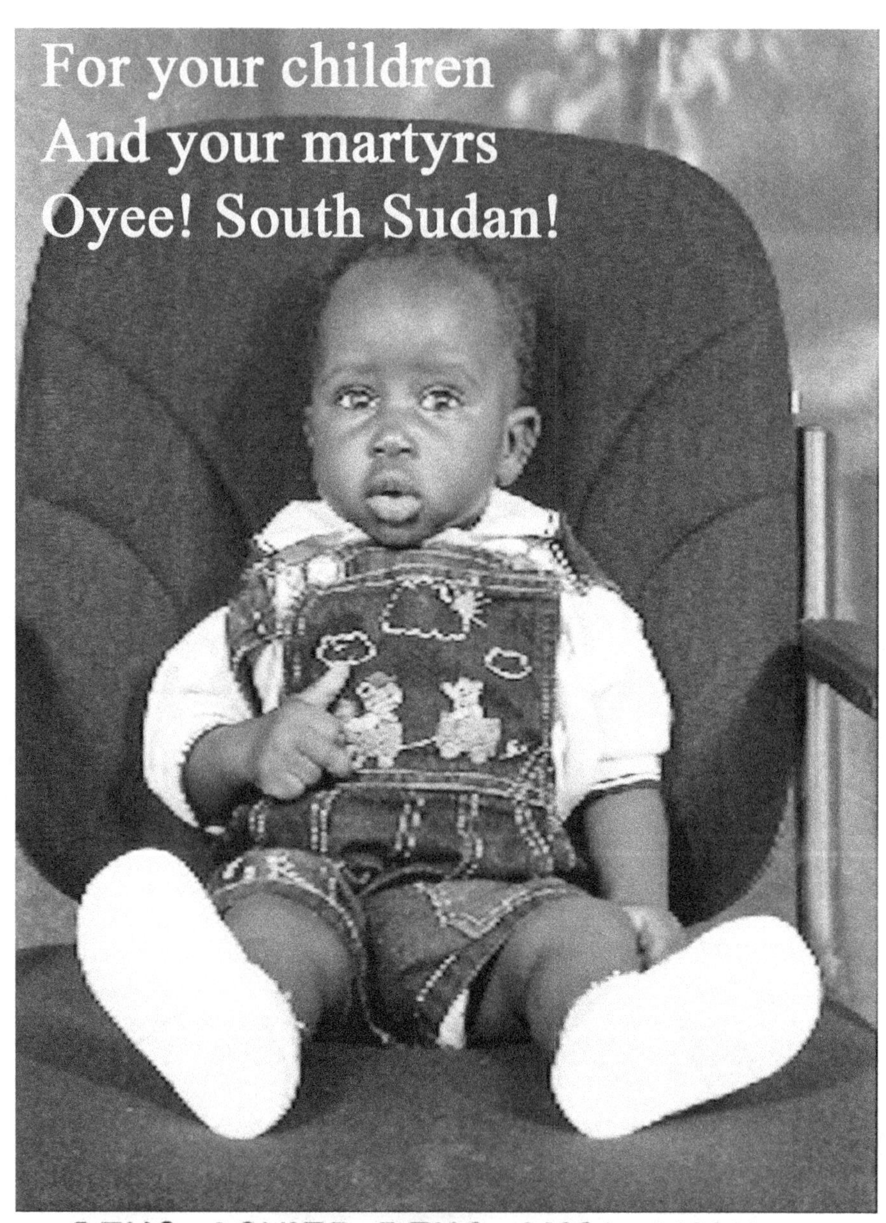
For your children
And your martyrs
Oyee! South Sudan!

DENG ACHWER DENG AKOL AYAY
(DHUKBAAI)

S1 OUR STRUGGLE CONTINUES UNTIL OUR FREEDOM IS ACHIEVED

Transcribed by Miss Akuac Abur Nhial of Inheritance Katiba of Nyacigak Battalion

Our struggle continues until our freedom is achieved

The day we raise the flag
Our death for our generation
And in memory of our martyrs
For the land is the guarantor. The revolution is our revolution
To be shown to our children and the end of our freedom
The trend of the flag with the peace, we strengthen our struggle
The peace of our land
From it is our nation and our nation is our Sudan
In it is green for agriculture
And black for the soil, the soil of our land and in it is Nile, the sign of life
Oh! The flag wave and you are the symbol of our revolution
The star is the symbol of our collective participation
The star is the symbol of our collective participation

S2 CONDITIONS OF THE LAND

By Daniel Maror of Katiba Banat of SPLA

Translated by Akuac Abur and Awar Ring Malek

Conditions of the Land
However it compels us

We must serve our Land
If we had come to our Land
Our Sudan, we fight, we fight
You the land of our Soldiers, We fight forever and ever

Leave and Come and Come
To the way and let us try

For the Land of the Soldiers, let us fight

Forever and ever

Everywhere, we saw, we saw our Leader Dr John Garang, You
the Commandant
You the Commandant
You our Revolutionist
You the Commandant
You the Land of the Soldiers
Our Commandant Doctor and Hero
The history of our Land will be remembered
For the liberation of the Land

S3 NO LAND BECOMES BEAUTIFUL ON ITS OWN

Recited by Miss Martha Ahok Ajiek Amet, a youth pioneer of SPLA/M
During the visit of Dr. John Garang and Salva Kiir to Gogrial

You See! No land becomes beautiful on its own
You see! No land becomes beautiful on its own
You can never find a land that becomes beautiful
on its own
You can never find a land that becomes beautiful on
its own

Even if our hearts differ, we should not concede and let our
land down.
Any one of us that will survive can pick a pen, can
pick a gun,
And raise it up and say: This is our land! This is our
land!

Our Land of South Sudan!
Our Land of South Sudannnnnnnn!
Let us welcome the leader
Let us welcome the leader

The coming of a leader is eagerly anticipated
The coming of a leader is eagerly anticipated

We are welcoming you, Our Leader John Garang, Our leader has come
We will welcome the leader in a festival style like when Jesus was borne;
The festival of God is eagerly anticipated.

We are so happy; for the coming of our leader is a blessing
A blessing for our lives

Oh! Our elders! You who are taking care of our land Sudan, we salute you
Good Morning! Good Morning our elders!

A leader is praised; a leader is praised for doing something good
John Garang we praise you, together with our leader Salva who deputises you
And Lual Diing that follows both of you in hierarchy

You our leaders of entire Sudanese People, a heart is kept okay
All of you, please rule the land well, for a heart is kept okay

We are the youth of Gakrial
The youth of Kuajok and beyond
You have come to our area
The great area of breath of life
Our Gakrial, the great area of breath of life

So let us now laugh ah ahaa,
For we are happy in our land

And survival of children is known by the leader that owns the land
Oh! Our leader John Garang de Mabior! Survival of children is known by the leader that owns the land
Oh! Our leader Salva Kiir Mayardit! Survival of children is known by the leader that owns the land
Oh! Our Leader Riek Macar Teny! Survival of children is known by the leader that owns the land
Oh! Our Leader James Wani Igga! Survival of children is known by the leader that owns the land

Oh! Our leaders! Survival of children lies in the hands of leaders that own the land

S4 BAAI ACIE DHE□ AROT (TRUNCATED)

S5 WHO IS MOST OFFENDED IN THE SOIL OF SUDAN?

An SPLA Song by Magiir of Tuek Tuek Battalion of Muor Muor Division

Who is the first person that is most oppressed and marginalised in Sudan?
He is the colonel Dr. John Garang De Mabior…is the one who is looking to liberate his land of Sudan.

We are prepared to sacrifice our lives for this land.
We have accepted death; we the army of Dr. John Garang.
We are the ones that want to capture and liberate Malakal and Port Sudan and Kosti which will be resolved by the international community as the border.

Garang Mabior fetch us Kalashnikov; if it is death, we are prepared to die. That is why we came all the way from the soil of Bahr-el-Ghazal.

S6 OUR LEADER JOHN

An SPLA Song by Vilpam Battalion of Koryom Division

A victory song after the fall of more than twelve areas to gallant SPLA forces

Our Leader John gave us a mission forward
Yei, Kapoeta...
The fire burnt on the attack of Kaya, Morobo;
A must for the war of the soil

We are marching forward
We are advancing in war
We arrived Yambio, Maridi, Tambora, and Western Equatoria

S7 VILPAM BATTALION

An SPLA Song by Captain Lual of Ngok Lual Yak of Vilpam Battalion of Koryom division

Koryom Oyee!
Koryom Oyee!

One does not abandon one's own Land
The Arab says false agreement is to be made; but Garang Mabior will not accept it. How will he while his Land is destroyed

One does not abandon one's own Land
The Arab says false agreement is to be made; but Garang Mabior will not accept it. How will he while his Land is destroyed

The previous mistake will never be repeated. There are now enough forces: Vilpam and Bongo. When we return to Sudan, all the areas will fall to our forces.

Vilpam Oyee! Will use all tactics; Vilpam Battalion has no mercy; even your father you shoot him

S8 BRIGHT STAR CAMPAIGN (BSC)

By Salva Mathuc Ayay Akol Ayay of Majnun Batallion of Zal Zal (Earthquake) Division

Long time
Long time
We have been behind in our Sudan
Today we have found Kalashnikov
The revolution is marching forward

We shall not change our objectives and we will not retract backward

Congratulations, our Commander Dr. John
Congratulations, our Leader Dr. John
Congratulations for the victories BSC
Congratulations, the revolutionaries of New Sudan
The revolution is moving forward
The revolution is moving forward
Starting from Nimule
Up to Halfa Jadid
The end of liberation of Sudan is at Halfa Jadid

S9 BROTHERS AND SISTERS,
LET US UNITE

Recited by Salva Mathuc Ayay

Brothers and sisters
Let us unite

Unity is much better
To get the freedom of New Sudan
Southern Sudan is a winner all this time

We are crying SPLA
SPLA Soldiers be ahead
We are behind you
SPLM Ohyee
SPLA Ohyee

Backbone
Backbone New of Sudan
Surely we shall win

S10 SIGNAL AND MI

A marching song

Recited by Salva Mathuc Ayay

Signal and MI to unite comrades
Unity is very important to unite comrades
To defeat Beshir
We are the backbone of the movement
We are the backbone of SPLA
SPLA surely shall win Beshir
We are the backbone of the movement
We are the backbone of SPLA

S11 COMMANDER IN CHIEF 101 COMMANDO

By Kon Ayay Deng Akol of C & C 101 Commando

The struggle between the North and the South mimics that between Apiin, Flies, and Akolmagar

Akolmagar wanted to erect a hut, but Apiin objected saying: "I cannot leave the hut to you."

They dragged on the case for ten days till they got exhausted without resolving it.

SPLA is like Apiin. The army being commanded by a great leader called John Garang, the doctor son of Mabior.

John Doctor Garang Mabior aspires for his land to be powerful. If he captures it, it will be mighty.

The South we will never give up.

S12 WHY WE WENT TO THE BUSH

Transcribed by Zeinab Daffala

We went to the bush, including women and girls and young boys
Then the thirst challenged us to be the killer
But the cold argued to be the one that is the killer
So the mosquito exclaimed and ululated saying it is also a killer
Then famine emerged and asserted itself saying, "Who doesn't know me? Let me tell you my notorious nickname. I am the Great Destroyer. I will destroy all of you now."

S13 THE ONLY THING THAT WENT WRONG

By Deng Kuot Thiec

Transcribed by Dr. Victoria Anib Stephen Majur Achut

The only thing that went wrong, we seem not to know it. Oh! The land of the South, What is it? What is it? You the people abroad, you do not know. You people abroad.
You have forgotten it and that is not fair. You go about dividing the land when it is only one land. You split twice and then divide it again ten times.

Muonyjang with cows and sheep believe they are rich. Others with cassava and honey think they are wealthy.

Every group prefers its own. Everyone likes own words. Rivalry, Rivalry is the one destroying the land. Mere pride is the one destroying our land.

We will be praying to God and to the Land of Deng,

We will pray and pray for a blessing so that we think as one. Who ordered the split? Why, why divide the land before we even ignite the cooking flame?

We heard in the past
What prophet Ariath, Ariath Makuei said
He prophesized that the land will be destroyed while it is still being ruled
It will settle after a thousand years and it will be by the White people, the very ones that ruined the land last time; how paradoxical!
So you people of the South, everyone alone, everyone alone, is it good to be divided?
Words that are not compromised are lack Ha! Ha!

Disunity lacks laughter
Disunity is bitter
Disunity pushes people backward

The reason we are now suffering with no education in Sudan, is it not the arrival of two foreigners: The Turks and the English that came later
The English were even better for teaching us canniness

Leave this little education in South Sudan that we use to backbite ourselves
What about cattle keepers who lack that education, are they not surviving now without it?

People stay without a homeland, simple land, between foreigners and those that claim to be educated!
(Song truncated

S14 SUDAN HAS BEEN OUR LAND EVER SINCE

By Deng Kuot Thiec

Sudan and it has been our land ever since;
Even now, the Land needs its owner

Sudan and it has been our land ever since;
Even now, the Land needs its owner

These are things said all the time
Ngun Deng said them
Ariath Makuei said so
Cier Deng Thiepduok
And Ajingdit now says them in the land
And until now the land is still searching for its owner

Sudan should not be ruled by anyone who is selfish; only John Garang Mabior Atem Aruai who is patient and determined. He is looking forward and behind, left and right. Do not aim to steal and do not aim to remain slaves forever.

You who thinks that a black person cannot say a right thing; YOU WILL BE SURPRISED!

S15 OH! DON'T AGAIN PANIC, DON'T AGAIN PANIC I HAVE HATED YOURS!

By Akut Kuei, reproduced by Miss Ann Awien Nyang Dhieu

Oh! Don't again panic, don't again panic
I have hated yours!
All you have been doing to me is hated by the children of the land

When you came as a guest and our ancestor welcome you and hosted you at home, with a heart free of antagonism, and you turned to be the god that murders us, is hated by the children of the land

Your greed when you came and found food being cooked in my pot and you snatched the scoop and sat down and imposed yourself to distribute it, and you only gave me a tiny share when it was not your pot, is hated by the children of the land

The black bull of black cow is furious and marched to the bush and when a person steps into the bush, he breaks the foot of the person and you go back limping on a stick. Don't again limp on a stick. Why did you after all step on the soil of Deng Nhial, the soil of Ajang Duor and Ayal Baak, the burring soil of maternal uncle; people live in a land but it belongs to its owner seriously!

Oh! What took way the cattle, the god that dragged away the cattle when the cattle are the ones that nurture Muonyjak... and kills the women leaving children needy and yet we stay and stand aloof, what sort of death is it? Is it not the same death that leads to a grave?

What kills old men and kills old women until the cry "Oh God! Where are the youth!" and yet we stay and stand aloof, what sort of death is it? Is it not the same death that leads to a grave?

A hero (heroine) is killed in war and a coward survives and still dies afterward— is it not the same death that leads to a grave?

Men who help by simply weeping and resemble women who cry out when things go wrong and make noise.

Cowards whose eyes tremble and when scared they return, people cannot run away from death and even if we escape, it will still find us; just like last time, last time when the red flame (fire) reached a monkey that ran to the top of mahogany hoping to escape the fire; when the fire arrived, it was roaring, clearing away all grass and trees leaving nothing behind. When it caught up with it, eh! It burned the monkey together with the mahogany!

My right hand, my right hand, my right hand will surpass me; when I release my hand on a person; my right hand will surpass me and if I release my hand it will serve a fatal blow on the unwary; its joint strike, our joint strike, oh! Our God all of us!

S16 LET US NOT FORGET ONE ANOTHER

By Miss Nyankol Mathiang Dut of Ngok Abyei

South our Land; South Sudan our Land
Oh! South our Land; South Sudan our Land!!!

Peace has come
The Land is emerging

SPLA has accomplished its mission
What is left is our role to play for South Sudan

We should never concede
Let us remain vigilant
Let us focus properly
Let it not again defeat us
Let it never again torment us

These horrible people
Let us leave them
Those destroying peace
Let us throw them away

Child, single person, wife and her husband
Child, single person, wife and her husband!
The hyena said
The hyena, the hyena asserted

The hyena (Mr. Brown and White) stated
"Oh! God! help me to enter a hut
As for coming out, I will see"

Child, single person, wife and her husband
Child, single person, wife and her husband!!!

The Land needs work
The Land needs work
Let us concentrate on how to work
Let us focus our minds on how to work
Let us unite our hearts to work together

Child, single person, wife and her husband
Child, single person, wife and her husband!!!
During the six years, let us hang on
During the six years, let us hold on
Let us stop taking only and concentrate on work
Let us stop talking only and focus fully on work
Let us always think of what to do
And implement what we say

Child, single person, wife and her husband
Child, single person, wife and her husband!!!

You are there to help one another
To help people left behind
To help people left behind

Let us help one another
Our South! Let us help one another

Let us tolerate ourselves
Our South! Let us tolerate ourselves

Let us hold our arms together
Our South! Let us hold our arms together

Child, single person, wife and her husband
Child, single person, wife and her husband

You are there to help one another
To help people left behind

You should really help one another
Especially those left behind

Let us help one another
Our South! Let us help one another

Let us keep ourselves up
Our South! Let us keep our selves up

Let us hold our arms together
Our South! Let us hold our arms together

Child, single person, wife and her husband
Child, single person, wife and her husband

Let us engage our minds
Our South! Let us engage our minds

Let us put our heads together
Our South! Let us put our heads together

Let us guide ourselves
Our South! Let us guide ourselves

Child, single person, wife and her husband!!!

Let us tolerate ourselves
Our South! Let us tolerate ourselves

Let us hold our arms together
Our South! Let us hold our arms together

Child, single person, wife and her husband!

Let us hold our arms together
Our South! Let us hold our arms together

Let us engage our minds
Our South! Let us engage our minds

Let us hold our arms together
Our South! Let us hold our arms together

S17 YOUR LAND THAT YOU ARE NEGLECTING MAY DEFEAT YOU ULTIMATELY

By Nyankol Mathiang Dut of Ngok Abyei

Your land that you are neglecting may defeat you ultimately
Your nation that you are neglecting may defeat you ultimately

Eh! You will be like a lion and a human being
You will be like a lion and a man

A lion entered a house and a person followed inside the house When the man groaned, agonizing with pain being inflicted into his body inside the house, he was still being asked in Jieng Language why he was moaning severely. The person answered that "That thing has not gone away; it is staying with me."

Your land that you are neglecting may defeat you ultimately
Your nation that you are neglecting may defeat you ultimately

Eh! You will be like a lion and a human being
You will be like a lion and a man

If anything divides people, it will be resolved by the South alone
If anything divides people, it will be resolved by the North alone
If anything divides people, it will be resolved by the South alone
If anything divides people, it will be resolved by the North alone
It will be resolved by the South alone
It will be resolved by the North alone

Black-Hide! I am strong! I have a great homeland! I the owner of Sudan!
Black-Hide! I am strong! I have a great homeland! I the owner of black skin!

Small children are suffering
Old people are exhausted
The youth are finished
The dust of the dead martyrs will judge
The dust of the dead martyrs will liberate our land
So that we seize the land with right hands, this Sudan

Black-hide! I am strong! I have a great homeland! I the owner of Sudan!
Black-hide! I am strong! I have a great homeland! I the owner of black skin!

Oh! Black-skin! I the black skin, I the owner of Sudan
Oh! Don't you see I am the owner of the land, I the black skin; I am the owner of Sudan

Oh! Black-skin! I the black skin, I the owner of Sudan
Oh! Don't you see I am the owner of the land, I the black skin; I am the owner of Sudan

Oh! Black-skin! I the black skin, I the owner of Sudan
Oh! Don't you see I am the owner of the land, I the black skin;
I am the owner of Sudan

S18 THE LAND IS LAGGING BEHIND; OUR LAND IS LAGGING BEHIND US, OUR LAND

By Miss Nyankol Mathiang Dut of Ngok Abyei

The Land is lagging behind; our land is lagging behind us, our land

Oh! Our children of Sudan, how can we develop it?
My sister teach your child to survive
My brother teach your child to survive
When I move around and see my black people suffering, my eyes fill with tears and I break down
My sister, come on
My brother, come on
Let us leave mishandling life
And handle life well
Let us teach our children to learn

The Land is lagging behind; our land is lagging behind us, our land

S19 PEACE HAS COME TO OUR LAND LIKE A DREAM

By John Kudusay of Mading Aweil

Peace has come to us like a dream
To our Sudan of black people, for us to unite
Who else will again be called to rule us; it is us to rule ourselves. It is the child of the Land that either destroys or builds it

Peace allows you to wake up with a free mind
Peace allows you to walk with a free mind

Peace allows you to sleep with a free mind
Peace allows you to do whatever you can with a free mind.

S20 LEADERSHIP IS NOT A GAME TO PLAY

By John Kudusay of Mading Aweil

We are happy to dance on 16 May
The people that have gathered to celebrate were the ones who founded SPLM.

If you find a brother or sister, do not ignore him or her. Do not deny that you know him as if he is rivaling you in power. But nobody hates power.

Do not ignore your brother or sister. Do not say you do not know him or her.

I am saying this to people who rash in to rival over power. But, in my case, I will not advise people on how to acquire leadership. However if you aspire to become a leader, learn to govern your own self first.

Do not consider leadership like a simple dance that everybody flocks in to participate.

Leadership is not a game to play.

S21 WE NEED A CHANGE

By The Bees Group, a Choir of South Sudanese of Ahfad University, Khartoum

We need a change, change for the better
We need a change in the world.

The illiterate child no shelter nothing to eat victim
of poverty
He needs a change /she needs a change
The heavy loaded women of Africa
Women of the world facing discrimination
They need a change, they need a change.

You and I must bring that change
Old or young, men and women bring that change.

The war affected soldiers, casualties
The war affected places, fire tortured
No green trees the soil made barren
They need a change, they need a change.

The frustrated kinsmen
Oppressors, cold-blooded people no humane feelings
They need a change, they need a change.

The ill hearted people
Opportunists, selling their people in favour of money
They need a change, they need a change.

You and I must bring that change
Old or young, men and women bring that change.

S22 CRY FOR PEACE IN SUDAN

By The Bees Group

Oh yes, my sisters and mothers, don't be worried.
You are subjected to this world of war yet you must
Focus on the future.
There is hope, hope, deep in our hearts that one day
Things will be alright.

Ohm, ohm, ohm, ohm

I know of a woman who lived in a war zone, displaced from her happy home to live in a camp of poverty, she starved, starved all her life seeking only for the basic needs, she can only think of one essential thing and that is to keep up her life.

Ohm..........

I know of a woman who lost her husband in war, she remained a widow and a mother, of unlucky sons and daughters she tried all these and that to keep up her poor family she can only think of one essential fact and that is to keep her family's life.

Ohm.........

I know of a woman who lost her occupation in war she remained a non-working professional stirring up all ways to earn money she tried, tried all this and that yet no luck or fortune came her way, she can only think of one essential thing and that is to keep up her life.

Ohm..........

An abandoned soul, mother, widow crying out, the non-working victim of sorrow is a woman from the tongues of war.

No, no, no, I know, I know she's got no choice she's got no choice.
No, no, no, I know, I know she's got no choice she's got no choice.

War is the highest enemy, to any development; people lose all that they have built up to the mercy of bombs and cans.

Oh yea, we cry, we cry, again we cry, we cry for peace.
Oh yea, we cry, we cry again we cry, we cry for peace.

S23 I HAVE A CALL

By The Bees Group

I have a call, to you my people to you far and near let's bring our hands together and lift up our nation there's a call.

There's a call comes ringing from the bottom of the burning land, calling unto all the nations, there's a call, woo.

I have a call to you my people to you far and near, let's bring our hands together and lift up our nation there's a call.

There's a call comes ringing from the orphans and the broken hearts calling unto all the people there's a call woo.

There's a call to you my people to you far and near let's join our hands together and lift up our nation there's a call.

There's a call comes ringing calling unto all of us woo, woo, woo. Let's join our hands together to build up our nation, woo, woo, woo.

S24 WOMEN WERE THERE FROM TIMES OF CREATION

By The Bees Group

Women were there from times of creation, they are the builders of a nation.
We wonder how all things where made we wonder why women are despised.
It's amazing of women work aha, it's amazing, and how people look at them.
Sometimes they cry, sometimes they joke; it's education that can make change.

Here in Africa, here in Africa, here in Africa, here in Africa, we pray for the women to be saved in Afri, Afri(5), aha.

We must do the work for our country to make a change in our society.
Here in Sudan, here in Sudan, here in Sudan, here in Sudan, we pray for the women to be saved in Sudan, Sudan(5), aha.
Women were there from times of creation

S25 NO MORE SLAVERY OR BRIBERY

A Song by Miss Nyankol Mathiang Dut

Translated by Dr. Achier Deng Akol

South our Land; South Sudan our Land
Oh! South our Land; South Sudan our Land!
Peace has come
The Land is emerging

SPLA has accomplished its mission
What is left is our role
We civilians of South Sudan

No more slavery
No more bribery
Let us remain vigilant
Let us focus properly
Let it not again defeat us
Let it never again torment us

These horrible people
Let us leave them
Those destroying peace
Let us throw them away

Child, single person, wife and her husband
Child, single person, wife and her husband!!!

The hyena said
The hyena, the hyena asserted

The hyena (Mr. Brown and White) stated
"Oh! God! Help me to enter a hut
As for coming out, I will manage."

Child, single person, wife and her husband
Child, single person, wife and her husband!!!

The Land needs work
The Land needs work
Let us concentrate on how to work
Let us focus our minds on how to work
Let us unite our hearts to work together

Child, single person, wife and her husband
Child, single person, wife and her husband!!!

During the six years, let us hang on
During the six years, let us hold on
Let us stop talking only and concentrate on work
Let us stop talking only and focus fully on work
Let us always think of what to do
And implement what we say

Child, single person, wife and her husband
Child, single person, wife and her husband!!!

You are there to help one another
To help people left behind
To help people left behind

Let us help one another
Our South! Let us help one another

Let us tolerate ourselves
Our South! Let us tolerate ourselves

Let us hold our arms together
Our South! Let us hold our arms together

Child, single person, wife and her husband
Child, single person, wife and her husband

You are there to help one another
To help people left behind

You should really help one another
Especially those left behind

Let us help one another
Our South! Let us help one another

Let us keep ourselves up
Our South! Let us keep our selves up

Let us hold our arms together
Our South! Let us hold our arms together

Child, single person, wife and her husband
Child, single person, wife and her husband

Let us engage our minds
Our South! Let us engage our minds

Let us put our heads together
Our South! Let us put our heads together

Let us guide ourselves
Our South! Let us guide ourselves

Child, single person, wife and her husband!!!

Let us tolerate ourselves
Our South! Let us tolerate ourselves

Let us hold our arms together
Our South! Let us hold our arms together

Child, single person, wife and her husband!

Let us hold our arms together
Our South! Let us hold our arms together

Let us engage our minds
Our South! Let us engage our minds

Let us hold our arms together
Our South! Let us hold our arms together

S26 HOLD—LOVE—TAKE

A song by Achier Deng Akol

Yours! Yours!
Hold Yours
Love Yours
Take Yours

She is a lover
Offered to glow
In you forever
From head to toe

Let her steal
Your heart beat
Let her feel
Your warm heat

Feel her eh!
She is your own
Touch and kiss her
She is your own

Hold tight
Every day

Every night
Every way

Hold Yours
Love Yours
Take Yours
Forever

Don't let her slip
Off your hands
She is your strip
Of love strands

Hold her
Nicely
Love her
Sweetly

Hold Yours
Love Yours
Take Yours
Yes! Forever!

Oh! Daddy!
Will it be forever?

Oh! Mammy!
Will it be forever?

Hold Yours
Love Yours
Take Yours
Yes! Forever!

Oh! Daddy!
Will it be forever?

Oh! Mammy!
Will it be forever?

Hold Yours
Love Yours
Take Yours
Yes! Forever

S27 YIN AYA YIOK TIT H□N (TRUNCATED)

S28 I TELL YOU WAIT FOR ME

Recited by Miss Martha Ahok Ajiek Amet of Kuac Area

To a sweetheart that I would like to wait for me

I tell you wait for me
Child of my land, wait for me

Beautiful crane, wait for me
Then fly to the sky above
With your gorgeous body
And your lovely panama

And I desire
You join my family
And I want so much
To join your family

So that you can call my father daddy
And you can call my mother mummy
So that I can call your father daddy
And I can call your mother mummy

Even if my father refused
Or my mother objected
It is your skin
That I so much loved
In our homeland

Oh! The beauty of your heart!
And the wisdom of your mind!

S29 METHEE YIN AC□L DHUKBAAI (TRUNCATED)

S30 OH! OUR CHILD, WE HAVE NICKNAMED YOU RETURNING-HOME

By Dr. Achier Deng Akol and his wife Awit (Anok)
To all newly born children of South Sudan

Oh! Our Child, we nickname you Returning-Home
Oh! Child of Our Land

For it is our land that we have returned to
Now that peace has come

When our land was in war
We were thrown to bushes and Diaspora
Now we have returned home

So Deng Awit
Deng Achier
Deng our son
We call you Returning-Home

For it is our land that we have returned to
Now that peace has come

The children we give birth to
Are the seeds that will lift up our land

Deng of Pareu
Deng of Kuajok
Deng of South Sudan
You are called Returning-Home

For it is our land that we have returned to
Now that peace has come

They say when an elephant ages
It returns its task home
Young or old, we have returned home

Deng of gray colour
Deng like an elephant
The returning gray
You are called Returning-Home

For it is our land that we have returned to
Now that peace has come

Oh! Our Land
Oh! Our Soil
Oh! Our South

Wau our home
Is where we have returned
Juba our home
Is where we have returned
Malakal our home
Is where we have returned
Now that there is peace in our land

Aweil our home
Is where we have returned
Yambio our home
Is where we have returned
Bor our home
Is where we have returned
Now that there is peace in our land

Rumbek our home
Is where we have returned
Torit our home
Is where we have returned
Bentiu our home

Is where we have returned
Now that there is peace in our land

Kuajok our home
Is where we have returned
Abyei our home
Is where we have returned
All our areas are where we have returned
Now that there is peace in our land

Even if we starve, we suffer
We weep, we are poor
We will not abandon our land

For it is our land that we have returned to
Now that peace has come

And the hunger will decline
Suffering shall diminish
Weeping will reduce

For it is our land that we have returned to
Now that peace has come

In Diaspora, we were reduced to beggars
Now even if one cultivates a small piece of land
One can lift up his head and say I am proud of my land

Oh! Children, Oh! Youth
Oh! Fathers, Oh! Mothers

Oh! Our Land, Oh! Our Soil
Oh! Our Folks, Oh! Our People

Let us endure, let us not scatter again
Let us have courage, let us not disperse again

For it is our land that we have returned to
Now that peace has come

S31 OUR HERO STILL ALIVE

By Emmanuel Mark Kembe of Kreish from Raga

Transcribed from CD with help of his mother Honourable Veronica Dominic, his sister Mary, and Brother Levi in Juba

Our Hero still alive
Dr. John Garang still alive
He still lives on in our hearts
The Lord gave and the Lord has taken away
And the name of the Lord be praised

I have the high regards for the hero of our history
I have the high regards for our founding father Dr. John Garang
Because of his love for the marginalised and for constant peace and justice in Sudan

The Angel when we were suffering Ouch!
To give people like me and others get up for the life of joy and freedom

I said equality is not about religion ouch!
And it is not about tribe or about economy ouch!
But it is simply about freedom for everyone irrespective of religion and affiliation.
That is why I say our Hero is still alive
The Hero of our Heroes is still alive
He still lives on in our hearts
The Angel when we were suffering Ouch!
To give people like me and others get up for the life of joy and freedom

Our Hero still alive
Dr. John Garang still alive
He still lives on in our hearts
He rests in peace
He's still alive
He still lives on in our hearts

Our Hero still alive
Dr. John Garang still alive
He still lives on in our hearts

S32 SOUTH SUDAN ANTHEM

Composed by Dr. Achier Deng Akol

Oyee! South Sudan!
Of African Stars
Around River Nile

From Kush Kingdom
Of brave warriors
Where civilization began

Now fully free!
You will rise
To the top

For your children
And your martyrs
Oyee! South Sudan!

POEMS

A Land So Amorous

Beautiful South Sudan
Shall thrive with glamour
Once again as before
It will shine with power
Like a star or even more

PO1 COME AND LIVE WITH US

By Achier Deng Akol

Come and live with us
For even a single day
You will know instantly
How good a people we are

Visit any part of South Sudan
When our cottages are re-erected
You will not be neglected
To sleep in the cold outside

Knock on any door
Of a South Sudan home
When you are thirsty
You will be offered
The last drop of water

Now you have given us hope
Now you have suspended bloodshed
Now you have brought us peace
Now you have given us value

All UN Convoys
All National Envoys
All Tactful Mediators
All Expert Facilitators
Lazarus, Lazarus Sumbeiywo
John, John Dan fort
Alan, Alan Goulti
Colin, Colin Powell
Hilda, Hilda Johnson
To mention few examples

You people of IGAD
You Friends of IGAD
You African Supporters
You International Helpers

Come and live with us

Now you have given us hope
We who were ignored
By most of the world
We who were mal-projected
As valueless and cultureless

Come and live with us

All who helped us
From Nigeria
To Bageria
From Abuja
To Naivasha
From Arabia
To Caucasia
From Africa
To America

Come and live with us

In our hearts
You will live
In our minds
You will stay
Forever

Come and live with us
For even a single day
You will know instantly
How good a people we are

PO2 BEAUTIFUL SOUTH SUDAN

By Achier Deng Akol

Beautiful South Sudan
Shall thrive with glamour
Once again as before
It shall shine with power
Like a star and even more

It will grow
From a weakling
To an independent bow
With a mighty string

Its dry plains
Will become green
To produce grains
As it had been

Rivers lakes and streams
Will fill and flow
Rusty golden beams
Will begin to glow

All destroyed cities
Like Malakal, Juba and Wau
Will be re-flourished
New ones like central Ramkiel
Will be established

Multiple Wonderful Flowers
Will spring up once again
With spectacular colours
To relieve longstanding pain

The painful years
Of long war

With miserable tears
Of absolute poor
Will change to cheers

Dying forests
Destroyed plantains
Ruined harvests
Eroded mountains
Will all blossom
Once again

It will be time
Of utmost prime
Time for love and marriages
Time for constructive strategies
Time to produce more children
Time to replace lost kindred
Time to rename the martyrs
Time to reform the families
Time to rebuild the motherland
Time to own the fatherland

Beautiful South Sudan
Shall thrive and glamour
Once again as before
It will shine with power
Like a star and even more

The Heavens will open
The rain will pour down
And hibernating frogs
Will leap out
In full excitement
To join the celebration
Cocks will crow
In every home
That keeps them

To wake people up
And the chicks will run
Behind the mother hen
Waving their small wings
In additional celebration

All astonishing butterflies
From over the whole world
Will flock in their millions
Into the Heart of Africa
To join their counterparts
For a special ceremony
And taste South Sudan nectar

Dogs will shake
Their own tails
To welcome visitors
With touching gestures
And funny noises

All the wartime heroic victims
Like amputees, widows and orphans
Physically and emotionally traumatised
Will be comforted and motivated
And every martyr of the South
Should be remembered forever

The few children
That survived the war
Will run, sing and play
In the Southern fields
In their small numbers
Till they are joined
By more to come

For horrible slavery
Will become history

And terrible oppression
Will be in total extinction

Beautiful South Sudan
Shall thrive and glamour
Once again as before
It shall shine with power
Like a star and even more

PO3 THE CPA AND ANYA-NYA, SSLF, SPLA SOUTH SUDAN ARMIES

[By Mogga SJ]

There is no Peace without Development,
There is no development without Security
Therefore,
There is no Security without Well armed Army
Therefore
Worthy to spend and
Spend BIG on Well Armed Army
Otherwise
You end up with Army without Arms
An Army that cannot match their enemies
An Army that will run away instead of running into Battlefields
No matter how long Battle hardened

An Army that can protect no Land
And that causes Insecurity
And lack of Peace

PO4 MISSING HOME

[By Mogga, SJ]

The world is fast
My Bunad is first

Every tide fast, every wave fast
Let's abide by what we know
The world here, people there know
The rainbow you see, people there know
Fjell, Created by word power
Changed by fire
How can we sailors know?
How can my gracious Savior Show?

The meek and lowly hearts
That Spirit does impart
The things which freely do impart
We talk about ends of Earth apart
From Earth, you depart
From hurt heart

Take care, brethren
Your wrongs forgiven
Our names in heaven
Hearts are laden
By Askladen
Curse Bin Laden
Oh Heavens

What do you have?
Keep what I have
Soul to Save
Sight to live,
Account to give!
Watch and pray
My trust Peace betray
This boat I sailed away
Like Fish, I'll shy away

(Bunad A colorful Norwegian national dress)

PO5 ARROW OR LEAF OF PEACE?

[By Mogga, SJ]

Sometimes
You feel
Down, then
Pretended, Sometimes
Rejected, and then
Become afflicted!
A humiliation, an Observation
Someone Rested by incineration
Incarnation, life's oblation
Problems are like Painful tumors,
Extirpated by Surgical Operation
This night, Blessings of the light!
Oh the Arc Sund, Oh the Boat of Sund

Keep me, O keep me, Boat of Boats
Arc of Arcs, Mighty King of Kings
Behind us are thy own mighty wings.
By letting us doing every good things
Praise all creatures by Songs we sing;
We light and set our candles glowing;
Praise Father, Son, and Holy Ghost
Flying, Crying, Singing, Springing
The Arc of Sund
The Flag of Rainbow
Cultures Meet
People Seek
People Meet
People Joy
Freedom
Forever
After
Bullets
Killed
Many

V

PO6 ULULATE

By Miss Apuk Ayuel Mayen

Ululate, my daughter
Ululate
My throat is dry from years
Of wailing and screaming
And now that the day has come
To rejoice
It has failed me and denied me
The pleasure of ululating
So ululate, my daughters
Ululate

Ululate for all the fallen sons and daughters
and for all the martyrs
Ululate
For all of the innocent children
And for all who longed for today but perished
yesterday
Ululate, my daughters
Ululate

Let your voices accompany their spirits in their
ascension
For the day has come for our rivers to abandon their
discoloration
And for the blood to evaporate off of our soil
Ululate
For this is a day of cleansing and of the
discontinuation of mourning
Ululate

Let your voices erect memorials for the victims of the
war

For we will no longer name the dead
Ululate, my daughters
Ululate

May your powerful voices
Echo our prayers to all the corners of the earth
May it carry with it the joy, and the grief
The hopes and the dreams of a nation
Ululate
May it testify of the suffering, and enduring
Of my children
May it denounce the curses of evil spirits
Who are conspiring in broad daylight
Ululate, my daughters
May your voices raise up a fortress of protection
Built by the spirits of the innocent children
Who have longed to live,
now forever guarding the precious lives of the unborn
Ululate, my daughters
Ululate

Yes, peace has come
But let your voice announce caution
And denounce complacency
For I have once ululated decades ago
But it was for a pseudo peace
My sons were intoxicated by the promise of false power
And the quest of titles
They failed to notice that the agreement
Had a rotten and rat infested foundation
They were lured by the prospect of peace
But we were denied justice
Ululate, my daughters
Ululate

There is no peace without justice
Must be your cry

There is no peace without justice
Raise your voices high

My throat is dry,
Give me salt water
For I must join you daughters
In Ululating
For our collective voices
Have much to carry
Today we ululate
And tomorrow we shall continue the struggle
For a lasting peace
One that is fortified by justice
Ululate

Let's Ululate
Raising our voices to heaven
Ushering in peace everlasting
In God's willing

PO7 A CRY FOR FREEDOM

By Sunday Taabu

Oh S. Sudan, my beloved country S. Sudan
S. Sudan my motherland
Oh S. Sudan Let there be you, the S. Sudan I know
The land of the Black
Let you be the land you used to be
A land divided by the might Power of River Nile
From the source through Lake Victoria cutting through
the plains
Wounding its way to the Delta
Oh S. Sudan, you are rich and fertile
It is this rooted desire that hunts me day and night
Oh motherland S.
Sudan

The land of the brave
The land of martyrs
I'm crying and seeking a home that is free
O S. Sudan let you be that great land of Love
Let you be that great land of Peace
Let you be that great land of freedom
Let you be that land of liberty
Let you be the land of opportunity and equality

PO8 POLITICS

By Deng Awur Wenyin, LLB Khartoum, LLM Leicester UK

Politics is a prostitute
Politics is an adulterer
Politics is spying
Politics is a conspiracy
Politics is a betrayer
Politics is a dirty game
Politics is a friend
Politics is an opponent
Politics is an enemy
Politics is a critic
Politics is an opportunist
Politics is an embezzler
Politics is a blindfold
Politics is an eye-opener
Politics is a compromise
Politics is a human rights activist
Politics is diligence
Politics is vigilance
Politics is malice
Politics is lies
Politics is vengeance
Politics is void
Politics is mirage
Politics is the possible

Politics is the impossible
Politics is invasion
Politics is colonization
Politics is alliance
Politics is self-determination
Politics is secession
Politics is independence
Politics! Politics! Politics!
Politics is nothing
Politics is something
Politics is everything.

PO9 THE NILE

By Deng Awur Wenyin

I was born on the Nile
But I don't drink from the Nile
I was raised in the Nile basin
But I don't eat fish from the Nile
I ply over the Nile every morning
But I don't swim in the Nile
Strangers sport in the Nile
But I sport on rough ground
My ancestors knew the Nile
But at school I am taught
That the Nile was discovered by a tourist

Dengdit—with you numerous brothers
Like Nyikang, Dumo and Yonder
I don't believe in discovery theory
Tell me: Who created the Nile?
Not you? With your brothers yonder?
Who filled the Nile with water?
Not you? With your brothers yonder?
Who enjoys the Nile?
Why do the Pharaohs gauge the Nile?

Dengdit give me might
To regain control over the Nile
Dengdit—didn't you send a dream?
To your son Ngun-Deng?
To visualise a long dug hole?
In the Nile basin?
Meandering toward the Old Kush?
Oh! They want swift water
Your sacred bull will have no toc
It will die of thirst and hunger
If I want to drink from the Nile
It's said that's war on the Pharaohs
Dengdit—give me might—to rectify the situation.

PO10 GONE ARE THE DAYS

By Deng Awur Wenyin

Gone are the days...
On the African Continent
When governments mowed down
Their own citizens
And the world watched
Pretext...internal...domestic affair

Gone are the days...
When the Nile bathed in blood
Indeed the Nile turned red
Fish drank the blood...
Frogs laid eggs in skulls
Pretext...domestic blood halal

Gone are the days...
When the world was a million
Million miles...miles apart
Now...new ideas...fresh ones
Computer...Internet...Sudatel
Yes! New big ideas!

Gone are the days…
The world is a village
Really? Like Pacong? Kagwada?
Good news! Do they hear?
Events at Pacong?
Oh ya! Why not?

Gone are the days…
The sun awakes from the East
The sun sleeps in the West
The wind blows from the East
The wind settles in the West
Pouring down rain of redemption

Gone are the days…
But with what do they
Drink water here?
Is it koz? Glass? Calabash?
This koz! How much water does it now hold?

PO11 TRIBUTE TO WALTER SISULU

By Deng Awur Wenyin

Sisulu—technological news carried your death
We could have wept and wailed
But we have no forum for weeping
For our local oppressor is more vicious and worse
Than the White oppressor you fought against
Sisulu—we are indeed bereaved
For you are a relative in struggle

Sisulu—you and Mandela charged: AMANDLA!
The wananchi roared in Union: YETU…
Albertina, your wife, was always by your side
A combatant, wife, mother, and inspirer
Indeed great women make great men greater

Zwelakhe—your son—was in the front line
Sisulu—we are indeed bereaved
For you are a relative in struggle

Sisuslu—history will preserve the Rivonia Trial
You, Mandela and the rest of those gentlemen
Stood firm and confident before the oppressor
You know—the oppressor has no uniform colour
Though yours was White—it makes no difference
In this locality, mourning for your match is high treason
Sisulu—we are indeed bereaved
For you are a relative in struggle

Sisulu! Papas, mzee, monydit, sleep well!
Have you seen Viko and the Sharpeville youth?
In the distant border, have you found the uhuru men?
Mwalimu Nyerere, Ndugu Karume, Mzee Kenyatta?
Ndigo Kabisa! Meet all our ancestors
Tell them of our prayers...and aspirations...
Sisulu—we are bereaved
For you are a relative in struggle

Sisulu! Daddy Wangu, you were a torch in the dark
African forest and green valleys
Even for Algeria, the Saharawi, the whole Desert
In the further distant between the Desert and Equator
Have you met William Deng Nhial? Aggrey Gadein?
Dominic Muorwel Malou? Saturnino Lohure? Paul
Logali?
OO! Those Grass Curtain men: Sisulu, we are bereaved
For you are a relative in struggle

Sisulu—you were very lucky—indeed lucky
For you saw your folk through freedom
We don't know whether some of us will have the same luck to
see our folk in freedom
Beg the ancestral spirit to let that happen

Very soon…very soon…very soon…
Sisulu—we are bereaved
For you are a relative in struggle

PO12 KOFI ANNAN...KUDUAL

By Deng Awur Wenyin

Kofi Annan…kudual
Kofi Annan…madang
Kofi Annan…malee
Kofi Annan…mede
Kofi Annan…salamat

Kofi Annan…son of Africa
Son of the Land
Son of the Continent
The sun goes to sleep in your land
Waking up in my wretched land

Kofi ...brother of Nkrumah
Kofi…nephew of Sengor and Nyerere
Kofi…cousin of Kaunda and Moi
Kofi…son of Mandela and Sisulu
Kofi…Welcome! Welcome to Soudan

Kofi...see what is being done
To your own folk
By your own folk
It happened before…in South Sudan
Isn't it too much?

Kofi…we have suffered during the last five decades
Tell our relative…Colin Powell
Conditions his granddad experienced
Still exist in this Biblical Land

Kofi…I'm very confident
You'll see things in their colours
Kofi…I'm very confident
You'll see reality with real eyes
You'll stop atroci…geno…what's the name?

PO13 UNTIMELY DEATH

By Deng Awur Wenyin

What's timely for you
May not be timely for me
What's untimely for you
May not be untimely for me
Time is untime

In the Whiteman's mind
Time is money
In the Blackman's mind
Time is life, honour and dignity
Time is up on the Nile

Untimely death…
Means death before childhood
Untimely death…
Means death before youthhood
Youthhood—the rose of life

Alas! Untimely death…
Means death before liberation
OO! Untimely death…
Means death before decision
Decision to remain or part

Untimely death is death itself
Untimely death is conspiracy
Untimely death id cruelty

Untimely death is the child of politics
Untimely death is foreign politics

Nhialic Madhol…
What is this?
Untimely death…
Piny ace nhom gut ni lung!
Because time is money

PO14 TAKE MY BONES WITH YOU

To all that miss their homeland

By Achier Deng Akol

When you go back home
Take my bones with you
Do not leave them in a tomb
Among a distant foreign hue

Do not leave them to rust
Where the Nile does not flow
Do not leave them to crust
Beneath the ice and snow

Take them with minimal toil
To the sunshine of Savannah
Deep into the lovely warm soil
Within the heart of Africana

When you happily step down
Onto our precious motherland
Where African drums sound
Over our independent fatherland

Do not just gaze amazingly
At its beautiful landscape

Do not just stare astonishingly
At its wonderful forest-shape

Kneel down on the floor
Touch our precious soil
Kiss it more than a score
Then bury me in that soil

Singing: Die-heart of South Sudan
We have not left you in foreign land
We have brought you all along
To rest forever where you belong

PO15 WHO CHANGED OUR ORIGINAL NAMES?

By Achier Deng Akol

Cairo is not Cairo
It is Kar rou
Which literally means
In African Language
Where two rivers divide.

Khartoum is not Khartoum
It is Kar tuom
Which actually means
In the same language
Where two rivers unite.

Don't you know
I am a black seed
That regressed
From Kar rou
To Kar tuom
And beyond?

Who changed our original names?

PO16 GIVE ME MILK, MUMMY

By Achier Deng Akol

I know you care
With all your heart
But I have no teeth
To chew any leaves
I am just a little baby
With no teeth, Mummy
To chew any leaves

Give me milk, Mummy

I know you care
With all your heart
But these wild roots
Are unbearably too bitter
Too bitter, Mummy
Too bitter for me to swallow

I know you care
With all your heart
But I can't stand
Yes I can't, Mummy
I can't at all stand
The smell of urine

Give me milk, Mummy

I know you care
With all your heart
But mud in saliva
Mud soaked in saliva!
Can't reach my throat

I know you care
With all your heart

But don't you dare
Don't you dare, Mummy
To give me blood

Give me milk, Mummy

I know you care
With all your heart
But your final cuddle
Feels cold and painful

Give me milk, Mummy
Give me…Give me
Give me milk, Mummy

PO17 THANK YOU, MAHOGANY

By Achier Deng Akol

To our protective bushes

Freedom fighter tree
Extra natural protector
Help us free
From oppressive dictator

Your strong branches
Taller than camels
Were ancestral defences
Against wild animals

Your thick leaves
Now shield us
From bomb heaves
Dropped on us

Your bitter roots
Are our tablets
And our boots
Are your leaflets

Aren't your seeds
Like other weeds
As alternative nutrition
Better than starvation?

Isn't your presence
In thick wood
Saving our existence
Anyhow for good?

You constitute bushes
With all giant trees
For defensive ambushes
By freedom gallantries

Without bush cover
We'll be exposed
We'll lose power
And be disposed

Strategic forest sanctuary
And green camouflages
Against inhuman savagery
And terrorist damages

You are protective
You are majestic
You are supportive
You are fantastic

Thank you, mahogany

PO18 LET ME TOUCH YOU, SOUTHERN SUDAN, HEAVEN ON EARTH

By Achier Deng Akol

To all who lost vital parts of their bodies during the war
Like my own blind brother Joseph Aguer Deng Akol

They say the sky is extremely beautiful
With blue colours and various clouds
Or dark space filled with shiny stars
But all I feel is cold air and dry winds

Many say a forest looks wonderful
With green leaves and multiple flowers
Plus various birds on different trees
But all I hear are roaring of angry lions

You say oceans and seas are marvellous
With endless horizons lined with rainbows
And spectacular fishes animals and plants
But all I detect are frightening sound waves

They keep telling me this world is full
Of many lovely and attractive ladies
Coupled with a lot of handsome men
But all I enjoy is the touch of their hands

People say the world is very rich
With money, diamond, gold and silver
And food which can feed everybody
But all I feel is an empty stomach

I believe there is real Heaven
And there is Southern Sudan
That is like Heaven on Earth
But all my eyes can see is darkness

Let Me Touch You, Southern Sudan, Heaven-on-Earth

PO19 TEARS ALONE CAN'T SAVE US

By Achier Deng Akol

Are you weeping or praying
Because we are starving
Is your heart seriously aching
Because we are dying?

Tears alone can't save us

Weep for us you may
Pray for us anyway
But don't only weep
Donate whatever you reap

Stop weeping only
Do something more
Keep praying surely
But fetch a food store

Tears alone can't save us

I know you're a carer
Your heart is tender
You are sympathetic
And also empathetic

Yet don't weep merely
Think and think really
Of ways to rescue us
Of means to feed us
Sing and sell a cassette
If you have a voice
Pick your own pocket
If you have a choice

Move and move very quickly
Before it becomes too late
Don't waste time weeping only
We may soon have no heart rate

Tears alone can't save us

Weep for us you may
Pray for us anyway
But don't only weep
Donate whatever you reap

Tears alone can't save us

PO20 TEARS OF ESPLEES

By Achier Deng Akol

To all people who cry for their land

Why do we weep?
For our motherland
When we think deep
About our destined trend
If you are tears of escapees
Now stop spilling over
If you are tears of esplees
Continue to flow forever

Why do we cry?
For our ultimate freedom
When we just try
Dreaming of future kingdom
If you are tears of hopelessness
Now stop spilling over
If you are tears of steadfastness
Continue to flow forever

Why do you drop?
Even when we're standing
On a beautiful hilltop
In New Sudan pondering
If you are tears of depression
Now stop spilling over
If you are tears of motivation
Continue to flow forever

Why do you flow?
Down our ecstatic face
When SPLA heroes blow
Enemy soldiers off space
If you are tears of endless slavery
Now stop spilling over
If you are tears of SPLA victory
Continue to flow forever

Why do we weep?
For our motherland
When we think deep
About our destined trend
If you are tears of escapees
Now stop spilling over
If you are tears of esplees
Continue to flow forever

PO21 HE IS A HEART OF GOLD

By Achier Deng Akol

He who offers buses
To little school children
To go to school from houses
Without being bothered by rain

He who pays visits
To the sick and bereaved

And consoles their spirits
From pain and grief

He who officially ranks
Number one as security
In government plans
For absolute public safety

He who grants a car
To be used by a volunteer
As a lifesaving star
To say please carefully steer

He who truly weeps
For people suffering
And gives what he keeps
To help them with something

He who does all that and more
Is beyond what can be told
Is truly an exception with lore
He is a Heart of Gold

And why would he not be so regarded
When his first name S means Saintly
His second name K means Kind-hearted
His last name M means Mindfully

SKM-Salva Kiir Mayardit
A Saint in character
Kind-hearted indeed
A Mindful Leader

He is a Heart of Gold

PO22 DON'T CRY, MY PEOPLE IS HE NOT ME?

By Achier Deng Akol

To all orphans of
Southern Sudan

Don't cry, my people
My father isn't dead
Look at me closely
Is he not me?

Who says his name
Will go with him?
Can I not call
My child after him?

Who thinks his intelligence
Which made him doctor
Shall disappear with him?
Haven't I inherited it?

Who wonders his missions
He aimed to achieve
Will all remain incomplete?
Can't I continue them?

Listen to me, please
Trust me fully now
Believe what I say
Have no doubt at all

That tomb you see there
Doesn't contain my father
It is completely empty
He is not there

His body isn't there
It is reflected in me
His soul isn't inside
It's already in heaven

Don't cry, my people
My father isn't dead
Look at me closely
Is he not me?

PO23 DON'T BLAME IT AT ALL ON ME

By Achier Deng Akol

My land speaks. Hear what it says.
Following the tragic death of our leader
Dr. John Garang De Mabior and others

I am the land
You're fighting for
When I stand
Please listen therefore

For now and again
My weather alter
Causing heavy rain
Which maybe harsher
And even my thunder
Never struck a helicopter

Don't blame it at all on me

My huge mountains
With my thick bushes
Were tough restrains
For our enemy forces

Weren't those the justifications
Owiny kibul of Anyanya warriors
And New Site of SPLA soldiers
Were chosen strong fortifications?

Don't blame it at all on me

If my weather
And my mountains
Are now faultier
Please forgive pains
For I your land
And you my band
Are parts and parcel
Of the same struggle

Don't blame it at all on me.

PO24 STAR OF ALL STARS

By Achier Deng Akol

To Dr. John Garang De Mabior,
Who died in a Helicopter tragedy
On 30 July 2005

There are names
That are normal
And other names
That are special

John, John the Baptist
Garang, name of Adam
Mabior, Colour of Peace
John Garang De Mabior

An SPLA founder
A tactful liberator

An SPLM leader
A peace originator
With a name
That is special

There are stars
And stars of stars
There are heroes
And heroes of heroes

Garang De Mabior
A Sudanese Saviour
Who knew the routes
That will yield fruits
A star of stars
A hero of heroes

There are hearts
That are bitter
And other hearts
That are tender
To all people marginalised
He was very affectionate
Insulted or wrongly criticised
He remained compassionate
With a heart that was tender

There are eyes
That see nearer
And other eyes
That look further

A truly gifted missionary
A real talented visionary
A New Sudan thinker
With eyes that looked further

There are lights
That darkle
And other lights
That sparkle

Brilliant Brainy liberator
Ensured referendum tackles
Legitimate Peace originator
A light that sparkles

John Garang De Mabior
Our beloved leader
That was so bright
You will glitter
As a spiritual light
In our hearts forever

Star of all stars

PO25 YE YE YE WHY?

By Achier Deng Akol

To all our martyrs

Ye Ye Ye Why?

Ye who can
Make mountains tremble
Ye who can
Stop sea-wave trouble

Ye who gives lives
To all on Earth
Ye who saves lives
And conquers death

Why did you take
Millions upon millions
Of our people away
From all of us?

Why did you
Take all of them
Before peace implementation
Before self-determination

Is it because
You want them
In your Kingdom
As additional security
For our freedom
To become a reality?

You who are a saviour
Why didn't you
Answer our prayer
To save them all?

Is it definitely because
They are your children
Who are to you so close
You need them in Heaven

Am I right to say again
You want them all up there
Near to the Angels and Saints
And not down here
Which is full of pains?

Ye Ye Ye Why?

PO26 LITTLE DO THEY KNOW!

By Dr. John A. Akec

12 August 2005
London, UK

Little do they know!

The assassins' bombs will cause us to bow
To them we will kneel,
And in despair we will sink
Or so they think
But no!
They are wrong.
To no man we will bow
No bombs or guns
Will cause us to blink
And whatever they do
We will never be cowed.

Little do they know!

Silencing our captain,
Stabbing our leader in the back
His vision will be dimmed.
His mottos will be slimmed
Or so they think
But no!
They are wrong!
Our faith in New Sudan will ever grow
On course we will stay
Where our leader wanted us go
To that place we will go

Little do they know!

One Garang may leave
In his place will spring a thousand Garangs
Even more
To his vision they will cling
From his wisdom they will drink
For Luther, Gandhi, Karl Marx and Lincoln,
From blow
They still enthuse and inspire
Generations upon generations of revolutionaries,
Of writers and thinkers
To rise up and fight for a cause,
That is noble and true
Little do they know!
They are wrong
They are wrong
Cause will open our wings
And soar
And soar
Up in the heaven
Above the earth
With our heads lifted high
Our flags flying on the Mount Imatong
To speak of freedom
Of liberty, of dignity
And true humanity
Overcoming evil
Forevermore

PO27 WHEN I THINK OF YOU

In memory of Comrade Dr. John Garang de Mabior, my Chairman

Dr. Mawien Akot

When I think of you,
I think of the New Sudan.
Of hopes, and dreams.
That have just begun

When I think of you,
I see your gentle grin.
The one that happens,
When the marginalised score a win.

When I think of you,
Always patient, Always full of vision.
I know your love for the land,
Is the forever kind!

When I think of you,
And your love for the New Sudan.
I know that heaven,
Will help your people reach the Promised Land.

When I think of you,
I think of Orphans and Widows
The very people,
Whose dreams and hopes are hijacked

When I think of you,
I can smell the freedom you always cherished.
You were always flying,
Flying high above for sake of freedom till you died

When I think of you,
I think of your accommodating heart.
You showed us true love and patriotism.
North, South, East, or West, you instructed us that Sudan is ours to lead
From all these things our Chairman,
I cry day and night and sometimes deny that you're truly gone.
I know they killed you,
But they blame your death on Imotong the mountain you always loved.

PO28 IN THEIR VOICES I HEARD THEIR FATHER SPEAK

By Achier Deng Akol

To all our people everywhere
Who kept their hearts strong
During the burial of our beloved leader
Dr. John Garang De Mabior
Particularly his wife, Rebecca, and children

Listen to what his children said
When they buried their own father
Dr. John Garang De Mabior
In the Southern soil of Juba

In their look I saw their father appear
In their love I sensed their father touched
In their statements I felt their father alive
In their voices I heard their father speak

Listen to what his children said
About his courage and his dream
You may drop tears openly like me
You may weep silently in your heart

Listen to fellow children singing in London
I had a dream! I had a dream!
Listen to our people singing in Juba
Oh my people! Who will free my people!

You will know deeply in your heart
John Garang De Mabior is not dead
He is alive in his wife and children
He is survived in all who cherish him

Listen to his children speak
When they buried their father

They did not appear weak
As they stood with their mother

In their look I saw their father appear
In their love I sensed their father touched
In their statements I felt their father alive
In their voices I heard their father speak

PO29 FIGHTING THE DEAD WHAT COWARDICE!

By Achier Deng Akol

When he was alive
You were submissive
Now he can't strive
You are aggressive

Fighting the dead
What cowardice!

After he is gone
He won't defend
You grew horn
To then offend

You are wise
To play safe
And only rise
Against a grave

Before funeral
You're hysterical
Without any wait
You took a sigh
And walked straight
With head high

Even drank beer
All night
With real cheer
Outright

Oh! Pathetic coward
You go on awkward
Tap the keyboard
Attack the dead
Jam phone cord
You are sad

When he was alive
You were submissive
Now he can't strive
You are aggressive

Fighting the dead
What cowardice!

PO30 YOU WONDERFUL THINGS OF SOUTH SUDAN, WE MISS YOU SO MUCH

By Achier Deng Akol

To all children of South Sudan
Who are scattered by the war
And miss their precious land

You wonderful things
Of South Sudan
We miss you so much

You precious water
Of the river Nile
We will enjoy you

You morning dew
Of green soft grass
We will touch you

You warm sunshine
Of tropical Savannah
We will feel you

You beautiful birds
Of South Sudan
We will watch you

You wonderful land
In the Heart of Africa
We will own you

You marvellous martyrs
That died for our freedom
We will meet you

Let all sceptics say
Whatever they like
Let doubting Thomases
Continue to doubt

You wonderful things
Of South Sudan
Listen to us now
Listen to our promise

We will see you
We will touch you
We will feel you
We will own you

Once again and forever
You wonderful things

PO31 HOW ELSE CAN WE REPLACE OUR OWN MARTRYS?

By Achier Deng Akol

To all our depleted or eradicated families

Had I seeds
Of various trees
That have perished
During the war
I would scatter them
All over the South
In order to regrow

Had I magnets
That can attract
Our lost wildlife
I would pull back
Rare white elephants
And great rhinos
Among other species
That have migrated

Had I machines
That produce children
I would run them
Every day and night
In order to replace
Millions of our people
Lost during the war

Had I powers
To convince my people
I would form another Katiba
Called Katiba al Walada
To shoot its Kalashnikovs
Every hour nonstop

In order to win another battle
A battle of al Walada

Had I millions of money
I would reward families
Who reach eleventh child
With special valuable prizes
And appoint them to become
Commandants in Katiba al Walada

Had I also luck
I would marry soon
A lover so sweet
To make me whole again
And serve my South Sudan

How else can we replace our own martyrs?

PO32 OH! YEAR 2012 PLEASE COME SOON

By Achier Deng Akol

Between my eyes
And the book
Is not emptiness

Between my head
And the pillow
Is not vacant

Between my body
And its shadow
Is not a vacuum

Between my life
And the soul
Is not nothing

You are the one

The one I see
Between the book
And my eyes

The photo I keep
Between the pillow
And my head

The air that flows
Between my shadow
And my body

The love I feel
Deep in my life
And my soul

The girl of my dream
The sunshine of my life
A product of my land

Oh! The year 2012
Please come soon
For me to marry
The girl of my dream
And feel a double joy
Of New Wife New Country

Oh! The Year 2012
Please come soon.

PO33 OH! MY PEOPLE DO NOT SLEEP

By Achier Deng Akol

You see
640 AC
To 2008

For 1,368 years
To be very precise
We shed tears
Of extreme demise

We Kush children
Along River Nile
True African kindred
With magnificent style
Have been
Surviving
So harsh
Suffering
So much
Fighting
So strong
And dying
So long

1,368 years
Without surrender
What real bravery! What a power
Despite misery

This alarm
I will ring
In the arm
I will swing
Is called and I yell
The Referendum Bell

From 2006 momentum
To 2011 referendum

Only five or so
Five years to go

Oh! My people
Do not sleep
Do not creep
Stand up
Double up
Strongly exert
Make a spurt
It's not all gloom
A new sun will rise
It will one day bloom
With joy and no cries

This alarm
I will ring
In the arm
I will swing
Is called and I yell
The Referendum Bell

PO34 GIVE ME YOUUUUUUU

By Achier Deng Akol

You can give me
Gold and diamond
To make me feel special

You can offer me
Billions of money
To make me rich

You can buy me
Anything on Earth
To impress me

But my darling
I don't want that
I don't want all that

The only thing
I really want
Is youuuuuuu

If you actually want
To give me anything
Give me you

Even South Sudan
That I so desire
Will feel empty
Without you

Give me youuuuuuu

Give me
Give me
Give me youuuuuuu

PO35 MILLIONS OF MILES AWAY

By Achier Deng Akol

To all lovers thrown apart by war
And other circumstances

Give me love arrow
That I can shoot
Millions of miles away
To enter my die heart
Where it will stick

Give me special heart
That pumps and speaks

Saying over long distances
She's mine she's mine
For sweetie to hear

Give me lengthy arms
That I can stretch
From abroad to Sudan
To touch my lover
Where she feels sweet

Give me extensive lips
That can both expand
Overseas and oceans
To kiss my sweetheart
Where she won't forget

Give me explosive waist
That can swirl afar
To engulf my darling
And shake her softly
Till she sees stars

Without love arrow
Without special heart
Without lengthy arms
Without extensive lips
Without explosive waist

Without these special parts
How can I show?
That I love her
From head to toe
Millions of miles away

When words over phones
Messages via e-mails

Cards gifts and letters
Pictures texts and tapes
All are not enough

How can I
Millions of miles away

PO36 VOTE ME FREE IN 2011

By Achier Deng Akol

Tell me you love me
Countless million times
I won't still believe you

Sing me love songs
Every day and night
I may still doubt you

Promise to jump down
From top of a mountain
It won't reach my ears

Just vote me free in 2011
Then I will believe you love me

For Words Words Words
Songs Songs Songs
Promises Promises Promises
All can be blown away
By the wind around

But your decisive vote
That vote for our freedom
No wind can blow it away
However strong that wind is

If you love me
Don't leave me a slave
In my own country

Vote me free in 2011

PO37 HAPPINESS

By Achier Deng Akol

Dive deep into the Ocean
Roam the entire Universe
Fly high beyond the horizon
You will not find happiness

Collect all precious metals
And all universal richness
Own all the world essentials
You will not find happiness

Happiness is not in far streams
And it is not simply a bank card
Happiness is a light that gleams
In hearts of those who work hard
To achieve their desired dreams

So now on our celebration row
Let the light of joy start to glow
All over our bodies and souls
And let the tears of joy flow
Over our faces and eyeballs

Let the drums beat
And the music sound
Let our bodies heat
And our minds mount
With joy and happiness
Today and forever

PO38 WHEN THE NIGHT DREW ITS CURTAIN

Reproduced By Dr. Victoria Anib Achut

When the night drew its curtains it became so dark
I felt alone and started to moan and groan.
But my sweetheart visited my dreams and lifted the strain.
He overflowed me with love that ran throughout my veins.
It circulated all inside me and was a remedy for every
bit of pain.
I lived the dream and defeated all constrains.
I persuaded him to stay and remain.
I opened my eyes and it went all in vain.
In spite of this I still felt him inside my heart
Where he dwells like a planted grain.
His love will be my song which I will sing again
and again.

PO39 THE SWEET WE

By Achier Deng Akol

Top Class
Top Gear
The Sweet We

Enhance our voices
To outshine stars
And top all charts
Day after day

Lend us tactics
To outplay Brazil
And win world cups
Year after year

Strengthen our muscles
To outclass Olympians

And sweep gold medals
One after another

Spark our brains
To surpass the USA
In world power
Now and forever

Then we will sing
Our national anthem
For all to hear
Wave Independence Flag
For all to see

And by the time they ask everywhere
Whose Anthem is that so wonderful?
Whose flag is that so spectacular?
We will have put our unknown land
Of South Sudan: The Heart of Africa
Onto the map of the world
And introduced our great people
To the entire Universe

Top Class
Top Gear
The Sweet We

PO40 WIPE YOUR FACE FOR US THE VISION IS STILL ALIVE

By Achier Deng Akol

When the sun falls
And darkness rolls
The air stands still
Birds sleep on hill
At midnight or so
You get up and go

To visit our late leader
Dr. John Garang De Mabior

You stand over his shrine
Bravely in no moonshine
You alone in the queue
Tears in your face accrue
Then you solemnly pray
You lament and say
Things are not bright
Issues are not right
The vision is threatened
The mission is weakened
Wish you were here
For our land Oh dear!

Wipe your face for us
The vision is still alive

Things will change
Joshua will arrange
For all of us to unite
And freedom will ignite
All is not dim
All is not grim
There is some light
Let us just hold tight

Wipe your face for us
The vision is still alive

I will not weep now you said
Because my husband is dead
I will only weep later you stated
If the vision is not implemented
Wipe your face for us
The vision is still alive

PO41 WHO SAYS WE ARE DEAD? MILLIONS OF OUR MARTYRS SPEAK

By Achier Deng Akol

Who says we are dead?
We millions that perished
Fighting South of Kar tuom
For your total freedom

We may have no bodies
But we are not dead
We may have no ears
Yet we are not deaf
We may have no eyes
Still we are not blind
We may have no throats
But we are not voiceless

We are with you
With you our people
We are original bodies
That transform into you
We are spiritual ears
That echo your prayers
We are invisible eyes
That look after you
We are the voices
That encourage you
We are the spirits
That inspire you
We are the Angels
Protecting the CPA

So listen to us now
Listen our sole survivors
Had we a chance

To appear in a glance
We would advise you
Only just thrice
To be very precise

Advice number one
For entirely every one
Your strength does not lie only
In fundamental Molotovs
Anya-nya pioneers invented
Nor in instrumental Kalashnikovs
SPLA heroes and heroines extended
It lies mainly in your unity
In your total and solid unity

Hear this too
Advice number two
Keep away disunity
That our enemy uses
Throw away animosity
That NIF abuses
Lest we all perish
Lest we all finish

Advice number three
Maintain the momentum
Vote all of us free
During the referendum

Remember us in our graves
Marsh bravely in huge waves
To vote for South Sudan Freedom
And throw away Slavery Kingdom

Who says we are dead?
We millions that perished
Fighting for your freedom

We may have no bodies
But we are not dead
We are with you
With you our people
We are the spirits
That inspire you
So listen to us now
Listen our sole survivors
Your strength does not lie only
In Molotovs or Kalashnikovs
It lies mainly in your unity
Your total and solid unity

PO42 THEY DID THEIR PART NOW IT IS OUR TURN

By Dr. Achier Deng Akol

They did their part
Now it is our turn

They joined the SPLA line
Leaving all they had
They marched to frontline
Not afraid of any ahead

Bombs poured
Bullets rained
Dynamites struck
Tanks rolled

Others shivered
And ran away
Traitors quivered
And chose to betray

But our martyrs shouted
SPLA Oyeeeeeeeeeee

And marched undoubted
For our Land Oyeeeee

For our total liberty
They loudly cried
For our sovereignty
They ultimately died

Yes! They died for us
Leaving their wives
As widows
And their children
As orphans

They did their part
Now it is our turn

PO43 CHANGE US, LORD

By Achier Deng Akol

From rippers
Of our parts
To keepers
Of loving hearts

From creatures
With enemy dust
To treasures
With Southern crust

From weepers
For dead kith
To sweepers
Of division filth

Everyday
Every night

All we do
For our land
For our people
Is weep
Weep
And weep

Change us Lord

Make us able
To saw love
To cultivate unity
In the hearts
Of our people
In the soil
Of our land

Give us power
To quench fires
Lit by enemies
Ignited by hatred

LRA fire
In Eastern Equatoria
Tribal fire
In Western Equatoria
Potential Earthquakes
In Upper Nile
Looming Volcanoes
In Bahr-el-Gazal
Serious Minefields
In Abyei and beyond

Give us planes
To transport lovers
Of South Sudan
All over the world

With millions
Of white pigeons
And white flags
With tanks
Of water
And barrels
Of love

To burning spots
In our homeland
To quench the fires
Of hatred
And the flames
Of bitterness

To release
The pigeons
Of love
And wave
The flags
Of peace
And unity

So that the sky
Of the South
Is cloudless
The air of the South
Is smokeless
The atmosphere of the South
Is warless
The floor of the South
Is bloodless
And the Soil of the South
Rests from burial
After burial
After burial

Change us, Lord

Every day we dread
To click the internet
To pick the phone
To open television
To listen to radio

For all we will hear
All we will read
Al we will see
Is another death
In our homeland
Even in peacetime

Others reading this
May simply think
It's just a poem
They won't know
Tears are flowing
Down our faces
Yours' there
And mine here
This very moment
And will continue
To flow day
After day
After day

Change us, Lord

From rippers
Of our parts
To keepers
Of loving hearts

PO44 OH! FLAG OF THE BRAVE! WAVE AND WAVE!

By Dr. Achier Deng Akol

Flag of the Brave
Brave New Kush warriors
Wave and wave
For New Sudan survivors

For existence and safety
For justice and equality
For democracy and liberty
For peace and stability

Oh! Flag of the brave!
Wave and Wave!

Wave in vital colouration
White for peace gesture
Red for blood of revolution
Green for agriculture
Blue for Nile Water Connection
Black for identity texture
Yellow for hope aspiration
The star for unification nurture

Unification that is indefinite
For our struggle continues
Until our freedom is infinite
Our own nation is continuous
Our vital resources are definite
And our future is non-ominous

Oh! Flag of the brave!
Wave and Wave

PO45 THIS SUDAN!

By Sirr Anai Kelueljang

Would you please stop pestering me
so that you and I
do not have to start questioning
each other's racial origin
—so that you and I
can live together in peace?

PO46 LISTEN!

By Sirr Anai Kelueijang

Listen!

You, Mohamed, and I, are not brothers.
You're the son of my aunt—You're my cousin!
Long ago your Arab father came,
with the Holy Koran and his traditional ways,
But without a mistress for his wife!

You, cousin Mohamed in the Northern Sudan,
are an offspring of my slave-aunt
who in her wretchedness stooped to conquer
—by blood-strength—
a reality as large as the Imatong Mountains!

You are no longer a pure Arab like your father.
You are the hybrid of Africa
The generous product
of many years of bloody war
on the African land

Your African Motherland!
My cousin Mohamed

says he knows everything
because he is educated.

When I sing songs
about Freedom, Justice, and Equality,
My cousin gets angry and shouts at me:
"You, Abid!

You also want to be free,
and be equal to me!"

PO47 SEASONAL MIGRATION

By Dr. Francis Mading Deng

Why are you after a soil as dark as the Dinka?
What do you want from the dark soil of the Dinka?

You are a people who simply go after grazing areas
in the three months of the dry season.

How can a person of three months' residence
dispute the land with the settlers of all seasons?

PO48 WHAT BUSINESS OF MINE?

By Dr Mairi John Blackings

I saw the Land Cruiser pull up at Chukudum
And did not leave until the chief
And anyone who stood by him was dead

Hakuna matata
So long as my chief is alive

One afternoon having nothing better to do
Laughing they dragged Joseph Ke'bulu out of a public bus
And pumped bullets down his belly near Kerepi

Hakuna matata
So long as I am not a SAPCO member
One Good Friday at Kobar Prison Khartoum
They took Arkangelo Iga and put a noose round his neck
We buried him same day at three like his Lord

Hakuna matata
So long as I am no trader

One day they found Joseph Oduho in a meeting
In his extended open hand of peace they slammed a
Hand grenade before riddling the body with bullets

Hakuna matata
So long as my father is safe

In Juba they came for the uniformed men
Prison, police, and wildlife Officers
Like lambs they took them to slaughter

Hakuna matata
So long as I am not in uniform

And simply for whispering too loudly for a homeland
Of our own they silenced Akuot Atem and Gai Tut
For good amid our adoring applause

Hakuna matata
So long as I remain a good cheerleader

Yesterday they ascended the Imatong Mountains
Looking for cattle rustlers
And left a whole village counting their dead
Hakuna matata
So long as I keep no cattle

A cracking noise pierced my silence this morning
I saw the Land Cruiser stop at my door

PO49 STARS OF THE SOUTH DO NOT DIE

By Achier Deng Akol

To Amal Juliet el Tahir, Manut Bol, Dr.Sampson Kwaje and Similar Stars

They say the sun sets and rises
When it hardly moves at all
It remains still in the premises
While the stars spring and fall

They say the sky is clear
When it is full of masses
Clouds may not appear
Yet it is loaded with gases

They say one thing
The truth is other
You see something
When it is another

Yes stars may appear dim
When they lose sun beam
Yet they remain really bright
As they gain true heavenly light

Stars of the South do not die

PO50 We Are Top Class People

By Achier Deng Akol

Oh! Imatong Mountain
Lift us all high up
To the top of the world
You are a mountain
So unique so special

Oh! River Nile
Float us all along
To the main stream
You are a river
The longest the best

Oh! Beautiful South
Promote us worldwide
As valuable and respectful
You are a wonderful land

Oh! Our People
Of South Sudan
Let us fight together
For our total freedom

Slaves or second class?
No Kar tuom No No No
We are second to none
We are top class people

Homeless Beggars?
No Egypt No No No
We may be suffering now
But just wait and see soon

Useless Refugees?
No Diaspora No No No
We are useful bright stars
From dear Southern Sudan

Valueless and Voiceless?
No the world No No No
We have a powerful voice
Just wait and hear soon

Slaves and Second Class?
Homeless and Useless?

Valueless and Voiceless?
No Kar tuom No No No

We are top class people

PO51 OH! MY NAVEL, FROM MY CRADLE, REMEMBER!

Oh! My navel
From my cradle
Remember!!!!!

You the noble
Believe no crockery
When they babble
To distort our history
When they falsely teach
"Dukul el Nas fi el Sudan"
Or nonsensically preach
"Entry of people to Sudan"

Oh! Please
Tell them this
"Fi ghariibeen
Al dakhalu"
"Wa fi muothaneen
Al gahdu"
There are strangers
Who entered
And real owners
Who existed

If they insist
Stress to them this
"Intum mush
Min al Kush"
You are not
From the Kush

Oh! My navel
From my cradle
Remember!!!!!
You are a black seed
Of Mid-African fruit
Not a strange breed
Of Mid-Eastern brute

Oh! My navel
From my cradle
Remember!!

PO52 LET US CONTINUE TO TALK

By Dr. Achier Deng Akol

Oh! Our People! Our Kiths and Kins!
Let us continue to talk day and night
But start to put some words into actions
To utilize our good ideas in deeds
For actions speak louder than words

Let us continue to talk
For talking is good
It creates ideas very tough
Yet it is not enough

A professor of languages can spend hours
Describing how Salva Kiir Mayardit looks
But a photographer can do that in seconds
With simple click of digital camera dials
For a simple picture goes a thousand miles

If SPLA/M only talked and talked since 1983
Without shooting a single bullet in New Sudan
The CPA we cherish containing self-determination
Could never have been realised in negotiation

So my leader Salva Kiir Mayardit
Continue to drive two types of trains
An overground train in the open
And an underground train hidden

The rest of us here and there
Let us join one of the two trains
Depending on individual abilities
And specific group capabilities

We can have an **NCP Interest Group**
Working hard in the underground train
To expose NCP hidden objectives
And propose effective counter-activities

We should start an **SPLM Image Group**
Based in the overground train
To show to the whole world ourself
That South Sudan can rule itself

We must also establish a **UDI Strategic Group**
Of course in the underground train
To quietly evaluate and polish this option
Just in case it may become our final decision

Above all let us form an **SPLA Strengthening Group**
With an underground MI and overground troops
To make SPLA invincible to enemies of peace
And protect our lives and our 2011 choice

In 1947 our people were outwitted
When we lacked degrees and experiences
Let this negative history not repeat itself
Now that we have what we lacked in the shelf

Oh! Our People! Our Kiths and Kins!
Let us continue to talk day and night

But start to put some words into actions
To utilize our good ideas in deeds
For actions speak louder than words

PO53 SOUTH SUDAN, ONLY YOU

By Dr. Achier Deng Akol

My Life
My Love
My Dream

Only You
I want
Heartily
Very badly
Absolutely

My fatherland
My motherland
My precious land
South Sudan

My Life
My Love
My Dream

Only You
I desire
To own
To love
To cherish
Forever

African Beauty
African Heart

African Total
African African
Only You

Oil-rich
Tropical green
Warm Savannah
Beautiful South

My Life
My Love
My Dream

Beloved land
Of billion martyrs
For freedom
For justice
For equality
For democracy

My Life
My Love
My Dream

What more
Can I say?
For you
My Land

My Life
My Love
My Dream

South Sudan
Only You

PO54 JUST STAND UP STRONG AND PROCLAIM THE WORDS

By Dr. Achier Deng Akol

Oh! Salva Kiir Mayardit!
Where will you stand?
To declare our freedom

At Akon Elementary School?
Where you started education

At Kuajok Intermediate School?
Where you left to join the struggle

At Owiny Kabul?
The Capital of Anya-nya

At Rumbek Town?
The SPLA Capital

At original New-site?
Where our Leader fell

At the site of 1947 conference?
Where our elders tried their best

At Pibor Area?
Where SPLA began

At Vilpam location?
Where our martyrs trained

At Naivasha?
Where CPA was born

On the tomb at Aberou?
Of William Deng Nhial

On the shrine in Torit?
Of Father Saturnino Ohure

On the shrine in Juba?
Of Dr. John Garang De Mabior

Or at any site?
Where our martyrs fell

Oh Salva! Oh! Now our full President
Don't mind about the site
Just stand up strong
And proclaim the words
"I Declare South Sudan a Fully Independent Country!"

Then let those who want to jump up and shout
Those who want to ululate at top of their voices
Those who would like to say Oyee loud and clear
Like SPLA Oyee! South Sudan Oyee! Our People Oyee!
Those who prefer to start singing and dancing
Those who break down in tears of jubilation!
Tears of Relief! Tears of New Sunrise! Tears of Freedom!
Those who want to exchange wedding rings
In order to mark that day in style of love
Let them all express their joy and excitement
Any way they like and any style they choose

Oh! Salva! Oh! Now our full President!
Don't mind about the site
Just stand up strong
And proclaim the words

"I Declare South Sudan a Fully Independent Country"

PO55 A CELEBRATION BEYOND IMAGINATION

By Dr. Achier Deng Akol

If the decisive vote is secession
My GOD! What a party our land shall throw!
What a Celebration our people will make!

The bones of our martyrs shall shake
With joy in their graves
And their spirits shall dance
With jubilation in heaven
The birds shall sing wonderful songs
Fresh breeze of liberty shall blow
New sun of freedom will rise
The sky shall remain blue
And clouds shall come and go

New stars shall rise and shine
Old stars will rejuvenate
The heavens shall open
And rain will fall
Without dangerous strikes

Singers of the world
Shall converge and sing
Artists of the South
Shall display their skills
Drums shall sound
And dancers will rock

The young shall display
Michael Jackson styles
And the gray-haired
Will twist and bump

The blind will see
With their hearts
The deaf will hear
With their eyes
The lame will fly
On their hands

The amputees will clap
With their minds

Lovers shall hug
All night long
And kiss nonstop
Oh! If Africans do not kiss
They will break the law
And try how it feels
Just for that day!

Enemies shall reconcile
In the interest of our land
And become friends forever
Divorcees shall remarry
And bring more children
Named after our martyrs

Madam Ayen Parek
The wife of Deng Nhial
Mama Rebecca Nyandeng
The wife of John Garang de Mabior
Will hold the hands of all widows
And ululate together
In victory and glory

The first lady of Southern Sudan
Mrs Ayen Salva Kiir Mayardit
The deputy first lady of the South
Mrs. Angelina Riek Machar Teny
Along with Mrs. Nura Lero Igga
Will lead all the wives of our leaders
And the darlings of our commanders
To jump on the shoulders of their husbands
And say thank you for a job well done

On behalf of all the people of the South
The husbands of our female leaders

Will also jump simultaneously
Onto the shoulders of their wives

Celebrants will run and compete
To be the first to hoist the Flags
In all corners of South Sudan
Where a life had been sacrificed
For a celebration like this to happen

And when the night falls
The party shall not end
With stars shining in the sky
The moon glimmering
Coloured lamps glittering
And beddings shaking!

For some seeds
May be sown in the wombs
To mark that special night
The night of our independence day

Yes, South Africa celebrated
The release of Nelson Mandela
And disappearance of Apartheid
Yes East Timor and Eretria
Staged huge celebrations
Like other nations before them
For their independence days
But ours in South Sudan
Shall be an exceptional celebration
Never witnessed on this planet
Or any other planet in the Universe
A party unlike other parties
A celebration beyond imagination

PO56 I CAN EVEN DIE OF HAPPINESS ON THAT DAY

By Dr. Achier Deng Akol

Where will I find a voice so nice?
To sing a special song
On that day

Where will I find a style so unique?
To dance a wonderful dance
On that day

Where will I find a clothe so beautiful?
To dress a spectacular dress
On that day

And I tell you this
I promise you this
On that day

Although I have no voice
That can sing so nice
Since I was born
I tell you this
I will find one
On that day

Even though I have no style
That ever impressed others
Since I started dancing
I promise you this
I will find one
On that day

I may even wear leaves
If I cannot afford

A top quality dress
And put on beads
If I can't find gold
On that day

And I tell you this
I promise you this
Even though I am dead
I will still wriggle my bones
Inside my grave
And jiggle my soul
In the sky above
When my people celebrate
For generations and generations to come
On that day

All I need
All I pray for
Is for that day to come
The day our trees
And our rivers
The day all our living
And our dead
Will become independent

And I tell you this
I promise you this
I can even die
Of happiness
On that day

CONCLUSION

A Land So Victorious

Oh! Salva!
Just stand up strong
And proclaim the words

As I stated earlier, when an African drum sounds, all beauty starts to flow in a stream unseen elsewhere on Earth, especially when it sounds in the Heart of Africa, in South Sudan to say to the world: Our African culture that is threatened here in this land will never be killed. It will never die against all the wishes of our enemy anywhere.

In protection for this culture, our own survival on this planet and this beautiful piece of land called South Sudan, we have fought for over a thousand years (640-2005) which makes ours the second longest war on Earth after that of Israel and Palestine. During this long war, millions if not billions of our people have perished and not just the few millions usually quoted for the more recent wars. Many more have lost vital parts of their bodies to become people who are dead alive.

Our beauty is not only shown by how we look in addition to our land. It is reflected more in our sustained courage, strength, ability and perseverance to continue to defend ourselves and our land against any enemy forces as we did over many generations; our enormous readiness and ability to sacrifice our own lives and vital body parts for our land and our people. If our land was not so precious and beautiful, why would millions of our people sacrifice all they had for it?

Thank You, God, for this gift of exceptional beauty. A lot of it may have been destroyed by the long war for our freedom but no human beings can beat nature. Indeed trees have died. Even roads to walk on have disappeared. Wildlife has migrated to other countries. Rivers and lakes have dried up. A countless number of our people have died. Many families have been completely eradicated. Happy cultural ceremonies have been converted into funerals. The war indeed has taken a great toll on our Beautiful land and its resources. But nothing will eradicate our beauty. Nothing will take it away from us. It is in us, with us and around us. It can be seen on glamorous natural flowers that spontaneously spring on the graves of our martyrs that were lucky to be buried and in plains and forests where others withered away unburied.

Some may think South Sudan is just an ugly war-torn land and shall remain so. They are pretty wrong and maybe among those who might not have had a chance to see it before the war. In fact, I should correctly assert that they are those whose ancestors have not had the opportunity of seeing our land two thousand years ago before any war erupted. Yes, two thousand years ago for, I repeat, our war is over a thousand years old.

Others may assume too that this beauty is gone forever, knocked away by the successive hostility of war. They are wrong as well. It is not gone. It is there in the dry leaves that will become green again, the seeds in the soil that will grow, the livestock that will regenerate, our birds that will fly back without any flu! It is there in the sound of the drums and horns that we shall beat and blow...It is not gone. It is there and has always been...in our freedom that we shall secure and the development with prosperity that shall ensue...It is permanently engrained in our hearts and bestowed in our souls. It is transmitted from the womb to every new born baby and appears straight away in the colour of their eyes and glamour of their skin once the debris acquired along the birth canal is wiped off. It remains in the tips of their fingers ready to transcribe into artworks and arts craft. Indeed, it is that beauty which is now draining down my body through the tips of my fingers as I write this book so that our generations who missed seeing it and others who do not know about it can read it here. And the book is indeed the right place it should drain into so that when I join my parents in the sky where the war of our long struggle has taken them, it will remain and continue to tell the story.

I feel that those beautiful clouds that you see moving across the sky or standing still are mixed with spirits of our martyrs. Behind them are angels of goodwill. The millions that sacrificed their lives for us are not in their graves. They are up there looking down upon us. Making sure we are doing the right things for our land. Inspiring us day and night, keeping us united in the face of any enemies. I call them Angels of CPA, for without their sacrifice this vital peace agreement could never have been reached.

The birds you hear singing beautifully are reminding us to remain alert all the time. Any lapse in vision or thought could prove disastrous. Thunder strikes with the flash of a second. Earthquakes shake the entire land into pieces in moments. Volcanoes erupt in minutes. We must remain forever vigilant.

Let us not ignore the warnings black crows give us nor call owls, simple wizards. We are all struggling side by side with our trees, birds, snakes, mosquitoes and more. Yes, they occasionally bite us. More often they attack our foes.

The fresh air that touches us at dawn and dusk is not just air. It is a gift delivered to us from the Heavens in reward for our long endurance. Oh! That cool, lovely fresh air after rainfall! Nowhere else have I ever felt it that nice despite travelling to various places around the world, thrown here and there by our fate.

Yes my parents, Deng Akol Ayay and Adut Wol Dut, along with millions more from our land have perished prematurely along with other parents, but our beauty will last forever surely. I still remember them arguing sweetly that early morning when I was woken up at dawn at the age of five. Good Angels please fly up there and tell them that the little fingers of their last born have grown. His little fingers have grown big enough to firmly grasp a hoe and cultivate. Much more, they are now in the process of waking up other children of our land wherever they are not to sleep but to spread and saw seeds for our freedom... seeds of the Beautiful South Sudan, the Heart of Africa.

We, South Sudanese in general are indeed, a unique beauty that the Almighty Creator offered to the Universe. We are here to stay as a people in our own land forever, together with our startling domestic and wild life. Our staggering butterflies and flabbergasting birds shall continue to fly. Dumfounding springs, ponds, pools, lakes, streams and rivers will refill and reflow. Honeymooners and tourists all over the world will be visiting to enjoy with us on this beautiful land that I rightfully call Heaven on Earth. We can compete and, dare I say, beat the rest of the world in natural beauty.

Nevertheless, Beautiful South Sudan shall naturally regrow and re-flourish, especially now that another peace has been signed and I pray that it holds this time. You, my beautiful land, are a natural gift to us as a people no one will take you away from us, Our Land; for you are Our Life, Our Love, and Our Dream.

For, if the CPA survives, I believe the cry for South Sudan Freedom will be positively answered. Our people of South Sudan will achieve ultimate freedom in 2011 unless of course unity of the whole Sudan is miraculously made attractive to them before then. And what a special day it will be, the day that our land will gain its full independence. I can't wait for that day to come. Indeed, I can even die of happiness on that day!

I can even die
Of happiness
On that day

By Dr. Achier Deng Akol

Where will I find a voice so nice?
To sing a special song
On that day

Where will I find a style so unique?
To dance a wonderful dance
On that day

Where will I find a clothe so beautiful?
To dress a spectacular dress
On that day

And I tell you this
I promise you this
On that day

Although I have no voice
That can sing so nice
Since I was born
I tell you this
I will find one
On that day

Even though I have no style
That ever impressed others
Since I started dancing
I promise you this
I will find one
On that day

I may even wear leaves
If I cannot afford
A top quality dress
And put on beads
If I can't find gold
On that day

And I tell you this
I promise you this
Even though I am dead
I will still wriggle my bones
Inside my grave
And jiggle my soul
In the sky above
When my people celebrate

For generations and generations to come
On that day

All I need
All I pray for
Is for that day to come
The day our trees
And our rivers
The day all our living
And our dead
Will become independent

And I tell you this
I promise you this
I can even die
Of happiness
On that day

Oh! If the decisive vote is secession, let me ask President Salva Kiir Mayardit this question: Where will you stand to proclaim the words "I declare South Sudan fully independent"?

Just Stand up Strong
And proclaim the Words

By Dr. Achier Deng Akol

Oh! Salva Kiir Mayardit!
Where will you stand?
To declare our freedom

At Akon Elementary School?
Where you started education

At Kuajok Intermediate School?
Where you left to join the struggle

At Owiny Kabul?
The capital of Anya-nya

At Rumbek Town?
The SPLA capital

At original New-site?
Where our Leader fell

At the site of 1947 conference?
Where our elders tried their best

At Pibor Area?
Where SPLA began

At Vilpam location?
Where our martyrs trained

At Naivasha?
Where CPA was born

On the tomb at Aberou?
Of William Deng Nhial

On the shrine in Torit?
Of Father Saturnino Ohure

On the shrine in Juba?
Of Dr. John Garang De Mabior

At Kurmuk?
Where thousands died

At any site?
Where our martyrs fell

Oh Salva! Oh! Now our full president
Don't mind about the site
Just stand up strong
And proclaim the words

"**I declare South Sudan fully independent**!"

Then let those who want to jump up and shout
Those who want to ululate at top of their voices
Those who would like to say Oyee loud and clear
Like SPLA Oyee! South Sudan Oyee! Our People Oyee!
Those who prefer to start singing and dancing
Those who break down in tears of jubilation!
Tears of Relief! Tears of New Sunrise! Tears of Freedom!
Those who want to exchange wedding rings
In order to mark that day in style of love
Let them all express their joy and excitement
Any way they like and any style they choose

Oh! Salva! Oh! Now our full president!
Don't mind about the site
Just stand up strong
And proclaim the words

"**I declare South Sudan fully independent**"

And when our Land of South Sudan is declared independent, we its children shall start to sing together our South Sudan Anthem as proposed below. The anthem specifies the name of the Country as South Sudan and maintains the heroic acclamation of Oyee! Or Long Live! used by Sudan People's Liberation Army and Movement (SPLA/M). This acknowledges the role played by the gallant SPLA forces and their predecessors, the Anya-nya Warriors in the liberation struggle over fifty years of contemporary war. It avoids the dubious definition of Old Sudan as an African and Arab State by specifying that South Sudan belongs precisely to African Stars. Indeed, it reflects South Sudanese as stars and no more second-class citizens in their own country like before. Then it shows its geographical location as around the River Nile and traces its origin to the Kush Kingdom of brave warriors where civilization began. This great historical origin, plus the defensive role played by ancient Kingdoms around the Nile must be imparted in the minds of all South Sudanese forever. Next the anthem aspires that South Sudan will rise to the top, now that it is fully free, implying that it will never again be impeded by previous marginalisation, oppression and slavery. The People of Kush were great before and nothing will prevent their offspring from becoming great again, if they remain united and continue to be innovative like their predecessors. Finally, for its children and martyrs, it again hails Oyee South Sudan! Or long live South Sudan! Thus it emphasizes the survival of the people of South Sudan having been threatened by historical genocide and attempts to annihilate them. Besides, the anthem recognises the enormous sacrifice made by millions of its martyrs that died for liberty and ensures they are remembered forever:

South Sudan Anthem

Oyee! South Sudan!
Of African Stars
Around River Nile

From Kush Kingdom
Of brave warriors
Where civilization began

Now fully free!
You will rise
To the top

For your children
And your martyrs
Oyee! South Sudan!

After the declaration of our Full Independence and singing of our National Anthem, My GOD! What a party this land shall throw! What a celebration our people will make! Surely, it will be a celebration beyond imagination:

A CELEBRATION BEYOND IMAGINATION

By Dr. Achier Deng Akol

If the decisive vote is secession
My GOD! What a party our land shall throw!
What a celebration our people will make!

The bones of our martyrs shall shake
With joy in their graves
And their spirits shall dance
With jubilation in heaven
The birds shall sing wonderful songs
Fresh breeze of liberty shall blow
New sun of freedom will rise
The sky shall remain blue
And clouds shall come and go

New stars shall rise and shine
Old stars will rejuvenate
The heavens shall open
And rain will fall
Without dangerous strikes

Singers of the world
Shall converge and sing
Artists of the South
Shall display their skills
Drums shall sound
And dancers will rock

The young shall display
Michael Jackson styles

And the gray-haired
Will twist and bump

The blind will see
With their hearts
The deaf will hear
With their eyes
The lame will fly
On their hands
The amputees will clap
With their minds

Lovers shall hug
All night long
And kiss nonstop
Oh! If Africans do not kiss
They will break the law
And try how it feels
Just for that day!

Enemies shall reconcile
In the interest of our land
And become friends forever
Divorcees shall remarry
And bring more children
Named after our martyrs

Madam Ayen Parek
The wife of Deng Nhial
Mama Rebecca Nyandeng
The wife of John Garang de Mabior
Will hold the hands of all widows
And ululate together
In victory and glory

The first lady of Southern Sudan
Mrs Ayen Salva Kiir Mayardit
The deputy first lady of the South

Mrs. Angelina Riek Machar Teny
Along with Mrs. James Wani Igga
Will lead all the wives of our leaders
And the darlings of our commanders
To jump on the shoulders of their husbands
And say thank you for a job well done
On behalf of all the people of the South
The husbands of our female leaders
Will also jump simultaneously
Onto the shoulders of their wives

Celebrants will run and compete
To be the first to hoist the Flags
In all corners of South Sudan
Where a life had been sacrificed
For a celebration like this to happen

And when the night falls
The party shall not end
With stars shining in the sky
The moon glimmering
Coloured lamps glittering
And beddings shaking!

For some seeds
Maybe sown in the wombs
To mark that special night
The night of our independence day

Yes South Africa celebrated
The release of Nelson Mandela
And disappearance of Apartheid
Yes East Timor and Eretria
Staged huge celebrations
Like other nations before them
For their independence days
But ours in South Sudan

Shall be an exceptional celebration
Never witnessed on this planet
Or any other planet in the Universe
A party unlike other parties
A celebration beyond imagination

In conclusion to this book, I would like to state this. Looking a thousand years beyond 2011, well beyond the first day of our independence, I predict that our land of South Sudan that is so wrecked by deliberate economic deprivation and devastated by disastrous war will ultimately recover. It will pick up and rise into a powerful, prosperous, and glamorous nation. For Beautiful South Sudan shall thrive with glamour, once again as before; it will shine with power, like a star and even more:

BEAUTIFUL SOUTH SUDAN

By Achier Deng Akol

Beautiful South Sudan
Shall thrive with glamour
Once again as before
It shall shine with power
Like a star and even more

It will grow
From a weakling
To an independent bow
With a mighty string

Its dry plains
Will become green
To produce grains
As it had been

Rivers lakes and streams
Will fill and flow

Rusty golden beams
Will begin to glow

All destroyed cities
Like Malakal, Juba and Wau
Will be reflourished
New ones like central Ramkiel
Will be established

Multiple Wonderful Flowers
Will spring up once again
With spectacular colours
To relieve longstanding pain

The painful years
Of long war
With miserable tears
Of absolute poor
Will change to cheers

Dying forests
Destroyed plantains
Ruined harvests
Eroded mountains
Will all blossom
Once again

It will be time
Of utmost prime
Time for love and marriages
Time for constructive strategies
Time to produce more children
Time to replace lost kindred
Time to rename the martyrs
Time to reform the families
Time to rebuild the motherland
Time to own the fatherland

Beautiful South Sudan
Shall thrive and glamour
Once again as before
It will shine with power
Like a star and even more

The Heavens will open
The rain will pour down
And hibernating frogs
Will leap out
In full excitement
To join the celebration
Cocks will crow
In every home
That keeps them
To wake people up
And the chicks will run
Behind the mother hen
Waving their small wings
In additional celebration

All astonishing butterflies
From over the whole world
Will flock in their millions
Into the Heart of Africa
To join their counterparts
For a special ceremony
And taste South Sudan nectar

Dogs will shake
Their own tails
To welcome visitors
With touching gestures
And funny noises

All the wartime heroic victims
Like amputees, widows and orphans

Physically and emotionally traumatised
Will be comforted and motivated
And every martyr of the South
Should be remembered forever

The few children
That survived the war
Will run, sing and play
In the Southern fields
In their small numbers
Till they are joined
By more to come

For horrible slavery
Will become history
And terrible oppression
Will be in total extinction

Beautiful South Sudan
Shall thrive and glamour
Once again as before
It shall shine with power
Like a star and even

DR ACHIER DENG AKOL AYAY

INDEX

Page

Folklore

History

Politics

Dedications

Songs

Poems

CPSIA information can be obtained
at www.ICGtesting.com
Printed in the USA
LVHW050106080322
712880LV00014B/620